W9-BMB-148

THE OPERA OMNIBUS

BOOKS BY IRVING KOLODIN

The Metropolitan Opera 1883–1935   (1936)

The Metropolitan Opera 1883–1939   (1940)

*The Story of the Metropolitan Opera, 1883–1950,
A Candid History*   (1953)

The Metropolitan Opera 1883–1966   (1966, 1968)

A Guide to Recorded Music   (1941)

New Guide to Recorded Music   (1947)

The New Guide to Recorded Music (International Edition)   (1950)

The Guide to Long-Playing Records Orchestral Music   (1955)

The Musical Life   (1958)

The Continuity of Music   (1969)

The Interior Beethoven   (1975)

In his study at home in Weston, Connecticut, master conductor Fritz Reiner said, "When I am doing opera, I always long for the symphony orchestra; but when I am doing symphony, I always miss opera." (*photo courtesy RCA*)

THE
OPERA OMNIBUS
Four Centuries of Critical
Give and Take

IRVING KOLODIN

E. P. DUTTON & CO., INC. | NEW YORK

To

EC

HC

MDC

Library of Congress Cataloging in Publication Data

Kolodin, Irving, 1908–
  The opera omnibus.
  Includes bibliographical references.
  1. Opera.   I. Title.
ML1700.K65   782.1   76-40

ISBN: 0-8415-0438-5

Published simultaneously in Canada
by Clarke, Irwin & Company Limited, Toronto and Vancouver

DESIGNED BY JEANETTE YOUNG

Acknowledgments

Grateful acknowledgment is made to the following for permission to use copyrighted materials: *Franco Abbiatti.* From *Giueseppe Verdi* by Franco Abbiatti. Copyright © 1959 by G. Ricordi & Co., Milan. Reprinted by permission of the publisher. *Edward Albee.* From *Who's Afraid of Virginia Woolf?* by Edward Albee. Copyright © 1962 by Edward Albee. Reprinted by permission of Atheneum Publishers, the William Morris Agency, and Jonathan Cape Ltd. *Adolphe Appia.* From *Music and the Art of the Theatre* by Adolphe Appia. Reprinted by permission of University of Miami Press. *J. M. Barrie.* From *The Complete Plays of J. M. Barrie* by J. M. Barrie. Copyright 1928 by Charles Scribner's Sons. Reprinted by permission of Charles Scribner's Sons. *Sir Thomas Beecham.* From *La Bohème* (brochure). Reprinted courtesy Angel Records. *Mosco Carner.* From *Puccini: A Critical Biography* by Mosco Carner. Copyright © 1958, 1974. Reprinted by permission of Gerald Duckworth & Co. Ltd., London. *Henry F. Chorley.* From *Thirty Years' Musical Recollections* by Henry F. Chorley. Copyright 1926. Reprinted by permission of Alfred A. Knopf, Inc. *Lorenzo da Ponte.* From *Memoirs of Lorenzo da Ponte* by Lorenzo da Ponte, trans. by Elisabeth Abbott, 1959. Reprinted by permission of Dover Publications, Inc. *Henry-Louis de La Grange.* From *Mahler* by Henry-Louis de La Grange, trans. by Herbert Weinstock, Johanna Harwood and Wendela Schurmann. Copyright © 1973 by Henry-Louis de La Grange. Reprinted by permission of Doubleday & Company, Inc. and Victor Gollancz, London. *Giulio Gatto-Casazza.* From *Memories of the Opera* by Giulio Gatti-Casazza. Copyright 1941 by Leon Schaefler. Reprinted by permission of Charles Scribner's Sons. *Donald Jay Grout.* From *A Short History of Opera* by Donald Jay Grout, 2nd edition, New York: Columbia University Press, 1965, by permission of the publisher. *Edward Heath.* From The London *Sunday Times.* Copyright © 1961 by *The Sunday Times.* *W. J. Henderson.* From *The Art of Singing* by W. J. Henderson. Copyright 1938 by W. J. Henderson. Copyright renewed © 1966 by Julia W. Henderson. Reprinted by permission of the publisher, The Dial Press. *Spike Hughes.* From *Glyndebourne, A History of the Festival Opera.* Reprinted by permission of the publisher, Methuen & Co. Ltd., and Curtis Brown Ltd. *Dyneley Hussey.* From *Verdi* by Dyneley Hussey. Copyright © 1963 by J. M. Dent & Sons Ltd. Reprinted by permission of Farrar, Straus & Giroux, Inc. and J. M. Dent & Sons Ltd. *Irving Kolodin.* From *The Composer as Listener: A Guide to Music* by Irving Kolodin. Copyright © 1958. Reprinted by permission of the publisher, Horizon Press, New York. *Robert Lawrence.* From *Opera News.* Copyright 1952 by the Metropolitan Opera Guild, Inc. Reprinted

vii

by permission of the publisher. *Edward Lockspeiser*. From *Debussy: His Life and Mind* by Edward Lockspeiser. Copyright © 1962 by Edward Lockspeiser. Reprinted by permission of Macmillan Publishing Co., Inc. and Cassell & Co. Ltd. *John Livingston Lowes*. From *The Road to Xanadu* by John Livingston Lowes. Copyright © 1955 by John Wilbur Lowes. Reprinted by permission of Houghton Mifflin Company. *Edmond Michotte*. From *Richard Wagner's Visit to Rossini* by Edmond Michotte. Reprinted by permission of The University of Chicago Press. *Modeste Petrovich Musorgsky*. From *The Musorgsky Reader* by Modeste Petrovich Musorgsky, ed. and trans. by Jay Leyda and Sergei Bertensson. Reprinted by permission of Jay Leyda. *Ernest Newman*. From *The Life of Richard Wagner* by Ernest Newman. Copyright 1939. Reprinted by permission of Alfred A. Knopf, Inc. and Mary E. and John W. Parkin. *Charles Osborne*. From *Letters of Giuseppe Verdi*, sel., trans., and ed. by Charles Osborne. Copyright © 1971 by Charles Osborne. Reprinted by permission of Holt, Rinehart and Winston, Publishers and Curtis Brown Ltd. Also from *The Complete Operas of Verdi* by Charles Osborne. Copyright © 1969 by Charles Osborne. Reprinted by permission of Alfred A. Knopf and Curtis Brown Ltd. *Alexander Pushkin*. From "Eugene Onegin" in *The Poems, Prose and Plays of Alexander Pushkin* by Alexander Pushkin, ed. by Avrahm Yarmolinsky. Copyright 1936. Reprinted by permission of The Modern Library. *Jean-Jacques Rousseau*. From *The Confessions* by Jean-Jacques Rousseau, trans. by J. M. Cohen. Copyright 1953. Reprinted by permission of Penguin Books Ltd. *Clara Schumann*. From *Clara Schumann, An Artist's Life* by Clara Schumann. Reprinted by permission of Breitkopf & Hartel, Wiesbaden. *Robert Schumann*. From *On Music and Musicians* by Robert Schumann, trans. by Paul Rosenfeld, ed. by Konrad Wolff. Copyright 1946. Reprinted by permission of Pantheon. *George Bernard Shaw*. From *London Music in 1888–89* by George Bernard Shaw. Reprinted by permission of The Society of Authors on behalf of the Bernard Shaw Estate. *Desmond Shawe-Taylor*. From The London *Sunday Times*. Copyright © 1975 by *The Sunday Times*. *Geoffrey Skelton*. From *Wagner at Bayreuth* by Geoffrey Skelton. Copyright © 1965 by Geoffrey Skelton. Published by Barrie & Jenkins, Ltd., London and George Braziller, Inc., New York. Reprinted by permission in Georges Borchardt, Inc. and Barrie & Jenkins. *Richard Strauss*. From *Recollections and Reflections* by Richard Strauss. Copyright 1949 by Atlantis-Verlag, Zurich. English translation copyright 1953 by Boosey and Hawkes, London. Also from *A Working Friendship* by Richard Strauss and Hugo von Hofmannsthal, trans. by Hanns Himmelmann and Ewald Osers. Copyright © 1961. Reprinted by permission of Random House and William Collins Sons & Co. Ltd. *H. H. Stuckenschmidt*. From *Maurice Ravel* by H. H. Stuckenschmidt. Copyright © 1966 by Suhrkamp Verlag, Frankfurt am Main. Reprinted by permission of Calder & Boyars, London. *Francis Toye*. From *Rossini: A Study in Tragi-Comedy* by Francis Toye. Copyright 1934. Reprinted by permission of Alfred A. Knopf. *Richard Wagner*. From *My Life* by Richard Wagner. Reprinted by permission of Tudor Publishing Co. (Leon Amiel Publisher), New York. Also from *Tristan and Isolde* by Richard Wagner, trans. by Stewart Robb. Translation copyright © 1965 by Stewart Robb. Reprinted by permission of the publishers, E. P. Dutton & Co., Inc. *Frank Walker*. From *The Man Verdi* by Frank Walker. Copyright © 1962. Reprinted by permission of Alfred A. Knopf. *John Warrack*. From *Carl Maria von Weber* by John Warrack. Copyright © 1968 by John Warrack. Reprinted by permission of Macmillan Publishing Co. and Hamish Hamilton Ltd., London. *Herbert Weinstock*. From *Vincenzo Bellini: His Life and Operas* by Herbert Weinstock. Copyright 1946. Reprinted by permission of Alfred A. Knopf and Weindenfeld & Nicolson Ltd.

Contents

Illustrations

Preface

The beginning of my operatic life can be dated to January 1908. This would suggest that the experience somehow predated the beginning of physical life itself, which is, in too many sources to be refuted, assigned to February 21, 1908. The statement still stands. It has been family legend over decades that my mother visited the top gallery of Oscar Hammerstein's Manhattan Opera House some weeks before I was born (the walls of the building may still be seen on West Thirty-fourth Street, though the portion occupied by the theater has long since been adapted to other purposes). In such circumstances I could hardly avoid being present.

I am inclined to doubt that I was present, prenatally, at the performance of Charpentier's *Louise* with Mary Garden on February 19 (two days before my own, personal debut). However, I mention this particular work and performer because it was an experience my mother was fond of talking about years later. Actually, she could have gone to the performance of January 3, 1908, in which *Louise* was first heard in America, or to one of several later repetitions during January.

I have, however, an obstinate preference for February 19. It would please me to think that my mother would have gone to an opera house two days before bearing a child. That would have been in the true operatic tradition of the great Ernestine Schumann-Heink. As a young singer in Hamburg, Schumann-Heink performed in an opera until 10 P.M., then went home and gave birth to one of her eight children after midnight. When this story was circulated in the years of her great success, she did not deny its truth, but explained, "I sang even a few hours before Hans was born" because she needed the five-dollar fee she was paid.

Without regard for exactly when it occurred, my unconscious, involuntary first visit to the Manhattan was followed by a much more conscious, voluntary one to the Metropolitan a decade later. It was my tenth birthday, a self-explanatory reason for the upgraded environment. The place, however, was still the top gallery (called, grandly, at the Metropolitan—now, as then—the "Family Circle"). The opera was again French, which was wholly accidental. Indeed, my mother's partiality to *Louise* was only distantly related to its language or to Charpentier's music, and it was not due, altogether, to its star, Mary Garden. Her preference was, rather, related to its "working-class" heroine, who wanted to escape from the sewing room of the dress shop in which she was employed. Both the profession and the desire for independence catered to my mother's own background. On my first visit to the Metropolitan, the opera was *Carmen*, with Geraldine Farrar, Giovanni Martinelli, and, if I read the records of the season correctly, Clarence Whitehill (as Escamillo).

I do not count either *Louise* or *Carmen* among my true opera-going experiences, except, perhaps, as B.C. (Before Consciousness). The first I could not, of course, have heard. The second I could—technically speaking—have heard. But my only recollections are visual. No vocal impressions remain, which is just as well. Carmens of today hardly need, in addition to all their other problems, a critic with the memory of still another Carmen—especially so feminine a one as Farrar.

It was not until several years later that I began to gather operatic memories worth talking about. Then it was not in the exalted surroundings of the old, time-tinted Metropolitan or some comparable shrine. I had been taken to live in Newark, New Jersey, where a sometime burlesque theater was utilized, on Sunday evenings, for opera. Now its location would be ascribed to "the inner city." Then it was just downtown. Once again, the opera was *Carmen*. My musical recollections of this event are quite generalized. I do, however, recall my early teen-age indignation at being asked to believe that the "soldiers" who marched in front of and around the painted backdrop of a bull-ring in Act IV were part of some large, impressive military group. They were, clearly, the same ones, over and over again.

This rising gorge of incredulity may well have been my first exercise of critical judgment. I cannot precisely recall. But it was on the order of the disillusionment I had experienced half a dozen years before when I realized that it was one's parents, not Santa Claus, who were responsible for Christmas gifts. The only difference, I might add, is that I have since totally discounted Santa Claus: I still go to opera with faith, hope, and even charity.

The foregoing may suggest that I had a musical upbringing largely conditioned by opera attendance. Nothing could be further from the truth. I was brought up as a violin-playing snob, conditioned to sonatas and concertos, quartets and trios. Opera came via a horn-variety phonograph from which—amid the dulcet tones of Jascha Heifetz playing Schubert's "Ave Maria" (joy transcendant!) or Fritz Kreisler and John McCormack sharing the soaring line of Braga's "Angel's Serenade"—there emanated an occasional sobbing sound from an individual with the mellifluous name of Enrico Caruso.

The name clearly gave warning of an Italian, thus of a person not to be trusted with "higher musical values" (Arturo Toscanini had not yet returned from Italy for his second American career as a peerless conductor of symphonic music, and to give artistic credibility to names ending in *o* and *i,* of which he had both). I regret now the missed opportunity to have heard such a deity as Caruso in the famous Ocean Grove, New Jersey, Auditorium during July 1918. He performed there on the last Saturday of that month, a rare instance of Caruso's presence in America during the summer (like many other famous musicians, he had been unable to return to Europe during that agonizing last summer of World War I). The opportunity (presented by my parents' preference for adjacent Asbury Park as a watering place) was sacrificed on the altar of prior allegiance to Mischa Elman, a violinist whom I would hear, repeatedly, for *decades* after Caruso's lamentable death in 1921.

When, eventually, opera did assert its preordained attraction it was, again, on the snobbish side. Wagner's *Walküre* and *Tristan,* Weber's *Der Freischütz,* Lauritz Melchior's American debut in *Tannhäuser,* lovingly caressed performances of Smetana's *Bartered Bride,* and the mystical apparition of Chaliapin as Boris were my preferences as long as my maturely immature tastes were in ascendance until force majeure, in the form of a newspaper job as an apprentice critic, came my way, and the "lighter" Verdi (an exception had been previously made, in my scheme of things, on behalf of *Otello*), Puccini, Rossini, Gounod, et al., were countenanced. This was the beginning of the pleasures and the pangs, the delights and the debacles I have since experienced. They can be embraced under the general title of *The Opera Omnibus,* and an explanatory subtitle: "Four Centuries of Critical Give and Take."

Irving Kolodin
September 23, 1975

ACT I

I

Overture

1

A taste for opera could be variously cataloged as an aberration, a delusion, a deception, a delight, and a despair—and all would be right. Of course, these assessments would not all apply to the same opera or operas—and that is the abiding fascination of this queen of hybrids. Why not king of hybrids? There is no rational reason I can offer in ready refutation, which is exactly proof of the point. I think of opera as the queen of hybrids because it is alluring, attractive, seductive, and, on the whole, fatally irresistible. Someone else might argue that it is the king of hybrids because it is of courtly descent, tempestuous, imperious, and capable of overcoming any resistance. Perhaps it is best described as the royal androgyny of hybrids, thus satisfying the claims of both sexes.

Opera is, in any case and without regard for legality or regality, a hybrid. Some aestheticians have extolled opera as the highest of art forms because it combines within itself music and poetry, dance and theater, the human voice, scenic design, and lighting. When the combination of all these elements produces Gluck's *Orfeo*, perhaps such a characterization is admissible. When the outcome is Ponchielli's *La Gioconda*, in which the *same* elements are present in methodically measured, irrefutably equal degree, the characterization is less than inadmissible. To assess *La Gioconda* in terms of an art form would be a pretension masquerading as a premise. Or, to put it in musical terms, as far on the aesthetic scale as "The Dance of the Blessed Spirits" (in *Orfeo*) is from "The Dance of the Hours" (in *La Gioconda*).

There are some of us who have a preference for one opera or

3

another but, perhaps because of overexposure, no real capacity to resist any. I would rather hear a good performance of *La Gioconda* than a poor one of *Orfeo*. This, some may say, is an aesthetic cop-out. By reaching for such qualifying words as "good" and "poor" one is avoiding the responsibility for declaring oneself unequivocally on the merits of one or the other. But it is no more a cop-out than to say that a well-cooked hamburger is preferable to a poorly cooked steak. It is a statement of basic fact: to wit, that *Orfeo* no more exists of and by itself for consumption by someone hungry for it than food does. It, too, must be prepared, processed, and converted into a palatable form before it can be consumed.

To be sure, if you are German-oriented and can at least pronounce *Gesamtkunstwerk*, a strong case can be made for opera as "the combined art form." But, immediately, a host of questions intrude. Where is dance in Wagner? The one ballet with which his name is associated was imposed upon the Paris production of *Tannhäuser* in 1861 as the price for having it done at all. As Wagner insisted on finding a "logical" place for the ballet—which meant the Venusberg scene of Act I—the dance episode was over and done with before the late-arriving members of the Jockey Club (whose taste for ballerinas made ballets *de rigeur*) put in their appearance. Their anger at Wagner's "arrogant" disregard for custom had its predicted consequence: an outburst of whistling and name-calling which brought on a famous fiasco. (Verdi faced the same requirement more realistically several decades later when *Otello* was to be performed in Paris. He inserted his ballet in the elaborate ensemble scene of Act III, where it could be readily absorbed and arouse no hostility.)

Certainly the gyrations of the Flower Maidens in the second act of *Parsifal* offer little that a choreographer would call "dance," and the little steps that the Apprentices execute in the third act of *Die Meistersinger* are simple enough for even the corps de ballet of an opera company to perform.

So much for *Gesamtkunstwerk*. For those wholly devoted to it as practiced in Wagner's self-designed theater in Bayreuth, participation must be total and complete. No day-to-day dalliance with a taste of *Tosca* or a soupçon of *Samson*. One takes the *Ring* like a cure at Baden Baden, so much per twenty-four-hour period. If one does, in the end, feel cleansed and regenerated, the reasons may be all too similar to those engendered by any other form of purgative.

My preference is for a well-rounded diet of operatic proteins and carbohydrates and an avoidance of overindulgence in the pastas (*Aida*,

Turandot, etc.) and the pizzas (*Cavalleria Rusticana* and *Pagliacci*) which may cause a rise in spiritual cholesterol and induce hardening of the mental arteries. An offsetting infusion of elixir d'Offenbach for every serving of *Elisir d'Amore* could do much to correct an imbalance of intake. This, however, is akin to urging iced tea on one who is addicted to Coca-Cola. To more than a casual number of enthusiasts, a craving for one kind of opera may be as habit-forming as food.

Such an unbalanced diet leads, all too familiarly, to the second stage of the affliction: attachment to a performer who then becomes the guiding star amid encircling gloom. Should the choice incline to such a luminary as Birgit Nilsson, the devotee may, at least, be drawn through her to a range of operas as wide as her own versatility: *Tristan* as well as *Tosca, Elektra* no less than *Fidelio, Götterdämmerung, Turandot,* even *Don Giovanni* (she has been known to sing a first-class Donna Anna). On the other hand, if favor is magnetized to a singer of another type, the poor fan or fanette may be doomed to eternal shuttling between *La Bohème* and *Un ballo in maschera, Madama Butterfly* and *La Gioconda.*

This may, in fact, lead to the terminal state of the operatic ailment, when the performer, for so-called good reasons of her own, decides to embrace such a tawdry specimen of the species as Cilèa's *Adriana Lecouvreur* or Leoncavallo's *Zaza.* The ensuing test of loyalties may determine whether an opera enthusiast survives or succumbs. When those who worship at the shrine accept the values that serve the performer's momentary purpose rather than measuring them objectively against works of greater substance and true distinction, little hope for recovery remains. Only severe shock treatment, in which the vanity of the adored one is revealed for what it is, can be prescribed.

If I have appeared to paint a dire picture of what lies in wait for one whose interest in opera has been aroused, it is not wholly unintentional. It is done with a purpose, somewhat in the spirit of the "indoctrination" films shown to new members of the armed forces. For those who have been denied that experience, it may be described as a discourse on the perils of promiscuity accompanied by a photographic display of the worst examples of gonorrhea and advanced syphilis that the clinic can provide. The purpose can hardly be to discourage an interest in sex, because it hasn't worked yet. The purpose, rather, is to counsel "Forewarned is forearmed," or "What you don't know may hurt you."

Promiscuity in a love affair with opera may not be as risky as indiscriminate intercourse, but the principle is more or less the same.

Each is capable of providing lifelong satisfactions, providing that the pitfalls are mapped, charted, and otherwise pointed out by one who has been around the track a few times. I limit my observations to the operatic—insofar as one can exclude from a subject concerned with gods and goddesses, saints and sinners, poets and peasants, the mammoth attraction that serves, inevitably, to bring them together.

Opera at its best is a noble offspring of the marriage of the visual and the aural arts. Opera at its most familiar is the crazy mixed-up kid of a love affair between egotists, conceived in haste and dedicated to the proposition that singing is the most absorbing form of megalomania ever created.

Both forms may have their delights, provided the attendant knows why he is where he is, every time he goes to an opera house. Like the other zoo, where they keep the four-footed beasts, the operatic menagerie has its canines, felines, and some reptiles who should be not be confused with each other.

There are even a superior few who started in life with training at the keyboard and thus have both an advantage and a disadvantage in their operatic careers. Not many have the extraordinary gifts of a Marcella Sembrich (who was a capable violinist and pianist as well as an outstanding soprano) or of a Teresa Carreño, who sang Zerlina in a Boston performance of Mozart's *Don Giovanni* in 1876 on the way to becoming one of the greatest pianists of her time. But it is certainly an advantage to be able to accompany oneself while studying a new role or reactivating an old one. The disadvantage, for such a well-versed performer, is the need to "collaborate" with the run of opera singers who are where they are almost exclusively because of a God-given vocal talent.

On the infrequent occasions when a decade produces a performer with some musical education and a voice of the qualities to make the most of it, I am tempted to ask, upon encountering one socially, "What is a good musician like you doing in a house like this?" It was, after all, Gustav Mahler who called the Vienna Opera (in its greatness of his time) a "cesspool" and Arturo Toscanini who characterized the Metropolitan of 1913–14 (when he worked there) as a "pigsty."

2

Of course, the foregoing is concerned with what happens after the curtain is up, when the pride of Canton, Ohio, who is the evening's embodiment of a Spanish cavalier, and the offspring of a coal miner in Wales, who is the fair maiden luring him—all unintentionally, of course—to destruction, have come into view. It is important to realize that much of what is paradoxical, contradictory, and sometimes confusing about opera may occur before the curtain is raised.

It is not without reason that the music which comes before some operas is known as "a curtain raiser." This may be exactly its function, as Eric Blom suggests in an essay on the subject in the Fifth Edition of *Grove's Dictionary of Music and Musicians:* "In early nineteenth century Italy the overture was merely a piece of music to usher the audience into the theater with a cheerful noise and to accompany its chatter."[1]

Some overtures of that description are still to be heard, and they would not be spoiled by discreet conversation. But there are many, many more that would. Inasmuch as few audiences can be trusted to discriminate between one and the other, it is sound practice to treat them, masterpieces and curtain raisers alike, with the same respect. Certainly the now widespread custom of restricting latecomers from being seated during an overture—and far into the evening if there is no pause for applause—is an acceptable price for guaranteeing equal enjoyment to all.

In this practice, the late arriver at least knows where he stands (and when he sits). It is more humane, certainly, than the treatment I encountered in Vienna when I misread the hour for the beginning of Verdi's *Don Carlos* and arrived when it was well under way. My seat was at the end of a row adjacent to an exit, and the usher agreed I would disturb no one if I entered during the applause after the next aria. The awaited moment arrived. But the aria had been so indifferently sung that there was but a patter of applause. The usher shrugged helplessly—and didn't let me in.

From Beethoven—who wrote three *Leonore* overtures for a work titled *Fidelio* (Leonore is the name of the heroine) and then composed a fourth called *Fidelio* before he had the problem resolved to his satisfaction—to Rossini—who wrote one overture that served him for three different operas (*Aureliano in Palmira* and *Elisabetta, regina d'Inghilterra* before it attained lasting fame as the bubbly predecessor to *The Barber of Seville,* for which it was never intended)—composers have traditionally left to the last what is heard first.

Among the few examples to the contrary that I can recall—thus testifying to the generality of the last-minute concentration—is Wagner's *Meistersinger* overture, which burst upon him almost fully born one day in 1862. He had, he acknowledges, been jotting down ideas of what he planned to do, and during the writing of the text (which he did himself, of course) words would suggest musical phrases to go with them. But, he writes in his autobiography: "As from the balcony of my flat, in a sunset of great splendor, I gazed upon the magnificent spectacle of 'Golden Mayence,' with the majestic Rhine pouring along its outskirts in a glory of light, the prelude to my *Meistersinger* again suddenly made its presence closely and distinctly felt in my soul. . . . I proceeded to write down the prelude exactly as it appears today in the score."[2]

This is the kind of extraordinary happening that, once experienced, must arm a composer with the conviction that he was, indeed, meant to compose, and that if he perseveres, it might happen again.

The basic reason for what may appear to some to be a perverse order of priorities is that, more often than not, an opera may begin to stir in a composer's mind what material related to anything *but* its beginning. In the instance of Wagner himself, another quotation describes the opposite case. The work was *Lohengrin*, of which he later recalled: "I first of all completed the third act."[3] This, it may be recalled, includes the scene in the Bridal Chamber, with its permanently inescapable Bridal Chorus. One of the consequences of this order of inspiration is a somewhat elliptical stylistic progression. That is to say, after the gathering strength of Acts I and II, Act III suggests—to those unacquainted with the facts—a regression to an "earlier" musical style.

With *Der Ring des Nibelungen*—whose only overture is the uninterrupted 136 minutes of *Das Rheingold* (the timing for the Bayreuth performance directed by Karl Böhm in 1967, as issued on a Philips recording)—Wagner worked both backwards *and* forwards. As a fairly young composer, he conceived the idea of treating the Norse saga of the indestructible hero, as *Siegfrieds Tod*. More than a decade passed before he became seriously involved with the subject. Then he recast the text as *Götterdämmerung*. To explain what had happened prior to the events recounted in *Götterdämmerung*, he wrote the text of *Siegfried*. Upon further thought, he decided that this, too, needed clarification, so *Die Walküre* came into being. The action still contained inexplicable circumstances—such as the power of the Ring and the curses attached to it—and *Das Rheingold* was created as a Prologue to the Tetralogy.

The music, however, grew in the way it is performed when the cycle is given complete, save, that having written *Das Rheingold, Die Walküre*, and half of *Siegfried*, Wagner took time out to write such more "practical" operas as *Tristan* and *Die Meistersinger* before going back to finish *Siegfried* and write *Götterdämmerung*.

The inevitable consequence of this backward-forward order of creation is a fair amount of repetition and textual prolixity that, repeatedly, gets in the way of Wagner's music. Each "night" of the *Ring* begins and ends impressively, but along the way each has to tarry for one of those tedious episodes in which somebody—Wotan, Brünnhilde, the Norns—tells somebody else what happened "before." A great artist can make an absorbing experience of Wotan's narration to Brünnhilde (really, for the benefit of the audience) of what happened before she was born. But it is inherently an inept detail among an awkward series of non-solutions to a cumbersome dramatic plan.

I would, sometime, like to see a performance of the *Ring* in which, after the 135 minutes of *Das Rheingold*—say from 7:00 to 9:15 P.M.— one had an interval of 45 minutes. This would be followed—from 10:00 to 11:01 P.M.—with the first act of *Die Walküre* (the longest sustained stretch of great music in the whole cycle). On the following evening, the audience would be greeted with the great opening of Act II of *Die Walküre*, Brünnhilde's "Hojo-to-ho!," with the last two acts of this work followed by the first act of *Siegfried* (as Brünnhilde lies asleep on the mountain in punishment for having defied her father's instructions). Evening three would be made up of the last two acts of *Siegfried* and the opening Norn scene of *Götterdämmerung*. This would enable the final evening to begin on the high note of the parting duet of Siegfried and Brünnhilde, and do away with at least one repetition of "what happened before" from the Norns.

As an expression of human endeavor, the *Ring* is unquestionably a staggering accomplishment. But with all consideration for the magnitude of his creation, Wagner falls humanly short of making the two elements with which he was working—text and music—into wholly compatible parts of a balanced equation. Fundamentally, the problem with which he was confronted was to write a sequence of four interconnected works, each of which could, nevertheless, be performed as a self-contained entity. It would have been a task of superhuman magnitude for Wagner to have made one version of the *Ring* for Festival purposes and another for repertory usage. But I never heard that this had even occurred to him.

3

If the occasional performance of "Depuis la jour" as a concert aria strikes your ear as summing up everything about *Louise* and attaining a concentration of expression that Charpentier never quite equaled else-where in his music drama, the reason is not without explanation. It was the very first thing he composed for his heroine—Charpentier was one of the post-Wagnerian composers who emulated the master's example by writing his own libretto—and it encouraged him to embark on an effort in which he never quite recaptured that impulse.

Strauss had better luck with *Salome,* his first real operatic success (there had been several earlier efforts which had been honorable fail-ures). He tells us in his *Recollections* and *Reflections* that he had seen a production of Oscar Wilde's play at Max Reinhardt's "Little Theater" in Berlin and arranged to have a libretto made for him: "I could not make up my mind to start composing until one day it oc-curred to me to set to music *Wie schön ist die Prinzessin Salome heute Nacht* straight away."[4] This phrase, which occurs in the fourth measure after the swift curtain rise, gave Strauss just the lyrical mood he wanted to convey the admiration of the young soldier, Narraboth, for Salome. It was a supra-*normal* tinge of ecstasy from which to digress further and further to the abnormality of Salome's necrophilic ap-petite for the head of John the Baptist.

Verdi, on the other hand, had the delightful experience of reacting to the sketch which Arrigo Boito had submitted to him for *Falstaff* with the triumphant announcement: "I'm amusing myself by writing fugues! Yes, sir; a fugue . . . and a *comic fugue,* which would be in place in *Falstaff!* You will say: 'But how do you mean, a comic fugue? Why comic?' I don't know *how* or *why,* but it's a *comic fugue!*" Adds Verdi's biographer, Frank Walker: "It thus seems likely that the concluding fugue 'Tutto nel mondo è burla' ['All the world is a hoax'] was the very first part of the opera to be written, before he even had the words."[5]

Thus Verdi had, as the reward for the more than fifty years he had invested in learning how to write an opera, the final satisfaction—in his very last opera, produced when he was past eighty—of having al-ways before him the objective toward which he was striving. He was freed of any uncertainty, relieved of all concern, and liberated from any worry of wondering how he would finish what he had set in motion.

Over that long stretch of time and out of the tremendous diversity of subjects he treated, Verdi evolved his own attitude toward overtures, how and when they would serve his purpose in a particular work. At the outset he was faithful to the practices of his revered predecessors, Rossini and Donizetti in particular, in writing a preliminary sinfonia (the Italian term for an orchestral piece, without regard for what we know as the "symphony"). But unlike Rossini, who felt that the sinfonia need not necessarily embody any music of the work to follow (as in the instance of the *Barber of Seville* overture previously mentioned), Verdi was instinctively impelled otherwise. The first of his great successes, and the work that might well have determined whether or not he would have a career as an opera composer, was *Nabucco*. And the determining factor in that success was a melody that went straight to the heart of the Italian public, the great chorus "Va, pensiero, sull' ali dorate."

Here, the Jews enslaved by Nebuchadnezzar (Nabucodonosor in Italian, which is long for Nabucco) send "flying on wings of gold" their longing for the homeland of which they have been deprived, amid remembrances of "when our land was free." The immediate artistic effect was inherent in the music Verdi wrote, but he had, all unintentionally, aroused a deeper identity among his listeners—the yearning of the Italians for the freedom of their own land from foreign influence. Verdi instantly became the popular embodiment of the urge to Italian unification, which was not achieved until nearly thirty years *after* the premiere of *Nabucco* in 1842. When, another cycle of time later, his cortège passed the crowded square before La Scala on a winter's day in 1901, the melody of the dead Verdi that spontaneously came to the lips of the thousands gathered there was the eternally living "Va, pensiero."

One would assume from the legend surrounding the effect of "Va, pensiero" in *Nabucco* that it had burst on the audience unexpectedly in Act III. But they had already heard it once, carefully planted with all premeditation in the overture, where it provides a balm of melodic unguent between the bruising dramatic material that precedes and follows. Here Verdi demonstrates that, at the age of twenty-nine, he was already possessed of the composer's intuition that an audience once warned is an audience doubly responsive to a great melodic strain. It would remain for the action to tell the listener how the melody would serve the drama, but all ears were alert to its promised recurrence.

The best known of Verdi's overtures are, curiously, not uniformly associated with his most familiar operas. Neither *Rigoletto* nor *Il trovatore* has anything describable as an overture. *La traviata* does have the famous preludes (Verdi's own term for them) to Acts I and III, but the purpose in each is to set the scene, musically, for what is to follow, rather than to arouse attention. The best of the more customary sort of Verdi overtures are those for *La forza del destino*, with its churning proclamation in the strings of the agitated figure which later announces the soprano's sumptuous "Pace, pace," and for *I vespri siciliani*.

The overture to *Forza* was not a part of its original conception, as introduced to St. Petersburg in 1862. It was written "last" in a more than figurative way—for the opera's first Italian performance at La Scala, seven years later. It was a great adjunct to a work whose first scene is brief and, though dramatic, contains no outstanding music. The audience applauded it hugely, and it has rarely been greeted otherwise since.

Several years later, when *Aida* was produced at La Scala after its Cairo premiere, Verdi again wrote an overture especially for the occasion. But there is no "well-known *Aida* overture" for the reason that Verdi decided, after hearing it rehearsed, that the quieter, more reflective music he had previously composed for the purpose was more appropriate. Those who know it in the place it still occupies will agree—especially after hearing an occasional performance of the planned "replacement"—that Verdi's judgment was never more correct.

Neither *Don Carlos* nor *Simon Boccanegra* and, of course, neither *Otello* nor *Falstaff* has an overture. It is thus cumulatively clear that, as he grew older, Verdi tended more and more to spare his audiences long stretches of instrumental music, to plunge them at once into the action. The whipcrack that sends *Otello* on its way is a jagged slash of sonority in strings and winds echoed by timpani strokes; together they are suggestive of the lightning and thunder which separate Otello's tempest-tossed craft from its safe harbor on Cyprus. In *Falstaff* the onset of sight and sound are almost simultaneous, a ripple of rhythmic pulsations accurately predicting the mercurial merriment to follow as the curtain rises on the Garter Inn.

Both beginnings are classic examples of terseness, and both no doubt had their lesson for the maturing Giacomo Puccini. The curtain rise on the attic of *La Bohème* is preceded by a fanfaring figuration to be counted in measures rather than even a page, and the overwhelming initial impact of *Tosca* comes from the ominous brass chords that symbolize the menacing presence of Baron Scarpia even before the action begins. Only *Madama Butterfly* is introduced by something more lengthy in the way of orchestral effect. That is, of all things, a bustling *fugato* which would hardly strike one as in the least suggestive of Japan or the Japanese. But, once heard, it does have a lasting association.

None of these "prefatory remarks" cost Puccini anything like the effort that went into Verdi's more ambitious overtures. The tendency thereafter among Italian opera composers has been to the premise "What was good enough for Puccini is good enough for me." Verdi did, however, reap a merited reward for the time he spent on one opera of the 1850s. The fine overture to *I vespri siciliani* kept the name in being and the appeal of its principal melodies intact until—in the 1970s—*Vespri* is having an international favor it had never previously attained.

4

Does the presence of an overture confer a benefit lacking to a work without one? This is a question akin to the one posed to Lincoln: "How long should a man's legs be?" To which he replied, "Long enough to reach the ground." In other words, the length would vary from man to man. So, too, would the presence or absence of an overture vary from opera to opera.

I have said, of the fugal prelude Puccini wrote for *Madama Butterfly*, that there is nothing in the least Japanese about it, but, once heard, it has a lasting association. This strikes me as a very good qualification for a passing grade in the overture test. To be a satisfying work of art (in any form) the whole of it should represent the equally reasoned judgment of its creator in every part. To Puccini, the bustle and scurry of the fugal pattern said "Japan," and with all the confidence of a man who had never been there, he risked the gamble that it would to the listener, also. Certainly it brings on the opening scene so well that surprise would now come from its absence, not its presence.

When Beethoven said yes to the convention of his time which held that an opera was incomplete without an overture, he did not write "an" overture and consider his duty done. *Leonore* No. 1 was discarded even before the first performance, and *Leonore* No. 2 (somewhat longer in its treatment of the same material) made ready in its place. For the revival of the following year (1806) Beethoven put himself out to produce the titanic *Leonore* No. 3. This, too, eventually had to be superseded: not because it wasn't a masterpiece but because it tended to dwarf the work it was meant to complement.

Beethoven might have left forever unhappy those in love with the materials of *Fidelio*, but discontent with their usage, had he not received an unexpected third chance to review the subject nearly ten years after the premiere of the first version. He not only restored to the 1814 version some material heard at the 1805 performances but omitted in 1806, he created some of the music now most closely identified with the opera's fame, broadened the action, and fused the whole of it anew in the heat of the fresh creative effort.

Even so, the first performances of 1814 were heard with an amiable triviality (from the incidental music for *The Ruins of Athens*) serving as—most noxious of terms!—curtain raiser, because a successor to *Leonore*s 1, 2, and 3 had not been completed. Beethoven persevered to produce what he finally concluded the work needed: not a prelude on the Olympian scale of the *Leonore*s to summarize the drama to come, but a work of lighter, more terrestrial temper to prepare the audience for what they would see at the curtain's rise (the modest surroundings of Rocco, the jailer, in which the first scene is played).

The existence of the great music contained in the *Leonore* overtures remained, for decades, a tantalizing temptation for opera conductors not content to leave them to the concert hall. The final, predestined scheme for *Fidelio* came about many decades after Beethoven's death when a particularly perceptive conductor of the nineties—some say Anton Seidl, some say Gustav Mahler—performed *Leonore* No. 3 between the end of the dungeon scene and the jubilation that follows. To this initiative the world of music lovers and interpreters has given nearly unanimous consent. It brings together all the eloquence of Beethoven's thinking on the subject of *Fidelio*, and with each part in its most suitable place.

Perhaps if Carl Maria von Weber had lived longer (he died at thirty-nine in 1826) the prodigious invention he lavished on such works as *Oberon* and *Euryanthe* might also have been reconsidered, to the benefit of posterity. Weber's overtures are classic examples of creations *too good* for the purposes they were meant to serve. Exhilarating to hear in the concert hall, where they test the great symphony orchestras of today to the fullest of their virtuosity, they are discouraging to hear before even the best festival productions of the operas for which they were written.

This is because there will come, in the performance that follows, a moment when a vocalist will be required to "sing the overture": the big tune of Rezia's "Ozean du ungeheur" in *Oberon* or Adolar's "O Seligkeit, dich fass' ich kaum" in *Euryanthe*. Not only is the difficult vocal line a challenge to the stoutest singer, we will inevitably be reminded that even the greatest soprano does not have the power of the trumpet, nor are there many tenors with the built-in flexibility of the flutes and clarinets Weber called upon to show off these tunes in his overtures.

We learn from biographer John Warrack in his comment on *Euryanthe:* "Weber" [as usual] "wrote the brilliant overture last."[6] This assured him of three enduring masterpieces for the orchestral repertory, but—together with inept libretti—robbed the opera literature of two fine works. *Der Freischütz*, fortunately, is not nearly so impractical in its vocal requirements and is heard as often as there is an impresario with the good taste to make the effort.

It might have been well, had Weber been predestined to write all his opera overtures *last,* for him to have followed the example of his illustrious kinsman Mozart (whose wife, Constanze, was a Weber and a niece of Weber's father) in the creation of *Le Nozze di Figaro.* He, too, wrote his "brilliant" sinfonia—as he called it—last, but he let his fancy roam as it might to invent a whole new family of chattering themes to gossip about the intrigues to follow. This left to the singers the music he invented specifically for them.

Bedřich Smetana created one of the greatest of operatic comedies and most endearing of musical outpourings in any form in *The Bartered Bride*, and did it in a manner wholly his own. It was in the mid 1860s that the poet Karel Sabina—with whom Smetana had collaborated previously—sent him the outline for a musical work embodying a comic treatment, in folk style, of "the long-lost son" (one of the standard dramatic subjects through history). Here he is Jenik, who outwits a marriage broker scheming to buy him out of marrying a girl he loves.

Says František Bartoš in his introduction to the postwar revised edition of the score: "The creative impetuosity . . . of Smetana's conception is testified to by the altogether exceptional circumstance that he composed the overture spontaneously even before he received the definitive text of the libretto."[7] Sabina's modest plan for a work in one act impressed Smetana as inadequate, and he suggested an expansion to two. *The Bartered Bride* only attained its final division into three acts five years later. In all forms, the overture remained as it was originally written, not only because it is an immensely cheerful piece of music, but also because its allusions to materials in the opera are never at the expense of those who will sing them.

Overtures thus come in many guises, under a variety of names, and in numberless different musical forms. Prelude, *Vorspiel*, sinfonia, intrada—call it what you will, an overture by any other name is an overture still. The fugal features of Smetana's *Bartered Bride* overture (a triumphant example of a work perfectly suited to both the concert hall and the opera house) are quite different from Puccini's in the nameless matter that precedes the rise of the curtain in *Madama Butterfly*. One relates to a meadowland in Bohemia, the other to a never-never land near Nagasaki, but they are alike in the crucially important respect that each satisfies the ear as well as engaging the imagination.

Wagner's prelude to *Lohengrin* is, formally, simply a long crescendo and decrescendo foretelling the Swan Knight's arrival and departure, which can be rendered graphically by the symbol $< >$. On the other hand, his *Meistersinger Vorspiel* (as he called it) is a masterful example of sonata form. Wagner's supreme skill in using the ground plan associated with innumerable first movements of symphonies, string quartets, and, of course, sonatas of all description, gives the well-informed opera-goer another dimension of enjoyment. He becomes an involved participant in the themes as they are exposed, developed, and finally woven into a jubilant recapitulation in which segments of the Prize Song, the March of the Guilds, and the stately motif of the Meistersinger are heard *simultaneously*.

In some circumstances, even the medley type of overture will suffice, given such "hits of the show" as are embodied in Johann Strauss's overture to *Die Fledermaus* or Donizetti's to *Don Pasquale*. One might even find delight in what could be called a "vocal" overture, such as the "Prologo" to *Pagliacci*. It was composed by Leoncavallo because Victor Maurel, a great performer (he was also the first Iago and Falstaff) whom he valued highly for the premiere as Tonio, complained that his role lacked a proper aria. This innovation may have been prompted by a partial precedent in *Cavalleria Rusticana*, in which Mascagni leads his instrumental prelude to an offstage serenade sung by Turiddu as the curtain rises on a square in Sicily. Here is another of the affinities that predestined the two works to journey into eternity together.

What an overture should not, cannot, and must not be—as history has demonstrated—is overbearing (*Leonore* No. 3), unsuitable (*Aida*), or counterproductive (*Oberon, Euryanthe*). Of the three eminent composers responsible for these works, two made the right judgments, the third did not. Which composers are which is self-evident from the names of the works that endure in the repertory.

II

Recitativo

1

The moment for which you have been waiting is now at hand. Settled comfortably in your seat (ideally, not too close to the stage to thwart illusion, or too far away to be removed from contact with it) and having enjoyed a satisfactory performance of the overture, you are about to experience the ever-mystifying miracle of theatrical rebirth. That is the moment when the composer—Gluck, Mozart, Wagner—has adroitly led the music through the raising of the curtain directly into the action, with no pause for applause.

But there can be an intrusion despite the most careful planning by the composer to circumvent it. I was settled comfortably and, in all respects, expectantly, awaiting the first scene of a Mozart opera that opened the first Vancouver Festival in the late fifties, when the music suddenly stopped. What unforeseen event had intervened, I wondered? I could see the conductor calmly in his place, with no evidence of a mishap to someone in the orchestra pit.

In a moment it was clear that nothing unforeseen had caused the action of *Don Giovanni* to be delayed. The stoppage had been *pre-planned* to permit late-arriving British Columbians to find their seats! It took some of us more than the length of Leporello's "Notte e giorno faticar" to reawaken expectancy and to realize that Donna Anna's anguished outcry to the predatory Don "Non sperar, se non m'uccidi, ch'io ti lascio fuggir mai" ("Do not hope, unless you kill me, that I will ever let you go") was being delivered uncommonly well by a little-known soprano not previously heard in the Americas, Joan Sutherland.

The jagged sequence of notes in which Donna Anna's determination is conveyed is not nearly as hummable as Leporello's "Notte e giorno faticar" or a dozen other pearls in Mozart's fabulous string of melodic gems. But, let us remember, without a strong supporting thread, there can be no necklace. This is also to say that without the *recitativo* (pronounced re-chi-ta-*ti*-vo) that connects its melodic pearls, there could be no such *Don Giovanni* as has enthralled audiences worldwide since it was conceived nearly two hundred years ago. It is even more revealing of character and far more difficult to deliver with conviction than some of the much lauded show pieces.

One can argue that any well-trained baritone can give a creditable performance of the Serenata, the "Champagne" aria, or the insinuating "Vieni . . ." with which the Don lures Zerlina to leave with him in the Ballroom Scene. But it takes a true vocal craftsman, a man who can shape a word to mean more than its literal sense, or inflect a question to the equivalent of a command, to give back to Mozart what he put into his treatment of the *recitativo*.

As conceived by Mozart and emulated by many later composers, *recitativo* is something more than the strong supporting cord on which he has suspended his charm of brilliants. It is nothing more nor less than the lifeline by which the scheme of the drama is held together. It is, let it be remembered, in a *recitativo*, not in a famous melody, that Don Giovanni expresses the innate charm and insinuating personality that inadvertently identifies him to Donna Anna as her attacker. Or, as the action progresses, by which he conveys his courtly grace and self-esteem to Zerlina, and eventually gives expression to the inbred hospitality with which he receives a guest in his home, even when the visitor is a stone statue he has last seen in a cemetery. In short, the words and tones of *recitativo* are the building blocks with which Mozart creates the pedestal on which to mount his likeness of Don Giovanni—or, if the performer lacks aptitude, does not.

Much else about the characterization may come more easily to a Don Giovanni, even to one so widely admired as the late Ezio Pinza. When he first ventured the part in the late twenties in New York, Pinza sang some of the music well, but was found wanting in the "elegance, the grace, the adroitness, the magnetic charm" of a true Giovanni (in the view of Lawrence Gilman, critic for the *Herald-Tribune*).[1] In the opinion of an even more penetrating Mozartean, Pitts Sanborn in the *Evening Telegram*, the problem went to specifics: "His treatment of the 'dry' recitative, which should be both glib and subtly colored, is prevailingly heavy and drab."[2] Not until five years later, after restudying the part (for Salzburg) under the expert tutelage of Bruno Walter, did Pinza discover that the opera could be "an enchanting experience" (to quote Pinza's biographer, Robert Magidoff).[3] He had, with Walter's assistance, found the key to unlock the door that barred him from his objective.

2

Why, to revert to Sanborn's perceptive comment, "dry" recitative? Is there more than one kind and, among them, a species to which *Don Giovanni* has a particular affinity? The answer, in all cases, is "Yes!" The basic word is Italian for "recite" and spells out the long-standing distinction, in opera, between something recited or spoken, and something sung (*cantare*). When the earliest writers of opera, as we know it, attempted to revive the lost art of Greek tragedy in 1597, the first vocal element was "what now came to be known as recitative" says the *Concise Oxford Dictionary of Music*. The seductions of song were joined to the candor of recitative by Monteverdi, in his *Orfeo* a decade later.

In the decades that followed, "dry" recitative, or what is more formally known as *recitativo secco* (*sec* is "dry" in French, *secco* is "dry" in Italian) came to be the apt term for rapidly articulated syllables pitched closely to the spoken sound itself. It is *recitativo secco* because instrumental accompaniment is of the lightest. To avoid muffling the audibility of the words, which are articulated in a "dry" manner lacking full vocal resonance, the accompaniment is mostly chordal, played on the first (and perhaps third) beats of the measure by a harpsichordist, with a supporting double bass. Together the instruments are the *continuo*, which leads the music from the key in which the *recitative* began to the one in which the composer wants to write the next, more melodic, segment. *Recitativo secco* serves beautifully Mozart's purposes in *Don Giovanni*, because it lends itself so well to the mercurial, electric, unpredictable volatility of the principal character's personality.

Mozart was also a master of *recitativo stromentato* (stro-men-*ta*-to), which is to say, accompanied *recitativo* or instrumented recitative. This is the kind in which the voice articulates much the same kind of matter to be heard in *recitativo secco*, but is supported by orchestrated chords or commentary. It came in about 1630 and hasn't gone out yet, thanks to the imagination and ingenuity which have been applied by countless composers to exploit its possibilities. In both *recitativo secco* and *recitativo stromentato*, the conductor cedes his leadership responsibility to the singer. He *leads*—within reason—as the spirit moves him on a particular occasion, and the conductor either plays the chords of the continuo on a harpsichord, or cues the player of it, as he cues the orchestra to enter as the supporting element in *recitativo stromentato*.

Prevailingly, *recitativo stromentato* differs from *recitativo secco* in being not merely a connecting link from one episode to another. It is more likely to appear when the next scene has been reached and a prefatory statement to the impending vocal solo is in order. The recitative thus forms a bridge, from a dramatic destination already reached to the exposition of what happens, at that point, melodically. Often the instrumented recitative is accompanied by an instruction in the score reading *colla parte* or *colla voce*. This means that the instrumentalists should not expect strict time values to be enforced, but "go with the voice." This requires quick reflexes and a response to the exercise of individual options in a singer's treatment of *recitativo stromentato* which differentiate the expert members of a fine opera orchestra from "symphony" men . . . and women.

Mozart is so widely acclaimed for the perfection of his artistry across a broad range of instrumental and vocal music that he is rarely recognized also as an innovator and, indeed, as a revolutionary. In less than a decade, from 1782 until his death in 1791, Mozart more than transformed the writing of both German and Italian opera. He left examples of style enriched by genius which stood as models of procedures to composers on both sides of the Alps through the nineteenth century, and, as utilized by Strauss and Stravinsky, into the middle of the twentieth.

Though the solecism of performing *Le Nozze di Figaro* in German (*Figaros Hochzeit*) has been perpetuated at, of all places, the Salzburg Festival, there are precise and cogent reasons why Mozart wrote certain of his works in German and others in Italian. At the heart of the matter is the treatment of the nonmelodic text—that is to say, *recitativo secco* and *recitativo stromentato*, or some variation of them. The most logical variation to these procedures would be the text minus *any* form of accompaniment, or spoken dialogue. And that is precisely what we have in two of his famous works, both with German texts and titles: *Die Entführung aus dem Serail* (*The Abduction from the Seraglio*) and *Die Zauberflöte* (*The Magic Flute*).

The two last named ascended, through the power of Mozart's imagination, from a lower species of German entertainment known as *Singspiel* (song-play). The title was arrived at by a procedure no more scientific than the one in the 1940s which described as a "musical" something that could no longer be called a "musical comedy"—*Street Scene, Carousel, South Pacific*, up to and including *My Fair Lady* and *A Little Night Music*. A "song-play" contained songs connected by spoken dialogue and was evolved by German composers after the successful production in Leipzig in 1764 of the English ballad opera *The Devil to Pay* by Charles Coffey.

The underlying, causative reasons for Mozart's preference for German in some instances and Italian in others was well stated in an article by the long-lived New York music critic W. J. Henderson, in the New York *Sun* of November 22, 1930. It was occasioned by the reappearance at the Metropolitan of the production of *Don Giovanni* with Pinza alluded to previously. Said Henderson:

> *Recitativo secco* is not for the German tongue, but for the Italian it is perfectly suitable. It was created by the Italians.
>
> When Mozart eliminated *secco recitativo* from his German operas he drew a line which was the first mark of the boundary between German and Italian opera. He was—perhaps unconsciously—recognizing the difference between the genius of the German tongue and that of the Italian. The "soft bastard Italian" is essentially a legato speech; the strong, original and independent German is rugged, bristling with aggressive consonantal attacks. When Mozart wrote German recitatives, he wrote them in the heroic vein and with the orchestra, not a harpsichord, under them.[4]

Henderson's point could hardly be more clearly stated, or more inclusively. For, in defining the reasons that inclined Mozart to one course in one *creative* circumstance, and another in a different creative circumstance, he also defined very specific considerations in *re-creative* circumstances. That is to say, German singers, or singers schooled in Germanic methods, usually make sorry specimens of Don Giovannis or Almavivas (in *Figaro*); equally, Italians schooled in legato are not likely to command the guttural attack for an Osmin in *Die Entführung aus dem Serail*, or for Sarastro's "In diesen heil'gen Hallen," in *Zauberflöte*.

There can, of course, be exceptions. Richard Tauber was a fine Don Ottavio in *Don Giovanni*, though he was a native of Linz, Austria. Elisabeth Schwarzkopf sang the finest Donna Elvira of her time—in

Italian, of course—though her birthplace (Jarotschin, near Poznan, previously Posen) was in the cusp between Germany and Poland. And today's Teresa Zylis-Gara, wholly Polish, has the qualifications to replace the now-retired Schwarzkopf in her specialty. But these are eminently the exceptions. A generality that can be confidently ventured, with small likelihood of contradiction, is that Mozart's great Italian operas—*Don Giovanni, Le Nozze di Figaro* and *Così fan tutte*—fare best with an international singing cast (Italians, Americans, Welsh, English, perhaps a Continental woman or two) but a *non*-Italian conductor.

The gift of tongue which makes an Italian singer superior to others in Mozart's Italian operas does not confer a comparable benefit for Italian conductors. Did I hear someone say "Carlo Maria Giulini"? A fair *Figaro*. A creditable *Don Giovanni* (for an Italian). But not, to my taste, on the level of a Bruno Walter or Erich Kleiber of yesterday, or a Georg Solti, Colin Davis, Charles Mackerras, Karl Böhm, Erich Leinsdorf, or Eugen Jochum of today. I would not impute a lack of *capacity* to the Italians. I would, however, insist that the non-Italian conductors I have named have a far greater *broad* indoctrination in the music of Mozart. From it they derive a much keener appreciation of the presence, in his operas, of the Mozartean mind that also produced his symphonies, concertos, serenades, and so on. It should suffice to say that when the Mozart operas were begging for a new musical orientation after nineteenth-century abuses, they found them not in Italian conductors but in two Germanic ones: Gustav Mahler for *Don Giovanni* and *Le Nozze di Figaro* and Richard Strauss for *Così fan tutte*.

3

Mozart's mastery of recitative as the fuse that contributed to the explosion of comedy in Italian opera is altogether evident in the world esteem for Rossini's *Il Barbiere di Siviglia, L'Italiana in Algeri*, and *La Cenerentola* (he wrote as many more of equal quality which are, unfortunately, less often heard). Rossini's birth, on February 29, 1792, followed by only a dozen weeks the death of Mozart on December 5, 1791, and a mystical attachment associated them through Rossini's lifetime. It was Rossini who said, after a visit to Vienna that included a viewing of the manuscript of *Don Giovanni*: "I would kneel before this precious relic. He is the greatest . . . the master of them all, the only composer with as much science as genius, and as much genius as science. . . ." On an occasion late in life when he had long since completed his catalog of nearly forty operas, Rossini was asked by an admirer: " 'Which of all your operas do you like best?' *'Don Giovanni!'* came the rapier-like reply."[5]

The practices of Mozart, in recitative and ensemble, particularly, filtered through Rossini's vision so much so that it was Mozart-Rossini when it became Donizetti's turn to invoke his tragicomedy spirit in the laughter of *L'Elisir d'Amore* and *Don Pasquale*. The New York critic who complained of the late Fritz Busch's conducting of *Don Pasquale* as "too Mozartean," was, in fact, rendering it the highest possible praise. When Verdi found in *Falstaff* the comic subject for which he had been searching all his life, he recaptured, for Italy and Italians, leadership in the high art of fun and frolic which Mozart had earned (in part) with Italian precepts absorbed during his teen-aged stays in Milan and other music centers of the peninsula (Rome, Mantua, Bologna).

From the application of *spoken* recitative and inimitable song in *Die Entführung*, Mozart created a model which he even more greatly glorified in *Die Zauberflöte*. From such enlargements of the *Singspiel* tradition flowed the impulses that impelled Beethoven's *Fidelio*, Weber's *Der Freischütz*, and a host of works by Lortzing and Marschner which entered into the conditioning of Wagner. Wagner, in turn, eventually conceived the innovation of "endless melody" (theoretically minus recitative *or* spoken text) that infiltrated not only Germanic but all European opera in the second half of the nineteenth century. From his early status as "la fille de Gounod," Jules Massenet became celebrated as "Mlle Wagner" when his masterpiece, *Manon*, made its appearance with a full line of leading motives. But the work still held rank as an *opéra-comique* because, in such passages as the one in which Des Grieux makes his first, flirtatious approach to Manon, it is not in some honeyed melodic phrase but in his own *speaking* voice saying ". . . Pardonnez-moi! Je ne sai . . . J'obéis . . . Je ne suis plus mon maître . . ." ("Pardon me! I know not . . . I obey . . . I am no longer master of myself"), while Massenet uses the violin to drip the nectar that sweetened the words to Manon's ear. This, in effect, was a combination of spoken and accompanied recitative exactly suited to the circumstances.

In recent years, not only *opéra comique* but the Opéra-Comique itself (the theater on the Rue Favart which historically housed the activity) has entered the limbo of lost causes, esteemed for the glory of its past rather than the adornments of its present. What, it might be asked, caused the sickening and death of a once healthy, flourishing stage specimen? I would cite, among primary considerations, the needs of the export market. *Carmen* was born speaking French as well as singing French, but when she was invited to accept the hospitality of her first foreign host (Vienna) it was on the condition that she forget about speaking, and only sing. Whether or not Bizet would have approved will never be known, for he died (on June 3, 1875) not long after the opera's premiere, and the first performance in Vienna did not occur until October of the same year. The accompanied recitative (in German) required for the Vienna production was provided by his close friend and interpreter Ernest Guiraud (a native of New Orleans). Guiraud did his work so well that the popular appeal of *Carmen* was much accelerated.

A contemporary effort to restore the "integrity" of *Carmen* by dispensing with Guiraud's recitatives and returning to the spoken text may be an acceptable alternative in such a metropolitan center as New York, where the most recent production of *Carmen* included spoken text. But I do not hesitate to predict that the *next* new production will return to the Guiraud recitatives. Meanwhile, it is likely that in smaller communities, *Carmen* will remain an all-singing, non-speaking, opera.

What can explain the importance to a successful opera of something that cannot be sung, whistled, or hummed as the patron is leaving the theater (the ordinary criteria for what is important in a stage performance with music)? Many opinions could be assembled, but they would hardly be as responsive to the question as the statement made decades ago by Henderson in the article previously cited: "What is learned by composers in solving the problems of recitative inevitably becomes the basis of their entire musical style. Gluck formed the style of his high artistic period by a searching examination into the phonetic and expressive character of the language. Lully developed his operatic idiom from a close study of the declamation of Racine, a master of the melody of French verse."[6]

In these few sentences are contained some profound truths about the nature of opera, and a root reason why all the performable operas of today were written by little more than a hundred gifted men, of the thousands whose names appear in the index of Alfred Loewenberg's definitive *Annals of Opera 1597–1940*. To paraphrase Henderson, one might say: "To solve the problem of writing recitative is to achieve the basis of a musical style." Negatively stated, it would read: "Failure to solve the problem of writing recitative would inhibit the achievement of a musical style." I wouldn't push the analogy far enough to declare that the writing of good recitative is the equivalent, in opera, to Maggie Wylie's characterization of "charm" in J. M. Barrie's *What Every Woman Knows:* "If you have it, you don't need anything else; and if you don't have it, it doesn't matter much what else you have."[7] Nor would I recommend an evening of the most sparkling recitatives ever written as the answer to a musical gourmet's inner craving.

But it is unquestionable that imitative operas have come and gone because men who could write pretty, indeed beautiful, melodies had not mastered the dramatic problem of writing an opera—beginning with recitative—and thus did not achieve a style of their own. Samples of luscious tunes are numerous and a scattering may be cited in several voice ranges: the "Lamento di Federico" from Cilèa's *L'Arlesiana* and "Magische Töne" from Goldmark's *Die Königin von Saba,* both beloved of tenors; "Ebben ne andrò lontana" from Catalani's *La Wally* kept alive by sopranos (not to mention "Marietta's Lied" in Erich Wolfgang Korngold's *Die tote Stadt*); and "Sonst spielt' ich mit Zepter" from *Zar und Zimmerman,* and "Nun ist's vollbracht" from *Undine* (both by Lortzing), a pair of arias favored by German baritones.

My personal test of the true operatic composer is contained in the question "Does he, as his career matures, develop a truly personal style of treating recitative, thus breeding, in turn, a wholly personal way of writing operas?" The single exception—other than Mozart, who is the exception to all rules—would be Rossini. He chose to retire from the creation of theater music at the age of thirty-seven. He might have reasonably reckoned that, after treating a variety of subjects from *Otello* to *Semiramide* and arriving at the fulfillment of *The Siege of Corinth, Le Comte d'Ory,* and *Guillaume Tell* in 1829, before he was forty, there remained little for him to prove—though he lived, well and happily, until 1868.

4

Verdi revered Rossini to the point of urging other Italian composers of the late 1860s to join with him in writing a Requiem in memory of their idol. The plan fell through, but the great *Manzoni* Requiem that Verdi wrote five years later evolved from the eloquent "Libera me" he had conceived for Rossini. From time to time, in moments of exasperation with librettists, impresarios, and singers, Verdi talked of writing "finito" to his career as a composer of operas and of tending the gardens and cabbages of Sant' Agata. But deep in his being he felt differently than did Rossini about the art to which they were both devoted. Rossini cheerfully confessed to "a passion for idleness"; self-improvement was an equally strong impulse in Verdi, who was impelled to write as long as he had something to say—which was as long as he lived.

And the longer he lived, the higher he set his standard for textual materials. Ultimately, he was collaborating only with "Papa" (as he called Shakespeare), thanks to the intercession of Arrigo Boito. A multitalented man, Boito was a good enough composer to create *Mefistofele*. But he took time out from his own creative work to apply his literary gifts to serving Verdi. He was motivated by the quite selfless belief that Verdi's genius merited the kind of material he evolved for him in *Otello* and *Falstaff*.

The distance from Temistocle Solera, who wrote the text for *Nabucco*, to Shakespeare-cum-Boito is hardly greater than the distance between Verdi's first dramatic success and his last. It might be likened to the distance from Mozart's *Die Entführung* to Wagner's *Die Meistersinger*. In each instance, a model was derived from a foreign source. For Mozart-Wagner, it was the transformation of the *Singspiel*, with its English antecedents, into the most abundant of operatic comedies. The model that first served Verdi was "melodramma," whose prototype was the French *mélodrame*, created by Jean-Jacques Rousseau in 1770. A German adaptation was composed by Jiři Benda and first performed in 1779.

The concept of "melodramma" to describe a combination of words and music became so imbedded in the Italian tradition that, by the mid 1800s, it was the prevalent term for what we call opera. The Italian score of *Rigoletto* describes it as "Melodramma in tre atti." Stretching into the distance behind it were such "melodrammi" as Bellini's *La Sonnambula* and even *Il Barbiere di Siviglia*, which Rossini called a "Melodramma buffo." *Ernani* could also be affiliated with this tradition, which brought with it *recitativo* designed to embody the turbulent emotions of the character who delivered it.

Difficult as it is for the dramatic sopranos of today to move their voices as flexibly as such an aria as "Ernani, Ernani, involami" ("Ernani, Ernani, fly me away") requires, they are even more vexed by the *recitativo* that precedes the aria. In substance, "Ernani, involami" is a classic of three-part construction. It takes in the opening recitative describing the circumstances which confront the singer; the *cavatina*, in which she expresses her hope for a brighter future; and a *cabaletta*, painting the joy that will be hers when she is united with Ernani. Each section illustrates a classic form of vocal discipline: declamation (for the recitative), sustained legato (for the *cavatina*), and exuberant facility (in the *cabaletta*). Such versatility was a common attribute of singers in Verdi's time. Of recent performers, only Maria Callas was educated to the awareness that emphasis in recitative should go to the *words* rather than the notes. Such others as Leontyne Price, Joan Sutherland, and Montserrat Caballé are disposed to dwell on the beauty of their vocal sound and let the words—if audible—speak for themselves.

At the outset of his career, Verdi accepted the textual material that came his way (along with commissions), grumbled, and did the best he could with it. This included recitative in the prevailing tradition (of Bellini and Donizetti) which was often stilted, rarely forceful. As his skills matured, so did his perception of what could be done by imagination, ingenuity, and taste to make recitative a more organic part of the action than it had previously been.

In the great trio of operas with which Verdi made his reputation in the 1850s, *Rigoletto* (the first of them) begins with a scene in a ducal palace and *La traviata* (the last) at a soirée in the salon of Violetta. Music and dance are built into the action of both, always a desirable *milieu* for operatic treatment. The animation and vivacity which have given them enduring life, are not merely a consequence of the musical response the subject aroused in Verdi's heart, but a product of the creative mind that controlled its application. Text and words, dialogue and asides are all carried buoyantly on a surging undercurrent of orchestral sound.

La traviata is even more successful in sustaining a forward flow than *Rigoletto*, which has a built-in need for a dramatic declamation in Act I by Monterone, who is being led off to jail for objecting to the Duke's more than playful interest in his daughter. The first matter labeled "Recit." in the score of *La traviata* does not occur until the beginning of Act II. It comes with the entrance of Alfredo, and it is so springy, so resiliently framed in the orchestral writing *around* it, that it bounds on directly into "De' miei bollenti spiriti" with never a sense of separation or even of preparation.

Tenors by the dozen have sung the opening words "Lunge da lei per me non v'ha diletto" ("Away from her, there's no joy for me") as if mentally and spiritually impatient to have done with them and get on to the following aria. Jan Peerce was one who lingered on it, savoring every word and syllable, especially in performances that followed his participation in the celebrated broadcast directed by Toscanini. It was Toscanini's common practice to prepare the orchestra—which was not conditioned to operatic performance—by vocalizing *every role* in the score as they went through the score together. As a result, there is a celebrated (private!) recording in which he can be heard vocalizing this episode. Hoarse? Yes. Throaty? Of course. But still a model of style.

To me—and to more than a few others, I suspect—the most inspired moment of *La traviata* comes not in the dashing "Sempre libera" for the soprano in Act I or the tenor's aria and the baritone's "Di provenza il mar, il suol" in Act II, great as they are. It comes in Verdi's treatment of the excerpt from Alfredo's letter which Violetta delivers at the beginning of Act III. A mere forty words in length, it can make or mar any performance of *La traviata*, according to the intonation and timbre its Violetta brings to the spoken words, over the sighing sound of two solo violins recalling a strain from Act I. Intonation? Timbre? Can such terms be applied to a spoken sound? They can indeed, when the spoken sound has been so closely involved with the musical as it has here by Verdi.

Many sopranos who can flit through the brittle music for Violetta in Act I, or accommodate themselves to their portion of "Dite alla giovine" with Germont in the next scene, fall far short of an acceptable standard in Act III. They have, to haunt them, almost any opera-goer's memory of perhaps the greatest performance of this scene ever recorded: by Claudia Muzio, of course. Thousands who were not alive when Muzio died in 1936 (aged only forty-seven) are convinced that she must have been the greatest Violetta of her time. In this they would have concurrence of Hermann Devries, critic of the *American* in Chicago (where Muzio spent much of her American career), who described her as: "without doubt the greatest Violetta of them all."[8] In New York the verdict was less emphatic: a good Violetta, among others. She did, in any case, have an extraordinary flair for this feat, which her recording of the mid-thirties has aggrandized for all operatic time. To be sure, it is easier to etch a sound into wax, as Muzio did, than to make it equally immediate for thousands in the theater. Bori,

Bidú Sayão, Licia Albanese, Callas, and Renata Tebaldi were all capable of performances far above the average, but this will remain Muzio's scene as long as a recording can be played.

It will also remain to Verdi's credit that he and his librettist, Francesco Maria Piave, created an operatic tradition with their treatment of the letter read by Violetta (the earlier letter read by Lady Macbeth, is not nearly as successful). There is a letter-*writing* scene for the Countess and Susanna in *Le Nozze di Figaro*, but it is of quite another, less dramatic character. Such letter-*reading* scenes to come as Tatiana's in Tchaikovsky's *Eugene Onegin*, or Charlotte's in Massenet's *Werther*, or Geneviève's in Debussy's *Pelléas et Mélisande* (not to mention Périchole's in Offenbach's *La Périchole*), all owe something to Verdi's demonstration that such an episode is dramatically valid, and aurally viable. Perhaps this is why he chose not to call *La traviata* a "melodramma." It is, by his own words, an "Opera in 3 atti."

By whatever name, *Il trovatore* must be rated the retrogressive one of the great Verdian trio. This is not only because it is, at bottom, just another variation on the theme of the "long-lost child" or that its characters lack the emotional reality of Rigoletto's fatherly feeling for his ravaged daughter or the hectic vivacity of the disease-racked Violetta. It is rather more because it has the least creatively conceived text of the three. In the opening episode we are back—courtesy of the librettist, Cammarano—to the tedious, time-worn device of having a person in the drama (Ferrando) recount to a chorus (and the audience) "what happened before" the action begins. Save in Italy, this is a wasted exercise, supplemented by many covert glances at a libretto, by those who would be at a loss to know, otherwise, what Ferrando was saying. The first *Recit.* comes on page 2 of the piano-vocal score, and the text moves slowly downhill thereafter, arrested and driven upward only by the furious musical energy Verdi brought to it.

As his experience grew and his authority mounted, Verdi expended considerable quantities of the same vehemence on the men who wrote librettos for such later works as *Un ballo in maschera, Simon Boccanegra, La forza del destino,* and *Don Carlos,* urging them to give him something closer to what he desired. But his success in no instance could be termed total.

To the librettist for *Ballo* he wrote: "I prefer a good recitative to a poor piece of verse"[9]—though there is no assurance that he had his preference satisfied. To the librettist for *Forza* he exploded: "For God's sake, my dear Piave, let's think about this carefully. We can't go on like this: it's absolutely impossible with this drama."[10] On the subject of *Don Carlos*, derived from Schiller, Charles Osborne, author of the excellent book entitled *The Complete Operas of Verdi*, says: "What his librettists were forced to omit [from the original five-act drama], Verdi was able to restore in music; but, where they actually altered or invented, it was usually for the worse."[11]

It is basic Verdian lore that he married young (twenty-three), had two children who died in infancy, and lost his wife before their fifth wedding anniversary. It is not so well known that, having survived these disasters, he eventually acquired a lifelong relationship with Giuseppina Strepponi, who had been the Abigaille of his first success, *Nabucco*, during a distinguished career as an operatic soprano. At the outset, they simply shared his rural home in Sant' Agata, both being mature enough (in their forties) to value companionship but wise enough to realize that an indivisible bond might not, eventually, suit the convenience of one or the other. They were, actually, married in 1859 and had nearly forty years of "respectable" life together. Giuseppina died in 1897, when Verdi was eighty-four.

One can hardly imagine a woman better suited to be a composer's wife—especially an opera composer's wife—than Strepponi. She knew and shared the values to which he was devoted. She knew the misbegotten world of opera in which he had to function and armed his resistance to it. She was personally versed in every pitfall and defile that lay in wait for him and sought to aid him in evading them. She was even capable of such excellent advice as she offered (in 1853) when Verdi was riding the crest of *Rigoletto* and *La traviata*, with *Il trovatore* finished, and complaining about what he had to do next: "In your position, I wouldn't tie myself in any way for the present. I should look for a libretto I liked and set it to music *without any engagement and in my own time!* . . ."[12]

This was, obviously, too good advice for any man to take from a woman, especially from one he loved. But eventually, and in the fullness of his creative wisdom, Verdi came to the conclusion "on his own." That it came to be *Aida* in which he would immerse himself at his leisure was, in part, an accident of circumstances. The price which Verdi cited to the Khedive of Egypt, who had approached him to write an opera for Cairo, was pitched astronomically high—$20,000— with a view to discouraging him from pursuing the subject. But the Khedive was not to be discouraged and proceeded to make the necessary arrangements for payment. It was, however, Verdi's interest in the synopsis of a story that was submitted, which led to his acceptance of 150,000 francs.

The form in which the text was written and the manner in which it related to Verdi's music were in no way accidental. It was, in the nature of a project undertaken when Verdi was nearing sixty, a proving ground for all the theories and principles of recitative which Verdi had argued over with the many librettists he could pressure but not command, bully but not transform. The opera would be done his way or it would not be done at all.

As a result, almost from the outset of *Aida* one is galvanized, transfixed, rendered attentive by—recitative. But it is recitative crackling, alert, not merely martial but militant, as Radames responds to the information from the High Priest (Ramfis) that the country is threatened and a young warrior will soon be selected to lead its defense. When Ramfis leaves, on his way to confer with the King on the warrior's identity, Radames gives voice to his hopes, perhaps even his expectations:

> Se quel guerrier io fossi!   If I were that warrior!
> Se il mio sogno si avverasse!   If my dream came true!

Yes, this too is recitative—a Verdian form of *recitativo stromentato*. But the *stromentato* is a blare of trumpets (after the couplet quoted above) which alerts the ear to a state of mind, a range of possibilities, a whole vista of action which has rarely been associated with that term before. All this, it might be added, is by way of preface to the famous "Celeste Aida," an aria which Verdi dared to introduce at an early moment of the drama considered indecently premature by many performers. (The good repute of the great Jean de Reszke, so greatly admired for his Tristan, his Siegfried, his Faust and Roméo, is somewhat tarnished by his inclination to omit "Celeste Aida" when he sang Radames, because it was too early in the evening.) Most people listen to "Celeste Aida" to determine whether or not the performer is really a good tenor. I listen to "Se quel guerrier io fossi" and what follows, not merely to determine whether the Radames we are in for that night is a good tenor, but whether he is a *warrior*.

If "Se quel guerrier," etc., and all the verbal byplay that follows in *Aida* are indeed galvanizing, transfixing, and inescapably magnetizing, it is, in large part, because Verdi injected himself into the writing of the text from the outset. He did not pressure, did not cajole or remonstrate, but *demonstrated* to his collaborator what it was he wanted. He invoked his vast credentials as an opera composer to place in the balance his judgment on what was verbally suitable to the music he had in mind.

What it was, in a phrase, was what Verdi termed the *"parola scenica"* (the "word of the scene"), or as he explained to his librettist in a letter of August 17, 1870, "the word that clinches the situation and makes it absolutely clear. . . ." He then cites a passage from the second-act duet of Aida and Amneris as rendered by the librettist, and, in the more pointed, specific language he would prefer, adds: "But what about the verse, the rhyme, the strophe, you exclaim? . . . When the action requires it, I should abandon rhythm, rhyme, and strophe altogether and use blank verse to say exactly and clearly what the action requires. There are many moments in the theatre when poets and composers must have the talent to write neither poetry nor music. . . ."[13]

In these proud, trenchant words, Verdi wrote his own Declaration of Independence from all the inanities in operas that had preceded—including some of his own—and articulated a Bill of Rights for all the Italian composers who followed. The extent to which they would implement the freedom he had articulated remained to be demonstrated. Of the existence of it, however, there was not the least possibility of doubt.

The composite Radames I have assembled, mentally, from the dozens I have seen and heard is—as is true of many "ideal" operatic characterizations—a virtue of this one, a distinction of that one. Some were good tenors, who had been great tenors (not, unfortunately, within my hearing), some were overpowered by their surroundings. But not many were warriors. At one point, Mario del Monaco might have qualified, had he ruled his passionate outbursts with a firmer hand. As of his first appearance in New York (in Puccini's *Manon Lescaut*), his was the closest likeness to the fabled Martinelli sound that I had heard from anyone, including Martinelli himself. That great singer's days as a heroic tenor were behind him when I started to write. But, as Radames, Martinelli bore himself like a warrior—if, perhaps, of five-star rank rather than one anxiously awaiting his first command.

Ramon Vinay had qualities to admire as Radames, and Carlo Bergonzi had perhaps the suavest approach to the top tone (B flat) of any. Unlike most other singers, this was close to his best effort of the evening, for the power to override the charging brass of the Nile Scene was not at his command. Oddest, perhaps, of all who stood with hands clasped to chest was Jess Thomas. He was pressed into duty in an emergency and his aria came out "Holde Aida" because he wasn't yet sure of the part in Italian and insisted on the translation with which he had become familiar in Germany. That was not a prime night for Verdians. Nor, may I add, were those on which Jon Vickers weaved and bounced on his toes, as though shadow-boxing the part rather than singing it.

5

The instance of Wagner is of special interest because he wrestled with the double dilemma of composer *and* librettist. He wrote the texts for the music he composed and composed into reality the texts he had written. He thus faced the dubious delight of multiple success or duple failure. There is some evidence to indicate that he was prouder of his accomplishments as a poet than he was of his attainments as a composer. Or, perhaps, he assumed his greatness as a composer was self-evident, but felt he had to prove his literary abilities once again with every new project.

I would have given much to be present—astrally, of course, as a misty, invisible spectator—on the May evening in Paris in 1860, when Wagner, with his disciple Karl Klindworth at the piano and the great, but hardly Wagnerian, singer Pauline Viardot as the voice of Isolde, performed the second act of *Tristan* for an audience of two. One was a wealthy female patron, the other was Hector Berlioz. Of the end, Wagner, who had intoned the music of Tristan, records in *My Life*: "Mme. Kalergis remained dumb. Berlioz merely expressed himself warmly on the *chaleur* [ardor] of my delivery."[14]

As Berlioz had already expressed his lack of enthusiasm for the *Tristan* prelude when it was performed in a Paris concert several months before and had no real knowledge of German, it would have been a memory to cherish to observe him as he reacted to what he heard. At that, he was much more fortunate than those who were rounded up to sit through an evening's recitation by Wagner, *sans* music, of whatever new work the *Meister* was contemplating.

The most famous occasion, of course, was the one to which the eminent Viennese critic Eduard Hanslick was bidden (in 1862) to hear Wagner read his current version of *Die Meistersinger*. It was familiar gossip in Viennese musical circles that the script contained a character named Hanslic*h*, though not much information about his part in the play had been circulated. Whether or not, by the time of this reading, Wagner had renamed the character Sixtus Beckmesser, it is certain that the mere association of Hanslick with the pettifogging, faultfinding town clerk was sufficient to convert an adversary into an enemy.

From these and a dozen other similar seances—including the reading of the text of *Parsifal* to a gathering of idolators in Bayreuth—it may be inferred that Wagner attached considerable importance to his texts as things in themselves, in addition to the function they served him musically. For this, it strikes me, there is rarely a contemporary justification. Even Ernest Newman, whose esteem for Wagner caused him to dedicate a good share of his life to documenting the music dramas and their creator, described him as a "versifier" rather than a poet.

As an instance, he cites the words in which Wagner conveys the rapture of Tristan and Isolde at their reunion early in Act II:

TRISTAN: Isolde! Geliebte!	Isolde! Beloved!
ISOLDE: Tristan! Geliebter!	Tristan! Beloved!
Bist du mein?	Are you mine?
TRISTAN: Hab' ich dich wieder?	Now do I have you?
ISOLDE: Darf ich dich fassen?	Dare I embrace you?
TRISTAN: Kann ich mir trauen?	Can I believe it?
ISOLDE: Endlich! Endlich!	At last! At last![15]

and so on, and on.

Newman observes: "If this telegraph style, as Emil Ludwig calls it, is poetry, then we shall have to give the word a meaning it never yet had."[16]

For Wagner, such words served the necessary function of verbalizing the ecstasies of his characters where the real rapture was boiling up from the orchestra. He could bend and shape the syllables as suited his purpose, with the assurance that the "poet"—himself—would always be in agreement.

This was, however, by no means the only kind of word-spinning of which Wagner was capable. It varied greatly in quality over his career, beginning with *Rienzi* and *Die fliegende Holländer*. In these, and the succeeding *Tannhäuser* and *Lohengrin*, the language tends to be formalistic and ponderous, giving rise to squarely cut phrases in recitative and repetitious rhythmic patterns. It was not until he had approached close to the beginning of the *Ring* (with the texts of *Götterdämmerung* and *Siegfried* already in being) that he achieved, on behalf of Siegmund and Sieglinde in the first act of *Die Walküre*, a flow of words evocative of the emotions of the humans with which he was concerned.

It is precisely here that we sense a new maturity in the music of Wagner (the score of *Das Rheingold* had preceded, of course, but it is still in many ways transitional from *Lohengrin*, and blemished by the five years of compositional inactivity during his residence—1849-54— in Zurich). The first act of *Die Walküre* is a mighty miracle among the many miracles for which Wagner was responsible. It stands almost alone in embracing, between curtain rise and curtain fall, a self-contained drama. It is, moreover, done with only three performers, who comprise the characters of the classic triangle.

A distraught, weaponless man bursts into a hut to take refuge from a raging storm. It is apparently empty, but a woman, attracted by the sound of the entry, offers the stranger a reviving drink. Their eyes meet in a glow of recognition neither can understand. The noisy arrival of the woman's husband from a day of hunting interrupts their conversation. A gruff man, he soon recognizes the intruder as a foe of his clan. It is he, not game, they have been hunting. The husband retires, with the warning that they will settle their differences on the following day. When he has fallen asleep, the wife reappears to tell the stranger he should escape while he can.

In a series of incidents that ensue, the stranger asserts his love for the woman, is confirmed in the hope that she shares it, and retrieves a sword buried deep in a tree trunk long before by a mysterious visitor. Armed not only with the sword but with the knowledge that the woman is the sister from whom he has long been separated, he proclaims her "Braut und Schwester" ("Bride and Sister") as they dash off into the spring night together.

Almost all of this is carried on amid a singular blend of vocal and instrumental writing in which the melodic line is now in one, now in the other. The words are close to the most poetic Wagner ever wrote, and they evoked from him a gush of music with a new spirit, a new flexibility, even a new, flowering freedom. There are, in the ebb and flow of it, shreds of narrative, much in the German form of declamation Beethoven wrote in *Fidelio* and Weber in *Der Freischütz*.

But the true source of the new melodic urgency in the interchanges of Siegmund and Sieglinde is the great outpouring of German *Lieder* (art songs) that had been accumulating during the four decades before *Die Walküre* was written in the mid 1850s. One doesn't have to know many examples of such songs to sense the similarity between the storm music that precedes the opening of *Die Walküre,* and one of the greatest by Schubert, his setting of Goethe's "Erlkönig." It is also audible fact that Siegmund's growing affection for Sieglinde is phrased in terms very similar to those employed by Schumann in many songs, especially "Widmung."

Out of this background grew Wagner's elaboration of a device that can be considered Schumann's own personal contribution to the art of the *Lied.* That is the art of using the piano, not merely to paint a background mood or picture, but to carry the melodic line when it soars beyond the range of the voice. A famous example is the setting of Heine's "Ich grolle nicht," where the piano plays the rising climax of the cresting melodic line. The optional, small notes inserted by Schumann are attempted by some hardy performers, but, in all circumstances, the tones are there in the piano to secure the tonal objective.

Wagner's exploitation of this overriding urge of the instrumental line to assert itself as the vocalist sinks back to countertones in a lower register is not a discovery of mine—much as I would like to claim it—but one that was noted decades ago by no less well versed a composer of songs (and admirer of Wagner's music) than Edvard Grieg. Writing in the *Century* Magazine for January 1894, Grieg observed: "In his treatment of the piano, Schumann was furthermore the first, who in a modern spirit, utilized the relation between song and accompaniment, which Wagner has later developed to a degree that fully proves the importance he attached to it. I refer to the carrying of the melody by the piano, or the orchestra, while the voice is engaged in the recitative."[17]

The recitative! Grieg's casual intrusion of this term into a discussion of Wagner is both arousing and amusing. Was it not Wagner who proclaimed his aim to be "endless melody" into which there could be no classification of aria or recitative? On the other hand, is it not a fact that, in this first act of *Walküre* itself, Wagner was inspired to write "Winterstürme wichen dem Wonnemond" for Siegmund, and the responsive "Du bist der Lenz" for Sieglinde? Each is, in every terminology but the Wagnerian, an aria. Grieg's reference to the orchestra carrying the melodic line while "the voice is engaged in the *recitative*" is a refreshingly candid reminder that there *is* recitative in Wagner's mature works and of where it may be found.

What was it that Henderson was saying to the effect that a composer who had solved the problem of writing recitative had evolved the basis of an entire musical style? Wagner may be said to have solved his recitative problem right here in the first act of *Die Walküre* and, in so doing, to have found his musical style.

6

It is also curious, and revealing, to find in the same article a comment by Grieg which bears directly upon the German *Lied*, upon Schumann's contribution to it, and upon a notable performer who was, in herself, a bridge from Schumann to Wagner and to a century and a half of outstanding interpreters of the music of both.

Writing of Schumann's disposition toward a melodic line that begins in the lowest part of a vocal compass and soars almost beyond the highest note it can be expected to contain, Grieg comments:

> Two instances among many occur to me—*Ich grolle nicht* and *Stille Thränen*—for which one will scarcely ever find an interpreter who can do equal justice to the beginning and the end. But if, on the other hand, a singer has a voice at his command capable of such a feat, he will produce the greater effect. Thus, I remember as a child in 1858, having heard Frau Schröder-Devrient, then fifty-five years old, sing *Ich grolle nicht*, and never shall I forget the shiver that ran down my spine at the last climax. The beautiful timbre of the voice was, of course, lacking, but the overwhelming power of the expression was so irresistible that everyone was carried away.[18]

The name and the fame Grieg has evoked could hardly be more central to the subject. Wilhelmine Schröder (she acquired the Devrient by marriage) was chosen, at the age of eighteen, by Weber to sing Agathe in *Der Freischütz* when he conducted it in Vienna for the first time in 1822. This prompted Beethoven to select her to sing Leonore in *Fidelio* when it was revived in Vienna later in the same year.

From this emerged *Fidelio*'s first round of successes in other European cities, especially when Schröder-Devrient was available to perform the leading role. Such an occasion occurred when *Fidelio* was heard for the first time in Leipzig in 1829. Included in the audience was the sixteen-year-old Richard Wagner. He was so impressed with what he saw and heard that, as he has written, he became a lifelong devotee of the performer as well as the work. Indeed, he sent Schröder-Devrient a letter so warm with praise that she recalled it a decade and a half later when they met in Dresden, where Wagner had gone to produce *Rienzi*. She was Wagner's choice to be not only the first Adriano in *Rienzi*, but also the first Senta in *The Flying Dutchman* and the first Venus in *Tannhäuser*.[19]

Clearly her opera credentials were of the highest, the reader may impatiently interject. What else did she do? In 1830 she visited Weimar and sang Schubert's "Erlkönig" for the poet whose words Schubert had set. Goethe, whose prior estimation of the song was hardly high, said that for the first time he understood what Schubert had done with it.

In 1840 Schumann—like Berlioz, not only a composer but one of the most prominent critics of his time—wrote of a concert given in Dresden by Franz Liszt: "From beginning to end he played alone and accompanied [Liszt invented the piano "recital," even the term itself]. . . . Only Madame Schröder-Devrient—almost the only artist capable of asserting herself in such company—toward the end of the concert performed Schubert's *Erlking* and some of his smaller songs together with Liszt."[20] Finally, it may be noted that 1840 was Schumann's "song year" (he had written few settings of poetry before). Having heard Schröder-Devrient, he changed the climaxing phrase of "Ich grolle nicht" to include the optional top tone (after the song was in proof) which does, indeed, complete the vocal line and aroused Grieg's admiration when he heard her, and it, as a boy nearly twenty years later.[21]

The clear indication of all this is that Schröder-Devrient was not only a brilliant and distinguished figure in the concert and operatic life of the mid-nineteenth century, but the mother superior for a host of singers who have professed the same faith, unto the present. To be a fine Leonore in *Fidelio* and an admired Agathe in *Der Freischütz* is, almost automatically, to be an outstanding Sieglinde in *Die Walküre*. Schröder-Devrient was born too early and died too soon (1804–60) to perform in the *Ring*. But there is little doubt that her performance of the leading female roles in two of his favorite works "laid out" in Wagner's mind many of the specifications for Sieglinde.

Lotte Lehmann's American career came too late for Agathe in *Der Freischütz* to be included among her roles. Leonore in *Fidelio*, of which I heard a memorable performance (conducted by Richard Strauss) at a Salzburg Festival in the 1930s, she did not sing in New York because it had been revived for Kirsten Flagstad (Lehmann said at the time that she felt she merited precedence because of her close identity with the role in many European centers). As with some distinguished predecessors—including the great Lilli Lehmann—the extension of the Schröder-Devrient line led her directly to Sieglinde. When the later (unrelated) Lehmann made her Metropolitan debut as Sieglinde in 1934, she was acclaimed, by one who had heard *every* New York predecessor, with the words "It is not injustice to her predecessors to say that she must be placed in the foremost rank." And, of course, as a *Lieder* singer—up to and not excluding "Ich grolle nicht," of which she gave one of the noblest of all performances, including the top tone—she was the greatest of her time.

Concurrently, Flagstad's Sieglinde was cherished by some even more than Lehmann's; she was a fine Leonore in *Fidelio;* and she had sung Agathe earlier in her career. She was also much enjoyed as a recitalist. Neither as Leonore nor as Sieglinde did Flagstad approach the intensity of Lehmann, but the beauty of her sound was something to cherish when heard, in all its splendor and accompanied only by piano, in such ideal acoustical surroundings as those of Carnegie Hall.

Two of the finest Sieglindes of the last decade are, without question, Birgit Nilsson and Leonie Rysanek. Each is also a famous Leonore in *Fidelio,* and both were heard as Agathe in the early years of their careers. Nilsson has been heard in many song recitals, Rysanek in relatively few. Perhaps for lack of application, neither has matched Lehmann in this specialty.

If you are confronted with the option of hearing or not hearing a new Sieglinde when the next one comes along, ask three questions: Is she a fine Leonore in *Fidelio?* Does she sing Agathe in *Der Freischütz?* Has she a good reputation as a *Lieder* singer? If the answer comes up, two out of three, "Yes," my injunction is "Go!" Even if she isn't a superior Sieglinde, you will, at the least, have a story to tell your grandchildren about the gifted lady who, for all her attributes, didn't follow through on what Schröder-Devrient started.

It might also be mentioned that, for an entirely different category of opera singer, Schröder-Devrient was a prototype of another sort. It has been written of this "Queen of Tears," as she was known, that her singing showed "a discrepancy between the delicate organization of her voice and the passionate energy of her temperament."[22] She may thus be affiliated with a whole Legion of the Damned—those with a fine voice too small to convey the emotions by which they were driven, or too large to consort with the small frame they possessed. Ferruccio Tagliavini is an instant example of a tenor who wanted to do more, as Edgardo in *Lucia di Lammermoor,* than his lovely sound could convey. Teresa Stratas is a case to the contrary point: vocally programmed to be a "Queen of Tears," she was restricted by physical size to the fate of being called the "Baby Callas." For such as Tagliavini and Stratas, not the Olympian heights of Wagner, to which their temperament might suit them, but the demi-world of Puccini to which their physical attributes restricted them.

7

Within that demi-world, for those who must embrace it as their part of the operatic bargain, there is another order of values, another set of objectives, and governing musical mores all its own. Unquestionably the most popular composer among the widest range of opera-goers of today—Wagnerites come when Birgit Nilsson sings Turandot, Verdians come when Luciano Pavarotti sings Rodolfo, and everybody would come if Placido Domingo sang Pinkerton in *Madama Butterfly*—Puccini is patronized by some, denigrated by others, and deified by those who love him for what he was: an outgoing embodiment of the Italian capacity to be both artistic and wholly unintellectual.

By this, of course, I do not mean unintelligent. I do mean that he could no more have written *Götterdämmerung* than Wagner could have written *Tosca*. Puccini would no more have thought of addressing himself to writing *Art and Revolution* than Wagner could have spent an afternoon duck hunting (remember the Swan slain by the innocent arrow of the guileless Parsifal?). In the aggregate, it is simply another instance of the abundance of nature in apportioning attributes so wisely that one talent rarely overlaps another altogether.

Puccini's talent was not for the monumental but for the microcosmic. His was an instinctive aptitude for detail, for nuance, for marginalia. He could, when necessary, sketch with broad strokes, but like his painter Cavaradossi in *Tosca*, he liked to retouch and refine. Sir Thomas Beecham recalled that "he had a positive mania for going about and hearing his own operas, whether they were played in a town twenty miles away in Italy, or in my country, a thousand miles off."[23] When he visited England in 1920, for the premiere there of *Il Trittico* (*Il Tabarro, Suor Angelica*, and *Gianni Schicchi*), Sir Thomas engaged him in a page-by-page discussion of *La Bohème*. He came away with a score full of markings additional to those in print—as Puccini's addenda to express every nuance and shading he really wanted but had not included in the original edition.

Puccini's practice relates, in part, to an order of composition consciously contrived to be reasonably loose, semi-improvisatory, and subject to the urgencies of the moment. Primarily, however, it relates to a desire to permit the ultimate in freedom to the principal performers, lest there be an external constriction to hamper the interplay of self-expression between Rodolfo and Mimi, Tosca and Cavaradossi, Pinkerton and Cio-Cio-San. The colloquial is almost always close to the core of Puccini. Even in *Turandot*, amid the high-flown language of the Princess and her ministers, of Calaf and the priests who are called upon to adjudicate his answers to the riddles, it is the simple, artless personality of Liù that restores us to a ground zero of emotion when the others threaten to take it too far into the artistic empyrean.

At the outset of his career, in *Le Villi*, Puccini inflamed Italy with the power of his promise and the possibility that a new man had arisen (1884) to occupy, far into the future, the place that the aging Verdi would, eventually, relinquish. There was considerably less cohesion in *Edgar*, which followed five years later and caused some influential members of the publishing firm that had been supporting Puccini to suggest that his stipend be ended. But the one who bore the name of the founder, and thus was the most influential, disagreed. "No," said Giulio Ricordi, "he is the Crown Prince, he will succeed"[24] (both for the firm, and to the laurels of Verdi, one presumes he meant). Ricordi encouraged Puccini to proceed with a project to which he had been attracted—a treatment, from another point of view, of the Abbé Prévost's *Manon Lescaut*, which had already served Jules Massenet well.

No one even then doubted Puccini's ability to evolve a melodic line which was supple and succinct, even succulent. *Manon Lescaut* is not long under way before Des Grieux launches into the soaring phrases of "Donna non vidi mai, simile a questa!" ("Never did I behold so fair a maiden!") in praise of the handsome heroine. The open, frank appeal of the melodic line has the quality that caused an Italian critic to hail it with the embracing word *paganesimo*, meaning "of our race."[25] It is sufficient to arouse the enthusiast to exclaim, "Aha! The real Puccini."

The more cautious might demur: *is* it the real Puccini, or is it more of Catalani or Cilèa, who could also write a beautiful melodic phrase? "Donna non vidi mai" has a charm and an ardor impossible to resist. But it is only an element of an opera, not the essence of one. That indispensable entity spreads its glow midway in Act II, with the episode beginning "O tentatrice, O tentatrice" ("O fatal temptress, O fatal temptress" is the translation in the piano-vocal score). It is melodic and it is expressive. But above all, it is exactly expository of the situation in which the hero-victim Des Grieux finds himself—entangled in the tentacles of a temptress from whom he cannot escape, helpless to resist what he knows will be his undoing.

Moreover, when the sweet-faced villainess takes Des Grieux's hand in hers and sighs (appropriately, Puccini marks it *pp*) "È fascino d'amor; cedi, cedi, son tua!" (" 'Tis love's own magic spell; your own am I, am I, forever!") it is the *orchestra* that carries the bewitching thought forward on the melodic line Puccini has devised for it, as Des Grieux exclaims: "Più non posso lottar! Son vinto!" ("I resist you no longer, I am vanquished"), with the voice sinking down to the lower octave to three repeated Gs on "Son vinto!" This is two ways clever: it gives the orchestra a chance at a sweeping statement of the big melody and it provides an opportunity for the tenor to gather himself for the duet with Manon that follows. This begins, incidentally—by no accident at all—with a reference to the melody of "Donna non vidi mai" sung by the "donna" herself, Manon.

Says Beecham, in the same comment cited previously: "The evolution of a Puccini style embodied the development of a quasi-melodic, yet narrative style which serves so well to carry the action along in his greatest works. We can see the style evolving in his earlier *Manon Lescaut*, which is in many ways a charming piece. Given a tenor of high quality, it can have quite a success. Puccini's gift for melody is apparent in the tenor's song in the first act. . . . But the other order of things only emerges in Act II ("O tentatrice, O tentatrice")."[26]

The "other order of things" just described was no manic inspiration of Puccini's but his rational, reasoned reaction to what had been happening in the opera world while he was growing up (Puccini was born in 1858, a year that straddled the birth of Verdi's *Un ballo in maschera* and the creation of Wagner's *Tristan und Isolde*). What was happening had as much to do with recitative as it had with melody, and when Puccini began his student years at the Milan Conservatory in 1880, the new ideas were as much a part of the atmosphere as the air he breathed.

Puccini, as has been suggested, was nonintellectual but far from unintelligent. That he was well versed in the works of Verdi was to be taken as a matter of course. That he had been indoctrinated in Wagner is evident from the appearance in *Manon Lescaut* of liberal segments of the *Tristan* vocabulary. As *Tristano e Isotta* (with an Italian text by Boito), Wagner's revolutionary score had made its peninsular debut in Bologna in 1888, two years before Puccini began work on *Manon*

Lescaut, and a year after his visit to Bayreuth in 1889. But students are invariably in the vanguard of the *avant-garde,* and Puccini was no exception in being familiar with Wagner's innovations.

Thus, whether Puccini had any awareness of Schumann's part in the generation of this kind of writing or not, he was exposed to it, not only in Wagner's appropriation of it, but in Gounod's imitation of it (in the Garden Scene of *Roméo et Juliette,* in which Roméo sighs ecstatically on a repeated C as the strings carry the melodic line forward) and in several episodes in Massenet's *Manon.* The free flow of instruments in and around the voice came to be perhaps the commonest denominator of Puccini's practices. Doubling the voice part with instrumental unisons an octave above or below was still another. Interrupting the vocal line altogether and carrying the thought through with a solo violin or horn or oboe came to be Puccini's nicest way of telling a singer that, much as he liked her/him, there was an instrumental color to be invoked at this point to fine-line the character sketch more precisely. Indeed, there is hardly a resource exposed in Wagner's use of voices in Act I of *Die Walküre* that was not inspected, rejected or accepted, externalized, and Italianized to Puccini's purpose.

The result, in *Manon Lescaut,* is a score not to be characterized as mature or immature, perfect or imperfect. It is music suspended for all time in a solution of impulse and enthusiasm that outruns even the skill of the composer who brought it about. While it was being written, Puccini took shelter in a town near the Italian-Swiss border, across from a house in which Leoncavallo was also busy at work. To symbolize his project, Leoncavallo hung out a drawing of a clown, to signify his immersion in *I Pagliacci.* Puccini responded with the outline of a hand, symbolizing "la mano," or "Manon." Two works more redolent of youthful talent can hardly ever have come to birth in such close proximity.

It might be assumed, in the aftermath of the success of Puccini's *Manon Lescaut,* that it was enthusiastically welcomed by interpreters of Massenet's heroine as a double dividend on a single character study. A soprano, preferably pretty, who had penetrated to the heart of one could, reasonably, be expected to have privileged access to the heart of the other. They would appear to be sisters not merely under the skin but under the satin of one costume exchanged for another.

This would, however, disregard the first fact that Jules Massenet, in the words of Nellie Forbush for Émile Debecque in *South Pacific,* was "a cultured Frenchman" and that Giacomo Puccini was an impulsive Tuscan. They were driven by different impulses directed toward unlike objectives. The vastly experienced Massenet's first impulse in writing *Manon* was, as he mentions in his *Recollections,* to realize a "dream" which had "haunted me for a long time."[27] That was another way of saying that he yearned to convert the subject matter in a way that would seduce the readily susceptible clients of the Opéra-Comique into still another acquiescence to his talent for pleasing them. Puccini's commitment in writing *Manon Lescaut* was much more earthy and fundamental—to establish beyond doubt of his reluctant underwriters (the directors of Ricordi's) and the public, his right to pursue his chosen career.

The difference in the conditioning of the two composers finds its way, inevitably, into the manner of treatment pursued by Massenet and Puccini in one detail of a scene they share in common: the square at Amiens where the principals have their first encounter. In Massenet's treatment of the libretto by Henri Meilhac and Philippe Gille, Manon has priority—as a title character should—as well as the first solo statement: "Je suis encore tout étourdie" ("I've seen so much that amazes me") in which we learn more than a little about her.

In Puccini's transformation of a text by Marco Praga, Luigi Illica, and Domenico Oliva (among others) we are awash in a sea of melody from the curtain rise. Des Grieux is on stage almost at once, and before five minutes have passed, he has served an *hors d'oeuvre* to the evening's musical repast: "Tra voi, belle, bruna e bionde" ("Among you, dark and fair beauties"), an arietta addressed to a bevy of chattering girls. Before five minutes more, he has launched into the sinuous, arching theme that later becomes the aria ("Donna non vidi mai") previously mentioned. Between and around them, Manon Lescaut has been on and off stage without so much as an arioso. If there is a suspicion from this that Puccini's opera is really more about "Renato des Grieux" (as he identifies himself) than it is about Manon Lescaut, it is not quite true. It is merely a confirmation of Puccini's one abiding conviction that there is nothing more compelling or less resistible to a woman than hot Italian blood, melodically conveyed. Bypassing all the intermittent details, there is no question that each approach arrives at the same outcome: Des Grieux's degradation and Manon's demise. But it is the "intermittent details" that make horse races, and operas.

Indeed, it is these "intermittent details" that have deflated the previously mentioned expectation that a skilled interpreter of Massenet's *Manon* might readily adjust herself to Puccini. There is, to be sure, a language difference which might give rise to a problem, but the weight of sound that differentiates Puccini's heavier vocal line from Massenet's more delicate detail and the orchestral treatment that enters into one *vis à vis* the other are more urgent considerations. Both Manons begin their adventures in the square at Amiens where they have been deposited by coach, but they go their separate ways thereafter.

Among the few who have ventured both operas and achieved success were Frances Alda, a Massenet Manon first (c. 1910) and a Puccini Manon Lescaut a few years later (her recording of "In quelle trine morbide" is still among the best); Lucrezia Bori, who reversed the order, singing the Italian version first (with Arturo Toscanini, in 1912), then the French (in the 1920s); and Eleanor Steber, who achieved this "double" between 1947 and 1955, with French preceding Italian. It should not be lost on students of artistic adaptability that *none* of the sopranos mentioned above was ethnically related to one Manon or the other—Alda was a New Zealander, Bori of Spanish descent, Steber American-born. It is thus a double distinction for Licia Albanese, born in Bari, Italy, that she mastered the Massenet Manon in 1947 before adding the Puccini in 1949.

Of contemporary sopranos, Dorothy Kirsten remains the most qualified exponent of the subtle differences that best define one treatment from the other. If she should, sometime, be moved to perform *both* parts within a week, she might be credited with the psychological, physiological, and musicological credentials that Bori earned when she sang *Manon Lescaut* on October 28, 1929, and *Manon* on November 8. Amid a multiplicity of other Massenet Manons, including Grace Moore, Bidú Sayão, Jarmilla Novotna, Victoria de los Angeles, Anna Moffo, Mary Costa, and Beverly Sills, Bori remains, for me, the ideal embodiment—vocally, visually, and textually—of the girl its composer christened "a perfidious darling."[28]

In his subsequent projects, as they matured, Puccini found more and more ways of telling his story musically and of employing his singular gift for making his narrative flow through words that reach the ear clearly, as the orchestra drapes garlands of melody around them, rather than burying them in blankets of sound. How much there is that is *conversational* in the three great works of Puccini's forties—*La Bohème* (1896), *Tosca* (1900), and *Madama Butterfly* (1904)—which parallel Verdi's production of *Rigoletto, La traviata*, and *Il trovatore* at roughly the same age! Virtually the whole first act of *La Bohème* evolves in this vein, setting the tone and temper of what is to follow. The procedure is extended to both Acts I and II of *Tosca* and all three acts of *Madama Butterfly*, which are, more often than not, one sustained conversational interchange between Cio-Cio-San and someone near her.

This conversational conception was cleverly converted to stage advantage by the Fujiwara Opera Company of Tokyo in the production they brought to the New York City Opera's stage in the 1950s. This remains one of the most engaging stagings of an opera I have ever seen. The action was, of course, highly stylized, but it was the treatment of the text that made all the difference between the merely exotic and the uniquely satisfying.

When the Japanese characters in the opera were conversing with each other, they communicated in a vernacular—*their* vernacular—translation of the text. When foreigners were present, they reverted to the Italian of the original. This was, among other things, an interesting affirmation of the premise that the Japanese use language to conceal, rather than reveal, meaning. Perhaps the most exquisite moment came in the "Flower Duet," when Cio-Cio-San and her maid, Suzuki, decorate their dwelling in anticipation of Pinkerton's return. Not only was the language piquant to the ear and an additional spice to Puccini's clinging thirds and sixths; enticing Harue Miyake and her house-companion Shizuko Kawasaki performed their decorative ritual in a willowy dip and glide, with a complete absence of angularity, that could only be described as choreographic.

Not too many Butterflies have the advantage of such physical aptitudes, even when exposed to such authentic surroundings as those designed by Motohiro Nagasaka for a Metropolitan production of the 1950s, in which the action was supervised by Yoshio Aoyama. About all that remains of that excellent venture a decade and a half later is that everybody still takes their shoes off before entering Butterfly's dwelling.

In *Tosca*, the conversational aspects are so artfully embedded in the flow of the music line in Act I that all too many performers of the title role are inclined to treat it, if not as an aria, then at least as an arietta or arioso. That is obviously a misreading of Puccini's purpose, and of the character herself. She is, after all, a reigning queen of the Roman stage and would, as a mere matter of professionalism, have more consideration for the spoken word and what it should convey.

Here, perhaps, Puccini should be held accountable for part of the blame—for having his recitative almost too palpably palatable. In his great middle trio the thin line of separation between recitative and aria has almost disappeared. The most famous aria he ever wrote for a tenor is, without doubt, what is known to most performers of it as Rodolfo's "Racconto." This merely means Rodolfo's "Narrative," which is self-evident reason why the next subject for consideration is clearly at hand.

III

Aria, Da Capo and Otherwise

1

If recitative may be described as a penance, in advance, for pleasure to come, *aria* is the embodiment of that promise—which may be deferred or diluted, as well as fulfilled. The possibilities in it are threefold because the involvements are triple, taking in composer, performer, and listener. If the composer serves only his own selfish purpose, it may be a pleasure deferred; when the aria caters only to the performer's privilege, it is likely to be a pleasure diluted. But when the aria serves the best of both purposes and rewards the listener with something indeed worthy of attention, then it can be exactly what is meant by a delight.

If, in the beginning there was *recitativo*—in Peri's *Euridice* of 1600—it was not long before it was joined by *aria* (or "song," which is the English equivalent)—in Monteverdi's *Orfeo* of 1607. They have been wedded to each other ever since, and, as in all such arrangements, not always happily. Though I have not meditated deeply on the sexual elements in that relationship, I tend to think of *recitativo* as manly and outspoken, *aria* as feminine and a little fickle. Certainly *aria* has seduced more composers into excess than recitative and incited more performers to acts of infidelity to good taste. Were there such a thing as a musical Domestic Relations Court, the docket would be loaded with endless cases of recitative charging aria with impropriety and extravagance.

In its inception, the arrangement was private and aristocratic. Peri and Monteverdi both wrote for the cultivated nobility of mid-Italy, who were their patrons and primary audience. Word soon began to circulate that there was something going on at court that other people

49

1733, the work endures today, aged nearly two hundred and fifty, to pleasure audiences at festivals and during regular opera seasons worldwide.

If the seventeenth century belonged exclusively to the male singer, the eighteenth saw the rising star of the soprano, which reached its zenith in the nineteenth. And for every artist such as Alessandro Scarlatti, a master of every musical means (including the *aria da capo*) who wrote 115 operas for the male-dominated Italian stage between 1679 and 1725, or Handel, who responded to the beauty of Caffarelli's voice to write the gorgeous sustained phrases of "Ombrai mai fu" (the famous "Largo" of *Serse*, in 1738), there were dozens of artisans willing to provide the castrati and, eventually, their female counterparts with what would bring crowds to the theater.

In many instances, what was provided might be the mere melodic line, so versed were such singers in the modification, elaboration, magnification, and perhaps the desecration of what they performed. There is a pretty tune by Paisiello named "Nel' cor più non mi sento" which is remembered by some as the subject for a series of suitable variations for piano by Beethoven. There is also a written record of the manner in which it was performed by a celebrated soprano of the eighteenth century, Angelica Catalani. Paisiello himself might have had some trouble in recognizing, under the runs, grace notes, and other fancy work imposed upon it, the real line of his melody. When Adelina Patti, as a young woman, paid Rossini a visit to show off her flashy version of "Un voce poco fa" from *Il Barbiere di Siviglia*, the bemused composer commented, "A nice tune. Who wrote it?"

Amid the numerous varieties of aria which had sprung up by the beginning of the eighteenth century—*aria cantabile* (sustained song), *aria di portamento* (slow, long notes, amenable to demonstrations of breath control), *aria di mezzo carattere* ("serious and pleasing," says one commentator), *aria di bravura* (which is self-explanatory)—why should *aria da capo* be singled out for bad marks?

It did, unfortunately, lend itself perfectly to purposes of individual alteration, as Baldassare Ferri was presumably the first to demonstrate in a theater, in the mid 1600s. In an *aria da capo*, the first melodic strain is succeeded by a second, contrasting one, usually more dramatic. Then, in response to a marking in the score reading "da capo" (meaning "return to the head"—*capo*—of the music) the first strain would be reprised. There is nothing inherently evil in the design; it served dozens of eighteenth-century composers for hundreds of minuets and trios, including all those by Haydn and Mozart bearing the mere instruction "Menuet D.C." "Erbarme dich" in Bach's *St. Matthew* Passion is an *aria da capo,* as is Handel's magnificent "Waft her, angels" for the tenor in *Jephtha.*

What came to be evil in the design was the latitude for abuse that it embodied, the open-ended opportunity for introducing leaps, runs, shakes, swells and diminuendos, divisions (splitting up the notes of a tune into shorter tones), and other devices into the reprise.

As a phenomenon in itself, improvisation is not without interest. It can be entertaining, amusing, even exciting, as has been demonstrated by jazz musicians for decades. As part of a drama, however, it could tend to be intrusive if Nicolai Gedda imposed his own ideas on how to vary the repetition of the opening strain in Mozart's "Il mio tesoro" on one night and Stuart Burrows countered with his in the next performance of *Don Giovanni.*

The final decision of the Church to eliminate castrati from liturgical usage left the public stage bare of them after 1861. No great loss, some might say. That would have my concurrence, even though no way has been found to persuade nature to produce, genetically, what society no longer allows to be produced surgically.

However, on an occasion when a fine mezzo of today such as Janet Baker might venture to challenge *Orlando,* with its Mad Scene, or Beverly Sills applies her art to a revival of *Giulio Cesare,* one yearns for wider circulation of the great stocks of Handel operas (forty!) in something closer to the original sound. For all their good intentions, when the music written for an altered male is performed by an unaltered female, one has to conclude—as one castrato replied, when he was asked to comment, candidly, on the state of his being—"something is missing."

2

For those to whom the dominance of the performer over what was being performed was a day-to-day condition of life, there was also "something missing" from Italian opera as a category (the only one that had international circulation in the mid 1700s). What was missing was a link, a likeness to or a trace of, the purposes defined by Peri and Monteverdi. These fastidious folk deplored the rigidity of *opera seria* (with its set sequence of aria, and at least one per act per performer), its obligatory dance elements, its artificial verbiage and static characters.

They longed for greater freedom, more poetry, a closer relationship of text and music.

The one designated by fate to become the voice of this discontent and to write the first full-length opera still regularly performed was the son of a forester-gamekeeper. Born in the Upper Palatinate in 1714, Christoph Willibald Gluck gave evidence of musical talent in his youth. He worked at prosaic jobs while studying; at twenty-three he acquired a noble patron who took him for a lengthy stay in Milan. Here he profited from studies with Sammartini, a master of instrumental composition. Gluck's inclinations were primarily to the stage, and he studied the models of the time with sufficient success to have works produced in Milan and Venice. In the mid 1740s he went to London, to join the numerous composers competing with the great Handel. Gluck was not much more successful than the others.

In 1750, after visits to Copenhagen and Prague, Gluck settled on Vienna as his home, married, and went to work at his trade of composer. His impulse toward reform or revolution was slow to mature and he did not soon become known as an innovator. He had, nevertheless, a latent capacity for substance. When he encountered a dismaying lack of success in London, he asked Handel—his lifelong idol—for a few words of advice. As recounted in Herbert Weinstock's *Handel*, the response was: "You have taken far too much trouble over your opera. Here in England that is a mere waste of time. What the English like is something they can beat time to, something that hits them straight on the eardrum."[4] (That may perhaps be why, after Handel's death in 1759, the English did not develop a creditable opera composer for a hundred and fifty years.)

The "suddenly wise Gluck"[5] (to quote Weinstock's description of him) was engaged, stimulated, and finally aroused when he was sought out in 1761 by Raniero da Calzabigi, a literary man and courtier who had written a text on the Orfeo legend. He had offered it to the Vienna Court Theater and been told that it required music. Gluck, it was suggested, might be a possible composer. Many years later, Calzabigi wrote: "I thought that the only music suitable for dramatic poetry . . . was that which would most nearly approach natural, animated, energetic declamation. . . . I read my *Orfeo* to him. . . . I begged him to banish . . . everything that was Gothic, barbarous and extravagant in our music. M. Gluck shared my views. . . ."[6]

In the creation of an *Orfeo* that would conform to a credo sometimes attributed to him ("All efficient music must be the peculiar

expression of some situation") Gluck disavowed no resource introduced before he was born, or during his lifetime. With Calzabigi, he
applied himself to select or reject, include or exclude, whatever contributed to their purpose. Text, vocal as well as instrumental music,
dance, mime, stage design—all the arts of the theater were welcomed.
Recitative is a strong element in Gluck's *Orfeo* as it had been in Peri's
Euridice; aria, which had served Monteverdi in his *La Favola d'Orfeo*,
is present and healthily accounted for; a chorus is utilized to humanize
Orfeo's despair and to rejoice when Euridice is restored to him.

To pretend that Gluck was aiming to reform opera is probably to
sound a moral tone he didn't profess. But to say that it was his aim to reform the elements of opera as they were utilized in 1760 into something more dramatically compact and musically consistent is to describe
in exact, factual terms what he and Calzabigi accomplished. They took
the best of what presented itself to them, and, by subtraction and addition, reformed it into something better.

For the Orfeo he had in mind, Gluck did not ever discard the
singularly suitable sound of the castrato. He selected the contralto castrato named Gaetano Guadagni, who was capable of an extraordinarily
disembodied vocal timbre, somewhere between the recognizably male
and the unmistakably female. What Gluck did discard was the castrato's privilege of adding *his* ideas to what the composer had written
for him to sing. He simply performed, with all seriousness and no
intrusive embellishments, the music of Gluck as written.

Guadagni may or may not have been a willing participant in this
singular example of forbearance. But it is a certainty that he was not
tempted to indulge the star singer's *aria da capo* privileges in that
morsel of melodic morsels "Che farò senza Euridice," in which Orfeo
laments the loss of Euridice. For all that it may suggest one, this is *not*
an *aria da capo*. The beautiful strain with which the aria begins is followed by a contrasting one. The two are both heard again. But when
the opening appears a third time, it is not as a repetition *pro forma*
or *da capo*. It is *written out again by Gluck*, with a last restatement of
the melody in a finalizing way that leaves no place for unsolicited
assistance.

Indeed, if you search the score of *Orfeo* aria by aria, as I have
recently, you will not find, among the dozen or so it contains, one
single *aria da capo*. Such a singular vote of no confidence in a device
which had served countless composers for decades could hardly fail to
have an effect on Gluck's contemporaries (especially in a work which

circulated as widely as *Orfeo* did). *Aria da capo* remained in being—for a while, anyway—and Gluck himself used it when it suited his purpose (as in "O Toi qui prolongeas mes jours" in *Iphigénie en Tauride*). But an alternative had been articulated, an option exemplified.

What Gluck invented, as he set *aria da capo* aside, is exemplified in Orfeo's rapturously beautiful greeting to the Elysian Fields, "Che puro ciel." Gluck is not content to leave all the ecstasy of which he is capable to the celestially beautiful vocal line. He adds, to the quiet murmuring in the orchestra (descriptive, perhaps, of an invisible brook) exquisite exclamations of pleasure for solo flute, oboe, and bassoon. This is the first look ahead to the symphonic synthesis of voice and orchestra in Mozart in the later years of the eighteenth century, and its eventual endorsement, on virtually every side, in the nineteenth.

That Gluck implemented many of Calzabigi's excellent intentions in *Orfeo* is beyond question. That he forged a strong link from opera's past to its future is equally evident. But the most distinctive of his accomplishments may be ignored, glossed over, or otherwise escape mention because it is so plain, so basic, even perhaps so obvious.

Orfeo endures because it is among the earliest and greatest examples of *the power of music to persuade*. The secret weapon with which Orfeo is armed to achieve the impossible—retrieve his wife from the dead—is not a sword with the magic properties of Nothung, or a spear wrested from the evil hand of a magician. *Orfeo* endures because Gluck possessed the power to write music which persuades *the listener* that it could subdue the Furies, gain consent of the gods to Orfeo's urgent purpose and, finally, their agreement to return her to him a second time. As often as one may rehear *Orfeo*, Gluck's power is so persuasive that the miracle is instantly regenerated.

There are only a few other instances I can think of in which an opera composer has ventured the same high-risk gamble and won. There is the moment in *The Magic Flute* when Tamino stands up to the menacing wild beasts around him by playing a flute solo of such ravishing sweetness that they are reduced to docility. And when the "barbarians" who serve Monostatos close in on Papageno, he responds with an enchanting phrase on the glockenspiel that charms them into a dance of delight.

Wagner joined this exclusive company in the course of composing *Die Meistersinger*, when Walther appears in the workshop where

Sachs has been ministering to the anxious Eva's needs in footwear and launches into the final stanza of the song he hopes will win the contest and her hand. "Lausch', Kind!" says Sachs smugly to the incredulous, enraptured bride-to-be. "Das ist ein Meisterlied!" ("Listen, child! That is a Mastersong!"). If it wasn't, the opera might as well have come to an end right there. *The proof is contained not in what is said, but in what is heard.* But Wagner knew he had won his gamble. He had written the words that made the claim, and the music that justified it.

Because such power inheres in the music, Orfeo is one of the most difficult of all singing roles for a performer to make convincing. When the French refused to permit a castrato to perform at the Paris premiere in 1774, a tenor was substituted. It was not convincing. Not until Berlioz agreed, in 1859, to reassess the problem and produced a version in which the principal role was restored to the alto range and Pauline Viardot accepted the challenge to be the first "Orpheus with *her* lute" was the present practice of a female Orpheus evolved.

It is every producer's dream to find an Orfeo capable of looking like a Greek husband, and sounding like a Greek husband who also happens to be the son of the muse Calliope, and Apollo, god of Music. Or, if his aspirations are tempered by experience in the operatic bargain, to find a woman with an overwhelming ability to sing the music irresistibly, and hope that this will outweigh other considerations (which are, in some circumstances, likely to be of considerable weight in and of themselves).

Of the dozen or so performers of Orfeo I have seen, I would nominate one of the most recent, Grace Bumbry, as among the most persuasive in appearance. She could have been a male Orfeo (who married young), she wore the short Grecian tunic well, and moved beautifully, with a trancelike detachment as reserved as it was uncommon. And she sang some of the quieter music exquisitely. But good as she was as Eboli (in *Don Carlos*) or as Carmen (my preference among recent performers), she could not muster the power to intimidate the Furies. And, in that, she failed to make explicit in the performance what Gluck had made implicit in the music.

Sigrid Onegin (born Hoffmann in Stockholm, of a German father and a French mother) was a classic Orfeo of the thirties and perhaps the most formidable of all to hear. She was, by the time I saw her, also one of the most formidable to contemplate. Anything male discerned in her appearance would have been wholly by courtesy. Kerstin Thorborg, a splendid Swedish singer of Wagnerian roles in the forties, presented an admirable composite, though she was a little too wifely to pass as husbandly. Giulietta Simionato, whose power of utterance was directly inverse to her petite figure, might have succeeded very well as Orfeo, but her promised New York stage appearance never materialized. A single concert performance (1960) was a model of vocal deportment, with one coloration for "Mille pene, ombre sdegnose" and quite another for "Che puro ciel."

On balance, the most satisfactory Orfeo in all respects should have been Risë Stevens, who had a good bearing, a well-formed figure for the purpose of male impersonation (her particular specialty was Octavian in *Der Rosenkavalier*) and a sensitive appreciation of what the role was about. However, her appearances in a production of *Orfeo* conducted by Pierre Monteux cut across a period in which she was constantly appearing in *Carmen*. As a result, she had neither the power to tame the Furies nor the well-focused sound to sing "Che farò senza Euridice" with the calm command of her performances in other circumstances (and on an earlier recording).

It might have caught the attention of some that the Pauline Viardot for whom Berlioz designed his edition of 1859 was the singer who participated two years later in the epochal audition of the second act of *Tristan* for Berlioz. Some singer? The youngest daughter of Manuel del Popolo Garcia, one of the great vocal pedagogues of the nineteenth century, Viardot's repertory not merely included, in addition to Orfeo (and Act II of *Tristan*), but encompassed Rachel in *La Juive*, Norma, Lucia, Amina in *La Sonnambula*, Azucena, Donna Anna, and Zerlina.

Lest it be supposed that *Orfeo* was the end as well as the beginning of Gluck's operatic influences, it should be noted that he preceded Mozart in breasting the tide of two operatic traditions, and causing them to flow into new channels. When *Orfeo* was produced in Paris in 1774, Gluck put himself out to make it more attractive by improving the instrumentation behind "Che puro ciel," writing the famous flute solo now heard in the "Dance of the Blessed Spirits," enlarging Orfeo's "Che farò," and otherwise endearing himself to the French public. The success of *Orphée et Eurydice* brought on the production, with a French text, of *Alceste* (originally written in Italian) whose splendid "Divinités du Styx" gave new character to a dramatic dissertation in that language. Gluck then wrote, exclusively for Paris and directly to a French text, *Iphigénie en Tauride*. The union of sung, declaimed, played, and danced values evolved by Gluck remained a lonely signpost on the road to a revitalized French opera until the way it pointed was followed first by Luigi Cherubini, then by Hector Berlioz (as well as several lesser others).

As for Mozart, it was his proudest pleasure to report from Vienna to his father in Salzburg (in August 1782): "My opera [*Die Entfüh-rung aus dem Serail*, which had just been introduced] was given again yesterday—and that too at Gluck's request. He has been very complimentary to me about it. I am lunching with him tomorrow."[7] Should the conversation have been carried on in their native tongue, the two could have complimented *each other* in German for reforming Italian *opera seria*, projecting the French *opéra* to come, straightening out the German *Singspiel*, and, perhaps, even discussing the possibility of doing something about Italian *opera buffa*, an objective that Mozart was to realize within the elderly Gluck's lifetime, in *Le Nozze di Figaro* only four years later.

3

Whatever other subjects they might have discussed at length, the probability is that the future of the "number opera" was not among them. A term rarely defined in opera encyclopaediae (of which I have more than a few), it is just what the inner circle of opera enthusiasts know it to be: an opera consisting of an indefinite number of separate "numbers" (*Orfeo* has fifty-three) sequentially set forth in a list at the beginning of the score, with a page number identifying the place where the beginning of each may be found.

This formulation served Gluck for all his operas, and Mozart for his. By this procedural term, Beethoven's *Fidelio* is a "number opera" and so also is *Carmen*. Whatever the substance, the list of number operas includes Massenet's *Manon*, Tchaikovsky's *Eugene Onegin*, Bellini's *Norma*, and Wagner's *Flying Dutchman*. Even more remarkably, Berlioz' *Les Troyens* is a number opera—all five acts of it—totaling fifty-one numbers spread over the divisions of action between Troy and Carthage. This is two less than *Orfeo* and only six more than the total numbers that separate the overture from the exit march in Rodgers and Hammerstein's *The King and I*.

An average opera-goer confronted with this partial sample of a much larger total might say, "Why should Gluck and Mozart discuss the matter? Apparently all the great, and a lot of very good, favorites of mine are number operas." Only, I would interject, to a point. Save for *Rigoletto* and *La traviata*, the list is sparse with middle or late Verdi, with Wagner beyond the *Dutchman*, Puccini, Leoncavallo, Mascagni, Debussy, Berg, and so on, without whose works the operatic repertory would be even more restricted than it is.

The particular characteristic of the number opera—assisted by that useful table of contents—is that every element of it is separated *physically* from what follows, usually by a double bar. For every instance of a Gluck writing *attaca* ("go on") at the end of No. 13 in *Orfeo* (which is an aria for Amor) there are hundreds which end definitively, giving way to something, perhaps a pause, an exit, the introduction of a new character, or a change of scene. If everybody is lucky, what the concluded number gives way to is applause.

Was anyone ever applauded for a brilliant, forceful, imaginative performance of a recitative? Hardly. But audiences regularly and enthusiastically applaud effortful, colorless, uninteresting performances of arias. When they actually hear an extraordinary performance, they may applaud for minutes. The number opera enables them to fulfill this impulse—up to a reasonable point—without interrupting the action.

This might be construed as the ideal compromise between the desirable and the undesirable: an arrangement that affords the least possible intrusion on the drama without depriving the performer of that soul food on which his spirits soar or sink, whose presence or absence sustains or starves the artistic appetite—applause. Alas! As with the outmoded *aria da capo*, the number opera, for all its adaptability, has a built-in susceptibility to abuse. To say that it sickened and died of such abuse would be an exaggeration; the many many number operas which sustain the needs of half the repertory of every opera house are proof to the contrary. But it is no exaggeration to say that composers from the 1840s on looked wistfully for an alternative to the formulation, because of the twin sisters C by which it was beset, the ones named Cadenza and Cabaletta.

The offspring of that troubled *mésalliance*, recitative and aria, they grew up clinging to Mother Aria's skirts and, in time, tended to pre-empt her importance (as growing children may). Cadenza was the less offensive of the two, because she was smaller, more compact, and when her turn was over, could be forgotten. Cabaletta, however, was much bigger, more garrulous, and possessed of a greedy appetite that got to crave attention all the time.

For those to whom these related forms are not altogether familiar, it may be mentioned that cadenza was named for her habit of hanging around the "cadence," or final chords with which most musical pieces end. At first she liked to express whatever was on her mind at the moment, but as she grew up, things began to be written out for cadenza's use.

The source of cabaletta's name is somewhat less explicit. Some people say it is a corruption of *cavatina* or *cavatinetta*, meaning a "little song," but I find this unconvincing.[8] I am more partial to another attribution, which reads: "Cabaletta. Sp [Spanish] Melody in rondo form accompanied in triplets, imitating the footfalls of a cantering horse: short final movement of an air."[9] This has a greater ring of probability. What does happen at the end of numerous nineteenth-century airs (or arias) in an Italian number opera is such a cantering, perhaps even a galloping, finale. Whether originally used for expressive purposes or not—source material is hardly abundant—a cabaletta very soon came to be not merely an awaited but an expected occasion for the performer to excel any prior vocalism, in a transport of untrammeled virtuosity.

I am not curmudgeon enough to say that there is no place for either cadenza or cabaletta in opera. I would propose, meekly, that they be reserved to a place where they are tolerably appropriate, and not dragged in merely to make the next break in a number opera louder and longer, by the kind of applause that only a vocal frenzy induces.

I would say, for example, that in the two works of Bellini which I would rate highest among all those written during the *bel canto* period—roughly 1815–1845, when the greatest exponents of "beautiful singing" flourished in never-duplicated quantity—there is both palatable and unpalatable *cabaletta*. I accept it with relish and digest it with pleasure when it is well served in *La Sonnambula;* I find it doesn't go down as smoothly or leave as pleasant an aftertaste in *Norma*.

As both works are by the same enormously gifted man—in some moments, the greatest of vocal composers—the issue cannot be joined on the merit of one vs. the merit of the other. The issue is, rather, which cabaletta is more in keeping with the happenings of the moment.

La Sonnambula is concerned with the case of a young woman who innocently sleepwalks her way into the bedroom of a man she barely knows and is accused by her "beloved" of deceiving him. The cabaletta to which I refer occurs when she reperforms her somnambulism, this time in the view of the whole village, and is, of course, forgiven. Joy reigns supreme, especially in Amina's concluding lap of a veritable cross-country course of vocalism, in as arduous an evening of singing as the repertory contains. The unrelenting Bellini expects his heroine to be at top form throughout, but saves his most chilling test—the hedge and water jump—for the very end. In effect, "Ah! non giunge" is a cabaletta to a whole evening of singing, not simply to the aria which precedes it. When the sentiment it contains ("On the earth where we live We will make a heaven of love") is performed as well as it has been by Joan Sutherland, up to the dazzling C-topping high E flat at the end, it makes a delicious dessert to a rich repast.

In *Norma*, on the other hand, the cabaletta to which I take exception follows "Casta diva," one of Bellini's most sumptuous inventions, a flowing arch of sustained melody which has been rarely surpassed. Here Norma, as the Druid priestess, invokes the "chaste goddess" (the Moon) as the Queen of Heaven, to shed love upon those who worship her. In its leisurely, languorous wake come the allegro proclamations of "Ah! bello a me ritorno," a cabaletta which sounds for all the world like a militant proclamation of rejoicing. It is, rather, Norma, the woman's, plea to the same Deity to "restore to me, beautiful in your first true love," the man by whom she had borne a child, though her vows forbid it.

It is brilliant, it is dazzling, and the same Sutherland sings it as fluently as she sings "Ah! non giunge." The difference is that one series of dazzling vocal passage writing is entirely appropriate to the circumstances, the other is not. In justice to Bellini, it may be noted that the great final scene of *Norma*, in which that sorely tried heroine assumes full guilt for bearing a child fathered by the hated proconsul, is one of the most nobly beautiful of all operatic ensembles—a rising tide of solo and choral voices in which were engulfed and carried to their individual destinations both the later Donizetti and the Verdi to come. No cabaletta!

But not necessarily no embellishment. What was provided by the composer in that solemn resolution was not the end of what the singers bred on the cadenza and the cabaletta considered their due. "Nothing," as Oscar Wilde so well said, "succeeds like excess." The liberty of the cabaletta gave way to the license that all outstanding singers of the time invoked on behalf of their performances. Nor were they necessarily only female.

Of Giambattista Rubini, "king of tenors" between 1825 and 1845, one may read in the greatest documentation of the singing of that time, Henry F. Chorley's *Thirty Years' Musical Recollections:* "He ruled the stage by the mere art of singing more completely than any one, woman or man, has been able to do in my time." Despite this sweeping statement of high esteem, the level-minded critic of the *London Athenaeum* between 1833 and 1863 continues: "His taste in ornament was often questionable. . . . He revelled in embroideries of the phrase in ritarded time which occurs just before the close, which, however ingenious and wonderful as vocal displays, I always felt to be super-abundant."[10] (The reference is to Paolino's aria "Pria che spunti" in Act II of Cimarosa's *Matrimonio Segreto*.)

Thus, to embellish or not to embellish is hardly the question. The questions are, rather: why, where, when, and in what taste? In his introduction to the republication in 1926 of Chorley's text, the late Ernest Newman asked: "Who today, for example, can understand the old passion for 'ornaments' in vocal music?"[11] In the ebb and flow of time and custom, individualized embellishments had all but gone out of style in the twenties and thirties. But they are back in vogue in the sixties and seventies, and questions of taste are once more an issue.

Little in present-day embellishment can be ascribed to an "impulse of the moment," for vocalists, like performers of Chopin, carefully prepare their impromptus. They are written out, memorized, and fitted into the structure of an aria or cadenza or cabaletta as carefully as anything else. Nor is it likely that any of the three women who have recently or presently made a reputation for florid singing are wholly responsible for the style of the embellishments they favor, or even for the detail of them.

For Maria Callas, who reintroduced the world to the pleasures of the seldom-heard Bellini operas (even to *Il Pirata*) in the fifties, to the unfamiliar Donizetti (*Anna Bolena*) and the long-neglected *Medea* of Cherubini, the fount of style and the source of wisdom was the late Tullio Serafin, who was born in 1878 and lived on until 1968. He made his debut as a conductor in 1900 and absorbed, from the older musicians of his youth, what was best in the Italian practice of the nineteenth century. When Callas was only a child in New York, Serafin was at the Metropolitan coaching Rosa Ponselle not only in how to sing Norma, but also Giulia in *La Vestale* (by Gasparo Spontini, a predecessor of both Rossini and Bellini). Had Serafin not encountered Callas in Italy in the late 1940s, when she was drifting directionless, and discerned in her the all-purpose soprano of which he had been dreaming, her career might have been quite different.

When I first heard Joan Sutherland in Vancouver, I asked, at a social occasion a few days after her debut, "Who coached you in

Donna Anna?" She answered, "My husband—he is also from Australia. But we couldn't afford for him to come on this trip." "My husband," now as then, meant Richard Bonynge, who has earned a considerable reputation as a student of nineteenth-century opera, not only on behalf of his wife but in other projects as well. He has acquired an awesome library of rare scores containing the written-in embellishments of eminent singers of the past. These are the materials from which he has evolved the embellishments sung by his wife. His knowledge is wide, his judgment sound, his taste reliably good—save, of course, for a natural disposition to favor a form of vocal exhibitionism of which his wife is so skilled an exponent.

For Beverly Sills, singing begins and ends with the influence of her longtime teacher, coach, and shaper of vocal manners Estelle Liebling. A singer in her youth (briefly at the Metropolitan, where she made her debut as Marguerite in Meyerbeer's *Les Huguenots*) Miss Liebling was one of the most sought out vocal teachers in New York until her death in 1970. Their association was indeed almost lifelong, for Sills became a Liebling pupil at seven and achieved her belated success during her mentor's lifetime, and with her constant assistance. For accessory advice on ornaments and embellishments, Miss Sills has sometimes relied on coach-conductor Roland Gagnon, more recently on others.

The ladies agree, in their mutually shared repertory (Bellini, Donizetti, some Verdi) that embellishment is desirable. But they disagree sharply on not only where and when but how and why. For Callas, "why" is summarized in the meaning of the *word:* embellishment is, first of all, a way of intensifying meaning, underscoring emotion and highlighting drama. With Sutherland, "how" tends to edge "why" out of first place. The "how" is concerned, in Bonynge's input and Sutherland's output, with devising embellishments that will produce the most beautiful arches and parabolas of sound possible with an instrument of extraordinary range and flexibility. Words? Sutherland's production hardly permits a phrase to be understood in "Home! Sweet Home!" The chances, therefore, of hearing the text in "Casta diva" or "Ah! non giunge," when decorated and bejeweled, are nil. With Sills, however, how, what, where, and when are bundled up into one big grab bag of joy, to be dipped into whenever and however the results will produce the most astonishing testimony to her skills, and induce the shared enthusiasm in which she is not so much a recipient as a participant.

As an instance, in the common ground of their recordings of

"Regnava nel silenzio" in *Lucia,* Callas puts a moving accent on the recitative and sings aria and cabaletta well, though not as fluently as Sutherland, to whom the recitative serves nicely to flex her vocal muscles for the aria to follow. The Sills version is competent in recitative, the ornaments introduced almost as soon as the melody of the aria itself, where the skyrockets of sound peak around C or D, thus displaying brightly her top register.

It would, however, strike me as an elementary principle of music that embellishments should be deferred until the line of the melody has been clearly projected to the listener, that he may have straight in his mind what it is that is being varied. Jazz musicians do it, pop singers do it, even old rock-'n'-rollers in Detroit do it.

This curbstone opinion was recently raised to a point of law when I encountered a comment by Gioacchino Rossini directed to a celebrated soprano of the nineteenth century, Clara Novello: "The repeat is made expressly so that each singer may vary it, so as best to display her (or his) peculiar capacities: therefore the first time the composer's music should be exactly given."[12]

Emboldened by this precept (actually to be found within a definition of *cabaletta*), I offer my own inclusive Rules of the Road for Artistry in Embellishment:

a) Allow the composer's melodic line to be heard clearly and completely before you embellish.
b) Embellish within a vowel sound, not across it.
c) Don't embellish against the meaning of the word. If there is some implication of tragic meaning, don't add a frivolous decoration to the serious meaning.
d) Put aside the temptation to sing your *highest* note before the end of the aria. It will be upstaging the climactic effect where it is most wanted—at the climax.
e) And finally: if the composer's climax tone doesn't strike you as high enough, or as high as you can sing, leave it alone. He knew enough to write all the rest of something worth singing, so let him have his way at the end.

The last of these comments was aroused by a soprano in a recent revival of Cherubini's *Medea* (Maralin Niska) who ended the second act with a top C rather than the F (below it) in the score, thus imitating the practice of Maria Callas. At the London performance I saw in 1959, Miss Callas paid for her misdeed by missing the note altogether. Miss Niska reached it, but not too well. In either case the singers were serving their interests. Stylistically they violated the composer's, by making a vocal demonstration of what should have been a dramatic affirmation. Performances of *Medea* are relative rareties, but the same disservice is constantly heard at the end of what is unquestionably the greatest aria-and-cabaletta ever written. I refer to Violetta's scene at the end of Act I of *La traviata*. It contains all the classic components: opening recitative, "È strano! è strano . . ." ("How strange! how strange!"); the slow segment or cavatina, "Ah! fors' è lui . . ." ("Ah! perhaps he is the one"); the dramatically contrasting "Follie! Follie! . . ." ("Folly! Folly . . ."); and the cabaletta of all cabalettas, the precipitous, heedless, headlong allegro brillante: "Sempre libera degg'io" ("Always free I must be . . ."). For compositional, dramatic, and aesthetic reasons best known to himself, Verdi preferred his high C three measures *before* the last measure, and a middle-range A flat at the cadence. Most sopranos of today would be ashamed to sing it as Verdi wrote it, for fear somebody might allege they couldn't make it to a top tone at the end. (If Violetta has done her job properly, she has *already* sung ten top Cs in "Sempre libera.") As Callas has recorded it (to her shame) with a top E flat, Sutherland could hardly do otherwise.

Perhaps this is why Verdi increasingly eschewed the cabaletta (of which he was one of the greatest masters) and eventually the numbers game of number opera altogether. Writing to his collaborator Ghislanzoni during their work on *Aida* in 1870, Verdi observed: "I see you are afraid of two things: any bold theatrical stroke and of *not* writing cabalettas. I think the cabaletta should be reserved for a situation that demands it. In neither of these duets is it appropriate to the situation, especially in the duet between Aida and her father. . . . Aida in her state of terror and moral abasement cannot and should not sing a cabaletta. . . . After the terrible scene with her father she would be, as I say, incapable of speech. . . ."[13] When such a consideration was invoked on what became the *most performed opera* of the nineteenth and the twentieth centuries, the day of the caballeta and the number opera was drawing to a close.

4

Perhaps the end had been hastened by the overindulgence of the parents, Recitative and Aria. Perhaps the twins—Cadenza and Cabaletta—had "favored" their mother too much, providing more latitude for the singing side of opera than the dramatic. Even before Giuseppe Verdi, who cherished but was not in bondage to the traditions of Italian opera, was ready to give up the number opera, Richard Wagner, who had a much shorter, less extended tradition of German opera to contend with, did so on his own.

As of 1843, when *Die fliegende Holländer* was first performed in Dresden, Wagner was a composer of number operas (*Rienzi* had preceded). As of 1845, when *Tannhäuser* was first produced, he was something else. He had cast off the old skin and was looking for a new one—one that would be form-fitting to his purposes and designed to accommodate all necessary action without giving or constricting. At first it would be rather rough, perhaps clumsy, with the stitches and seams showing. Probably it would need work before it could deserve the name of music drama.

Indeed, as Donald Jay Grout suggests (without saying) in his admirably informative, succinct *A Short History of Opera* (for all that it is in two volumes totaling 707 pages), *Tannhäuser* is a number opera without numbers. Says Grout: "The division into numbers is still clear, though with more sweep and less rigidity than in the earlier works."[14] Among other details, the inventory of contents provided in *Die fliegende Holländer* is amended. In its place *Tannhäuser* presents a listing of scenes, with a page reference to the divisions within them. In Act II, two such well-known "numbers" as "Dich, teure Halle" (Elisabeth's great greeting to the Hall of Song) and "Blick ich umher" (Wolfram's entry in the song contest of knightly minstrels) are listed, but with no numbers.

Whatever Wagner was trying to accomplish, dramatically, in *Tannhäuser*, the strong suggestion to me is that he decided, midway in the process, to abandon the old system and evolve something else. But the intention that resulted in the much greater fluidity of action from scene to scene in *Lohengrin* and carries us through almost the full length of each act without interruption is clearly on the record, in Wagner's own words.

Wagner was barely through with *Tannhäuser* when he plunged into the planning for *Lohengrin* in 1845. When the poem was finished, late in the year, he arranged several by now "customary" readings for favored Dresden friends and sympathetic colleagues of whom—as of this time—Robert Schumann was one. As Wagner recounts in *My Life*, one reading was held before the "Hiller set" (Ferdinand Hiller was a prominent, conservative conductor-composer of the time). The poem of *Lohengrin* was "praised and pronounced 'effective.' Schumann thoroughly approved of it, although he did not understand the musical form in which I wished to carry it out, as he saw no resemblance in it to the old methods of writing individual solos for the various artists. I then had some fun in reading parts of my work to him in the form of arias and cavatinas, after which he laughingly declared himself satisfied."[15]

So here was Wagner, not yet the "old magician" but already equipped to conjure Schumann into the acceptance of a new art form, with the bland assurance that he was not going to banish aria and cavatina, just recast their relationship to what went on about them. Of the presence of recitative, of course, there could be no doubt after a reading of the poem of *Lohengrin*!

Nor does Wagner's success in achieving his dramatic intentions require elaboration. *Das Rheingold*, which followed *Lohengrin*, is prefaced by a statement of scenes, with no reference to internal divisions; and so it went ever thereafter. Musically, he sustained his allegiance to "aria and cavatina" without disavowing his fidelity to organic unity, accomplishing this either by weaving them into the texture of the music (as in the first act of *Die Walküre*) or building a structure of which they were the crowning detail (as in *Tristan* and *Götterdämmerung*).

There should, moreover, be adequate attention paid to the way in which Wagner's initiative penetrated the operatic world, and eventually compelled its consent. Much wordage has been spilled on "Wagnerism" as a system of leading motives or expanded use of an enlarged orchestra or submission to rigorous ideas of unity of time, in the Greek theatrical sense. Not enough attention, in my opinion, has been directed to the all-conquering power of his dramatic conception, the *elimination* of the number opera with its attendant encumbrances, not only in the German operas of Central Europe, but in Italy, and eventually in France.

So far as I can determine, *Il trovatore* is the last of Verdi's number operas. He thereafter tended to a listing of acts and their contents, without internal numbers. As for recitative, aria, cavatina, and so on, he treated them as circumstances warranted and his own impulse dictated. The longer he lived, the less he regarded the singer as possessed of any privileges, aside from the inestimable one of being allowed to appear in his works. Perhaps the subtlest, bluntest reminder of his aesthetic attitude comes in *Falstaff*, at the moment when Ford in his supercharged conclusion to the emotion-laden "È sogno o realtà?" ("Is it a dream or is it reality?") denounces his wife, and all women, for their perfidy. This is a virtuoso air if there ever was one, but Verdi holds the performer in the frame of the action, without intrusive applause, by striking home the dramatic point with pile-driver force in the orchestra and, *without a break*, shading it down to a mere whisper as Sir John appears in all his finery to be escorted by Ford (in his disguise of Signor Fontana) to the wives of Windsor. With elaborate mock courtesy each bows to the other: "Pray, do go first!" as they reach the door; then they agree to exit arm in arm. When the curtain falls on this choicely comic moment, the audience can applaud to its— and Verdi's—heart's content. But one can picture the fiery old man saying to himself as he plotted these details, "This is one scene they won't be able to ruin with an interruption after the aria!"

Ponchielli's *La Gioconda* (1876) is perhaps the last well-known opera to be written in the number manner (though without numbers). This, as much as anything else—despite its frequent melodic splendor and sonorous ensembles—may be the reason it strikes me (and a good many others) as curiously old-fashioned. All of Puccini's major works are carried through without preplanned breaks in the action— although there almost always are breaks in the performance, by audience fiat and failure of the conductor to exercise his authority. As for Giordano's *Andrea Chénier*, its sections are identified (with an austerity to challenge *Das Rheingold*) only as "quadro primo," "quadro secondo," etc. ("Tableaux one," "Tableaux two," etc.). Debussy's *Pelléas et Mélisande* breaks with all French opera tradition—*comique*, *grand*, or *numero*—in being a line-by-line setting of Maeterlinck's play.

The number concept has occasionally surfaced in recent opera (it endures as the most familiar form of "musical"), most often when deliberately chosen by a composer to evoke a style or to serve a special purpose. Stravinsky's *The Rake's Progress* is written as a number opera because he was matching his musical manner to the Hogarthian period (eighteenth century) of the action. Benjamin Britten's *The Turn of the Screw* is another kind of number opera: two acts, each of eight scenes, with a Prologue, and a Theme and Variations I to XV before, between, and after.

If not all the recitatives and arias written by Puccini, Giordano, Cilèa, Mascagni, Menotti, *et al.*, have been in circumstances "dramatically true and musically valid," it is a certainty that the composers were, more often than not, thinking in terms of such precepts. Musetta's waltz in *La Bohème* may not be exactly the sort of thing one would expect a young woman to sing in public on Christmas night to taunt her ex-lover (Marcello), but Rodolfo's "Che gelida manina" is, after all, a self-descriptive *Racconto* ("Narrative") to which Mimi responds in kind with "Si, mi chiamano Mimi" ("Yes, they call me Mimi"—though her name is Lucia); Tosca's "Vissi d'arte, vissi d'amore" ("Music and love I have lived for" is the sense of the Italian phrase) is a *Preghiera* ("Prayer"), and even "Un bel dì" in *Madama Butterfly* is Cio-Cio-San's projection to Suzuki of what will happen "one fine day" when Pinkerton returns. *Turandot* is unquestionably Puccini's supreme effort to create a consecutive drama with solos, duets, and so on, artfully inserted at points where they are dramatically defensible. To everyone's regret, Puccini did not live long enough to finish the concluding duet, but the structure he had previously evolved is sufficiently spacious to give a sense of fulfillment even without that finalizing detail.

Is there any way in which a curious opera-goer could identify a number opera, in performance, from any other kind? With a stopwatch, perhaps, he might make note of solos (followed by concluding chords) which are relatively brief and often preceded by an entrance or followed by an exit of the performer. This is especially true in works of a comedic character by Mozart or Rossini, Donizetti or Offenbach, Cimarosa or Paisiello. If the music comes to a full stop each time an aria or ensemble ends, that is the number opera in its local, rather than express, journey. All too often, the manners of the number opera intrude into a work in which the composer has made a determined effort to suppress them.

Even Wagner, with all the built-in protections he devised on behalf of dramatic cohesion, may not always be heard as he wanted—uninterrupted. This is a curiously localized contradiction: interruptions are rare in a performance of *Tristan* or *Meistersinger* but may crop up in *Lohengrin* or *Walküre*. I refer not to a tenor's farewell to the Swan or to a soprano's singing of "Elsa's Traum" or to Sieglinde's "Du bist der Lenz," but, rather, to the delivery by Ortrud of a few measures in which she denounces her antagonists and invokes her pagan gods to undo them, or to Brünnhilde, who exercises her agility in the battle cry of the Walküre. At some time, in some circumstance, a Schumann-Heink or a Lilli Lehmann may have delivered these measures in a manner that provoked applause in Hamburg or Vienna. It has now become what is known as a "tradition" that every Ortrud or Brünnhilde must have a burst of applause at this point or she will have a sleepless night. More often than not the outburst is begun by a husband, friend, or camp follower hoping to pick up a few persuadable others. I am glad to say the effort usually fails.

In too many instances of stoppages in other works where they were not intended (*Aida* as an instance, or *Samson et Dalila*) it is a matter of "business as usual"—meaning favoritism to the very present performer over the absent composer. There are not too many singers who would intellectualize the difference between a number opera and any other kind, and if they have sung a solo well enough to be applauded, God knows, they are going to expect their reward. Nor can the best-intentioned impresario curb the practice by admonishing the audience —by means of a printed note in the program—not to applaud while the music is in progress. (The ones who lead the applause probably don't read the program anyway.) The best that can be done is to establish house rules to prevent such an incident as happened when the audience applauded a tenor's performance of the "Air de Fleur" in *Carmen*. He stood up, took his bow, and knelt down again to rest his head in Carmen's lap. The happening was the more notable because the audience included Albert Einstein, a music lover as well as an eminent physicist, who must have wondered to what all this was relative.

In current practice, the singer is directed to maintain the posture that prevailed at the end of the aria and not to smile, nod his head, or otherwise step out of character. This procedure originally aroused some grumbling, for not many singers are as philosophically minded about it as was the late Richard Tucker. When I encountered him a few days after this order was issued at the old Metropolitan Opera House, I asked him what he thought of the rule. His answer was: "If it's the same for everybody, what difference does it make?"

Of course, the worst of all possible circumstances is the one in which the performer being applauded also has the next *word*. Tosca's "Vissi d'arte, vissi d'amore" is one famous example in which, after her concluding "Mi vuoi supplice ai tuoi piedi?" ("Must I kneeling beg for mercy?"), Tosca eventually sings: "Vedi" ("Behold me"). If she doesn't raise her head and look at the conductor—indicating her readiness to proceed—he is powerless to do anything with the following chords. A rare exception to ordinary procedure occurred when Montserrat Caballé, having sung very well the great aria "Arrigo! ah parli a un core" in *I vespri siciliani*, was resoundingly acclaimed by the audience. The applause went on so long, indeed, that, smiling to cover her embarrassment, Caballé motioned for the audience to desist and let the performance go on. I shall long remember that restrained but thoughtful gesture. Unfortunately, the same singer gave us, more recently, a negative reason for remembering her even longer. The opera was *La Bohème*, in which she appeared for the first time in New York in the same cast with Luciano Pavarotti. When the audience exploded in applause for his singing of the Racconto, Caballé, sitting on the stage of the Metropolitan Opera House in the costume of Mimi, graciously added her handclaps to all the others.

Of course, a singer can—in some circumstances—appear to be taking the law in his or her own hands, as happened on an evening when Zinka Milanov was singing in a performance of *La Gioconda* at which I was present. Midway in Act II, the Laura of the evening (Nell Rankin) was vibrantly applauded for her singing of "Stella del marinar" ("Star of the seafarer") which ends with a plea for the Virgin to "discenda la tua benidizione" ("bestow your benediction") on her love. When Milanov, apparently irked by the duration of the applause, walked onto it from the wings, the conductor had little choice but get on with the performance. What the score called for the soprano to deliver were the curiously appropriate next words: "E un anatèma" ("And a curse").

On balance, the operatic involvement may arouse human factors having to do with more than vocal aptitude and resource. It may include a compulsion for the appeasement of a deep-down psychological need, as was observed by a lady of the nineteenth century writing to a friend who had predicted the retirement of a soprano of their mutual acquaintance:

> As for your Invalid's intention of making an end in 1867, I don't believe in it all. Avarice, vanity and the exigencies of her disease will cause her to wander to all the corners of the earth until the boredom and disgust of those who will have, so to speak, suffer her, will force her to bring down the curtain.

The writer was speaking from a certain knowledge of the subject. She was the soprano Giuseppina Strepponi who had, by that time, become Signora Verdi. The "disease" to which she referred, says Frank Walker, from whose *The Man Verdi* these words are quoted, was "a craving for applause."[16]

To one singer, the presence of applause may be a greater satisfaction, as Leontyne Price has been quoted in an interview, than "being with a man." To another, the absence of it in a certain situation may cost a career, as soprano Gianna d'Angelo discovered during a performance of *Rigoletto* at the new Metropolitan in the late 1960s. She was having a not too good evening as Gilda, with an unsteady performance of "Caro nome"—but it was not significantly inferior to other performances by youngish sopranos which have been heard off and on in New York over the years. This one, however, encountered the presence of a. scattering of vulgar-minded listeners, who unloosed the rarest of sounds to be heard in an American theater: a chorus of boos. Despite the contrary, encouraging comments of those who thought she had been shabbily treated, Miss d'Angelo was so unnerved that she has not sung in a New York performance of opera since.

Fortunately, the issue is not invariably joined in the narrow musical Straits of Messina between the Scylla of recitative and the Charybdis of aria. There is an escape now and then to a broader, if perhaps more turbulent, water, where a challenge awaits that is some of each and a little more than both.

IV

Scena

1

If recitative and aria were the total vocal requirements for a satisfactory opera, Handel's *Serse* would have provided an ideal, permanent solution in the 1740s. For it, Handel conceived a sequence of thirty of one, thirty of the other: recitative and aria, recitative and aria, thirty times over. It is a scheme arresting in its simplicity and disarming in its symmetry. *Serse,* however, did not fare too well historically, even if one of its thirty numbers became the most celebrated melody Handel ever wrote (as the "Largo").

As an alternative to recitative and aria—or their spinoffs, cadenza and cabaletta—dramatic necessity and compositional craft evolved an artistic entity known, eventually, as the *scena* (*shay*-na). *Scena,* of course, also serves the Italians as the word for "scene." At its point of origin, the vocal *scena* would have borne the qualifying *drammatica* (dramatic scene) or *comica* (comic scene). By the same law of usage which produced *opera* itself as a contraction for *opera musica* (meaning "musical work"), *scena* has evolved into a self-sufficient terminology for the purpose it serves: to denote a self-contained segment of an opera. Nor is it difficult to distinguish *scena* the scene from *scena* the musical piece. "His" or "her" *scena* means the composition, whether it is the performer or the character. Actually, the same usage long ago came into the English-speaking theater. To speak of someone as a "scene stealer" is to refer, not to a theft of a painted canvas, but to a performer adroit at making off with honors in a segment of a play or film.

Should the question arise "How can you tell a *scena* from an aria?" the only honest answer is "You can't, always." Nor are the reprinted scores of eighteenth- and nineteenth-century scores always dependable. Such scores are, in the main, unresponsive to any consideration but the commercial. Some are edited with more care than others, but even the best may not reproduce the precise words of the composer in identifying time and place of action, or sub-headings of content.

I do, however, have a rule of thumb to suggest. If the performer is on the stage alone, it is a good chance that what will ensue is a *scena* of some sort (more often than not, the equivalent of a soliloquy in a spoken drama). An aria is less likely to be performed by a person who occupies the stage alone; often the stage is shared by someone to whom the aria is addressed, and who will, eventually, make a response.

The *scena* is, in all instances, a testing ground for characterization, for projection of personality, for the demonstration of dramatic capability rather than lyric—though the two may coexist—and for focusing the attention of the audience on some essential part of the opera rather than a passing phase of it. Were it sung rather than spoken (and at somewhat greater length), Violetta's reading of the letter in the last act of *La traviata* would be an excellent instance of a dramatic scene. As it is, I would identify "Ritorna vincitor!" in *Aida* as the exact example. Aida is alone; she has picked up the last words of the preceding ensemble's celebration of Radames' appointment to lead the defense of their common country and turned them to an entirely different meaning. They are the exact symbols of her dilemma, as the new general's beloved *and* the daughter of a king he is about to oppose.

Verdi applies all his skill to placing side by side the negative and the affirmative, the crunch between love and loyalty. In the nature of things, the spotlight is not only on the character being portrayed, but on the performer herself. Can she hold the stage alone? Is she of the dramatic stature to replace the hundreds who have just left it? Will the drama move forward or be impeded by what she does? These are some of the values which make the *scena drammatica* the testing ground it is.

So far as I can determine, no composer ever sat down of a morning and said, "Today I am going to compose the first *scena drammatica*." The concept is one that emerged from a variety of dramatic circumstances, certainly in response to an operatic situation in which a central character is confronted by a turn of events challenging, troubling, angering, encouraging, or otherwise productive of conflicting emotions. What at first might have been tentative but promising, effective but incomplete, was added to over decades and centuries, enriched by the instincts of talent and the overriding thrust of genius.

I stress the factor of contrast because the *scena drammatica* is customarily painted on a broader canvas than an aria and embodies several changes of tempo to accommodate vacillations of impulse, with or without affirmative resolution. It may not always end with a vocal flourish and a top tone. It may shade down to a *pianissimo*, as befits a character brooding, lost in thought, and thereby draw the audience more deeply into his/her dilemma (as, indeed, "Ritorna vincitor!" does).

My nomination for a point of beginning of *scena drammatica*, both well known today and aesthetically valid—though I cannot vouch for historical primacy—is "Divinités du Styx" in Gluck's *Alceste*. This sublime episode contains many of the elements previously defined as characteristic of the genre: a character alone on a stage, a serious emotional problem, several vacillations of impulse—and a nonaffirmative outcome.

It is, moreover, an elaboration of what was previously known in French as an *air déclamé* ("declamatory song"). And Alceste does, indeed, declaim her intentions to the gods of the Underworld that she will, by forfeiture of her own life, meet their requirements for the recovery of her ailing husband, Admetus (an inversion, as is readily apparent, of the central situation of *Orfeo*). The scene begins and ends andante, with a dozen tempo changes in the many measures between. The word "aria" does not appear in the original score. "Scene" does.

In accordance with common practice of the time, Mozart used "aria" to identify the two solo segments for Donna Anna in *Don Giovanni* (a work that I think of as an eighteenth-century projection of a nineteenth-century fulfillment). The first (the recitative begins "Don Ottavio, son morta!") is an anguished outcry of Anna to her faithful bodyguard that she has recognized from his voice and manner, Don Giovanni as her father's killer, and that her honor demands his punishment. In the other episode, much later in the action, Donna Anna responds to Ottavio's complaint that she is being unfair to him by delaying their marriage with the words "Non mi dir" ("Do not tell me") and the melodic assurance that the wedding will come when her time of mourning is passed.

More often than not it is the stage director's prerogative to decide whether Don Ottavio remains on the stage when she launches into the florid segment of the air or quietly withdraws so that he need not hear again what he has heard so many times before. I, personally, am all for withdrawal, to avoid one of those typically operatic moments when a performer who has had no part in provoking applause (indeed, has to feign indifference to how well a partner is performing a difficult task) has to stand by mutely through the response that follows. Moreover, the brief recitative in which Don Ottavio comments on Anna's statement is often omitted, leaving him no further function in this episode. The result might be described as a *scena drammatica* in spite of itself.

Joan Sutherland has not, to my knowledge, yet performed Alceste publicly, but there is every reason to believe that she will, and well. Thus far the performance by which to judge other singers of the mid-century has been Kirsten Flagstad's, in the fifties. On the verge of retirement and with little other active repertory, she was, before and after "Divinités du Styx," a fine Alceste; during it she was a great one. She took the lower notes with the richness of an alto while reserving for the climax a B flat so bright in tonal metal it could have been assayed on a scale jewelers use to weigh gold. Add to this an inner strength and conviction that communicated themselves through a vocal delivery as effortless as it was irresistible, and the outcome was, in being, the classic style so much talked about and seldom heard.

In this time of Mozartean abundance—in quantity of performances if not of quality of performers—the public has been served by a series of superior Donna Annas. They range from Elisabeth Rethberg, Rose Bampton, Zinka Milanov, and Ljuba Welitch in the forties to Eleanor Steber in the fifties and to Birgit Nilsson, Leontyne Price, and Joan Sutherland in the sixties and seventies. One excelled in one part of the role, another in a different aspect of it, and almost all favored one or the other of the very different solo scenes. This was also true of the highly regarded Rosa Ponselle of the twenties. Her performance of the "Honor Air" ("Or sai chi l'onore") in Act I was much superior to "Non mi dir," whose florid detail in slow tempo was not comfortable for her.

Only Sutherland has been equally adept in every (vocal) requirement, by virtue of a voice more flexible than the average dramatic soprano's and more dramatic than the average florid soprano's. It is out of such odd and unusual attributes that standards are born. Sutherland has no need for apprehension that a fine performance of the first (dramatic) scene might founder on the rocks of the second (florid), or cause for regret that she hadn't done the earlier as well as she would the later. She is equally adept in both, a *singer* to whom the word "Mozartean" can be applied without reservation. What an Italian would think of her pronunciation of his language might provoke a word of quite a different kind.

2

From the patchwork that is the average "season" in any of the capitals of the world where opera is regularly performed, it is hardly possible, even after ten years' exposure, to fit together all the pieces and processes that have formed the repertory with which the Western world is familiar. Nor is recourse to library shelves, the abundant literature of recordings, or performances of obscure operas in concert (useful though all are) the answer. Even Schumann had to write to a "friend" (Felix Mendelssohn) after seeing *Tannhäuser* in the theater: "I have to take back some of the things I wrote to you after reading the score: from the stage everything strikes one very differently. I was quite moved by many parts of it."[1]

But twenty or thirty years of absorbing opera from all these sources does provide a perspective from which, if it is still not possible to put all the pieces together, it is possible to say what is lacking. This, in my view, is a larger indoctrination in French opera than has been offered to this generation—and to several of its predecessors—whether living in New York, London, Chicago, Buenos Aires, or Paris itself.

Unlike Italian opera, which was cradled by its own parents, or German opera, which sank roots in its own soil, French opera was not only a transplant but often tended by alien horticulturists and trimmed to conform to a royally dictated design, like the gardens of Versailles. That it did, nevertheless, give rise to a range of works as indispensable to an internationally well balanced repertory as French cuisine is to an international table is a tribute to the talent by which it was blessed rather than the sense by which it was propagated. Can one imagine the astonishment of Gounod, Massenet, Bizet—let alone Berlioz—were they to learn that the chief officer of the famous Théâtre National de l'Opéra (the official name for the Paris Opéra) was, in this enlightened era, the Swiss-born, German-oriented Rolf Liebermann? Their certain scorn would be no denunciation of him, but of the internal disintegration of the bureaucracy that brought his appointment about.

The two main streams of French opera, which have now been reduced, in creation, to a trickle, and in performance, to droplets, were *opéra comique* (not a description of content, but of method, the text being spoken, not sung) and *grand opéra* (descriptive of a work with sung text, spectacle, ballet, and so on). French opera all but began at the court of Louis XIV, where Jean-Baptiste Lully, a Florentine adept not only in vocal music but in ballet, devised—for the Sun King's pleasure—works fanciful to see and most agreeable to hear. To restore them to the stage in all their glory would require the restoration of the French monarchy—perhaps too high a price to pay. *Opéra comique* flowed from the artistry of André Ernest Grétry, a native of Liège (then an independent community not a part either of France or Belgium).

There were, of course, gifted Frenchmen who found an outlet in one operatic discipline or the other. One of the first was Jean Philippe Rameau, a lineal successor to Lully in importance, some fifty years after the latter's death. After the Revolution overthrew the monarchy, both kinds of *opéra* were institutionalized under government administration and support. They were bidden not to intermingle, so that each might be preserved in its integrity. A little cross-breeding might have contributed hardiness to a species now all but extinct.

Though French opera as a robust thing in itself may have disappeared from the world stages (save for the prime works of Gounod, Bizet, Massenet, and Debussy, with an occasional revival of Berlioz to convince us of what we are missing), what France gave to opera is with us all the time—in works by non-French composers. In part a testimony to the pervasive power of the French imagination, it is, in another equally large part, owing to the magnetic attractiveness of Paris to the European creative community during the nineteenth century, and to the earnings that a success in Paris could provide. Young men came to Paris to study, to dream, to create; older men came and came again, drawn by commissions and the promise of wealth they implied.

For both, Paris became a meeting ground of ideas, a testing ground for theories, a parade ground for aspirations. It held the promise, for those who achieved fulfillment, of the kind of heavenly happiness on earth characterized by its broad, tree-lined Champs-Elysées. For example, even though he came to Paris relatively late in life, Gluck's response to the whole background of theatrical culture, including the ballet collaborations of Molière and Lully, Voltaire and Rameau, became very much a part of his mature works. He also observed that French lyric expression preserved an identity with the *word* not to be found elsewhere. The restriction on *castrati* inhibited the spread of the wilder flights of improvisation and embellishment for which they were famous. The consequences on behalf of the *scena* were numerous. The opportunities provided by the *air declamé* have already been noted vis-à-vis *Alceste*. From there Gluck went on to the greater grandeur of *Iphigénie en Tauride*, not seen in New York since a production of 1916—a mere matter of sixty years!

What Gluck imparted to French opera found a responsive ear in Luigi Cherubini, who was born in Florence (1760) and came to Paris in his late twenties. He flourished artistically and endured physically to earn the extraordinary honor of being appointed director of the famous Paris Conservatoire at seventy. A landmark in French opera, Cherubini's *Médée* of 1797—much admired, long neglected, and only recently restored to public performance—carried forward what Gluck had started, impelling the art in a direction that enlisted the admiration of the young Hector Berlioz when he came to Paris to study in the 1820s.

In a return flow of influence, Cherubini's operas (first *Lodoïska*, then *Les deux Journées* and later *Médée*) brought back to Gluck's Vienna a startling new kind of post-Revolutionary French opera in 1802. Cherubini and what he represented—a blend, really, of Italian, French, and German elements—gave him high favor with Beethoven. His elevated style of vocal writing and the fine instrumental techniques represented in his opera overtures prompted Beethoven to endorse him as "the greatest dramatic composer of the age. . . ."

The wave of enthusiasm for Cherubini brought to Vienna in its wake a flotilla of other operas from abroad, either French or reflecting French influence. Among the latter was Ferdinando Paër's *Léonore*, based on a text by J. N. Bouilly (originally written as an *opéra comique* with an obscure composer named Pierre Gaveaux, and produced in Paris in 1798).

Bouilly has one place in a prime series of historical happenings, Paër another. Bouilly's text brings us abreast of a theatrical outcropping in the late eighteenth century known to the French as *opéra de la délivrance*, to the Germans as *Rettenoper*, and to the English-speaking as "rescue opera." The first of the line was composed in the late 1770s by Grétry. Titled *Richard Coeur-de-Lion*, it deals with the quest of the faithful troubadour, Blondel, for his master and Richard's *délivrance* from captivity. Plots based on searches and sacrifices, dangers and deliverances, flourished during the Reign of Terror, when subject matter was abundant. Paër's treatment of *Léonore* brought the subject to the attention of Beethoven when it was produced in Vienna in 1804. Whether or not Beethoven's well-known candor impelled him to tell Paër, when they met, "I like the subject of your opera. I think I shall set it to music," may be left to the reader's preference. It is certain that his well-known idealism and his compulsive belief in the goodness of women resulted in the adaptation of the Bouilly text that became *Fidelio*.

And from this quadruple play of Gluck to Cherubini to Bouilly (who also wrote the text for *Les deux Journées*) to Beethoven emerged one of the greatest of dramatic scenes to be heard regularly in the opera house. As noted, the French subject of *Fidelio* was categorically an *opéra comique*, genre *opéra de la délivrance:* in it Beethoven carries forward what Mozart made of the *Singspiel* in *Die Entführung* and *Die Zauberflöte*. It is hardly the first—and let us hope, not the last—time that two knowns have served a man of imagination to produce a previous unknown. Nothing on the scope of Beethoven's use of the orchestra in *Fidelio* had ever been ventured by a previous composer, nor had a German opera soprano ever been challenged by the risk and dangers assumed by Leonore (in the disguise of the male Fidelio) to discover whether her husband, a political prisoner, was still alive and could be rescued.

Not the least of these risks and dangers is the *scena* midway in Act I in which Leonore-Fidelio discovers that there is, indeed, a live political prisoner in a dungeon of the jail in which she has obtained a job, and that he will soon be put to death. Here is hope and here is uncertainty: there is no way for her to know whether the imprisoned man is her Florestan or not. In any case, the monster who threatens his life is to be denounced and the man whose life is being threatened must be saved.

As a pendant to an observation previously made on overtures—that what is heard first may be the last written—the first word of this famous *scena* and the one by which it is universally known, "Abscheulicher!" ("Monster!"), was almost the last word of the many hundreds in *Fidelio* to be written. Begun in the heat of enthusiasm for the French subject engendered by contact with Bouilly's text in 1804, the first version of *Fidelio* was produced in Vienna in 1805. It was in three acts, and did not play well. A second version, more compact and reduced to two acts, was produced in 1806. It still left much to be desired. There is a scene for Fidelio in Act I of the earlier version, but it is nonexplosive—which is to say, a dud. When the score was reworked for performance in 1814, it was clear that Beethoven, out of his relentless application and bulldog determination to succeed, had done many fine things and some great ones, to transform his unequal product. But the first act *scena* still did not fulfill its purpose. Not until the middle of June (in a sequence of performances that had begun on May 23, 1814) were all the elements present in the form that now exists, with "Abscheulicher!" as the fuse to detonate the finally explosive matter that follows.

But the driest powder, the tightest packing, and the longest fuse cannot produce an explosion if ignition does not occur, whether for a space rocket or an artistic experience. The fire to light the fuse must come from the performer, especially in the special circumstances that exist in *Fidelio*. For the first time since the action commenced—at least half an hour before—Leonore is able to address the audience as an anxious wife, rather than an oversized "boy." She has the stage to herself, and to her dangerous dilemma: resentment against the tyrant who threatens a man's right to live; a prayer of a hope that a chance exists to save him ("Komm, Hoffnung") ("O Hope"); a determination to see things through at no matter what cost. These, in short, are the components of the greatest *scena*s (for all that Beethoven called this one "Recitativ und Arie"): a character alone on a stage; a tempest of emotions; and the gusting, quartering, fluctuating winds of changing tempos which are their musical equivalents.

I grew up with a scratchy 78 rpm low-fidelity version of this episode—performer unrecalled. The disc had to be turned in mid-performance, and there was a throbbing sound in the background which could be construed as an orchestra. The orchestral sound I began to hear in performances of the late twenties (with vocal effects by several pseudo Fidelios, obviously well fed, but with unflattering figures for the knee breeches customarily worn in the part). A little later came Gertrude Kappel, a woman of conviction and musicianly impulses. But her voice was less than heroic and she tended to be gingerly with her tones in the flaring final scale in which Leonore voices total resolution.

The rewards of a trip I made to Salzburg in the thirties were many, but the one, the lasting, the imperishable memory is of *Fidelio*. I have mentioned that it was conducted by Richard Strauss, but not that it was in a manner to which the Vienna Philharmonic in the pit responded as though he were Beethoven himself. The cast was, in general, excellent.

The Fidelio was Lotte Lehmann. She, too, was a woman of conviction and musicianly impulses and her voice, also, was less than heroic. But she was not in the least gingerly in the use of her voice in the flaring final scale or in any other measure of the part where drama was of the essence. She was that ultimate, blessed, indispensable kind of interpreter who sang every performance as though it might be her last, and was determined—with every fiber of her body—to make it worthy of such a finality. It transcended music, art, and emotion. It was Lehmann vs. Beethoven. Both won.

In a sequence of subsequent experiences with *Fidelio*, there have been the two Flagstads, a decade apart: the first youthful, vibrant, pantsworthy, incredibly easy in the execution of everything written; the second aging, stolid, broad of beam, and not nearly so easy in the execution of everything written, but with a heartful of experience which gave her access to much that was unwritten. Since that time there have been more than a fair share of fine Fidelios. I would single out Inge Borkh, who deserves high marks as an actress (her training before she discovered she had a voice) and Christa Ludwig, who earned an I for involvement, though her voice is short for the top tones the part requires.

Along this way I have heard touchstones of beauty, models of endearing emotion, embodiments of such rare resolution as Nilsson's. But no other performer of the day has defined the two perimeters of the interpreter's problem as definitively as Leonie Rysanek. The first is the flint and steel of the outcry she commands to strike fire with "Abscheulicher!" The other is the heart's blood she pours into the last three words of the whole *scena*, in which Beethoven isolates them, syllable by syllable, on an upward surge of sound from low to middle E ("Gat-") then doubling back, still on the same syllable, from the middle to the top B, from which he drives down to the cadential D sharp ("-ten-"), F sharp, E ("-liebe"). "Gatten liebe" is "wifely love." Rysanek's holiest devotion to this concept was to interpose a short pause and a final exhalation of sound on "-liebe" to summarize, finalize, and incidentally, energize the by now almost intolerably delayed conclusion.

In manner and procedure, the draftsmanship of the scene now universally known as "Abscheulicher!" was bound to be arresting to young composers growing up in Central Europe when it was new. The first to respond in kind was Carl Maria von Weber, whose "Leise, leise" and the following allegro in *Der Freischütz* are not copies from, but fulfillments of, Beethoven's initiative. They are individualized and amplified in Rezia's "Ozean du ungeheuer" in *Oberon* and the great outburst of Lysiart in *Euryanthe*. Out of such source matter—and the concert arias of Mozart and Beethoven ("Ah! Perfido") which preceded them—can be traced the deviations that enter into the great Wagnerian soliloquies, from Vanderdecken's "Die Frist ist um" in the first act of *Die fliegende Holländer* to those of Hans Sachs in *Die Meistersinger*. For that matter, the tradition goes far into the Strauss repertory, from Elektra's opening ruminations on "Agememnon" to the reflections of the Countess in *Capriccio*, which Strauss wrote forty years later.

3

To elevate the *scena* from an "alternative to recitative and aria" to something with a "tradition" is to suggest that it acquired international acquiescence, diversified identity, and widespread usage from a standing start in the early years of the nineteenth century. Nothing could be more precisely true. Two elements contributed to that spread: the gradual, irresistible drift in operatic subject matter from the past to the present, from the mythological to the realistic, from the aristocratic to the folk, and the expansion of tonal and visual resources for realizing such subject matter on the stage.

If, as Donald Grout contends, "During the first half of the nineteenth century Paris was virtually the European capital of opera,"[2] this was in no small part true because she had not only the stage but the stages to accommodate it. There were the official homes of *grand opéra* and *opéra comique;* but there were also privately sponsored enterprises in the Théâtre de l'Odéon (where a butchered version of *Der Freischütz* had a run of 387 performances in the 1820s) and later, the Théâtre des Italiens, where new works not considered suitable for the state-sponsored Académie could be performed.

One of these numerous theaters provided the stage for *Robert le Diable*, which introduced to fame one of the most successful opera composers of the nineteenth, or any other, century. Its composer purveyed a talent as many-faceted as the name by which he became famous, Giacomo Meyerbeer. A native of Berlin (1791), he was no more entitled to call himself Giacomo than Meyerbeer. He was born Jakob Liebmann Beer, showed a talent for music at an early age, and was a contemporary, crony, and fellow-Bohemian-in-the-arts of Weber before either became well known. Jakob Beer changed his name to Meyer Beer to foster the favor of an uncle of that name who helped to underwrite his career. He contracted Meyer Beer into its familiar form and replaced Jakob with its Italian equivalent when, during a visit to Italy in the early 1820s, he found an audience for a style of writing that fed the Rossini vogue. Not that Meyerbeer was alone in being so tempted. In a letter of his youth, Weber wrote to a friend (from Darmstadt, where he was working at the court) that he had written a duet "in such a wretchedly Italianate style that it might have been by Farinelli: it was hellish successful."[3] Weber recognized his "Se il mio ben" (op. 31, no. 3) for what it was and aimed higher than being "hellish successful." Likewise, when Wagner was fighting the struggle for survival in Paris twenty years later, he undertook to produce a bass aria in the hope that an Oroveso with whom he had become acquainted would introduce it into *Norma*(!). When the plan fell through, Wagner wrote: "My relapse into the domain of Bellini's style . . . was therefore useless to me, and I soon became convinced of the fruitlessness of my efforts in that direction."[4]

But with Meyerbeer the case was rather different. As a part-time critic, Weber wrote of one of Meyerbeer's early Italian operas (1820): "There must be something seriously wrong with the digestive powers of Italian stomachs for a genius of such original powers as Meyerbeer to have felt it necessary not merely to have set nothing but sweet, luxuriantly swollen fruit on the table, but also to have sugared it over in this manner. . . ."[5] Meyerbeer was generous enough not to hold this condemnation against one who was, indeed a genius. When Weber died only half a dozen years after this was written (in 1826), Meyerbeer put himself out to be helpful to his friend's widow. In another half dozen years, when Meyerbeer had become not merely Italianized but Frenchified, he was so "hellish successful" that he could lay siege to the esteem that Rossini had won in Paris with *Guillaume Tell* a few years before.

In the decades that followed the great success of *Robert le Diable* (1831) and the even greater success of *Les Huguenots* (1836), Meyerbeer spent much of his time in Berlin, but continued to feed the French stage with works that provided much of its identity in the mid-nineteenth century: *Le Prophète* (1849), *L'Étoile du Nord* (1854), *Dinorah* (1859), and, finally, *L'Africaine*. The last of these is, despite its title, an interesting venture into India as an opera locale which occupied Meyerbeer for more than twenty years, but was not staged until 1865, a year after his death. *L'Africaine* was thus a kind of artistic mortmain in which Meyerbeer was enabled to retain his grasp of the French stage even from the hereafter.

To hear such a score as *Les Huguenots* today is to understand not only what made Meyerbeer, but what unmade him. Big choruses, gaudy solos, flamboyant orchestration—a viola solo behind a tenor aria, an unkeyed trumpet to suggest a ghostly voice were typical— ripping good tunes, actions (one almost adds: "Camera!") are popular goods in any market, and the Parisian market of the mid-nineteenth century was full of people ready to buy.

But these are procedural rather than substantive matters; they lent themselves not only to imitation, but to improvement. When Gounod wrote a catchier chorus for the soldiers in *Faust* than Meyerbeer had provided for his nobles in *Les Huguenots* ("Bonheur de la table"), one of his better cards had been trumped; when a bigger spectacle took the place of the top scene in *Le Prophète,* another underpinning eroded; and when Ponchielli added, to the explosion of a ship in *La Gioconda* and the tenor's "Cielo e mar" such other melodic induce- ments as "Suicidio," "Stella del marinar," "O monumento," "Voce di donna," *and* the "Dance of the Hours," the less appealing arias and the mere shipwreck of Vasco da Gama's craft in *L'Africaine* had all been faced down.

Meyerbeer's achievement could be described as the lost cord bind- ing together early-nineteenth-century French opera (including the *genre* works of Auber, Boieldieu, and so on) and its more enduring repertory of the latter half of the century. He could also be described as the most thoroughly cannibalized composer in history. Like me- chanics at a modern military airbase picking over some huge grounded aircraft for one part and then another, to keep other planes flying, opera composers of the time helped themselves first to one and then to another of Meyerbeer's innovations. Wagner reacted rather caustically to the charge that, in *Tannhäuser,* he had glorified Catholicism as Meyer- beer, in *Les Huguenots,* had glorified Protestantism. If this allegation can be laughed off, it is nevertheless a fundamental fact that there is more than a little, in early Wagner, that is a carry-over of his response to a Paris production of *Les Huguenots* (1841), which, he wrote: "dazzled me very much indeed . . . the extremely careful and effec- tive *mise en scène* gave me a grand idea of the great possibilities of such perfect and definite artistic means."[6]

Nor was Meyerbeer's greatest Italian contemporary immune to the contagion that spread from his works. In *Les Vêpres siciliennes* (to give it the name of its original production) Verdi was lured into writing for Paris an opera on the Meyerbeer plan (five acts, spectacle, ballet, and so on) with a text by the author of such successes as *Robert le Diable, Le Prophète,* and *L'Africaine,* not to mention the re-use of a tolling bell as a symbol for massacre borrowed from *Les Huguenots.* The experience was so frustrating Verdi vowed never to do it again. A dozen years later, he was tempted anew and did not refuse, because this time the subject matter was not by Eugène Scribe but by Friedrich Schiller.

If Verdi's *Don Carlos* could be described, in its original five-act form (with ballet), as the grandest of Meyerbeer's operas, it could be because it, too, has a religious motif, an *auto de fè* in which heretics are burned (offstage), a son who defies his kingly father's authority, stirring choruses, brilliant orchestration, and opportunities for spectacular *mise en scène.* The difference might be that, in this venture, none of the elements are synthetic.

In its original five-act form, *Don Carlos* brought together the imagination of a German playwright, the resources of the Parisian stage, and the genius of Verdi which transcended nationality. The form in which it is now customarily presented requires the audience to take on faith the love affair of Don Carlos and Elisabetta which was depicted in Act I (as written for Paris). Its omission deprives many audiences of a fine duet for its principals, as well as Verdi's initial impulse. Once under way, however, the grinding force of the dramatic machine is all but irresistible. Powering it are Carlos's losing contest for the love of Elisabetta, who has been forced to make a political marriage to his aging father; Philip II's suspicion that the tie between his son and the woman he now dutifully calls "Mother" may still endure; and the unshakable awareness that he will, as king, have to deal with Carlos's defiance of throne and church by his expression of sympathy for the rebellious Lowlanders.

Merely to sketch these human, political, and philosophic considerations is to comprehend the distance that opera had come from the first performance of *Alceste* on December 26, 1767, and the premiere of *Don Carlos* on March 11, 1867. But to hear the celebrated first part of Act III (as now reckoned), which brings together Philip's great monologue and the succeeding scene with the Grand Inquisitor, is to realize that what Gluck had set in motion a hundred years before in "Divinités du Styx" was still in being. It was, indeed, enormously expanded and fleshed out with a progression of means—in which Meyerbeer as well as Verdi had played a part—to give *scena drammatica* a new, inclusive meaning.

Here it has grown from a single element (the tense, introspective, soul-searching monologue in which Philip II confronts his situation and concludes that he will find peace only in death) to a series of unfolding, interconnected episodes which, together, bind music to words and truth to action in a manner rarely equaled.

Philip's "Ella giammai m'amò" ("I never won her heart!") are the opening words of the act, prepared by Verdi with a somber, brief prelude which is, in fact, the introduction to the sung measures that follow. Out of them emerges the regally flowing measures of "Dormirò sol nel manto mio regal" ("I'll sleep alone in my royal robes tonight"). They turn and they curl, but wherever Philip's thoughts lead him, they lead back to "Ella giammai m'amò" and the heartbroken recognition that "Amor per me non ha!" ("Love for me she never had!"). Barely has the audience reaction subsided—and Verdi wisely wrote a double bar at this point, knowing that what he had written would always be applauded, no matter how performed—than an attendant announces: "Il Grand' Inquisitor!"

The chamber where the scene takes place is narrow and high, almost cell-like, and reached by an equally narrow door. The more, then, to accentuate the gaunt greatness of the red-robed red-hatted Inquisitor—ninety, blind, and led by two Dominican friars. They retire. He takes a chair. Philip knows that he has to order the execution of his son. He shrinks from it, and hopes that the Inquisitor can ease his dilemma. The scene comes to a rare, Schillerian confrontation of power, temporal and spiritual, in which the Inquisitor not only commands that Philip fulfill his function as king, but demands that he treat subversion roughly, or the Inquisition will. The music is monumental in its grandeur and menacing in its inhuman undercurrent—a portrait in sound of a churchman who is both monumental and menacing.

Hardly have the friars returned and led their master away than Elisabetta appears in agitation to declare that she has been robbed of her jewels. Philip points to the casket on his table and orders her to open it. When she shrinks from the act, he seizes the box and breaks the lock. Carlos's picture lying atop the jewels is proof to the king that Elisabetta has deceived him. All her protestations that it is a memento of the time when they were engaged have no effect. She falls to the floor, weeping, as Philip summons her maid-in-waiting

Eboli. With her as escort is Rodrigo, Marquis de Posa, his son's best friend, whom the Inquisitor has decreed must also die.

In the emotionally taut, intensely compact quartet that follows, the main strings of the drama are drawn tight as Verdi gives voice to the driving emotions of each of his characters: the King, aware that he has unfairly accused his wife, cursing his temper; Rodrigo, sensing from the King's demeanor that his own life is in danger; Elisabetta, in despair, wishing that she had never left her native France; and Eboli, remorseful that jealousy of Elisabetta had caused her to steal the jewel box and bring its incriminating contents to Philip's attention. At the quartet's eloquent end there is nothing for the King to do but leave, followed by Rodrigo; for Elisabetta to listen in astonishment to Eboli's confession of her guilt, brought about by her secret love for Carlos; and for Verdi to conclude an unbroken stretch of half an hour's music with the greatest moment of all, "O don fatale," in which Eboli laments the "fatal beauty" which had caused her to act so unwisely. This Verdi calls an aria—all the preceding segments were designated *Introduzione e scena, scena, scena e quartetto*, and so forth. Thus, finally, have the content and the terminology come together, to remain indivisible in the works of Verdi to follow: *Aida, Otello,* and *Falstaff*.

As for Eboli's *aria*, Dyneley Hussey has a pertinent comment to make in his biography of Verdi (short, but extremely valuable, in the *Master Musicians* series): " 'O don fatale' breaks away altogether from the old aria form. There is no reprise of the opening section, but an entirely free sequence of contrasted sections culminating in a tremendous dramatic climax. . . . The same process is used in Aida's 'Ritorna vincitor' which, unlike Eboli's aria, is more accurately entitled a *scena* in the score."[7]

If the mind can be likened to a camera, much of what is inscribed "photographically" on the memory can be attributed to the candlepower of the images to which it has been exposed. The opportunities of this great *scena* in *Don Carlos* are many, and the manner in which they have been utilized in the great Bing revival of the fifties—more than seventy performances in New York over a twenty-two year period—have left images of performers as vivid as the colors of their costumes. In most respects traditional, as realized by Rolf Gerard, the costumes gave sight to sound in a most uncommon way—Philip's black beaver hat and costume, with a gold cord at the neck; the blood-red robe of the Inquisitor; Elisabetta's gold brocade; Eboli's emerald gown; the jaunty cut of Posa's ruff and jerkin.

Philip II has been admirably served by such warm-voiced, well-structured singers as Cesare Siepi and Jerome Hines, both of whom have had the comforting experience of finding it a role in which a basso can hardly grow too old. Others of quality have included Nicolai Ghiaurov (a little at a loss for the bottom notes of the role) and Giorgio Tozzi. As time passed, less and less of the gray in the hair was makeup, more of it authentic—a transformation that no one who treasured realism could regret. As for the Inquisitor, no basso ever grew old enough to play him without a whitening cream to suggest his pallid, waxlike skin. Dramatic credibility in this role has never been so well served as it was by the formidable Hans Hotter, a great Wotan and Dutchman, who had the height (six feet, four inches) to tower over almost any Philip II and the depth of voice to support any command he issued. Martti Talvela, of Finnish birth, has the inches to equal Hotter, if not yet the assertive manner, and John Macurdy's Inquisitor was unique in suggesting an Irish padre who might have been cousin to Boston's Cardinal Cushing.

Of course, if the Philip II were sung by Hines, the contest in inches would have been closer. He sang both roles (Philip and Inquisitor) well, if somewhat placidly. Big men, it is said, are often of gentle disposition— a truism for Hines. Paul Schoeffler was another master of both roles. In America, Schoeffler appeared only as the Inquisitor; at home, in Vienna, his Philip was by far the most memorable effort in a cast whose other members lacked candlepower to register on the camera of memory.

Few baritones of any time could have matched Robert Merrill's feat of repeating, at the opening of Rudolf Bing's last Metropolitan season (1971–72), the Posa he had sung twenty-two years before at the first *Don Carlos* of that administration, without looking an ounce heavier, an inch thicker around the waist, or vocally depleted. The quality of his voice had changed, of course—not as ripe, not as vibrant in "Per me giunto" (in the second scene of Act III)—but extraordinarily firm, still, for a man who had sung *forty* performances of this role alone among the 669 he had sung with the company (in New York and on tour). Tito Gobbi has also been a fine Posa in this period, as was the ill-fated Ettore Bastianini, a victim of cancer in his prime as a singer. They had, for all their physical and tonal differences, one quality in com-

mon: each bore himself like a man and a courtier who would give anything to a friend, including his life.

Elisabettas, however, have not been of true Verdian quality over
this span of *Don Carlos* in New York (nor elsewhere, really)—no
Tebaldi, no Price (I wonder why), and Callas only on rare, infrequent,
occasions. Antonietta Stella was perhaps the best, but her abbreviated
American career accommodated only two performances. Leonie
Rysanek had both the appearance and the dramatic pulse the role required, but neither the finesse of vocal line nor the steadiness of support
to meet Verdi's requirements. Ebolis, curiously, have been of con-
sistently high rank. My preference was for two performers who have
brought entirely different personalities to the emerald gown: Fedora
Barbieri, a perfect Dame Quickly in *Falstaff*, and Grace Bumbry, a
svelte, boylike Orfeo. Each was superb because each commanded not
only the voice for the laughing "Veil Song" of Act II and the tor-
mented "O don fatale" in Act III, but the personal presence to risk
the great gamble of betraying Elisabetta, and to rue the result. Shirley
Verrett could be the next of high quality—if she could accept the
proposition that great personal beauty *could* be a curse.

As for Don Carlos, there has been—for me—only one, worldwide:
Jussi Bjoerling. The late Richard Tucker had his admirers, and I was
one of them, in certain roles—but they did not include Don Carlos.
Bjoerling had both the special, certain splendor in his tone to complement the brilliant brass sound that Verdi—courtesy of Meyerbeer and
Berlioz—called upon in this score, plus an openness and candor of
manner that was, indeed, Carlosian.

Considering the success of *Don Carlos* in America in the fifties and
sixties (certainly over a hundred performances, adding those in San
Francisco and Chicago to the basic seventy-three by the Metropolitan
company), it is curious that this opera, during preceding decades, was
more prominent in Central Europe than elsewhere, including Italy.
Perhaps the derivation of the opera's subject matter from the literature
of the great Schiller had a part in the opera's appeal to the German-
speaking public.

Of the handful of performances that *Don Carlos* had in New York
during the twenties, one in particular would have been something to
treasure. That is not because Giovanni Martinelli sang Don Carlos or
Giuseppe de Luca was the Posa or Léon Rothier, a Hotter-sized French
basso, was a towering Inquisitor. It was because King Philip II was

portrayed by Feodor Chaliapin. Having had a gratifying success with "Ella giammai m'amò," he not merely rose to bow his thanks, but walked to the footlights, told the obsequious conductor where to find a point of beginning, and repeated the scene (what the Italians call a "bis"). Doubtless he had found a *da capo* under the double bar of his Russian score.

4

To speak of Chaliapin is, of course, to speak of *Boris Godunov,* and to speak of *Boris* is, inevitably, to speak of Russian opera in general and the special place in it of the *scena drammatica* at its most powerful. Russian opera has a tradition even shorter than German, but the out-pouring of its nineteenth-century composers produced one of the world's great repertories. At home, it is more than sufficient to sustain seasonal needs, year after year (not that the public is denied matter from other sources). Abroad, it has fared less well—to some extent because of language difficulties, but even more for reasons of style, of procedure, of content, and of philosophy. All of these require more adaptability of attitude than the international operatic audience is conditioned to provide.

It may strike some readers as a little odd that Verdi wrote *La forza del destino* on a commission from St. Petersburg in 1862. Actually, the tradition of Italian opera in Russia is older than the tradition of true opera in Russian. Opera was a court-bred and -supported activity, with the court's musical interests well cared for by the importation of works by Galuppi, Paisiello, Cimarosa, and Salieri (in several instances, the composers themselves came to St. Petersburg).[8] Native talent did express itself in the theater—the raw material of myth and folk song was too abundant to be ignored—but the cultivated courtiers and land-owners looked elsewhere for their diversion.

The prototype for all of the prominent Russian composers of the century-to-come was Mikhail Glinka, born in 1803, the son of a retired army captain, educated (as a gentleman should be) with a taste for music. He studied piano with the illustrious John Field, and was able to play a Hummel concerto at eighteen; but he was not to consider music as a career, let alone composing as a lifework. Of the usual alternatives for the well-born—the law, the military, or the civil service—Glinka chose the Ministry of Ways and Means.

His health was poor (he eventually died of syphilis contracted at some undetermined time), and at twenty-seven he went abroad, to a warm climate—which meant Italy. In Milan, hearing Pasta and Rubini in one of the earliest performances of Bellini's *La Sonnambula* had a lifelong effect on Glinka. It brought him to the realization that learning how to compose—he had written some songs and similarly brief works in Russia, without benefit of serious training—was the only thing he really cared about. Like Weber, Wagner, and Meyerbeer, he sought to imitate what was in the Italian air. But, like Weber and Wagner (if not Meyerbeer), he discovered: "It cost me some pains to counterfeit the Italian *sentimento brillante*."[9] He went to Berlin, where he found an able teacher and began to find his own way. He was thirty when his father's death required his return to Russia.

Within two years, Glinka had shaken off all submission to exterior example, plunged into the depths of his own and his country's character, and produced the first authentic Russian opera, *A Life for the Czar* (the name by which it is now known in the Soviet Union is derived from its hero, *Ivan Susanin*). Its first performance on November 7, 1836, was an epochal experience in self-recognition for the audience. For the first time, Russia had a composer who did more than merely reproduce folk songs; he used them as the substance of an idiom. Even the complaints from some that he had written "la musique des cochers"[10] ("music of the coachmen") did not disturb him. "What matter," he observed, "since the servants are better than their masters."[11]

To a listener of today, nearly a hundred and fifty years later, *A Life for the Czar* provides an extraordinary foretaste of Russian opera to come. Within a half hour of its first act, the grand design is in being: a hero derived from history, with a deep bass voice; powerful choral voices; a tenor who sings "above the staff" (in his highest register) much of the time; a sweet-voiced soprano heroine; much more ample use of the orchestra than characterized the Italian operas of the time (indeed, the Weber of *Der Freischütz* is very much in the picture). In every way, *A Life for the Czar* may be one of the best first operas ever written, as well as one of the most influential.

For those in whom this may arouse a desire for indoctrination in depth of what followed, I recommend the Modern Library Giant G 62. It is not a volume of opera libretti, nor is it a biography of composers. It is devoted to the poems, prose, and plays of the Russian Shakespeare—Alexander Pushkin. Within it you will find the sources of such operas-to-be as *The Stone Guest* (by Glinka's immediate successor, Alexander Dargomyzsky), *Boris Godunov* (Moussorgsky), *Eugene Onegin* and *Pique Dame* (both by Tchaikovsky), *Le Coq d'Or* and *Mozart and Salieri* (two subjects favored by Rimsky-Korsakov), and *The Covetous Knight* and *Aleko* (Rachmaninoff). The collection might—but does not—include the material on which Glinka based his second, celebrated opera, *Russlan and Ludmilla* (typified by its much-played overture), and on which he was hoping that its author would collaborate with him until Pushkin died after a duel in 1837.

As well as being Pushkin's first long poem (1818–1820) and the source of a famous opera, *Russlan and Ludmilla* contains, in its prologue, a parable of Russian art that endures to the present day. Pushkin speaks of the "famous and miraculous cat that, circling around a great oak-tree in the deepest forest, spends day and night in stimulating a belief in the fairies. When he turns to the right, he sings a song, when he goes to the left, he tells a tale. It is at his feet," says Pushkin, "that one must sit, if one would seek to know the ancient Russian legends, to hear about the 'russalki' [another opera by Dargomyzsky, later set to even better known results by Antonín Dvořák], 'the terrible Katschei' [the menacing magician of Stravinsky's *L'Oiseau de Feu*] and Baba Yaga in her hut on fowl's legs" (one of the creations of Viktor Hartmann that became a memorable part of Moussorgsky's *Pictures at an Exposition*). Concludes Pushkin: "I am seated under the oak and hear the cat's stories: this is what he told me."[12]

If what the cat told Pushkin made literature, what Pushkin told the generations to come made Russian opera. And if words can be said to sing, his almost wrote their own music. *Boris Godunov* is a play written in blank verse, which barely required more than compression and curtailment to make Moussorgsky's libretto. It is redolent with such phrases as "I am dying. Farewell, my son: forthwith Thou wilt begin to reign,"[13] which echo in the ear with Moussorgsky's music. In *Eugene Onegin*, Pushkin achieved the rare literary feat of a novel in verse, nothing less than *399* sonnetlike segments. No. XXXI in Chapter Three is Tatyana's Letter to Onegin, which is written in French. The reason for this the author explains in a preceding sonnet (No. XXVI, Chapter Three which reads (in part):

> Tatyana read no Russian journal
> She did not speak the language well
> And found it rather hard to spell;
>
> And so of course the girl decided
> To write in French . . . What's to be done?

> For lady never, no not one,
> Her love in Russian has confided;
> Our native language turns up its nose
> At mere epistolary prose.

In his sonnet introducing the letter itself, Pushkin gives Onegin these words descriptive of it:

> . . . like an air from Freischütz played
> By someone awkward and afraid."[14]

Both of the foregoing Pushkin texts—as well as many others—became the source for a famous *scena drammatica*, and the result tells us why the outcome is something more than merely operatic. Unlike Beethoven fusing the words of an obscure litterateur of Vienna with his own life's blood in order to galvanize the listener's attention to "Abscheulicher!" or Verdi trying to fit himself into the English Shakespeare's skin to re-create the emotion in the Italian equivalent of Othello's "Farewell the tranquil mind, farewell content!," Moussorgsky in *Boris* and Tchaikovsky in *Onegin* were (in a phrase used to me, in another context, by Luciano Berlio) "eating their own bread" in Pushkin, and thriving on it.

Moreover, the scenes from Pushkin's *Boris* and *Onegin* accord with the circumstances of the true *scena drammatica* as previously defined: the characters hold stage center virtually alone (Boris cradles the mute Tsarevitch in his arms and there are several silent Boyars in the background); each scene has a built-in latitude for a number of tempo changes to reflect the ebb and flow of emotion; each deals with a vital element in the drama rather than a passing phase of it; and neither is in the least operatic. They are evocations of *character*, such as one finds throughout the Russian opera we are privileged to hear now and then. *Pique Dame* is so rich in character portrayal that we have a hero, Ghermann, Russian enough to be unlucky both in cards and love; *Le Coq d'Or* is inimitable for the character of a King (Dodon), lovable and foolish like none other in drama; and Moussorgsky's *Khovantschina* is made up mostly of character sketches, beginning with another Russian monarch of the seventeenth century who worries about "aggression from the west" in an opera written in the nineteenth century.

The reasons why, of all Russian operas performed outside of Russia, Moussorgsky's *Boris* is the one most commonly heard and widely enjoyed, are many, of which one is transcendentally important: its music has a wider, more elemental appeal than that of any other stage work by a Russian. Also, *Boris* is cast in the form of a chronicle

play, which is to say it deals with its subject in interrelated, but uncon-
nected, episodes. Some might regard this as a liability; I would cite it
as an asset to the unindoctrinated, as the scenes change frequently and
the subject matter is thus more varied. Above all, it has as its central
figure one of the greatest creations of the operatic stage, which has
acquired over years of performance a set of standards as specific as
those related to a great Don Giovanni, a great Hans Sachs, or an
outstanding Golaud.

The legend and lore of Chaliapin might make one suppose that he
had been singing the role from the day *Boris* was born. They did,
indeed, share a time of birth (1873), but it was twenty-five years later
that Chaliapin began his unparalleled reign as the greatest basso of the
Russian stage. It would, therefore, have been after more than a thirty
years' indoctrination in his specialty that I had my first view of Chaliapin's Boris at the Metropolitan (c. 1928). He was, as I recall it, no
longer "dignified, colossal, the very personification of kingly authority,
in his superb robes of cloth, with the crown of Monomakh on his
head,"[15] as he was described by an authority on Russian opera twenty-
five years before. As he had aged, so the part aged with him; he was
a figure gaunt rather than colossal, menacing and Tartarish of face,
with a raspy voice torn by use and abuse. I have no other worthwhile
insights to convey. I was a standee without standards.

Of later performers of Boris, I was warmly partial to Ezio Pinza, but
more fulfilled by the performances of Alexander Kipnis and Georges
Baklanoff. The contention that a proper Boris should be tall—as Chaliapin, Pinza, and Kipnis were, and Siepi, Hines, London, Christoff, and
Talvela have more recently been—is sound, but not incontrovertible.
Baklanoff was not of much more than average height, nor is Giorgio
Tozzi. Both were among the best of their time, however, because there
are some roles in which gray matter can lend as much spiritual eleva-
tion to a performance as inches can to its physical dimensions. The
sense of character that Siepi conveyed—with or without premeditation—
when he put his hand affectionately on the Tsarevitch's head in the
Nursery Scene with his children, told us more about this Boris than
the highest-heeled pair of boots could.

The curious, finalizing fact about the *scena drammatica* is that it
provides the opportunity for *language* to play its part in the equation
of sung and played music. By its very nature, the *scena* enables the
performer to work with words, as is not always possible in aria, and
also does what recitativo cannot—hold the center of stage for minutes

at a time. The mine of Pushkin not only provided Russian composers of the nineteenth century with inexhaustible treasure, but pointed a way to composers of the twentieth century to find more of the same (as Prokofiev did in Tolstoy's *War and Peace*, with its great *scena* for Kutuzov).

Internationally, the example of Moussorgsky and Pushkin had consequences that neither could have imagined. Long before the work was first performed in Paris (in 1908), a musical traveler to Russia returned to France with a score of *Boris* which found its way into the hands of Debussy, in the nineties. Opinions still differ as to the amount of musical matter Debussy absorbed from Moussorgsky—I would say more, rather than less, especially in the treatment of words in a naturally declamatory way—but there is little doubt that it impelled him in the direction of a spoken drama when he came to write a Debussy "opera" (*Pelléas et Mélisande*).

This adaptation may well have influenced Strauss to discover, in Oscar Wilde's *Salome*, the material for his own first successful stage work, and renewed the life-span of play as opera, which dated to Mozart's treatment of Beaumarchais' *Le Nozze di Figaro*. It also gave rise, in *Elektra*, to the category of opera as play, in which, with the same Hofmannsthal as collaborator, Strauss evolved such masterly works as *Der Rosenkavalier, Ariadne, Die Frau ohne Schatten,* and *Arabella,* each with its own species of *scena drammatica*. Who, having seen it, can question the rightness of the Marschallin's second monologue as the one, the only proper way to finalize the first act of *Der Rosenkavalier*? But that is another subject—and one which has brought overture, *recitativo, aria,* and *scena* to their natural destination: *finale.*

V

Finale, Finaletto

1

If an overture is something that brings up the curtain and therefore can be known as a "curtain raiser," it would appear reasonable and logical that there should be a counterpart which brings down the curtain and thus be known as a "curtain dropper." Reasonable, yes, and logical, perhaps—but unoperatic. How an act of serious opera ends is wholly at the composer's discretion (assuming it is not a product of the *opéra comique* tradition which has its own house rules). Sometimes, as in the instance of Gluck's decision to end *Orfeo* with a chaconne (to be danced), the finale may be a director's indiscretion, undoing all that has been well done previously.

Curiously, there *is* such a solution to a vexing problem—in the least likely place one would expect to find it. Though much else about *opera buffa* (and its descendants *opéra bouffe* and operetta) is frothy, frivolous, even wayward, there always comes the moment when the serious business of being funny requires an organized attention to the resolution of the situation that has been created. That is the point— classically and dramatically—at which the finale begins.

It may also be the moment when the onlooker wonders why what has previously been loose, almost improvised, seems to settle into a sequence of diverting but well-defined episodes. I would liken the convention of a finale in an act of operatic comedy to the convergence, as a climax to many films, on "the chase." "The chase" was one thing to Mack Sennett, who invented it, and another to Mike Nichols, who reinvented it for *The Graduate*—one was pure farcical mayhem, the other, farcical mayhem with an overtone of social comment. Similarly, the operatic finale serves as a catalyzing moment to be utilized in as many ways as there are composers and librettists.

Invariably, the finale will have been preceded by a series of solos, in brief interchanges. There will have been considerable *recitativo secco* as the characters come and go, with a plan of action discussed, an objective defined, and the elements of intrigue, mirth, mistaken identity, and grandiose counterplotting which make opera *buffa* set in motion. At some point it becomes desirable for all the participants in the action to share the stage at the same time. That is where the finale serves its divine purpose: to combine and finalize.

Like the chase, the finale is an objective toward which composer and librettist plot their course, chart their direction, and plan their moves and countermoves to make the most effective use of the tools they deploy. This may utilize the classic convention of knotting the plot with an unexpected twist. Certainly the presence of numerous characters, rather than two or three, will enable the composer to combine them into an ensemble. In all likelihood, *recitativo secco* will be reduced in occurrence or set aside altogether, and when the finale is in full cry, the orchestra will take its place with the other characters in a total pattern of sound.

Hence the finale is there for the composer to make what he can of it. So many innovators have made so much of the challenge that the finale may, in certain specific works—such as Mozart's *Così fan tutte* or Rossini's *L'Italiana in Algeri*—be among the compelling reasons why people are drawn to the same opera again and again. Like those who were chilled by the climax of *North by Northwest*, without realizing that they were responding to Alfred Hitchcock's masterful variant on "the chase," so those opera fans have become involved with an artistically organized, highly individualized operatic finale, without even knowing that it has a name.

It is basic musicological history to say that *opera buffa* began with the three characters (two singing, one mute) of Pergolesi's *La Serva padrona* in 1733. But it would be more accurate to say that the genre dates to the dim recesses of time, wherever and whenever *commedia dell'arte* (or, to give its full Italian name, *commedia dell'arte all'improviso*, or a "comedy improvised by the acting guild") began. Pergolesi's two singing characters (the maid, Serpina, and her master, Uberto) are classic figures of *commedia dell'arte* (like Arlecchinno, Colombina, and Pagliaccio). The mute character who acts out his unwritten lines has been a favorite of comedic construction since antiquity—and as recently as Harpo Marx.

Perhaps the enduring charm of the comedy purveyed by Pergolesi is the spectacle of a servant getting the better of a testy master—especially if the servant is female. Uberto's continuing complaints of Serpina's lazy ways and arrogant airs prompt him, finally, to direct his mute male servant, Vespone, to find him a wife, any wife, so he can get rid of Serpina (whom he has been looking after since childhood). She, in turn, insists he will marry her or no one. So ends the first intermezzo given between the first and second acts of *Il prigionier superbo,* an *opera seria,* also by Pergolesi, in 1733.

In the second intermezzo, Vespone appears, disguised as a suitor for Serpina. They contrive so much nuisance for Uberto that he cannot decide whether to throw her out or give her a dowry and let her marry a dolt who can communicate only by stamping his feet. When Uberto demurs at a dowry, the disguised Vespone threatens him with a sword, loses his false nose, and discloses his real identity. The enraged Uberto decides that *he* is the one Serpina should marry—and the clever servant has had her way over the master.

All the appeal of Pergolesi's music—and it is considerable—would not seem sufficient to carry this elementary comedy very far. But the work was so new on the scene in the early eighteenth century, and, as reconstituted into a single, one-act sequence, so readily performable, that by 1750 it had crossed the Alps and been played in many parts of Germany (by Italians). Very soon afterward it came to Paris, with immediate amusement and lasting historical results. As Lully had introduced, from his Italian background, what would eventually become *grand opéra,* so his countryman Pergolesi provided, in *La Serva padrona,* the impulse for what would eventually flourish as *opéra comique.*

An on-site insight into the events as they were happening may be found in the least expected place for a musical commentary, *The Confessions* of Jean Jacques Rousseau. That is to say, unless the reader is already aware that, among his various other attributes, the versatile Rousseau was a fine musician and a capable composer. Among his best-known compositions was a stage work, *Le Devin du village (The Village Soothsayer),* which was first performed at Fontainebleau in 1752 and continued in the French repertory until the middle of the nineteenth century.

Concerning the impact of the Italian players and their fluffy *pièce de résistance,* Rousseau writes: "Some time before *The Village Sooth-*

sayer was performed there arrived in Paris some Italian comic opera singers who were put on at the Opera. No one foresaw the effect they were to have. Although they were execrable and the orchestra—at that time a most ignorant lot—performed wilful murder on the pieces they played, the Italians did not fail to do irreparable harm to French opera. The comparison between the two idioms, which could be heard on the same day and in the same theatre, opened French ears; absolutely no one could endure their drawling music after the lively and incisive singing of the Italians. Once these had finished everyone walked out, and they had to change the order of the playing and put them at the end. . . . Only *The Village Soothsayer* could stand the comparison and still pleased when played after even *La Serva padrona*."[1]

In addition to the categorical differences between the two modes of composition sharply defined by Rousseau—"drawling" for the native variety, "lively" for the foreign—his one specific distinction in *performance* between the two groups of nationals is worthy of emphasis: *incisive* (for the Italians). That is an instinctive response on Rousseau's part to his first encounter with that highly distinctive element of *opera buffa:* a pattern of pitches and a variety of rhythms devised by Pergolesi to follow, as naturally as possible, the inflection of the words as they should be *spoken*—in other words, a highly distinctive form of *recitativo secco*. This has remained the model for all—Paisiello, Cimarosa, Mozart, Rossini, Donizetti—who have subsequently written *opera buffa*. Each varied the pattern to express his own emphasis, but the old precepts—especially at the cadential point preceding an aria—remained valid (like certain formulations in the playing of improvised jazz).

The conflicts of rich and poor, servants and masters, remained diverting subject matter of *opera buffa* well into the nineteenth century. The variants were many. If Serpina, in *La Serva padrona*, viewed marriage as a means of legalizing her lazy ways and arrogant airs, there could be another young woman who was looking for more in marriage than was offered by her elderly guardian. The assistance of a clever artisan might be useful, especially if he had a variety of tricks at his disposal and a reputation for being the best barber in Seville.

2

To most opera-goers, a fast-talking barber means Rossini and Rossini means *Il Barbiere di Siviglia*. However, the amusing rascal who began twisting the tongues of Italian baritones in 1816 with "Largo al

factotum" ("Make way for the factotum") had already been entertaining audiences for nearly fifty years. A decade before Rossini was
born (in 1792), Giovanni Paisiello's *Il Barbiere di Siviglia* had begun
giving operatic pleasure with a character and plot that were first seen
and heard in a play (with songs) seven years before.

The man who made a literary name for himself through *Le barbier
de Séville* was born Pierre-Augustin Caron (1732) of a watchmaker
father. He grew up to be a wizard at that intricate trade almost before
he was out of his teens. In his early twenties, Pierre Augustin invented a
mechanism (in the escapement category) which added considerably to
the dependability of the timepieces worn at court and by wealthy
commoners. This opened the way for Caron to be appointed Clerk
Controller at the court of Louis XV (one of his principal duties was
to precede the meat to the royal table, a position functional as well as
ceremonial, because he assumed responsibility for its edibility as well as
its safe arrival). To accord with his new status, he added to his family
name that of a village in the province of Brie where his wife owned
property. He thus became Pierre-Augustin Caron de Beaumarchais.

The sequence of events by which Beaumarchais—as he was forever
after known—added to native wit and some talent for music a reputation in finance (including the procurement of arms for the Colonies
during the War for Independence) is too entertaining to be synopsized.
In addition to making a name for himself as Caron de Beaumarchais, he
made another (literally) for his most famous character.

The one, the only, Figaro is Beaumarchais' exclusively because the
name did not exist previously. According to E. Lintilhac (*Beaumarchais
et ses oeuvres*, Paris, 1887), the name of the immensely clever semi-
servant was evolved from "fils Caron" ("the son of Caron"). I have to
believe that the vastly learned Sir Thomas Beecham was versed in this
derivation. Always when he referred to one of his favorite operas, he
would pronounce it *"Le Nozze di Fee-ka-ro."* It never occurred to me
to inquire into what appeared to be merely an idiosyncrasy. When, in
the sixties, I discovered the possible reason, it was too late—Beecham
had died a few years before.

If the fantasy-fashion in which the one-time watchmaker became a
courtier, a man of international involvements, and a famous dramatist
beggars paraphrase, the manner in which one of his characters became
a dynamic force in an entirely different art form challenges credibility.
It takes in such unlikely elements as the French tastes of Catherine
the Great, the Russian habit of cultivating Italian opera, and the pres-

ence of Giovanni Paisiello as *maestro di cappella* (music director) in St. Petersburg between 1776 and 1784. It was out of these circumstances, and Catherine's pleasure when the Beaumarchais play was presented during a visit of the Comédie Française, that Paisiello was prompted to convert the French text into an Italian *opera buffa*. One of the great traditions of Italian opera thus began in the Hermitage of the St. Petersburg court on September 26, 1782.

Though Rossini's more muscular score has driven its predecessor out of the contemporary repertory, Paisiello's work merits—in properly intimate surroundings—a share of attention it is denied. Paisiello was a composer of considerable originality, as well as a master of many musical skills. Into his *Barbiere* he poured a treasure of imagery and invention, from the Gluck-like sinfonia (overture) with which it begins through the prime melodic substance, rhythmic verve, and artful balance of voices and orchestra which follow. Rossini's reputation as "Signor Crescendo" is slightly tarnished by the presence, in Paisiello's sinfonia of an opening sequence of bars beginning *piano*, rising to *cresc.* (as it is marked) returning to *piano*, and driving to a full *fortissimo* by measure twelve. And if the first sounds of each of the characters are familiar, it may because Figaro is a baritone, Almaviva a tenor, and Bartolo a basso, as they are in Rossini.

As befits the surroundings for which it was composed, Paisiello's *Il Barbiere* is, initially, a patrician affair, elegant in phraseology and refined in style. It is also mindful of its surroundings in suppressing some of Beaumarchais' more cutting commentary, which might have offended members of Catherine's court, especially the visiting French. There is a point in Act II (each of the two acts has two parts) when the pace becomes languid and the impulse runs down.

It is just here, however, that the mainspring of the plot—as befits a watchmaker-dramatist—is fully rewound, the tension thus generated driving the action to its resolution. It is historical fact that Beaumarchais designed his structure to serve the needs of *opéra comique*. However, one of the principal members of the Opéra-Comique had begun life as a barber, and Beaumarchais' work was turned down for fear of giving offense to that colleague.

In their adaptation, Paisiello (and his collaborator, Giuseppe Petrosellini) readily recognized the opportunities for having the performers *sing* together lines that they had to *speak* separately. Out of such opportunity was born the beautiful "Good Night" quintet (in which Almaviva and Figaro lull Rosina's guardian, Bartolo, into believing they are all going off to bed, rather than meeting at midnight to finalize the marriage they have been plotting).

Similarly, the catalytic purpose Beaumarchais meant the following scene to serve finds its true fulfillment in Paisiello's music. It begins at the point (after the "Good Night" quintet) when Almaviva returns, to reveal himself to Rosina not as the penniless student Lindoro, but in his own, noble identity. Surprise. Excitement. Delight . . . but also muted rejoicing because Bartolo might discover them at any moment. The Notary who arrives to marry Rosina and Bartolo is induced—by a purseful of money—to marry her to Almaviva instead. When Bartolo bustles in, it is all too late. The first great operatic finale has ended and with it all the "Useless Precautions" (Beaumarchais' play is titled *Le barbier de Séville ou les précautions inutiles*) Bartolo has taken to prevent young love for finding its own level.

Clearly, the finale parallels the *scena drammatica* in being designed to accommodate a variety of shifting moods and as many shifting musical tempos. Paisiello's finale demonstrates, with exquisite artistry, how each can complement the other and, together, the purposes of the drama. As though to underplay the action to follow, the finale begins *larghetto* (the Count's expression of love for Rosina), quickens to *allegro moderato* (the revelation of his true identity), slows to *andante* (the Notary's uncertainty as to who he is supposed to marry), and then picks up again to *allegro* (when Bartolo arrives to discover what has been happening). At the end, seven voices are joined in proclaiming: "Whenever young hearts beat in time to love, All precautions are useless."

3

Paisiello's *Il Barbiere* is a miraculous expression for its time and place— a Neapolitan frolic in St. Petersburg!—and a charming alternative, at any time, to the vastly more volatile, post-Revolutionary, hence more "contemporary" masterpiece of Rossini. But it is much more of a father to the infant art of *opera buffa*—which, only twenty years after its introduction in Paris by *La Serva Padrona*, had produced so credible an offspring for Paisiello's giant forward step—than is suggested by these perimeters. Between the two operatic *Barbieri* Beaumarchais pursued the further farings of his characters in not one but two stages: *La Folle Journée ou le mariage de Figaro*, also a play with songs, and *La Mère Coupable*. Both had operatic consequences of their own.

Certainly it was not the first time that a famous success had prompted further exposition. But it was a rare instance, in the case of *Figaro,* of a sequel as successful as its predecessor. Any successor to *Le barbier* would have aroused international attention; one which ran for more than two months in Paris piqued curiosity wherever theater flourished. In Vienna, Wolfgang Mozart, with the divine gifts of an Orpheus and the sharp practical impulses of a Sacha Guitry, suggested to his literary friend Lorenzo da Ponte that perhaps something could be done with *Le mariage.* They fell to work together in the fall of 1785, and within six weeks the project was finished.

Obtaining royal consent, however, to the production of an opera based on a play which had been forbidden production in German (it was "too licentiously written") took longer. Da Ponte mimicked some of the wiles of Figaro to persuade the art-loving Emperor Joseph II that he had, with foresight, "omitted or cut anything that might offend good taste or public decency" and baited the monarch's musical sweet tooth with the "secret" opinion that Mozart's score was "marvelously beautiful."[2] Court consent was eventually granted, and the premiere of *Le Nozze di Figaro* occurred on May 1, 1786, a few days more than two years after the Paris premiere of Beaumarchais' play.

It was, also, not much more than two and a half years after the Vienna premiere of Paisiello's *Il Barbieri* in August, 1783. No factual evidence exists to prove that Mozart heard the Italian's path-breaking work at that time. The usual letters to Mozart's father are lacking because Mozart was himself at home in Salzburg, showing off his recent bride, Constanze, to the family. But there is every musical evidence in *Le Nozze di Figaro* to suggest that Mozart was well acquainted with Paisiello's score. As much might be said of Joseph Haydn's astonishing *La fedelta premiata* (1780) long lost and only recently revived by H. C. Robbins Landon.

In their first collaboration, da Ponte showed a sure instinct for the kind of verbal imagery that would set Mozart's music flowing. Even more—perhaps on the basis of their mutual acquaintance with Paisiello's valiant example—he sensed the means of broadening Beaumarchais' situations to play on the bigger scale of full orchestra (the first *Il Barbiere* is scored only for strings), chorus, and a dozen solo voices. With the insight of genius, Mozart learned from Paisiello's improvement on Pergolesi's *recitative secco* how to make it his own.

The ferment latent in the juices of Beaumarchais, Paisiello, J. Haydn, da Ponte, and Mozart reaches the bubbling point midway in Act II.

The Count, no longer in ardent pursuit of Rosina, is aching to preface the official *Nozze* with his privilege—as "lord of the manor"—to enjoy the young servant, Susanna, sexually. The Countess Rosina is equally determined to protect her maid from a barbaric custom which the Count has himself renounced. During a strategy session in Rosina's boudoir, at which Susanna, Rosina, and the page Cherubino are present, Count Almaviva makes an unexpected appearance. Susanna hides, and Cherubino takes refuge in an adjacent wardrobe. Almaviva's attention is attracted to a noise in the wardrobe, which he finds locked. He goes to get tools to open it forcefully, taking the Countess with him. Here, then, is the point of beginning for one of the greatest ensemble scenes in all opera, moving ahead from the broad finale to Act I of *La fedelta premiata*.

In Beaumarchais' treatment, the action that follows covers 10 pages of an act printed in 36 pages. In Mozart's treatment, it occupies 64 pages of a piano-vocal score in which 110 pages are allocated to Act II. Thus the finale is nearly 60 percent of the total, thanks to the combined input of all—Beaumarchais, Paisiello, J. Haydn, da Ponte, and especially Mozart. What such a finale may contain has been inimitably described by da Ponte in his memoirs:

> This finale, which must remain intimately connected with the opera as a whole, is nevertheless a sort of little comedy or operette all by itself, and requires a new plot and an unusually high pitch of interest. . . . Recitative is banned from the *finale:* everybody sings; and every form of singing must be available—the *adagio,* the *allegro,* the *andante,* the intimate, the harmonious and then—noise, noise, noise; which, in musical jargon is called the *chiusa* ["close"] or rather the *stretta* ["drawing together" is the literal Italian meaning, but *stretto* is a musical term also meaning "gradually accelerating"]. . . . The *finale* must, through a dogma of the theatre, produce on the stage every singer of the cast, be there three or three hundred of them, and whether by ones, by twos, by threes or by sixes, tens or sixties; and they must have solos, duets, terzets, sextets, thirteenets, sixtyets; and, if the plot of the drama does not permit, the poet must find a way to make it permit, in the face of reason, good sense, Aristotle, and all the powers of heaven or earth. . . .[3]

Da Ponte's amiably exaggerated dissertation does not conceal the truer fact that he has given, in painstaking detail, the philosophy of the finale and its capacity for evil as well as for good. Well used, it can be an exhilarating acceleration, dramatically as well as musically, of what has preceded; ill-used, it can be a tiresome, repetitious straining for effect.

In Mozartean usage, the finale becomes a treatise on the higher art of operatic composition, deriving from the resources of all the compositional means he commanded. One can characterize the greater Mozart operas in terms of the latitude each subject provided for the inclusion of Mozart's *nontheatrical* aptitudes—a phenomenon, of course, congruent with the reasoning of *what* makes of *who* the best conductors of his *theatrical* works.

Don Giovanni is the symphonic opera; *Die Zauberflöte* is the churchly opera, in which the vocabulary of his masses and Requiem is invoked; *Così fan tutte* is the one that embodies the riches of woodwind sonority that Mozart poured into his serenades and divertimenti. *Le Nozze* is a comedy, but it is also his concerto opera, frequently close in method and texture to the great piano concertos (especially Nos. 23, 24, and 25) he was writing in this period. And nowhere is it closer to the polyphonic interplay of piano and orchestra than it is in the marvelously intricate, deftly diverting, endlessly enjoyable finale to Act II. It is here, incidentally, at the words "Dal balcone che guarda in giardino, mille cose ogni di gittar veggio" ("Every day from the window they throw down rubbish and stuff to the garden"), in which Antonio, the gardener, is describing the manner in which Cherubino jumped from his hiding place in the Countess' boudoir to escape detection, that the hand of Paisiello guided the pen of Mozart. This intrusion from the finale of the first *Il Barbieri* is a rare instance of Mozart reproducing anything identifiably related to another composer. But, in a subtle conversion, voices take the place of ten fingers on the keyboard as Mozart, the concerto-master, weaves Paisiello's pattern into his own texture, cues the characters in and out of their assignments, pulls the strings that make them puppets of his purpose, and, incidentally, memorializes forever his predecessor's contribution to the lore of operatic comedy.

Da Ponte could have, but did not allude to the kind of finale which does not erupt in "noise, noise, noise." Two of the best are to be found in the glorious fulfillment of his collaboration with Mozart: the two finales to the two acts of *Così fan tutte*. Inspired, perhaps, by the learning experience of working with the materials of Beaumarchais (whose symmetrical distribution of forces has been extolled by Etienne Souriau, among others) da Ponte evolved, in *Così*, a paragon of symmetry—six performers, equally divided between male and female. Two are sisters (Fiordiligi and Dorabella); two are their suitors (Ferrando and Guglielmo); and two are plotters (Don Alfonso and the maid, Despina). The latter pair have made a bet with the men that, in disguise and following faithfully the instructions given to them by Alfonso, each one's lady will respond to the approaches of the other's suitor. Each act rises to a climax of happy absurdity when Despina—one of opera's earliest soubrettes and one of its most enduring—appears in a disguise that will give the opera (in da Ponte's phrase) "a new plot."

In the first finale, Despina appears as a disciple of the then contemporary Dr. Mesmer (from whom the word *mesmerize* is derived). In accordance with his principles, she bears a huge magnet. When the magnet is waved over the recumbent figures of the two men—who have taken "poison" because, at this point, the ladies are still resistant—they rise slowly and begin to extol the beauty of the "angels" who confront them. In the second finale, Despina's guise is as a bumbling notary—false nose, large paunch, high-pitched voice *Pel naso* ("in the nose")—about to marry the now reversed couples, and to prove that the title ("They All Do It" is about as close as English can come to the feminine ending of "*tutte*") is all too true.

In this most chamber of chamber operas, da Ponte's manipulation of the verbal content of the finales is as pungent, resourceful, and sophisticated as Mozart's music. It reaches its zenith of suitability, not in the comedy, but when Don Alfonso gently tells the sisters they have been duped. In response to the loving words of reconciliation da Ponte has written, Mozart's music attains heights of consolation and forgiveness, which make *Così* unique among comedies. After a century of neglect (the nineteenth couldn't accept the "immorality" of the plot), *Così* now has more devotees than ever before. And in the aforementioned *La fedeltà premiata*, they may discover several musical manners it has parodied.

4

Save for the virtuoso effort required of Despina these finales are the domain not of the performer but of the director. It is he who determines the do's and the don'ts, the musts and the must nots, the touchables and the untouchables, of action, movement, and style. This is not confined to *Così*; rather, it typifies the customs and procedures of a genre in being reduced to one performer who acts, and five who react. Moreover, for every director who can be trusted to give a good and thoughtful, serious and understanding consideration to the necessities of operatic comedy, there are ten who will bend every word, stretch every meaning, contravene all common sense, and climb every mountain of absurdity they have made out of a molehill of a joke.

Each encounter with a new production of an old operatic comedy may be described as a competition between the director and the observer. The point at issue is to determine (a) how many old sight gags are included, and (b) how many very old sight gags are omitted. My scale of critical rating would be to award minus one for each old gag included and plus two for each very old one omitted. Thus, if the director is only *half* qualified for his assignment, but possesses some discrimination, he could wind up with a favorable rating for knowing what to leave out.

If, *mirabile dictu*, he comes up with a new, intelligently entertaining piece of business, this might atone for including everything commonly seen and omitting nothing that isn't altogether threadbare. The resolution of it all for the young critic would be: Expect only the worst—which is to say, everything commonly seen; if there has been a faint stirring of creativity at *some* point, the evening has been redeemed.

Proceeding further along the same line, it might be useful to offer a definition of what, in the world of operatic staging, could be described as "new." Mine is: something the observer hasn't seen before. Where the director of a production may have gotten his "new" idea is his secret to protect and the viewer's challenge to guess.

A classic instance was provided in New York during the sixties. The opera was, perchance, *Così fan tutte*, which had been brought back, several years before, from decades of obscurity, with a simple, handsome decor by Rolf Gérard and elegantly turned, beautifully stylized action devised by Alfred Lunt. It was a great and deserved success from the moment before the overture when the tall, highly mobile Lunt appeared in a powdered wig and silks to touch a taper to each of a dozen "candles" at the edge of the stage. To those bold enough to applaud he gestured sharply for silence. He then waved for the conductor to begin, and disappeared.

Some seasons later, when Lunt was unavailable to indoctrinate another cast, Rudolf Bing invited his old friend of Glyndebourne days, Carl Ebert, to take the task in hand. When the results were revealed, one prominent newspaper critic reproved Ebert for having appropriated much of the Lunt "approach"—whereas Ebert had indeed *originated* that approach for his famous productions in England, where he, Bing, and Gérard had been associated in the forties! .

The particular point of interest is *not* that the critic was unacquainted with Ebert's production of *Così* at Glyndebourne. That could happen to anyone. But he had no idea of Ebert's *identity* with the work, or where he ranked, historically, among directors of Mozart, Verdi, Berg, and so forth.

In a craft populated by adventurers and charlatans—New York has seen a good deal of both lately at the Metropolitan as well as the State Theater, where the City Opera performs, as have Chicago and San Francisco—as well as frauds and theatrical quacks no less misguided than Dr. Mesmer, Ebert was as rare as he was able. His credentials and conditioning will be dealt with at a later point, but veritable proof of them were presented in microcosm in a segment of a pre-season rehearsal I was fortunate enough to see in the Glyndebourne Festival Theatre in the early fifties.

Ebert was directing the scene in *Figaro* earlier described and just preceding the finale in the second act, in which Almaviva has taken the Countess with him as he goes to find tools to pry open the door of the wardrobe in her boudoir and Susanna has emerged from her hiding place to find a way of getting Cherubino out of the room before "his" employer returns. The Cherubino and Susanna were both young, both talented, and both inexperienced. The action calls for Susanna to persuade Cherubino to use the only available exit—the balcony—to jump to the garden below, then for the maid to take Cherubino's place of concealment and await Almaviva's return.

This calls for considerable agitated movement around the Countess's boudoir, as Cherubino dashes to the balcony, balks at the jump, rushes to a door and finds it locked, goes back to the balcony, and is literally pushed off to the ground below by Susanna. Ebert watched intently for a few minutes as the girls raced from spot to spot, to the sound of a rehearsal pianist, meanwhile singing their lines. When he stopped them, I was too far back in the dark theater to hear his exact words, but there was no mystery to his meaning. "You have to run and you have to sing" he said to both of them. "When you run," pointing to Cherubino, "you sing," and he pointed to Susanna. "When she runs," gesturing to Susanna, "you sing," he said to Cherubino. "Now," he said to the pianist, "let's have the scene again."

When they tried it and found that it greatly simplified the whole procedure, Ebert amplified his point: "If you run, you can't have breath to sing. And if you sing, you don't have breath to run." A simple, self-evident fact, one might say. To which I would respond, "Yes, as simple as knowing the right way from the wrong way to do anything—after someone has told you how to do it." Some singers go through half a career trying to do simple things the hard way, because no one has ever told them how to do it the right way. Nor is this at all related to lack of effort. Indeed, *excess* expenditure of effort is one of the commonest ways of doing things *wrong* in the theater, generally, as well as in opera.

In a circumstance involving a director less versed in the specifics of a work and a composer than Ebert was in *Figaro* and Mozart, it may be the experienced performer who knows a work and the composer but is forced into the wrong way, nevertheless. When the Metropolitan offered Verdi's *Nabucco* for the first time, I encountered Cornell McNeil on the way from a rehearsal and asked how things were going.

"Well," he replied, "pretty good." The hesitant response suggested some problem and I inquired what it was. "In the latter part of the opera," he explained, "there are two heavy scenes for Nabucco. One is in Act III, the other in Act IV. Now this director has the bright idea of doing the whole opera in three acts, so my scenes come one right after the other. In addition, he has switched around the sequence so that the choral scene [the famous "Va, pensiero" previously mentioned] comes *before* the first of them. Says it's better pictorially. Why hell, one reason Verdi did it the way he *did* was to give the baritone a rest between his two big scenes. Now I have to do them one right after the other." The only conclusion can be that *Nabucco* isn't given very often, and MacNeill knew a lot more about it than the director—who also happened to be a German, not an Italian.

If I have maligned the directorial craft in some previous comments, it is not because I would purposefully disparage their kind as disagreeable people, wife-beaters, or otherwise socially offensive. As a group I know them almost exclusively in their professional capacity, which, in some instances, may be very slight.

The question that arises, of course, is: "How do they become directors of opera?" My answer would be a paraphrase of Malvolio in Shakespeare's *Twelfth Night:* "Some are born directors, some achieve directorship, and some have it thrust upon them." The number of "born" opera directors is, regrettably, all too limited; the number who achieve that status through related circumstances—such as enabled Tito Gibbi, for long a brainy baritone with a talent for the stage, to make his first venture as a director or for George London to make a similar transition—is larger, but also restricted; but the number who have it thrust upon them is legion.

For every director now prominent in opera who had adequate

musical training for the work he does, there are two or three who began in some affiliated form of theater or films. From the work they have done, it would be difficult to tell who, among a representative group including Franco Zeffirelli, Giorgio Strehler, Josef Svoboda, Jean-Louis Barrault, Peter Ustinov, John Dexter, Cyril Ritchard, Jean-Pierre Ponnelle and Francis Ford Coppola, had serious musical schooling. They are, for the most part, the ones who have had opera directorship thrust upon them by a general manager or intendant at wit's end to find a man to match a subject, and suddenly possessed of an inspiration. The inspiration commonly consists of the conviction that a man with a suitability for a *stage* project might just possibly work well in an opera on a similar subject.

The theory has been put to the test many times, and it works with reasonable frequency—*for a single project*. It has worked well for a variety of projects, many fewer times. Margaret Webster, for example, was a successful director for a wide range of operas because she was imaginative and scholarly and had a broad cultural background. However, there are few Margaret Websters of either sex.

A successful venture with Gounod's *Faust* prompted Rudolf Bing to suggest to its director, Jean-Louis Barrault, that he do a production of *Carmen* for one of the early seasons of the company in its new home in Lincoln Center. The offer was accepted, with the further agreement that Jacques Dupont, who had designed the *Faust* production, would do the same for *Carmen*. Not until many months later, when the production plans were fully defined, was it discovered that, in Barrault's view, *Carmen* was a vaudeville, or perhaps a "café piece," and it might be nice to play it as though all the action took place in a bull ring, with Carmen as a matador and the various men with whom she is involved (Don José, Zuniga, Escamillo) as her victims. Not a bad idea—but not the opera Bizet wrote.

Even worse, when the scenes were arranged on stage, the public discerned that the amphitheater effect of a semicircular segment of a bull ring in the background would serve as the square in Seville, it would be visible in Lillas Pastia's tavern, not invisible in the rocky, mountainous scene for Act III, and of course, Act IV would be in effect inside the bull ring, rather than outside. All the crossed fingers, the high hopes that the performers could "turn the production around," didn't prevent the feared derailment when the vehicle was launched in 1967. The consequence: when the curtain rose on the first opening night, in 1972, planned by Bing's successor, the late Goeran Gentele, it was on *another* production of *Carmen*, by Josef Svoboda. The Barrault-Dupont version had been used many times fewer than any American theater would expect of a new production of so popular an opera as *Carmen*.

Clearly, this is a costly way to run an opera house. Why then, weren't the plans for the Barrault-Dupont *Carmen* amended or scrapped when the direction in which they were trending became evident? I don't doubt the issue was argued and some adjustments made. But, scrapped? The realities of the operatic bargain were all against it. Opera plans, for schedule and personnel, are made not months but years—two-three-four—ahead. The kinds of names and voices to perform twenty or so *Carmen*s in a season must be arranged for, and firm dates fixed, eighteen to twenty-four months before. Even if the Barrault-Dupont project had been called off—for a price—organizing a replacement to be ready when the singers would be reporting for rehearsal would have been all but impossible, and hideously costly.

I might mention, as another factor in the events that resulted in an opening with *Carmen* for the 1972 season and the Deutsche Grammophon recording that followed, that neither of *its* principals, James McCracken or Marilyn Horne, were in these parts because they were the best singers available for their roles. Many months before, when his successor was not yet engaged, Bing—in accordance with the realities of scheduling defined above—began to sign artists for 1972–1973. As a mark of merit for services rendered, he selected McCracken and Horne for the season-opening opera, *Tannhäuser*—in which McCracken would sing the title role and Horne would sing Venus. When the opening became Gentele's responsibility, he decided that an outmoded, rather dowdy production of *Tannhäuser* (Rolf Gérard's, vintage 1953) was not the way he chose to introduce himself to New York. The obligation to the singers would be honored, but, he insisted to the board, he required a new production of *Carmen* for them, which he would stage-direct himself.

Everything worked out according to Plan II, except that Gentele elected Sardinia for a midsummer holiday prior to the beginning of his first, arduous season—which never came to pass when he was killed in an automobile he was driving himself. A young assistant, Bodo Igesz, filled in as director.

5

Not much more than libretto Italian is necessary to know that a finale is a finale, a finaletto is a little finale. This might be construed several ways: a finaletto is something which precedes a finale, or something that is a pendant or tail to it. I would have speculated that it was one or the other—and I would have been wrong in both speculations.

I find that Rossini's *Il Barbiere di Siviglia* ends with a finaletto. I find that the first act of Alan Jay Lerner and Frederick Loewe's *Paint Your Wagon* ends with a finaletto. What connects them? Not only a hundred and fifty years' evolution of the *opera buffa* into the *opéra bouffe* and from the Viennese operetta to the Broadway musical, but common sense.

The finaletto in *Il Barbiere* comes at the point previously described in Paisiello's treatment at which Bartolo returns to discover that he has been outmaneuvered and that Rosina has married the Count. As Rossini had already resolved *his* plot, why finalize further? So, practical man and sensible genius that he was, Rossini merely finalettoizes it— he writes a bright, jubilant little wedding present of an ensemble "with love from Gioacchino to Almaviva and Rosina," in which Bartolo takes part.

Of the hundreds of *opéras bouffes* and *operettas* that were written between *Il Barbiere* and *Paint Your Wagon*, a cross-section I have scanned shows a finaletto in Karl Millöcker's *Gräfin Dubarry* (one of the greatest scores in the *operetta* literature), in Oscar Strauss's *The Chocolate Soldier*, and in Sigmund Romberg's *The Desert Song*. Finaletto is, clearly, a means to an end to be drawn upon, especially when the end itself is not to be drawn out to the length of a finale.

In the Lerner-Loewe musical, a finaletto is appropriate to Act I, where a finale would not be. The L–L finaletto is brief, and it is to the dramatic point. As Jennifer, the principal female character, leaves the stage, a reprise of the Loewe tune "I tell you my dreams" is heard. Julio and Steve, two of the principal male characters, exchange a few words. Here a stage direction in the score reads: "They look at each other meaningfully." Anytime two characters "look at each other meaningfully," it is time for a quick curtain to allow the audience to escape to the lobby for a cigarette, or at least for fresh air.

And so, too, with this finaletto, a curtain to Act I of this operatic *seria comèdia*, or *semi-seria*.

ENTR'ACTE

1

To speak of the hundreds who fill an opera house (1,620 in the reconstructed Staatsoper in Vienna, 3,880 in the Metropolitan in New York) as an audience is to indulge in a convenient misstatement. It is, also, to collectivize the many individuals who do only two things as a unit—arrive and depart. Perhaps the only occasion in history when an audience could truly be described as being "of one mind" occurred on May 11, 1866, in Munich's Court (now Bavarian National) Theater.

The one mind belonged to Wagner's princely patron, King Ludwig II of Bavaria, who was about to reap the rewards of his affection and extravagance—the world's first hearing of *Tristan und Isolde*. The records read that the public premiere of *Tristan* occurred on June 10, with Hans von Bülow conducting. The performance a month earlier was the *pre-premiere* presentation, also under Von Bülow's direction. It was primarily for Ludwig, but he waived exclusivity and permitted six hundred others (members of the court and a privileged coterie of Wagner disciples) to huddle in the darkness of the more than half-empty theater.

In ordinary circumstances, the audience rarely reacts as an entity, least of all during the entr'acte (interlude, interval, or intermission, according to which term is in vogue in a particular country). Individuality begins to assert itself almost before the house lights have come up at the end of an act. Invariably there are those who can hardly hear out the final chord or the dying sound of a *pianissimo* before they have sprung from their seats as though propelled by a pilot's eject mechanism. Among them are likely to be a few critics; the remainder appear to be motivated by the same kind of forthright reaction to what they have enjoyed or, perhaps, merely endured.

It would be a mistake to assume that a critic's prompt (*not* hasty) departure indicates rejection rather than acceptance of what he has heard. It is a reminder, merely, of a professional truism: his performance begins when the visual, audible performance ends. First priority of the well-organized critic goes to the thought-taking and the silent communion required to sort out the impressions derived from what he has just heard. Trial and error long ago persuaded me that the proper place for this is a quiet corner in a lobby, not in an aisle closely packed with other bodies. A prompt start allows at least a fighting chance of getting to the foyer before the aisle becomes congested.

More often than not, having sorted out such impressions as I have, and enjoyed a breath of air—outside pollution is always less than inside pollution—I return to my seat well before the last bell or buzzer sounds. I thus rejoin what is, to me, the most absorbing element of any group in a public place—the fractional part that does *not* leave the auditorium during an entr'acte. They are, by inspection, persons of sober habits, in need neither of nicotine nor alcohol; they are physically well adjusted; they clearly prefer the private contemplation of a program or a libretto to the public clatter of lobby conversation.

I may be in error, but I regard them as the inner core of operatic connoisseurs. They are the sort who know not only when to applaud during an aria, but when it is permissible (if ever) to whisper a word of comment to a companion when the curtain is up. Most crucially, they are well versed in the etiquette of behavior when the curtain is down.

This may strike some as a trivial point of protocol. It is, rather, the mark of distinction separating the opera lover from the opera-goer. The opera lover knows that, in a smallish but vital part of the repertory, the mere fact that the curtain is down does not mean that the performance is suspended. The opera-goer, on the other hand, assumes that if there is nothing worth seeing, there can be nothing worth hearing, and this is a "safe" time for a host to exchange opinions with a guest, for husbands and wives to catch up on the day's happenings, and for friends who recognize each other at a distance to wave programs.

Such "audience participation" may be more than an invasion of other people's pleasure—it may, in some circumstances, be nothing short of blasphemy.

I have in mind those operas in which the composer has put himself out to interconnect the flow of drama and music by writing the entr'acte music required to cover the scene shifts or when the curtain is lowered to denote a passage of time. If the heavenly introduction to the Countess's "Porgi amor" in Mozart's *Le nozze di Figaro* is being used to accompany the slow rise of the curtain on the second act, I want to hear it. If Berg has written interludes between scenes to sustain the mounting horrors in *Wozzeck*, his purpose is frustrated if talking interferes with listening. Certainly the orchestral passages that interrelate rather than merely join together the episodes of Debussy's *Pelléas et Mélisande* are as vital a part of its dramatic effect as anything heard from the stage.

2

As composers from the eighteenth to the middle of the twentieth century have continued to exert themselves on such instrumental interludes (Benjamin Britten as early as *Peter Grimes*, as late as *Death in Venice*), they clearly believe them to serve a functional part in an opera, of no matter what epoch. Somewhere, someplace, there must have been an audience sufficiently indoctrinated to give its full attention to a composer's purpose, whether the curtain was up or down. Was the proper behavior practiced in learned Vienna in the late nineteenth century? Were there better manners in bygone, genteel New York, in the time of dowagers and dandies?

While browsing through a volume devoted to the criticism Hugo Wolf was writing to supplement his pitifully small income as composer of some of the most beautiful songs ever created, I found the following:

> Two whispering neighbors seated behind me managed, by their inconsiderate behavior, to deprive me of all enjoyment of the overture. "Lackey-souls" is what Kreisler, the conductor [the fictional creation, many years before, of E. T. A. Hoffmann] once termed these disturbers of the peace, these creatures who whimper while the music is being played, rattle their fans, stare stupidly about them, greet their acquaintances, wave to their friends, slam their seats, snap their opera-glass cases open and shut, keep time to the music with their stamping feet, or drum out the tempo with their fingers, and perform countless other stupidities. . . .

In another vein, continues Wolf:

> the conversation is usually lively, and beneath the gaiety and laughter a distinct undertone of business is discerned. "It's going up," "It's

going down" [references to the Bourse, or stock exchange] are as frequently heard and exchanged in their talk as piano and forte in the orchestra. Figures are sprayed through the words, etc., etc., and if ladies are along family matters, too, are not omitted. The cook has a novel way of producing roast goose; the children are growing up to be *so* talented, clever, and promising. Elsie, the five-year-old can already play all of Mendelssohn's *Songs without Words* by heart! And little Sigismund, or it may be Siegfried, is writing poetry—[1]

The occasion for Wolf's comment was a performance of *Fidelio* in Vienna in 1884; as Hoffmann's fanciful sketches were written between 1814 and 1822, the "lackey-souls" referred to by Wolf characterized musical life many decades before.

If the conversational habits of Central European opera-goers did not change much between Hoffmann's time and Wolf's, those of their New York counterparts have remained much the same over a similar span of decades. Writing in a New York newspaper of the mid-1920s, W. J. Henderson observed:

> Perhaps some day local opera audiences will accept scores in which music without song or action seeks to preserve the continuity of the work. That day has not yet come. Well defined entr'acte pieces such as the "Meditation" in *Thaïs* and the "Intermezzo" in *Cavalleria Rusticana* are heard because people have been educated to sit up and wait for them. But the music connecting the scenes of *Petruschka* which prevents the mood from dying is rather indifferently treated.[2]

The reference to *Petrouchka* arose through its revival as part of a triple bill with Puccini's *Gianni Schicchi* and John Alden Carpenter's *Skyscrapers*. The comment could have as well been directed toward the audibility of the orchestral interludes in *Pelléas*—a work I was just beginning to hear that year (1926) in the same theater—where, because of audience conversation, it could not be heard as a whole.

Taken together, these happenings in Vienna and New York could be paralleled by others at the Colon in Buenos Aires in the 1960s or the Paris Opéra in Berlioz' time. They are not curiosities of a time or of a country. Ignorance is more likely to be a horizontal rather than a vertical phenomenon—it flows forward on the stream of opera itself, as it engulfs, from generation to generation, persons who find themselves in a place with whose manners and mores they are unfamiliar.

This contention may be validated by another series of observations by Wolf in the article previously quoted. It is sometimes stated, and written, that opera theaters in the Anglo-Saxon countries (England, the United States, Canada, Australia) are cursed, more than others, by people who come to be seen or to see others more celebrated than themselves, because opera is an alien art, performed in a language they do not understand.

Wolf's audience, on the contrary, was present at a performance of *Fidelio*, a German opera sung in German, the language in which it had been educated. Nevertheless, the types he describes are as familiar as those to be seen at any gala in Covent Garden or at the Metropolitan, nearly a century later:

> Even the best, most sensitive, most thoughtful of these lackey-souls attend the opera only to feed upon the striking scenery, the luscious hips of the ballerina, or the voice of a singer. . . . Second to them are those theatre-goers who attend the opera only to observe Society, fashions and the latest coiffures. . . . For them the chief role in opera is played by the virtuosos of opera-glass twirling. . . . But bad as they are, these lackey-souls are not the worst—the ultimate in the whole category of the species is achieved by those who attend the opera for no other reason than to let themselves be seen. . . .[3]

It might be said, then, that you can take an opera-goer out of a century, but you can't make an opera lover of him merely by putting him in an opera house in a different country.

Is there no hope, then, for those who dream of a *Pelléas* in which every note would be audible from beginning to end, a performance of *Les Troyens* in which "The Royal Hunt and Storm" would not be interrupted by unscored voices, or Delius's *A Village Romeo and Juliet*, in which "The Walk to the Paradise Garden" is listened to as attentively as it would be in a concert hall?

3

If the only hope were to result from the kind of "education" recommended on behalf of *Petrouchka* by the New York critic of the 1920s, it might as well be abandoned. One could have hardly corrected the habits of one generation of opera-goers before the next would be on the scene. Nor are shushing and angry looks the answers. They merely provide those *giving* offense with a moral "right" to express themselves.

Nevertheless, recent attendants at American performances of *Les Troyens*, *A Village Romeo and Juliet*, and *Pelléas* have had the dazzling experience of hearing all three without intrusion or interruption. The

Berlioz, Debussy, and Delius works have been performed before ordinary, non-festival audiences in New York and in Washington with no concession in cuts or in text. Nothing was added by way of indoctrination, preparation, or education. Nothing was sacrificed in illusion or stage action.

The triumph was not sociological, but technological. The miraculous result was achieved by the simplest of stratagems: the curtain did *not* come down at any time during an act. The stage remained visible, even in semi-dark. By use of projected, rather than solid, scenery; of backlighting and scrims; of pieces that rolled and swiveled; of side stages and revolving turntables, stagecraft in the second half of the twentieth century has, literally, bounded out of the Dark Ages into the blessed time of light that leads as well as shields, of the image that comes silently, swiftly, in place of another, and can itself be replaced, at the press of a button.

To date a time of transition, reference may be made to *Opera and Its Future in America* by the late Herbert Graf, known for decades as a stage director in Vienna, Salzburg, Florence, and New York, who was artistic director of the Geneva Theater at the time of his death, in 1973. He writes: "Work is being done to replace even painted backdrops by these methods, and in performances in Zurich, Paris, and various cities of Germany, there have been numerous experiments in this direction."[4] By "these methods" Graf referred to "projections," then (1941) at an early point of development, and dependable only for occasional usage and limited purposes.

From Adolphe Appia, at the end of the 1890s, on, farsighted designers have dreamed of the day when lighting would be a co-equal to sound and design, in the creation of illusion in opera. It would become part of the *mise en scène* which the great Swiss-born producer (Geneva, 1862–1928) defined as "a design in space with variations in time," a neatly phrased summation of the elements that combine to make opera: the visual arts, which exist in space, and the audible arts, which occur in a frame of time. Among Appia's immediately constructive innovations was the creation of what is now universally known as a "light plot"—a running, scene-by-scene, even aria-by-aria, record of exactly which lights are to be used and how. It serves the lighting supervisor as a scheme of action serves a stage director, as Labanotation serves a choreographer, or a score serves a conductor.

It was Appia's insight, first articulated when *Music and the Art of the Theatre* was originally published in 1898, that, as creatively as

Wagner had thought through his *musical* problems in designing his Festspielhaus in Bayreuth (the invisible orchestra, the split curtain that could be swiftly drawn up to the sides or slowly lowered at the end of a scene, the large area for the choruses), he had grossly failed to solve the scenic problems. In Appia's words: "When the curtain was raised, the settings *on stage* offered nothing whatever to correspond with what was wondrous in the scores."[5]

As well as Appia argued his case and as strongly as his theories appealed to an influential few at Bayreuth, there was no place for him in Wagner's theater as long as Cosima, the composer's widow (and a daughter of Liszt), ruled it. "Appia does not seem to know," she wrote to one of his partisans, "that the *Ring* was produced here in 1876, and therefore there is nothing more to be discovered in the field of scenery and production. Consequently all that is right in his book is superfluous, since it is in accordance with directions in the score, and all the rest is wrong to the point of childishness."

She did agree that "we now have electric light. . . . To carry through transitions, to bring out subtle modifications, for that there is need for a resourceful technician. But Appia must not ask for darkness where the text calls for brightness and vice versa. . . ."[6] As Appia aspired to be something more than "a resourceful technician," he had to seek out his opportunities elsewhere, in less promising surroundings. An Appia production of *Tristan und Isolde*, conducted by Toscanini in 1923, shows vast promise in the sepia reproduction of its designs, but it did not enjoy lasting favor at La Scala. Nor was a venture with the *Ring* at Basel in 1924–1925 a success. Bayreuth remained closed to Appia as long as Cosima reigned supreme. She lived until 1930, seven years short of celebrating her hundredth birthday in 1937. Appia died in 1928 at sixty-six.

He remains, nevertheless, a mighty motival force in the lore of stagecraft, at Bayreuth as well as elsewhere. His theories flowed into the work of such other producers as Alfred Roller, Mahler's great collaborator in Vienna, which means that they proliferated worldwide. Eventually they entered into the thinking of the creator of the postwar "New Bayreuth Style," Wieland Wagner himself.

In the program book of the 1955 festival, the older son of Siegfried Wagner (and thus the grandson of the composer) stated unequivocally: "What the Swiss scenic artist Adolphe Appia called for in his book *Musik und Inszenierung* [the German title of *Music and the Art of the Theater*] and created with his Wagner designs in the first quarter of our present century—the stage of stylized space arising out of the music and out of three-dimensional feeling, his conception of the symbolic power of colour and light in rhythmically controlled space—these are the first steps toward a reform of operatic production which has led logically to 'the new Bayreuth style.' "[7]

It was the gifted Wieland's sure insight, at the time Bayreuth was being reorganized in 1950 (after the disastrous wartime interruption), that *no* prior style—whether "old" or not—could be regenerated. Whether it was inspiration or accident that led him to his theories of "painting with light," I cannot say. I do know that I visited Bayreuth for one of the early postwar *Parsifal* productions in 1956. I was enormously impressed by its grandeur and its subtle relation to the space for which the work had been created.

Appia would have had no reason to complain (as he had in 1898) that "when the curtain went up on the scene of the interior of the Grail Temple, the painted scenery had to be sacrificed to the darkness necessitated by the scene change—imparting a marvelous life to the setting. As the lights started to come up, the illusion was continuously dispelled until finally, in the full glare of the border lights and the footlights, the knights made their entry into a paste board temple."[8]

In the Wieland Wagner ordering of things, there was not only no "painted scenery," there were no border lights or footlights. Save for minimal props—chairs, a round table, and so on—all else had been swept away to provide the vast, empty *space* which served Wieland Wagner as canvas to his lighting board.

My reference to "inspiration or accident" as a determining factor in these developments—out of which have flowed, of course, the Herbert von Karajan productions for Salzburg and elsewhere—has its origin in a comment I then (1956) heard at Bayreuth. It went to the point that when plans for the reorganization of the festival were being made in the late 1940s, German industry was asked to make contributions not only of funds but of *matériel*. The electrical industry had recovered from the war rather more rapidly than some others, and it made available, in abundance, lighting materials, from the "board" (control panel) to overhead lights of all sizes. Whatever the means that were provided, it was Wieland Wagner's *creative* use of them that swept away outmoded thinking and made for the Bayreuth Renaissance that has affected operatic production everywhere.

Wieland Wagner's death of cancer at the age of fifty in 1966 was a deprivation as dismal as any the art of opera has suffered since World

War II. It is not enough to say that it is a blow from which Bayreuth has not yet recovered: it is a blow from which Bayreuth cannot recover until another Wagner of his vision and talent matures. His brother Wolfgang does not qualify in either respect, but the young, fourth-generation Wolfi (Wieland's son) may.

4

As greatly as he succeeded in making Appia's preachments the source of his practice, Wieland Wagner's innovations were much more suitable for the mythological symbolism of the *Ring,* the psychological complexities of *Tristan,* and the pseudo-theological mysticism of *Parsifal* than they were to the workaday world (however exalted by poetry) of *Die Meistersinger von Nürnberg.* Either at its sparest or most embellished, Wieland Wagner's version of *Die Meistersinger* tended to turn Hans Sachs into a likeness of Richard Wagner, to probe under the surface of the opera for symbolic, even erotic, values, that were, perhaps, not there. The opera's humanity and warmth asked for what the producer was reluctant, or unable, to give—a simple evocation of a scene, a place, a time, that would rejoice the eye as much as the music ravished the ear.

Ever since the advent of *cinématographe*—the illusion of movement produced by the rapid projection on the screen of a great number of photographs taken sequentially—utilization of that medium for adding such realism to operatic staging has tantalized the experimenters. The Paris Opéra did it in the twenties with a filmed "Ride of the Valkyries," as a derivative from Wagner's own use of an unwinding roll of painted canvas to depict the changing panorama in the Transformation Scene in the first act of *Parsifal* as Gurnemanz and Parsifal—on a treadmill—appeared to be trudging along in front of it.

There was, in short, no lack of ideas. The problem, always, was to find technical resources sufficiently sophisticated to be reliable, and guidance systems sufficiently acute to match the split-second musical changes. But the early images jiggled on the screen, as the Valkyries bounced up and down rather than soaring through the air, or the painted panorama snagged in its lateral movement, and nothing changed as Gurnemanz and Parsifal plodded on and on.

The idea of a small image painted on a glass plate, illuminated from behind and projected on some form of rear stage screen (to replace huge painted drops) has been—as Graf noted in 1941—at large for decades (almost as long as the magic lantern, of which it is an off-shoot). But it, too, suffered from lack of reliability—the Pyramids would not remain rigid or a slide would be inadvertently inverted and the beautiful, sumptuously atmospheric rendering of the Nile would show the river running uphill.

Few arts have advanced so far, so fast, during the last two and a half decades, as photography. Out of wartime emergencies and space travel exigencies have been developed techniques infinitely more versatile, in color as well as in black and white, than were ever available before. New editing devices permit montages never before possible; magnification, intensification, and computerization have all contributed their share to predictability and dependability.

Even Appia's innovation of the "light plot"—which, he suggested, should be memorized by the director as a conductor memorizes a score—has given way to a device that memorizes it for him. Punch tapes and decoders, by which a light board can be preset for an entire production, permit creating at leisure what needs to be re-created in haste; moreover, they take all the possibility of human error out of the equation. If the projector is told properly what to do and when, it should perform its job as accurately a hundred times as it does once.

Specialists have opted, as specialists will, for stylistic innovations in which their own specialty prevails or is at least dominant. Lighting rather than projection was a Wieland Wagner specialty, and he was extremely good at it. There were, of course, times when a projection would have served the audience better than another beam of light. Others, who specialize in projected images, take delight in all manner of tricked combination of pictures when a spotlight would be more welcome.

To my viewer's taste, the scope of treatment should accord with the nature of the problem. No one has ever "seen" Valhalla: Wieland Wagner's evocation of it in shimmering, dazzling light had a poetry and majesty that touched the mind. Inversely, Troy *was* a city of walls and buildings, temples and fortifications: a producer of Berlioz' *Les Troyens* owes an audience something visually veritable—however sparse or abstracted—to satisfy a sense of place and time.

It was Berlioz' conviction, when *Les Troyens* was being shaped between 1858 and 1860, that somewhere, somehow a way could be found of performing its two long "Parts" (the Sack of Troy and the idyll of Dido and Aeneas in Carthage) in a single evening. This was before the revolving turntable, before stage elevators, before filmed projections, even before Cosima Wagner could say "we now have electric lights." All of these adjuncts to illusion were enlisted in the Metropolitan production of 1973 in behalf of providing Berlioz with the results he craved through resources he could not have imagined. The outcome was transfiguring.

Under the embracing direction of Peter Wexler—trained in the theater, rather than in the opera house—and with the visual supervision of Nathaniel Merrill to synchronize the action, the wheels and turntables moved their stately cargo forward in a time-span comparable to that of such a "repertory" opera as Wagner's *Götterdämmerung*. The uninterrupted flow of people and props created a mood of its own by evolving from scene to scene *in full view* of the audience.

When sizable, solid pieces to depict the walls and fortifications of Troy were appropriate, they were provided. For all their appearance of solidity, they were formed of a stage designer's most prized, contemporary adjunct—some such bulky but light material as foam rubber. They could be readily swiveled on casters, serving one function from the front view, another when reversed. A forest vista to evoke, pictorially, what Berlioz had permanently evoked, musically, in "The Royal Hunt and Storm" found its natural affinity in film. Combined with what was seen, what was heard was no longer the tip of an invisible iceberg. It was the smoldering cone of a subterranean volcano, ready to erupt when Berlioz supplied the spark.

On the other hand, the first American production of Frederick Delius's *A Village Romeo and Juliet* in Washington (1972) was no less well served by projections and film, with barely a built piece of scenery. Delius' score has long been admired for the quality of the music he wrote for Gottfried Keller's tale of nineteenth-century pastoral love in Switzerland. But since its Berlin premiere in 1907 it has been equally deplored for a slow-moving, almost actionless text. In the new production plan devised by Frank Corsaro and illuminated by Ronald Chase, a leisurely tone-poem-with-words was converted into an absorbing theater piece. This was due in no way to the discovery in it of new dramatic details, but to the use of contemporary technics to liberate and enhance those it always contained.

Berlioz dreamed of resources unknown at the time he wrote *Les Troyens*. Delius imagined, in *A Village Romeo and Juliet*, a multimedia experience before the category or the term were known. Each was rewarded, for having created the best music of which he was capable, by the invention of the necessary mechanical means to complement it visually. In the end, the Wexler-Merrill production scheme gave to *Les Troyens* the outer physical form its inner musical life required and Chase's marvelously flexible lighting scheme escalated to poetic half-light what Delius had restricted, for the most part, to semi-shadow.

As Chase called upon several innovative procedures to achieve his purpose, a moment might be spent in detailing the form they took. By a clever use of rear projections onto a screen and front projections onto a scrim—a thin, tightly intersticed, netlike material which can either hold an image projected upon it or be rendered invisible by back lighting—and with film clips displayed in the middle distance, Chase achieved Appia's ideal of three-dimensional effects by light alone. Used in conjunction with words and music, the lighting clarified the motivations of the feuding parents and revealed the reasons why Delius was impelled to write the music he did on behalf of the children whose lives they had ruined.

Chase saved his finest visual effect for the moment when it yielded the highest re-creative dividend. As the lovers stepped into the row-boat for their self-decreed journey from dissension to eternity, a faint flicker of moonlight played upon the little craft. Light-reflecting "waves" rippled into the distance as the boat drew away. As it disap-peared into the darkness, the visual imagery on the stage and the audible imagery from the pit were united in a single, engulfing illusion.

Desmond Heeley's production of *Pelléas et Mélisande* for the Metropolitan utilized a totally different kind of contemporary tech-nology for equally artistic results. German ingenuity has produced a plastic that can be applied almost like paint to designs on a net surface. When dry, the substance becomes translucent—that it is to say, it permits lighting from either front or back. It is also responsive to projections and is so light in total weight that it can be "flown" (raised to the space above the stage) in seconds. As utilized by Heeley, the stage was, with but one or two exceptions, never dark between scenes. The result—with Colin Davis's imaginative conducting as a generative musical factor—was the rarest kind of *Pelléas*: one in which Debussy's invasion of Maeterlinck's poetic world resulted not in willful rape but in artistic procreation.

5

If education alone were the answer to the riddle "How do you behave during an entr'acte?" the practical demonstration provided by such productions as *Les Troyens* and *A Village Romeo and Juliet* (or such others in the same spirit as Janáček's *The Makropoulos Affair*, like the Delius given in New York by the City Opera, or Heeley's *Pelléas* at the Met) should have resolved the question in at least one city for a generation: operas are meant to be enjoyed as entities.

But the animal instinct in a miscellaneous audience is not to be suppressed—let alone evicted—by precept alone. Remove the restrictive restraints and the old instincts to which herd behavior is prone are likely to reassert themselves. They might even afflict the "Intermezzo" in *Cavalleria Rusticana* were the curtain to be lowered during its performance, rather than remaining up, universally, enduringly, to display the empty plaza in the hot sun of Sicily as Mascagni specified.

In a recent round of performances of Alban Berg's *Wozzeck*, the Metropolitan revived a production introduced in 1957, derived, in turn, from a predecessor (also by Casper Neher) which Berlin saw in the 1930s. It utilizes a scrim to *conceal* the scene changes, not to keep the eye of the viewer occupied as they occur, and thus to concentrate his ears, as they properly should be, on Berg's orchestral interludes.

In the darkness that fell upon the audience with the descent of the scrim, the reaction was inevitable: "What's the story all about?" was the first query that rang from guest to guest. A little later, after a few scenes had accumulated, the question had shifted to "What are they saying? I can't make out a word"—proof beyond contravention that the German text was, indeed, being heard in an English translation.

As Act II uncoiled, the female voice I could hear from the row behind me had veered to a plaintive "It's got me so nervous, I could use ten milligrams of Valium *right now!*" Either Berg's mastery overwhelmed all objection in Act III or the overwrought attendant had departed. There was only silence after Marie's murder.

If I were an operatic impresario tempted to present one of those esoteric *spécialités* without which no repertory can claim respect, and with which it often courts disrespect, my first question to the production staff would be, "How do we handle the entr'acte music?" If somebody murmured, "Well, now we have an educated audience," I would respond, Dorothy Parker-like, "Education may be purer, but restraints are surer."

ACT II

VI

Mad Scene

1

If the discriminating opera lover we left scanning a program during the entr'acte were present at one of the more famous operas of Bellini or Donizetti, he could have been gathering information on a subject for which they had a common, contemporary affinity. Major contributors to the great growth of the Italian repertory during the decade 1825–1835, they were of almost identical age. Donizetti, born in 1797, was the older by four years. He was already launched on his career when Bellini's first opera was produced in 1825. But the younger man's extraordinary endowments quickly earned him a lasting, international identity, though his career was ended by death only ten years later.

What Bellini and Donizetti had in common, beyond a profound knowledge of the human voice and its capabilities, was a strong sense of the drama inherent in dementia, hallucination, mental derangement, or whatever English equivalent one prefers for *la pazzia*. Out of their mutual involvement came some of the greatest vocal music ever written.

Bellini was only thirty-three when he died in 1835 and was thus restricted to writing only two operatic Mad Scenes. The first venture, in *Il Pirata* of 1827, has only recently returned to public attention. Its successor in *I Puritani* was first heard from a demented Elvira on January 24, 1835, and was frequently performed as a solo scene until a recent revival of interest in Bel Canto literature brought the work as a whole to new prominence.

Donizetti endured to a riper fifty-one and had the energy and the interest to go to the operatic well more than *sixty* times. Sometimes the pitcher produced a clearer, fresher draught than at other times, but the average quality was no less than potable. Between 1823 and 1843 (when his productivity was terminated in queerly ironic circumstances —the onset of a mental disorder from which he died five years later) he wrote three or four operas a year, ranging from tragedy to *opera buffa* to *opéra comique.*

He thus can be described as having a practiced hand when his fifty-first opera was produced in Naples on September 26, 1835. By that time he had written two works with Mad Scenes: *Anna Bolena* in 1830 and *Torquato Tasso* in 1833. And he would write another for *Linda di Chamounix* in 1842. But neither these nor any other music by Donizetti stirred the furore (quite literally, because it came from the Latin *furor,* meaning "mad") that followed the first hearing of the Mad Scene in *Lucia di Lammermoor* that September night. There was still another ecstasy of delight to come—the closing scene in which Edgardo mourns the death of Lucia and despairingly takes his leave of the world.

The cheering throng which that night acclaimed Donizetti could hardly know that they were also participating in a requiem for the man who had, earlier in the year, written "Qui la voce sua soave" in *I Puritani,* the famous prototype for Lucia's Mad Scene. The news had not yet reached Naples that Bellini, residing in the Parisian suburb of Puteaux, had unexpectedly died a few days before (September 23). Bellini's frequent complaints of abdominal irritations had changed to agonies of pain from a massive inflammation that cost his life (the present medical belief is that he could have been suffering from cancer of the liver). The news did not reach the ankle of the Italian boot until early in October. Bellini's friends in his native Catania, Sicily, did not hear of it until several days later.[1]

The darling *fioriture* phrases Donizetti found for Lucia's dilemmas (they begin in Act I) and the opportunity for dramatic trauma contained in the Mad Scene made the role a favorite for many sopranos as soon as they could get their hands on the score and the music into their voices. By the time Lucia made her maiden voyage to America in 1843, she was already a much traveled lady. The first city to make her acquaintance after Naples was Vienna (where Donizetti had succeeded to the popularity long enjoyed by Rossini). Productions followed in Madrid, Paris, London, Malta, Berlin, Prague, Algiers, Pressburg (now Bratislava), Stockholm, Geneva, Havana, and St. Petersburg . . . all before 1840.[2]

In a retrospect of Donizetti's career, the indispensable Chorley wrote:

> *Lucia* would generally be named as Donizetti's best opera. I am not able to share in the admiration it has excited. Never, assuredly, was a story so full of suggestion for music as Scott's *Bride of Lammermoor* tamed into such insipid nothingness, even by an Italian librettist, as this. The supernatural tone of the legend entirely taken away; the dance on the bridal night, with its ghastly interruption, replaced by a sickly scene of madness, such as occur by scores in every southern serious opera . . . He who speaks ill of the third act, closed by its long-drawn death scene (the darling scene of tenor singers) may prepare himself to be stoned for heresy. . . ."[3]

If the readers of London's *Athenaeum* (for which Chorley was for many years a commentator on music) were stunned by this "heresy," they were sufficiently forbearing not to convert his audacity into a prophecy. Chorley remained unstoned. The comment that stays with me, more than a century later, is Chorley's reference to "a sickly scene of madness, such as occur by scores in every southern serious opera. . . ." One must be versed in Chorley's use of the term "southern" (as in his reference to Giorgio Ronconi, a fine baritone, as "this great southern man") to recognize it as a synonym for "Italian."[4]

It is not so much Chorley's characterization of the *Bride* (born in Scott's mind in 1819) as the subject for a "sickly" Mad Scene that immediately interests me, as his reference to such scenes as occurring "by scores in every southern serious opera. . . ." Chorley was given to hyperbole, and "every" can hardly be surpassed as an absolute. But there must have been more than a scattering of them to arouse such scorn from a scholarly gentleman. If so, they lacked the quality, interest, and durability of Donizetti's four or Bellini's two.

The suggestion that operas of the early nineteenth century swarmed with Mad Scenes is provocative, if exaggerated. There existed, simultaneously, a rising tide of interest in the same psychic phenomenon in other arts. The reason is readily available: opera never has and never can exist in a vacuum; it is responsive to the social order, or disorder, around its creation. Literary men write novels (such as Scott's) which attract the attention of composers, just as Beaumarchais' social commentary for the theater attracted the interest of Mozart in *Le Nozze di Figaro*. Contemporary life itself has been mirrored in operas as different as Beethoven's *Fidelio* and Leoncavallo's *Pagliacci*.

For me the curiosity really is: What liberates one kind of subject matter, rather than another, for attention at a specific time? Is it

chance, happenstance, or merely that one theatrical success begets another? All of these considerations have their part in a trend, or a
vogue. But the impulse that *creates* a vogue may be related to something
deeper.

Within the span of half a dozen years, madness as a subject for
treatment in the arts spread from two great manifestations of 1835
(*I Puritani* and *Lucia*) to the creation, in 1841, of the earliest nineteenth-century ballet still regularly performed today. Jean Coralli's
choreography for Théophile Gautier's ballet synopsis is based on a folk
tale he had found in Heinrich Heine's collection of German legends
(*De l'Allemagne*) and was first performed in Paris on June 28, 1841,
under the title of *Giselle*.

Giselle remains—more than thirty-five years after Cyril W. Beaumont, England's great balletic authority, stated it was—the "only ballet
which has an unbroken tradition of performance since its first production."[5] It is greatly treasured for its second act, in which the legend
that stimulated Gautier's imagination (the nocturnal appearance of the
Wilis, "affianced maidens who had died before their wedding day") is
depicted in dance. But it is not less avidly anticipated for the balletic
equivalent of the Mad Scene at the end of Act I.

This is the episode which determines Giselle's destiny to be a Wili.
It is a dance of dementia brought on by the discovery that her
"peasant" lover is a count she can never marry. The scene begins in
incredulity for Giselle and ends with incredible acts of visual bravura,
wild flights about the stage and leaps *en l'air* (comparable to a soprano's
staccato scales, octave jumps, arpeggios, and appogiaturas) that can
only bring on her collapse and death.

2

Heinrich Heine played the role of intermediary between a folk legend
of Germany and a balletic project in Paris, as Sir Walter Scott served
similarly as a link between a Scottish fantasy and an Italian opera. The
sheer expanse of these connections should suggest to a contemporary
opera-goer seated comfortably in his chair watching *Lucia* that he is
participating in something more profound than an entertainment. Each
performer is acting out a part of a social and artistic cycle that left
behind the balanced formality of eighteenth-century expression and
impelled it toward the more impulsive, much more flexible expression
of the nineteenth. Even more to the point, subject matter that had pre-

viously been taboo was now available for treatment, in a new surge of interest in humankind—its joys and woes, triumphs and defeats, strengths and weaknesses. Among the weaknesses to which man was prone, and which prior centuries had shown little capacity to comprehend, the most profoundly engrossing was mental instability.

The longest-held belief on this subject of which there is written record is Sophocles' "Whom Jupiter would destroy he first makes mad" (c. 450 B.C.) in the *Antigone*.[6] (The saying is most familiar in its paraphrase: "Whom the gods would destroy they first make mad.") This statement encapsulates the Greek belief that all deviation from normal or proper behavior was caused by supernatural beings. Only by placating such powers could there be hope for a cure.

In the early centuries of the Christian era, the doctrine of invasion and possession developed. Madness proclaimed the presence of evil spirits or the prime evil spirit, the Devil. Animal or human sacrifice to effect a cure was replaced by penance—fasting or prayer—which would induce a superior power to intercede and cast out the Devil.

Not until the middle and later years of the eighteenth century was there a general view that mental health and bodily health had much in common. A realization developed in medical circles that madness was a symptom of a sick mind, just as debility was a symptom of a sick body.

It was not until well into the nineteenth century—the century of Edgar Allan Poe as well as Sir Walter Scott, Pasteur, Lister, Paul Ehrlich, William James, and, eventually, Sigmund Freud—that an approach to a clinical treatment began to evolve. Three-quarters of the way through the twentieth century, the malady remains a social problem. But its organic components and hereditary connections are better understood, the techniques of diagnosis and the therapy of treatment for specific subdivisions of mental affliction far more advanced. Still it is unlikely that we will soon, if ever, know how mental illness can be eradicated as, for example, leprosy was all but eliminated from the European scene before the end of the sixteenth century.

The connection between leprosy and lunacy as the Middle Ages waned is by no means a random metaphor (any more than *lunacy* just happens to be something that was at one time connected with the lunar body, or moon). Michel Foucault's absorbing *Madness and Civilization* (with its inventive subtitle "A History of Insanity in the Age of Reason") begins with the words: "At the end of the Middle Ages, leprosy disappeared from the Western World. . . ."[7] Through confinement and control and restriction on migration from the East where the infection flourished, the spread of the disease was first checked, then all but eliminated. Says Foucault: "Leprosy disappeared, the leper vanished, or almost, from memory; these structures [the leprosariums] remained." In England, in France, in Germany, the buildings were converted into asylums for the "new plague of the social order: madness."[8]

What could have given rise to the multiplication of mental disorders to the dimensions of "plagues"? Among the many possibilities, high priority would have to be given to the steady increase of population, the rise and extension of urban life in such cities as London and Paris, the pressures of crowding and community living that produced dismal conditions of sanitation, and the lack of understanding of the part heredity played in congenital instability. It is not impossible that nutritional deficiencies which caused "St. Anthony's Fire" (eruptions and irritations of the skin) could have had "maddening" consequences. The April 2, 1976 issue of *Science* magazine reported that experiments at the University of California at Santa Barbara have produced substantial evidence that the kind of hallucination which resulted in the Salem Witch Hunts of 1692 might have been caused by contaminated bread.

Foucault cites the continuing conversion of French leprosariums into asylums for the insane well into the sixteenth century. A very famous early instance occurred in England in 1402, when the former St. Mary of Bethelem Hospital became London's first madhouse. By gift of Henry VIII, the institution became the property of the City of London in 1547. Its typically idling, helpless inmates attained enduring visual form when, by the artistry of the eighteenth-century William Hogarth, the crawling horrors of the place lastingly known (by the vagaries of local pronunciation) as "Bedlam" were reproduced.[9]

The awareness of a new flaw in the social order soon found its way into the drama and fiction of the time. It was early in the seventeenth century (1601, approximately) that Shakespeare depicted Ophelia's dementia in *Hamlet,* followed not long afterward by Malvolio and such trenchant commentary as "Though this be madness, yet there is method in it" (*Hamlet*); eventually, Shakespeare converted the ragings of *King Lear* into literature. And the Clown was available, to be used as a symbol of madness: remember the moonstruck Pierrot? Part I of Cervantes' *Don Quixote* appeared in 1605, imparting to the literature of aberration an inimitably appealing character, and a new word for eccentric behavior—*quixotic.*

There was nothing operatic to parallel these literary happenings in the works of the Florence Camerata (so called because they met in a room or chamber [*camera*] of a ducal palace). But the beginning of the public presentation of opera in 1637 brought a vast acceleration of the kinds of subject matter considered acceptable for operatic treatment. Among them was the first operatic Mad Scene.

Needless to say, it was not in Bedlam or in Cervantes that Pier Francesco Cavalli found his subject matter for *L'Egisto*. This opera followed by a year Claudio Monteverdi's famous *L'Incoronazione di Poppea* of 1642 (the first opera, says Loewenburg, to be written "on a historical instead of a mythological, biblical or poetical subject"),[10] but Cavalli was content to find his dramatic source—as he had for his previous *La Didone* (1641)—in antiquity. A pleasant example of Venetian opera which Raymond Leppard revived in the early 1970s for Glyndebourne and the Santa Fe, New Mexico, Opera, *L'Egisto* depicts the gods working their illwill purposefully but beneficently.

3

L'Egisto is uncommon for its time in presenting its musical discourse through half a dozen principals with no choral ensemble to speak of. It is also notable for imparting to the nascent art form of the Mad Scene a series of components which recur in the familiar examples of the nineteenth century. In Italian, "Delirare d'amore" means "to be madly in love." Appropriate to the many examples to follow, Egisto's dilemma stems from his discovery that the Clori he loves no longer loves him.

Both are natives of the island of Delos (in the South Aegean Sea) kidnaped by corsairs and taken to another island, where they become separated. When Egisto next encounters Clori, his emotional base has remained fixed, but hers has been transferred to Ipparco, who is the beloved of Dema. Already Cavalli has given a foretaste of one of the grandest of grand operas to come, twenty decades later; the plot suggests *La Gioconda*, in which he loves she, and she loves he, but each one loves another.

Having been irrevocably inflamed by one of Cupid's darts, Egisto vows (at the end of Act I) to become a "wandering madman." Late in Act II, Egisto's dementia erupts into a solo scene in which he compares himself to Orpheus in search of Eurydice. This is a nice period touch because few subjects rated higher in the affections of contemporary opera composers than Orpheus.

As the scene progresses, Egisto makes an appeal to the gods—and laughs! This is a sure sign of madness in any theater at any time. At length (and just in time for the final double bar) Clori's "truer self" has been invoked, and she vows fidelity to Egisto.

In the Mad Scene itself (which covers some four hundred measures and eventually brings together almost all the principals in an ensemble) Egisto's emotions fluctuate from a denunciation of Clori to apprehensions that harm may befall her. The writing cannot be described as florid—but, unlike most other examples of Cavalli's vocal line in *L'Egisto* (in which stepwise progression prevails), it bounces up and down, thus projecting emotional instability.

It will not be lost on the reader that Egisto is a male "inamorata" and that the first operatic Mad Scene was thus written for a tenor. Some years would elapse before a female would be presented in the principal part of a dementee, but the adventurous Cavalli did experiment with the one celebrated by Euripides as "wild with love." This was in *Il Giasone* (Jason) of 1649, which contains a wild incantation for Medea beginning "Dell'antro magico stridenti cardini" ("On screaming hinges, open unto me O ye portals"). The first full-length attention to the woman who strangled a serpent, dismembered her brother, and killed her father, all for the love of Jason, was presented at the Teatro San Moisè in 1675 under the title of *Medea in Atene* by Antonio Giannettini. In respect to time and place, it was more than likely a castrato Medea (contradictory as that may sound). In either case, neither Giannettini nor his Medea have an identity today. But both Marc Antoine Charpentier and his *Médée* of 1693 do.

Charpentier was an eminent French musician of the seventeenth century, better known as a composer of masses and motets than of operas. His *Médée* not only survived its time of prominence, but has been republished in a facsimile score. It has also been recorded (vocal excerpts under the direction of Nadia Boulanger on Decca DL 9678, a suite of instrumental excerpts conducted by Raymond Leppard on Oiseau Lyre S-300). To hear these "highlights" without knowledge of their source would hardly alert the listener to high tragedy or deeds of deep deception. The music is, for the most part, bright and smooth-flowing. In a treatment true to the operatic customs then prevailing in Paris, Charpentier's *Médée* begins with a prologue of praise for the reigning monarch. It also contains a ballet midway in the action.

The depiction of musical madness on the English stage, for all its prominence in the spoken drama, is a rarity in late seventeenth- and early eighteenth-century writing. An exception may be cited in Purcell's *Don*

Quixote Part III (1695) in which Altisidora plots to challenge the Don's fidelity to Dulcinea with provocative actions. When he responds, she entices him further with "From rosy bowers," which Edward J. Dent, in his illuminating *Foundations of English Opera* published in 1928 at the University Press in Cambridge (England), describes as a "Mad Song," and adds "the type is clearly derived from the Italian chamber cantatas, such as Stradella (1642–1682) often wrote." That is to say, a continuous vocal piece, perhaps in several movements, embodying a variety of moods and passions.

Handel's *Orlando* contains a well-known sample of his graphic powers, written for the celebrated alto castrato, Senesino. In his masterful documentation of the composer's career (*George Frideric Handel*, W. W. Norton & Company, Inc., New York, 1966) Paul Henry Lang praises *Orlando* as "a Baroque opera of the first water" and another, German source identifies the elaborate, highly dramatic depiction of Orlando's irrationality at the end of Act II as a *Wahnsinnenszene* ("Mad Scene" or "Scene of Madness"). The instigator of Orlando's delirium is Zoroastro, a priestly (1000 B.C.) "dealer in magic and spells" long before W. S. Gilbert's John Wellington Wells (in *The Sorcerer*). Handel's Zoroastro taketh, and also giveth, restoring Orlando's senses when it suits his purpose.

The continuing appeal of *Medea* for the musical dramatist brought a production in Paris (in 1713) of Joseph-François Salomon's *Médée et Jason*: and the Jiří Benda celebrated for an adaptation of *Pygmalion* based on Jean Jacques Rousseau, wrote a *Medea* produced in Leipzig in 1775. It was a one-act work described as "Ein mit Musik vermischetes Drama," or a variant of German *singspiel*.

It was not until the century was approaching its end and the stage had been, by the upheavel of the French Revolution, liberated for fresh subject matter that the character of the daughter of Aeetes and her savage sacrifices found a mind and heart worthy of them. Luigi Cherubini was born in Florence, but his true musical nature did not begin to assert itself until he settled in Paris at twenty-eight (1788) and began to produce the works for which he is remembered. There is, in this *Médée*, no prologue of praise for a reigning monarch. The only king to whom Cherubini owes allegiance is Orpheus, and to him his loyalty is unflagging. The music strikes the tone of tragedy from the outset and builds, in power, to a climax hardly precedented in opera.

As befits the universal symbol of enraged womanhood, Cherubini's *Médée* has a multinational heredity. It draws on the Grecian heritage from the other side of the Rhine—Gluck's Alceste and Mozart's Electra in *Idomeneo*—for vocal accents and orchestral emphasis, fused by an Italian's heat for purposes of the French stage. Médée's final outburst, in which her children by Jason become the victims of her fury, are the first seeds of musical madness to burst into full flower (1797).

Such a *Médée* was not for immediate favor in France. It found greater response in Germany, especially after the composer-conductor Franz Lachner replaced the spoken text of F. B. Hoffmann's libretto with sung recitative for a production he introduced to Frankfurt in 1855. It is in Lachner's version, and with an Italian text permitting it to be titled *Medea*, that Cherubini's score has become a part of the Covent Garden repertory, later that of the New York City Opera. Maria Callas had much to do with the former happening in the late fifties, as she had with the work's revival at La Scala earlier in the decade. Though the City Opera has not found its Callas, it has found an audience responsive to the proposition that the values in *Medea* can be served by an ensemble effort of quality and an energetic, technically secure, dramatic soprano.

The first mentionable operatic *Medea* to be heard in Italy (Cherubini's did not reach his homeland until 1909, at La Scala) was Johann Simon Mayr's *Medea in Corinto*, in 1813. A composer of German birth (Mendorf, Bavaria, in 1763), Mayr reversed Cherubini's progression by going to Italy to acquire knowledge, and remaining to earn fame. Mayr's was, however, an ephemeral fame until the recent revival of interest in the broad repertory of Donizetti (*Anna Bolena, Maria Stuarda,* and *Roberto Devereux,* as well as *Lucia* and *L'Elisir d'amore*) and Bellini (*I Puritani* and *Il Pirata,* as well as *Norma* and *La Sonnambula*) rearoused interest in the man who had taught one and profoundly affected the other.

After he had found Italy *simpatico* and Italians had found Mayr worthy of respect, he settled in Bergamo, where he became *maestro di capella* at Santa Maria Maggiore in 1802. When the town fathers decided to establish a conservatory a few years later, Mayr became its director. It was he who insisted that one of his teen-aged students, Gaetano Donizetti, be allowed to follow his "genius"[11] (the word he used to describe the boy's gifts) for music, rather than being forced into the law, as his father preferred.

As a composer, Mayr brought to Italian opera in the early years of the eighteenth century something it could well use—a Germanic sense of structure and orchestral identity. Possibly in emulation of the result

Mozart achieved with a solo horn part behind the soprano voice of Fiordiligi's "Per pietà" in his *Così fan tutte,* Mayr became known for combining instrumental obbligati with his vocal writing: a bassoon here, a clarinet there, an oboe elsewhere. Through Mayr's influence, Donizetti's gifts were preserved for the career he was born to pursue; and through his *Medea in Corinto, Elisa,* and other operas, he provided guidelines for both Donizetti and Bellini.

As much could be inferred from Bellini's early adulation of Donizetti, already afloat on the operatic mainstream when Bellini was still a student in 1822. Their lines of connection to Mayr are established in the recollection of a fellow-student who later became a distinguished scholar and librarian of the Naples Conservatory. Recalling, many years later, his and Bellini's exposure to Donizetti's early *La Zingara* in 1822, he wrote: "As is natural it was attended eagerly by . . . those young men who meant to enter the same musical arena, not least among them the very distinguished composer Carlo Conti, who said to Bellini and me one day: 'Go to hear Donizetti's *La Zingara* . . . you will find a septet that only a pupil of Mayr could and would know how to create!' We hastened to go, and the septet mentioned [at the end of Act I] . . . was what caught the attention and admiration of Bellini, who soon obtained a copy of it . . . keeping it on the stand of his cembalo, studied it and played it every day. . . ."[12]

The tie between Mayr and Bellini is drawn even closer by the participation of Felice Romani in the lives of both. His was a link both spiritual and temporal. In his long lifetime (1788–1865) Romani wrote more than a hundred libretti. Having contributed to Mayr's durable fame by writing the libretto for his final work, *Medea in Corinto,* he applied his knowledge to guide the inexperienced Bellini from *Il Pirata,* with its precedent-setting Mad Scene, through *La Sonnambula, Norma,* and *Beatrice di Tenda.*

In this flow of musical forces, Donizetti was both catalyst and beneficiary. He conveyed Mayr's precepts to Bellini and, in turn, discovered in Bellini's treatment of Imogene's tragedy in *Il Pirata,* that there could be fulfillment for him, too, in the otherworldly world of the demented. Or to quote the eminent Ferdinand Hiller (composer, conductor, close friend of Mendelssohn, and founder of the Cologne Conservatory): "*Lucia di Lammermoor* could scarcely have existed without *Il Pirata.*"[13]

Perhaps there were, in Chorley's phrase, scenes of madness in "every southern serious opera" previously, but there was nothing like

the divine melancholia Bellini invokes for the recitative in which
Imogene responds to the news that her husband, Gualtiero (*Il Pirata*),
had been captured and condemned to die. With its oboe obbligato (an
echo of the same instrument's use by Mayr in his *Ifigenia in Aulide*),
it hints at a new relationship of voice and instrument. When, at a later
point in the same scene, Bellini reaches for the silvery sound of the
flute to brush in, delicately, the line also being pursued by the soprano,
he was innovating on his own for the Mad Scenes of all to follow.
Climactically, the cabaletta that follows is not a roulade of exhibitionism or a frilly embellishment of the merely decorative, but a free-
standing specimen of dramatic declamation that inspired not merely
Donizetti but, in his turn, Verdi.

Donizetti's first preference for the instrumental obbligato to Lucia's
Mad Scene was the disembodied, barely resonant vibration of the glass
harmonica. Ways of producing pitched tones by causing a glass vessel
to vibrate had been known from biblical times, but the use of various
sizes of glass bowls to form a scale was developed in the eighteenth
century by a series of experimenters. Among them was Benjamin
Franklin, who devised a system by which *both* hands could be used to
produce sound. He arranged the bowls in descending sizes, one inside
the other, on a horizontal rod. This, in turn, was attached to a foot
pedal that caused them to rotate. When the edges of the rotating bowls
were touched lightly by a slightly dampened finger, a melodic pattern
with a ghostly, eerie timbre could be produced. But no "Armonica"
(as Franklin named it) could be found in Naples when *Lucia* was being
rehearsed, and the most famous of all soprano and flute duets came
into being unintentionally. Whether the Mad Scene was ever performed as originally written, in a theater, is unknown to me. It can,
however, be heard in the sound that Donizetti yearned to hear in the
recorded version directed by Thomas Schippers (ABC ATS 20006)
with Beverly Sills as Lucia and Carlo Bergonzi as Edgardo.

4

Despite the soul-satisfying finality of a Mad Scene in which a soprano
holds the stage alone (save for a sympathetic chorus, and infrequent
intrusions by the chaplain Raimondo and her brother, Henry Ashton),
Lucia di Lammermoor was avoided by some eminent singers of the
nineteenth century. This had little to do with technical difficulties or
vocal challenge. Grisi, for example, had every vocal requirement (she

was the first Elvira in *I Puritani* and the first Norina in *Don Pasquale*) but I cannot find mention of her as Lucia.

For some singers, this avoidance had to do with what might be called "philosophic" reasons. The part of Lucia does, indeed, end gloriously with a Mad Scene and the soprano's death, with the curtain down and the audience able, immediately, to express its pent-up pleasure. But the Mad Scene does not end the *opera*. There is still a final scene to go, with "Tombe degl'avi" and other matter of what Chorley has called that "darling scene of tenors." Thus the performer playing Edgardo would have the last chance with the audience, which also means it might go away talking of him (Edgardo) rather than her (Lucia).

To avoid a role for such shallowly self-centered reasons might strike some as an imbecility unworthy of an operatic heroine, let alone a woman with the brain power to master the intricacies of vocal discipline and stage demeanor to perform such a part. But it could be, as I have suggested, merely a matter of philosophy, according to that non-Golden Rule of Operatic Behavior: Do not allow others to do unto you what you would gladly do unto them (steal the show). Nevertheless, it has happened. History is clear on that point.

The subtlest solution to the whole problem of the "Mad Scene" vs. the "Tomb Scene" is the one associated with Nellie Melba, whose career spanned thirty-eight years between a debut at Covent Garden in 1888 and a "farewell" in the same theater in 1926 (much of the performance was recorded "live" by the primitive means then available and may still be heard dimly today on a disc called "Melba The Complete Recordings from her Farewell Performance: Covent Garden, June 8, 1926," Opus Records 84). Whether she invented the practice or not, she gave consent to the formula: *"Lucia,* ending with the 'Mad Scene.' " The first such historic happening in New York with Melba can be dated to January 14, 1895.

Earlier in the season, Melba had appeared in a full-length *Lucia* under the direction of Luigi Mancinelli (something of an opera composer himself) and with the great Francesco Tamagno (the original Otello, among other career distinctions) as Edgardo. Neither eminent artist was associated with the performance of January 14, for which the conductor was Enrico Bevignani (a routinier of the time) and the Edgardo was Giuseppe Russitano, a tenor-of-all-work. The New York public was nevertheless beguiled by the promise of hearing Melba and Tamagno on the same evening. Following the truncated *Lucia* came an all-star *Cavalleria Rusticana*, with Eugenia Mantelli as Santuzza, Mario Ancona as Alfio, and Tamagno as Turridu. For that matter, Melba was willing to sing the Mad Scene, by itself, at the drop of a bank draft. This occurred several years later (for her first time in New York) when she died twice on the same evening: first in a performance of *La Bohème*, in which she sang Mimi; then, as an encore, in the Mad Scene of *Lucia*.

In such circumstances it can scarcely be wondered that the Mad Scene was widely regarded as a flight for a vocal nightingale and nothing else. Detached from its dramatic consequence (the death of Edgardo), the death of Lucia obviously lacked dramatic reality. Clearly the great tenors of the time (such as Tamagno or Italo Campanini, whose performance of Edgardo in the Metropolitan's first season in 1883 caused it to be called a "tenor opera") would not willingly engage in such a compromise.

The turning point for New York (and America—for what was permissible in New York was the guide, at that time, to what was permissible elsewhere) came on November 23, 1904. On that occasion there was no Nellie Melba as Lucia, but there was Marcella Sembrich to share the Fountain Scene in Act I with the rising Enrico Caruso, permitting W. J. Henderson to observe: "Lucia ending with the Mad Scene is no longer seen on the theater bills."[14] Edgardo was once again being treated as a character rather than a convenience.

My own introduction to *Lucia* as a "tenor opera" came in the later thirties with the first appearance in America of a celebrated Italian Edgardo of the time, Galliano Masini. It was the role of his debut (late in 1938) after years in which the listener had suffered the light-voiced efforts of post-Martinelli Edgardos (even the blessed arrival of Tito Schipa—who had done most of his previous American operatic singing in Chicago—found his dramatic vigor compromised by declining vocal volume). One had to take, along with Masini's old-fashioned flair for intense emotion and impressive vocal stamina, some old-fashioned sobs and strangulated high notes. But Masini's eloquent tomb scene was a foreshadowing—for those who had been denied the sound of an Edgardo by Caruso or Martinelli—of what it would become again, in the voices of such performers to come as Jan Peerce, Ferruccio Tagliavini, Richard Tucker, Mario del Monaco, Carlo Bergonzi, and, most recently, Luciano Pavarotti.

A golden-voiced tenor (whose girth, unless curbed soon by stringent dieting, may make him the first six-by-six operatic eminence),

Pavarotti is something of a rarity among operatic singers known to me. He is a student of everything he can learn from the lore and the recordings of his great predecessors—which he absorbs and modifies to his own purposes. Asked (prior to his first performance of Edgardo in New York in 1973) if he would punctuate his sudden appearance in the Contract Scene by ripping his hat from his head and dramatically whirling it across the stage, in a gesture made famous by Schipa, Pavarotti responded, "No, I don't do that. You see, for Schipa it was very good. He was a short man, and it gave his entrance an impact it might not have had otherwise. I am tall, and I do not need that kind of action to attract attention. Beside, I would *not* wear a hat inside anybody's home. To walk into the hall of Lammermoor castle with a hat on, in those times, would be considered very bad manners."

Equally, for a Lucia of these times to venture a Mad Scene without attention to the dramatic content of Donizetti's writing, as well as to its technical demands, would be considered not only bad musical manners but poor judgment. When Joan Sutherland brought her Lucia to America for the first time—in a Metropolitan Opera production which had never been properly staged—she came prepared not only to demonstrate her technical mastery, but with a plan of action devised for her, at Covent Garden, by Franco Zeffirelli. This was doubtless a response to the example of Maria Callas and her many productive dramatic collaborations with film and stage director Luchino Visconti. In turn, Beverly Sills put herself out to make Lucia not only a credible heroine deeply dashed by the emotional assaults to which she was subjected by those around her, but a credible Scottish heroine.

All three artists stand in the forefront of Lucias for whom responsibility neither began nor ended with vocal mastery. Each can be admired, in their different ways, for confronting difficulties squarely and not evading them (so long as range remained intact) and for bending their talents to the needs of a difficult role, rather than bending the role—in the manner of a Tetrazzini, a Galli-Curci, a Pons—to their talents. The wheel of operatic fortune spins endlessly and may, for a time, provide a spot of success for a performer only marginally entitled to such rewards. Always, however, it will come full circle and give rise to a new, full-formed exponent of a given style of singing capable of showing a new generation of opera-goers what an older one has singled out to idolize and idealize.

No present-day Lucia animated by the examples of Callas, Sutherland, or Sills at their best would need to be reminded by a critic (as

Henderson reminded the young Marion Talley of the twenties): "The mad scene, to revert to that much admired field for the exhibition of vocal virtuosity, is, in this respect overrated. There is room for a combination of *bravura with real dramatic interpretation* [italics added] but yesterday's Lucia was too inexperienced to grasp the opportunity."

Continued Henderson, with the clinching peroration for which his critical perceptions were famous: "The truth is that in so far as technical ability to sing Lucia is concerned, every soprano finds her full test in the second air of the first scene, 'Quando rapito.' Donizetti has written a florid air and has set down all the necessary fiorituri and a cadenza." To which Henderson adds: "It was in this air that she [Talley] was plainly extending herself."[15]

The clear conclusion to be derived from these words is that a Lucia should display her vocal credentials in "Regnava nel silenzio" and "Quando rapita" (which succeeds it) and then build, through the solos and ensembles that follow, a characterization climaxed by the Mad Scene. This would honor the proposition that Donizetti was more than a concocter of vehicles for star singers—that he was a musical dramatist concerned with the stageworthiness of every participant in the works he created.

Is this a novel concept of the twentieth century, pioneered by such "innovators" as Callas, Sutherland, and Sills? It is as "novel" as the quality admired by Hector Berlioz when he first saw the Lucia of Jenny Lind in the 1840s. I have not traced his opinion to a written comment by Berlioz, but the gist of it has been preserved by Chorley in his recollections of the same performer's Lucia: "She was the only Lucia (as was pointed out to me by M. Berlioz) who prepared for the last dismal heartbreak, by her agony in the moment when she is impressed with the falsehood of her lover by her haughty and tyrannical brother. Her madness was fearfully touching in proportion as it had been foreseen."[16]

As one whose taste in dramatic action had been formed by the works of Shakespeare and the performance of their great female roles (especially the mad Ophelia) by the celebrated English actress Harriet Smithson (who became his first wife) Berlioz was well placed to observe and appreciate such a detail.

5

It should be evident from the foregoing that, for all their individual attributes, Donizetti and Bellini were products of a lineage, inheritors of a progression that predisposed them for the careers in which they found fame. They were exposed to an environment in which opera was the popular art form of the people, and even young composers could find their way. Donizetti wrote his first opera (a one-act comedy) while a student at the Liceo in Bologna; Bellini began in exactly the same way at the Conservatory at Naples.

They were supervised and counseled, not by theorists or academicians, but by men who were themselves composers for the stage (though their names would mean little, in the broad panorama of opera). The circumstances could be likened to the collegiate world of today in which former major league baseball players become coaches at such universities as Arizona or USC, imparting their knowledge to those who become, in turn, the major league stars of tomorrow.

By the beginning of the nineteenth century, opportunity for composers was so abundant, encouragement so readily accessible, that every talent had its chance at a chance. Even without Cherubini, Italy possessed an operatic composer of great merit in every decade of the nineteenth century, to rouse the public to cheers and younger composers to emulation. From 1800 to 1810, it was Mayr; then it was Rossini ("Il Maestro di Maestri"—"the master of the masters," as he has been called), beginning with *Tancredi* and *L'Italiana in Algeri* in 1813 to *Semiramide* in 1823, when he left for Paris; and Bellini, from *Il Pirata* in 1827 until his death after *I Puritani*, in 1835. Bridging the two decades from 1823 until 1843 was the incredibly facile and versatile Donizetti.

Ready and waiting in the wings as Donizetti took his last bows at a premiere—though he was still short of fifty—was the figure already hailed as Italy's "coming man." Giuseppe Verdi had been struggling for six years (against dismal personal misfortunes and professional mishaps) to write a work that would justify his choice of a career, as Mayr, Rossini, Donizetti, and Bellini had justified theirs. For him the year was 1842, the work *Nabucco*. However hard Verdi's way would be henceforth—and it was often almost unbearably hard—there could be no doubt that composing operas was the one, the only career for him to pursue.

As Bellini and Donizetti had learned from their predecessors, so Verdi profited from their examples to find an outlet for his own genius. Rossini was his deity, but Donizetti was his lay preceptor in the shaping of a work for the stage, especially in the adroit balance of arias and ensembles. By 1847, when he was thirty-four, Verdi was able to extend the Mad Scene to an area a step beyond what had been ventured before—into the strange, distorted area of the unconscious. He found the challenge in a subject that combined the somnambulism of Bellini's Amina (in *La Sonnambula*) with the political pressures that had unhinged the mind of Donizetti's *Anna Bolena*. Both possibilities for self-destruction were contained in the single person of Lady Macbeth. She possessed the fascinations to become the prototype of a new operatic demented: one driven to her acts of violence by the psychopathic and the psychological.

The seeds of disturbance in Lady Macbeth are not planted by an external force, such as the gods in *L'Egisto*, or by the plotting of another (Henry Ashton's preference for Arthur Bucklaw, rather than Edgar, as a husband for his sister, Lucy) or by the disappearance of a beloved (which drives Elvira to distraction in *I Puritani*). The compulsion is wholly and specifically of Lady Macbeth's own making—a wild urge to extend the area of her husband's influence. That it culminates in destruction for both is a pertinent instance of *Macbeth*'s appeal for the fatalist in Verdi.

It is also a prime example of Verdi's uncanny instinct that he recognized, in "Lady" (as he called her), a much more compelling figure than Macbeth. To realize this objective he required—at this time of his career—some special circumstance in which a commission did not carry with it the demand for a tenor in a leading role. This came his way in an offer from Florence, which carried no such specification and gave Verdi the freedom he required to make Macbeth (the leading male role), a baritone, and to develop Lady Macbeth into a part for a far-ranging, more than soprano voice to embody her vengeful character. When these decisions were made in 1847, Verdi was still six years away from the trinity of *Rigoletto, Il trovatore*, and *La traviata* that made him famous. He was serious, ambitious, unafraid to measure himself against a major challenge.

He was also inadequately equipped with the skill and experience to balance so complex a plot as Shakespeare's with the musical content to make it wholly acceptable. It was not until he prepared a new version for Paris nearly twenty years later that the score became what it is today: a flawed masterpiece, but a masterpiece nevertheless. At the core, however, remained the dramatic confrontation which he had personally extracted from Shakespeare and directed his collaborator, Francesco Piave, to put into Italian verse for singing purposes. Lady Macbeth, forceful, strong-minded, insatiably ambitious, was to be the driving force behind the irresolute, blundering, fear-ridden Macbeth, the power base on which to convert high tragedy in one art form to the requirements of another. At the apex of the structure would be the sleepwalking scene and its hallucinatory consequences.

For this climaxing scena there would be need for a new kind of performer, far from the light-voiced mistresses of *leggiero* (passage work) acceptable in *La Sonnambula* or *Anna Bolena*. When the opera was being prepared for performance in Naples in 1848 (some months after its fairly successful premiere in Florence) with a cast over which he had no direct control, Verdi wrote in alarm, to a friend who was participating in the preparation, these now-famous words:

> I understand that you are rehearsing *Macbeth* and as this opera interests me more than any other, I ask you to allow me to say a few words about it. Mme. Tadolini is, I believe, to sing Lady Macbeth, and I am astonished that she should have undertaken this part. You know how highly I think of Mme. Tadolini and she knows it too: but in all our interests I think it necessary to remark that she has too great qualities for this part! This may seem an absurdity! Mme. Tadolini has a beautiful face and looks good, and I would have Lady Macbeth ugly and wicked. Mme. Tadolini sings to perfection and I would not have Lady Macbeth sing at all. Mme. Tadolini's voice is the voice of an angel, and Lady Macbeth's should be the voice of a devil. Please bring these comments to the notice of the directors, of Maestro Mercadante, who understands my ideas better than anyone, and of Mme. Tadolini herself, and do what you think for the best.[17]

A soprano who has "too great qualities" for a part? A woman who is too beautiful? A role for which the composer prefers a woman I would not have "sing at all?" Here is a new charter of specifications for a principal performer in an opera. Yet the evidence is compelling that Verdi was looking for a woman as different from the average operatic soprano as what he had done was different from the average opera.

As set by Verdi, the sleepwalking scene is an exact Italian equivalent of Shakespeare's words. Elsewhere in the letter just quoted, he refers to the staging of a production of Shakespeare's *Macbeth* that he had seen in London (where he had gone to supervise the production of *I masnadieri* earlier in 1848). Taken together, these two commentaries by Verdi provide criteria such as Italian opera had not previously known: an Italian composer who set a scene exactly as Shakespeare wrote it and invoked stage practices of the playwright's own country!

Verdi's thoughts and the words he used to express them mark the Great Divide of opera's topography. On the older side, it is a landscape populated in large part by roles written to the measure of a particular performer. On the other, newer side begins the more challenging terrain of roles written primarily to the needs of the drama, to which a selected performer must make every effort to conform. In the far distance would come the time when Verdi himself would combine the two modes of procedure, by shaping his dramatic treatment of Otello to the great *tenor robusto* of Francesco Tamagno, or of *Falstaff* to the artistry of Victor Maurel.

On its own, however, Verdi's cry for credibility above all brought into Italian opera a new sense of dramatic values. Together with what Wagner was doing in Germany (1847 was also the year in which *Lohengrin* was nearing completion), Verdi's manifesto of purpose would find its way into the emerging schools of national opera as the nineteenth century was putting away the easy solutions of the eighteenth century and verged closer to the harder challenges—mental and spiritual—of the twentieth.

Lady Macbeth was only the first in a series of great musical and dramatic portraits to emerge from the psychological dilemmas of characters who appealed to Verdi. He long cherished the ambition to master the character of King Lear. Certainly King Philip II in *Don Carlos* is a monarch beset by difficulties (many of his own making) that almost destroy him. *Otello* is the ultimate in the explication of suspicion fed by poisons which become self-destructive. All these problems and their consequences were not visited upon small men helpless to contest the forces around them. They concern royalties—kings, queens, and ladies —made small by an inability to control their human frailties.

Out of Verdi's abundant example flowed the classic casebook in music drama of a guilt complex, paranoia, and hallucinatory delusion. None of these terms were known to Modest Moussorgsky when he created *Boris Godunov* in 1873, but all the symptoms had been known to Alexander Pushkin more than fifty years before, when he wrote his play. Combined with these predispositions in Czar Boris are a manic-depressive psychosis fluctuating between joy that his son Fyodor will eventually succeed him and panic that his ministers will take the rule of Russia into their own hands after his death. The play of forces and counterforces are of a towering magnitude for the best dramatic actor, let alone one who must also be a master singer.

If Lady Macbeth is nineteenth-century opera's greatest challenge to the female singing actress—I have not encountered, among a half dozen I have experienced in the role in America and Europe, a wholly satisfactory one—Boris is without question the most demanding part for the male singing actor. The musical qualities of Moussorgsky's score were warmly admired when *Boris Godunov* was introduced to America in 1913 under the direction of Arturo Toscanini. But the full measure of its dramatic content was not appreciated until Chaliapin appeared in the role a decade later. Unfortunately everything else was not in proportion to it, including staging and conducting. But one critic was impelled to describe Chaliapin's Boris as comparable to a "Russian Macbeth," thus directly affiliating the role with Verdi's pioneering predecessor. Another reviewer vowed that not since Albert Niemann's enactment of Siegfried's death in *Götterdämmerung* thirty years before had he seen anything "so thrilling in this line." Much else about *Boris* and the men who succeeded Chaliapin in the title role has been said before and will be said again; the opera is inexhaustible in its content, its contexts, and its connotations.

It may be said, on Chaliapin's behalf, that much of what he did in his other celebrated characterizations—in Boito's *Mefistofele*, as Don Basilio in Rossini's *Barbiere*, and Dosifei in Moussorgsky's *Khovantschina*—conformed closely to Verdi's specifications for a successful Lady Macbeth. He was a man who could look "ugly" and "wicked"; his was a voice that could sound "hard, stifled and dark"; if necessary, he could make a striking effect by "not singing at all." He was capable of all of these and even more—a superior King Philip II in *Don Carlos* and a poignant embodiment of the mad idealist in Massenet's *Don Quichotte*. Has any other basso ever matched Chaliapin's virtuosity in bestriding the peaks and valleys of the irrational, from the most terrifying to the least harmful? I think not.

6

The clear indication, in this synopsis of the Mad Scene in its most common manifestations, is that its appeal to the creative mind increased rather than diminished in the second half of the nineteenth century. What had originally been conceived as an *incident* in a drama took on the importance and diversity to become a *subject* for a drama. As social awareness of mental affliction, its numerous causes and possible therapy, became more acute, so did the manner of its artistic interpretation. The morphology of operatic madness would show an evolution from the *theological* (a manifestation of the gods), *demonological* (invasion by evil spirits), *pathological* (the result of sudden shock, infection, or illness), and *psychological* (disturbances created by the individual's unreasonable demands upon himself) to the *psychopathological* (a combination of the last two).

German opera, and specifically the German opera associated with Wagner, could be described as *hyperpathological*. Here, typically, a predisposition to a state of mind creates a condition in which mental transformation occurs. A voracious reader when he was growing up, Wagner's disposition to the opera was demonstrated, at fifteen, less by any musical aptitude—that came later—than by the creation of a "great tragedy."[18] Based on *Hamlet, King Lear, Macbeth,* and Goethe's *Götz von Berlichingen,* its hero "is so completely carried away by the appearance of the ghost of his father . . . that he is driven to fearful deeds of violence, and, with a series of murders on his conscience, he eventually goes mad." When Wagner was seventeen, he was exposed to Bellini's *Il Pirata* and, at twenty-three, as a young conductor in Riga, he became acquainted with "whole shoals" of contemporary operas, "among them Bellini's, Donizetti's, Adam's and Auber's."[19]

The Wagnerian predisposition can first be encountered in Senta's vision of the Flying Dutchman, whom she is resolved to save from his endless ordeal even before she meets him. The legend of the mariner condemned to roam the seas, with a landfall only every seven years, had, of course, existed for decades before it attracted Wagner's attention. It was very likely that Heinrich Heine's retelling of it (*Memoirs of Herr von Schnabelewopski*) first disclosed to Wagner a linkage of the Dutchman's fate to a woman who might sacrifice her life to save his. An even more pathological predisposition can be found in *Lohengrin.* In contemporary terms, Elsa's inability to control her desire to know Lohengrin's name and place of origin—though he had warned her in the most solemn terms not to ask—might be interpreted as the acting out of a death wish.

Such a desire for death is, explicitly, the inner dynamic force of *Tristan und Isolde.* At the beginning it is expressed by the heroine's decision to cause the death of her hated foe and herself, which is contravened when Brangaene substitutes the love potion for the fatal poison. But the goal is not abandoned, only deferred. After King Mark's discovery of the lovers together, when Tristan asks Isolde whether she will follow him to the land of his choice, all good Wagnerians know that he means: "If I choose death, will you die to be with me?" That, of course, is why he does not defend himself in the duel with Morold, courting the wound that will bring death closer, and also, after almost an entire act of delirium and ravings, why he tears the bandages from his wound to bring closer, through death, his reunion with Isolde. Her expiration at the end of the "Liebestod" is symbolic of much more than terminal operatic fatigue—it is expressive of the will to live with Tristan in death.

The streams of the psychological, the philosophical, and the hyper-pathological collide in many operas of the twentieth century. The sheer shock value in dementia or its ramifications are no longer sufficient to absorb a creator's brain power and artistic energy. Now he searches out subject matter that will bear on causes as well as results. This quest coincides with the investigation and research that have been applied to isolate the rationale of the irrational.

Richard Strauss found within his technical means the ways to articulate in music Oscar Wilde's depiction of necrophilia in the Biblical subject of Salome. Then he ranged back to the mother lode of all opera—Greek tragedy—to find in Hugo von Hofmannsthal's treatment of *Elektra* something even more profoundly psychotic. Flowing through the work is Elektra's longing for her brother, Orestes, to reappear and consummate the revenge for her mother's murder of Agamemnon, her husband and the father of both Orestes and Elektra. This will enable the daughter to die in peace. This could be described as a Mad Scene that begins with the curtain rise and ends only when it falls, nearly two hours later. In the 1950s, the whole cycle of music and madness came full circle when Igor Stravinsky's *The Rake's Progress* followed Tom Rakewell through all forms of Hogarthian fortune and misfortune into the place where insanity was first socialized, Bedlam itself.

For me, the single most intensely absorbing aspect of these elaborations and abstractions from the classical Mad Scene is that they rarely, if ever, have to do with the contemporary scene. For one *Street Scene* by Elmer Rice, Langston Hughes, and Kurt Weill which finds its frame for violence on a hot summer's night "in a mean quarter of New York," there is a massively disproportionate emphasis on works whose subject matter derives from antiquity, from Shakespeare, and from the Renaissance, directly or in such a transformation as occurs in Eugene O'Neill's *Mourning Becomes Electra*. Alberto Ginastera's coolly contemplative evocation of the Renaissance eccentricities of *Bomarzo* and *Beatrix Cenci* (the latter concerned with an overattractive young lady who is raped by her father in Act I and enjoys satisfactory revenge when he dies by knife in Act II), Robert Ward's excellent response to Arthur Miller's treatment of incantations and other addenda of the Salem witch trials in *The Crucible*, and Alban Berg's rendering of Frank Wedekind's sex fantasies of *Lulu* (from the plays originally titled *Erdgeist—Earth Spirit—*and *Büchse der Pandora—Pandora's Box*) are a few that might be cited.

It is thus not the newness of the material which stimulates the creative mind to a response, but the newness of each generation's insights into the afflictions of the human being—including his mind—which generate a reaction. I would describe this as a comforting peroration to a discomforting subject. There are sure to be operas written fifty years from now on subject matter which, though current today, will not convey its stimulation until 2020. It would be in keeping with the instances mentioned above, just as Thomas Mann's *Death in Venice* of 1911 did not encounter a responsive mind until Benjamin Britten's, in 1970.

One can imagine such a talent, perhaps one already born, being able to deal operatically with Edward Albee's *Who's Afraid of Virginia Woolf?* An equivalent to Lady Macbeth's mind-walking might be found in the episode that begins Act III: "I cry all the time, too, Daddy. I cry alllll the time: but deep inside, so no one can see me. I cry all the time. And Georgie cries all the time, too. We both cry all the time, and then, what we do, we cry, and we take our tears, and we put 'em in the ice box, in the goddam ice trays (Begins to laugh) until they're all frozen (Laughs even more) and then . . . we put them . . . in our . . . drinks."[20]

What might tempt Albee even more into such a collaboration (he is something of a musician himself and worked on a musical project with the late William Flanagan) would be to participate in an operatic realization of the eloquent scene deep in Act III:

(BOTH TOGETHER)

Martha	*George*
I have tried, oh God I have tried; the one thing . . . the one thing I've tried to carry pure and unscathed through the sewer of this marriage; through the sick nights, and the pathetic, stupid days, through the derision and the laughter . . . *God,*	Libera me, Domine, de morte aeterna, in die illa tremenda: Quando caeli movendi sunt et terra: Dum veneris judicare saeculum per ignem. Tremens factus sum ego, et timeo, dum discussio venerit, atque ventura ira. Quando caeli movendi sunt

the laughter, through one failure after another, one failure compounding another failure, each attempt more sickening, more numbing than the one before; the one thing, the one *person* I have tried to protect, to raise above the mire of this vile, crushing marriage; the one light in all this hopeless . . . *darkness* . . . our SON.

et terra. Dies illa, dies irae, calamitatis et miseriae; dies magna et amara valde. Dum veneris judicare saeculum per ignem. Requiem aeternam dona eis, Domine: et lux perpetua luceat eis. Libera me Domine de morte aeterna in die illa tremenda: quando caeli movendi sunt et terra; Dum veneris judicare saeculum per ignem.[21]

(END TOGETHER)

Basically, Albee's work is already done. He would, perhaps, be required to add or subtract a few words to suit his co-worker's musical scheme. What he has written is the one thing not yet attempted in this category: a Mad Scene *a due*, already fixed, frozen, and packaged in a form appropriate for male and female voices.

VII

Duet

1

Whether an operatic *Virginia Woolf* would, of itself, give rise to a new form of duet could not be foretold. Much would depend on the talent of Albee's alter ego—on the collaborator's point of view, on the extent to which his vocal line would enhance the blur of metaphor and the hysteria of verbiage (whether in English or Latin) and contribute to the advancement of the plot.

The last consideration is crucial to the proper "duet" as I conceive it. Two voices singing together do *not* a duet make. Were that true, the duet would be a child of the eighteenth century, when voices were often blended in fulfillment of musical purpose. The Countess and Susanna composing a letter in Act III of Mozart's *Le Nozze di Figaro;* Dorabella and Fiordiligi cooing to each other in thirds and sixths through many pages of *Così fan tutte;* Papageno and Papagena mutually extolling the joys of having found each other—these are musical highlights in any opera-goer's experience. But these couplings do not embody the passions which enter into drama, bear the seeds of propagation, and give rise to offspring.

Such requirements suggest why, perhaps, "duet" is a relatively late addition to the sequence of *recitativo, aria, scena,* and Mad Scene. The latter are essentially solitary activities, the prerogatives of individual performers, giving voice not only to personal problems, but with personal means.

The delinquence of duet in making its appearance relates to historical factors which have, from time to time, crept into this discussion.

The prevalence of classical Greek subjects among early composers, the domination of the stage by castrati, the conventions of structure (*recitativo, aria, recitativo, aria*) which characterized *opera seria*—all these were elements that minimized the possibilities of characters being presented in the one guise they all share (other than being performers): as human beings.

Save for such a rarity as Donna Anna opposing Don Giovanni's rapacious attack with physical force, contention and conflict in eighteenth-century opera are almost always conveyed by . . . *recitativo, aria, scena* (eventually Mad Scene). I think of "O namenlose Freude" ("O indescribable joy") in Beethoven's post-Revolutionary, early-nineteenth-century *Fidelio* as one of the first great dramatic duets. But it is so only to a limited extent—it celebrates the fulfillment of a *common* objective (Florestan's release from the prison in which he has been unjustly confined) through Leonora-Fidelio's persistent effort on her husband's behalf.

For all the magnitude of its dramatic impact, the *Fidelio* duet runs true to the convention of its time in being part of a drama of *individual* expressions. There is, to be sure, a beautiful canon quartet, which flows as smoothly and serenely as it does because the characters are extolling, for the most part, the *common* objective of compatible love (though, as it happens, not with each other), and Don Pizarro and Rocco have an interchange that might be considered a form of duet.

But when the villainous Don Pizarro appears on the scene and mouths his determination to destroy an unidentified enemy in the dungeon, it is in an *aria:* "Ha! welch ein Augenblick" ("Ha! what a moment"). This is, of course, overheard by Fidelio, who does not rush out to confront and comment directly, but waits until Pizarro has left the stage. *Then* she launches into her great scena: "Abscheulicher! wo eilst du hin?" ("Monster! What brought you here?") and so the scenes, and the opera, go their conventionally contemporary way.

There was, however, one form of operatic expression inhabited by real people, in which contention and conflict could be expressed by confrontation. Curiously it was not some form of serious opera previously unmentioned, but, somewhat paradoxically, *opera buffa* and its descendants. An irritable master and a contentious servant with whom he can neither live nor live without—these are the structural simplicities of a plot as viable today as when Pergolesi wrote *La Serva Padrona* in the 1730s.

The intricacies of the plot have already been spelled out. But it may be mentioned that, though much of the discourse is carried on conversationally, never does a voice overlap another until the finale (where such musical mischief is permissible). *La Serva Padrona* does, however, contain a duet of a certain, oddly suitable sort. This comes late in the course of the comedy when Vespone, posing as a mute suitor for the servant, actually engages in an "argument" with Uberto (their master), by stamping his foot.

Forty years and many *opera buffa*s later, Pierre Caron de Beaumarchais was bold enough to broach the idea of a male servant with the audacity to speak, even perhaps to sing, at the same time as a member of the upper class—moreover, one who had been the servant's former employer. Perhaps it should have fallen to Mozart to have the honor of being the first composer to deal, musically, with this trailblazing exchange, but the subject did not come to his attention until it had already been set by Giovanni Paisiello.

Several respects in which Paisiello's setting of *Il Barbiere di Siviglia* broke new ground in the treatment of the operatic finale have already been mentioned. It may now be entered to Paisiello's credit that he ventured the logical, if heretical, premise that what is permissible in a finale is equally acceptable elsewhere. Doubtless there were earlier instances of characters *not* in agreement singing at the same time, but Paisiello's example endures, and it can be re-evaluated any time the work is performed, or any time a listener chooses to consult a recording (such as Mercury SR 2 9010).

The situation arises in the play almost as early as Beaumarchais brings on his principal male performers, the Count and the servant. Paisiello could have let one speak and then the other, but he is—through a considerable background in the creation of earlier *opera buffa*s—well versed in the ensemble tradition of the finale. Why not bite the bullet and let them sing together as soon as it is dramatically desirable and musically feasible?

No sooner has the Count entered the scene with the purpose of paying court to Rosina than Figaro intrudes, busily engaged in writing a song to serve him (in two of his other guises than barber) as raconteur and entertainer. The two men have a mutual sense of recognition—but the night is dark, the distance between them deceiving. In addition, the Count is disguised (as the student Lindoro), which adds to the confusion. Figaro takes the initiative by musing, half to himself: "Ma! quel soggetto / L'ho visto altrove" ("But there's a face I've seen before"), and the Count also says, in an operatic aside: "Quella figura

/ M'e certo cognita" ("I know that face from somewhere"). Finally, they sing *together:*

<table>
<tr><td colspan="2" align="center">COUNT</td></tr>
<tr>
<td>
(Al portamento
Grottesco e comico
Certo è costui
Quel birbo Figaro.)
</td>
<td>
(From his strange
and comical behavior
I'm sure this must be
that rogue, Figaro.)
</td>
</tr>
<tr><td colspan="2" align="center">FIGARO</td></tr>
<tr>
<td>
(Quell'aria nobile
Io non m'inganno
E quello il Conte.)
Son io, signore. . . .
</td>
<td>
(That noble air,
I can't be mistaken
This must be the Count.)
It's me, sir. . . .
</td>
</tr>
</table>

The conventional device of [   ] for indicating, in a libretto, that the words so enclosed are delivered simultaneously, may be described, in this instance, as the brackets that launched a thousand duets. It may also be mentioned that the phrase "Quel birbo Figaro" has an echo in Mozart's *Le Nozze di Figaro*. There it is put in the mouth of Dr. Bartolo in Act I.

As noted, Mozart did not have the opportunity of joining dissenting voices for the first time in a work that endures. He was, however, the first great composer of comic *and* serious operas to blend the resources of one with the needs of the other. By importing from *Nozze di Figaro* the Haydn-influenced finale of Act II, he gave those crucial sections in the "serious" *Don Giovanni* and *Die Zauberflöte* a new, special distinction. It is a curiosity, but also an inevitability, that the real junction of the low road of comic opera and the high road of serious opera was plotted by the man who was, after Mozart, the next great master of both modes of expression, and the one who gave enduring identity to "quel birbo Figaro" and his escapades.

2

Gioacchino Rossini could be described as one of the most admired and least understood of great opera composers. Universally admired for such flavorsome fantasies of wit and high spirits as *Il Barbiere*, *Cenerentola* (*Cinderella*), and *L'Italiana in Algeri*, Rossini is unfortunately undervalued in the English-speaking world for such achievements in serious opera as *Tancredi, Semiramide, Moïse,* the first of all operatic versions of *Otello,* and, until recently, *L'Assedio di Corinto (The Siege of Corinth).* As for *William Tell,* it tends to be forgotten that it is the name of a great lyric masterpiece as well as of a beloved overture.

To the average opera-goer who knows anything about him, Rossini was a fat, jolly man with a sharp wit and a taste for food that resulted in the creation of *tournedos Rossini* (filet of beef surmounted by *foie gras*). He was, indeed, all of these things: but these things were far from all of him. A native of a portion of Italy that entitled him to be known as the Swan of Pesaro, Rossini's gifts were so extraordinary (both of his parents earned a livelihood either in whole or in part as musicians) that he had relatively little formal training. At a point when he was told that he required two more years of study to master canto fermo and canon, young Rossini decided that he could use the two years to better advantage by putting his talents to work. On the other hand, he had acquired, as a sub-teen-ager in the early years of the nineteenth century, such a fondness for the works of Haydn and Mozart that he was known as "Il Tedeschino" ("The Little German").[1]

The designation was, in a way, prophetic, for depending on great gifts if small training, Rossini acquired a stature among composers that made him a living link between Beethoven and Wagner. Of all the distinguished musicians who lived in the nineteenth century, only the younger Franz Liszt could claim a similar distinction—and his contact with Beethoven was limited to being kissed on the cheek by the great man, after performing for him on the piano at the age of twelve (in 1823).

Rossini's contact with Beethoven was of a different, more personal sort. Not yet thirty, but with a considerable series of successes to his name, Rossini came to Vienna in the spring of 1822 to participate in the premiere there of his *Zelmira.* He was a particular enthusiast for Beethoven's quartets and arranged to express his admiration for them personally to the deaf master. By 1822 Beethoven's hearing was all but gone, and "conversation"—if such it could be called—had to be carried on through written questions.

What was "said," therefore, can hardly be part of a written record; but it is known that Beethoven was familiar with the score of *Il Barbiere,* had heard it performed in Vienna (in 1819, when he still had some hearing), and regarded Rossini as "a talented and a melodious composer."[2] In later years, Rossini responded to proddings for his recollection of the visit with answers suggesting it was both brief and mostly ceremonial.

But to Wagner—nearly fifty years later (when he was in Paris in 1860 to give a famous orchestral concert which included the first performance there of the prelude to *Tristan und Isolde*)—Rossini was considerably more loquacious. Now it was the Italian master (aged sixty-eight) who received the German aspirant (aged forty-seven). The intermediary was Edmond Michotte, a wealthy Belgian-born music lover and amateur of the arts who had the forethought to take notes on the conversation and the goodwill finally to publish them in 1906 under the title *La Visite de R. Wagner à Rossini* (Paris, 1860).

The French *Souvenirs Personnels*, Michotte's two books of memoirs, had long been out of print and all but forgotten when, in the course of research for his Rossini biography, the late Herbert Weinstock came upon them. He brought together, in one volume, translations into English of *Richard Wagner's Visit to Rossini* (Paris, 1860) and *An Evening at Rossini's in Beau-Sejour* (Passy, 1858), which were published by the University of Chicago Press in 1968.

The Michotte text has been challenged by some (Ernest Newman, in particular) for minor errors of fact; but that eminent Wagner authority concedes "there seems little reason to doubt that he [Michotte] was present at the interview, and that the talk was substantially as he represents it to have been."[3] What Rossini recalled, in 1860, of his conversation with Beethoven nearly forty years before is then the faded flesh of the bones he had offered to other interrogators. Perhaps Rossini knew that Wagner had written (1840) eloquently of an *imaginary* visit to Beethoven, and he could fill him in on a real one.

The visit was brief. And it was corrupted by language barriers and communication gaps. But, according to Rossini, Beethoven said "brusquely in Italian that was comprehensible enough, 'Ah! Rossini, you are the composer of *Il Barbiere di Siviglia*? I congratulate you; it is an excellent *opera buffa*: I read it with pleasure and it delights me. It will be played as long as Italian opera exists. Never try to do anything but *opera buffa*; wanting to succeed in another genre would be trying to force your destiny.'"

Reminded that Rossini had already composed such *opera seria* as *Tancredi*, *Otello*, *Mosè*, Beethoven replied, "In fact, I have looked through them. But look, *opera seria*—that's not the Italians' nature. They don't have enough musical science to deal with true drama; and how could they acquire it in Italy?"

Rossini and Wagner had a laugh together over Beethoven's outspoken frankness, Wagner complimented Rossini on not taking Beethoven's advice and expressed high praise for many fine pages in *Moïse*, *William Tell*, and the *Stabat Mater*. Rossini conceded that he did, indeed, feel more "aptitude" for *opera buffa*, but spoke of his high regard for Haydn's *Seasons* and Mozart's *The Magic Flute* and mentioned that he would copy out the vocal parts, sketch in his own "accompaniments" and then compare what he had done with those of the great masters. Eventually Wagner queried, "Will you allow me to ask how your visit to Beethoven ended?"

Replied Rossini, "Oh, it was short. You understand that one whole side of the conversation had to be written out. I told him of all my admiration for his genius, all my gratitude for his having allowed me an opportunity to express it to him."

"He replied with a profound sigh and exactly these words: '*Oh! un infelice!*' After a pause he asked me for some details about the Italian opera houses, about famous singers, whether or not Mozart's operas were performed frequently, if I was satisfied with the Italian troupe at Vienna.

"Then, wishing me a good performance and success for *Zelmira*, he got up, led us [Rossini had been accompanied by Giuseppe Carpani, an Italian poet whose acquaintances in Vienna had included not only Beethoven but Haydn and Mozart] and said to me again: 'Above all, make a lot of *Barbers*.' "

Those famous words of farewell—"make a lot of *Barbers*"—have been reproduced many times, but rarely with a specification of where they had been said, and to whom Rossini repeated them. Nor should it go unmentioned that when Wagner spoke of his admiration for pages of such *opere serie* as *Otello* and *Mosè*, Rossini replied, "*I had facility and lots of instinct.*"[4]

In this sentence Rossini summed up the force of personal influence which enabled him to alter the course of Italian opera on both sides of the temperamental ledger: the *buffa* which Beethoven admired, as did Wagner, and the *seria*, which Wagner was sufficiently broad-based in his musical tastes to esteem as well. If it was facility that brought him to a point in his career at which he could challenge Paisiello's achievement in *Il Barbiere*, it was instinct that caused him to accept the best of its innovations—such as the duet involving Figaro and Almaviva—and to add his own resources to them.

These resources extend what is merely a sequence of measures, and a

few minutes, in Paisiello, to a scene covering nearly thirty *pages* (74–
111) in Rossini's orchestral score. Preceded by a page or two of recitative, it begins *allegro maestoso,* is escalated into *vivace* as Figaro
launches into some of the tongue tripping *appogiaturas* (grace notes,
etc.) which make the part treacherous for a non-Italian, has an *andante*
interlude, resumes tempo I, and finishes its breathless course with the
Count arching his flexible tenor tones over Figaro's punctuating
counterpoint in the bass register.

Thus the duet is no longer a throwaway (in the theatrical sense)
amid a pattern of arias, but an entity with an identity of its own. It
has—by use of several varying tempo designations—been enlarged into
the equivalent of the great solo scenas, with introductory recitative,
cavatina, accelerated coda-cabaletta. Indeed, this duet has such structural definition and musical content that it is regularly used—especially
in American opera theaters—as the finale of Act I, with Rosina's "Una
voce poca fa" beginning Act II (in Rossini's score, both are included
within Act I, with a change of scene from the outside to the inside of
Bartolo's house). The opera also includes two additional duets—one for
Rosina and Figaro, another for the Count and Bartolo.

Having demonstrated, with triumphant success, that he had the
facility to write such a duet for *opera buffa,* Rossini steadily thereafter
showed the instinct to adapt it to where it would work to advantage in
opera seria. Already he had written a duet in *Aureliano in Palmira*
(1813) which Toye describes as "beautiful in itself and interesting as
the model from which Verdi was subsequently to draw his favorite
device of expressing emotion by the repetition of a note."[5]

Now he went on to extend his command (in *Otello,* 1816) with a
duet for Emilia and Desdemona in Act I and another for Otello and
Iago in Act II. In *Armida* (1817) he allowed himself the luxury of
three love duets described by Toye as containing "some of the most
voluptuous music that he had ever composed."[6]

There are others, sequentially, one of the greatest of Rossini duets
being in *Semiramide* (1823) in which the "guilty Queen mother" who
has "fallen in love with her avenging son before she discovers his
identity" shares the stage with him. It is introduced, observes Toye,
"by some orchestral writing which seems to suggest that Rossini had
by no means forgotten his visit to Beethoven."[7] Already in being was
the first version of the work which, when finalized, contained a structure of duets that would make *L'Assedio di Corinto* (1826) a landmark
of the art.

Out of these currents, cross-currents, and conversations came a stream of energy that picked up the next wave of Italian opera and sent it surging on its way. It will not be forgotten that 1823 was the year *after* Donizetti began his promising operatic career with *La Zingara* in Naples and wrote the septet admired by Bellini. It was during the next decade that Bellini wrote his famous duets for Norma and Adalgisa, which bring together some of the most sumptuous lines of musical design ever given to a pair of women's voices. The object, however, is—as it was in Mozart's *Così fan tutte*—concord, not conflict. Soon after, Donizetti exploited the skills taught by Mayr to accomplish the sextet in *Lucia*, the greatest vocal ensemble in Italian opera to that time, and rarely excelled since.

In each of them, some line of connection to Rossini—if only spiritual —was present. A model had been created, a demonstrable way of drawing characters together established, a new point of dramatic direction in the planning of an opera defined. Sometimes, as in Donizetti's duets in *Lucia*, the treatment is one for which Donald Grout has a very good term. They are, he says, "for the most part simply *arias divided between two singers* [italics added] who unite in thirds and sixths at the close."[8] But a beginning had been made, the way cleared for a man with another bent.

3

The way that Rossini had blazed to draw characters "closer together" may have been a dead end to such great young contemporaries as Donizetti and Bellini (both were born and died during his lifetime), but he lived to see it become the highroad for another. Rossini could give thanks not only to God but to their common birthright for the emergence of an even greater Italian genius, whose greatest moments would be found in the relationships of mother and son, father and daughter, sister and brother, husband and wife—than which there are, really, none closer.

These are all clichés of the theater, commonplaces of drama, cheap coin of tear-jerkers—save when they claw at a man's vitals and impel him to expressions that give new life to each and a new understanding to all. At first but a random occurrence in the librettos to which Giuseppe Verdi put his hand (at the order of the impresarios who often dispensed subject matter along with commissions), the incidence of such relationships in his later works is too high to be coincidence.

Out of these choices—conscious or subconscious—flowed a pattern of writing that tended, more and more, to diminish the frequency of aria and increase the occurrence of ensemble. Indeed, to think of Verdi without the Verdi duet is to think of Keats without a sonnet or Shelley without a rhyming couplet. It is a tautology, a contradiction in terms, a simply cannot-be. Duet is a deep and urgent factor in the eternal appeal of all the Verdi operas with the familiar (which originally connoted the *familial*) subject matter: mother and son (*Il trovatore*); father and daughter (*Rigoletto*); further father and daughter (*Simon Baccanegra* and *Aida*); father and son (*Don Carlos*); husband and wife (*Un ballo in maschera, Otello,* and *Falstaff*).

The impulse comes to light as early as *Nabucco* and again even in such a transitional opera as *Luisa Miller*, in which the fiery presence of the real Verdi-to-come begins (as of 1849) to burn its way into the consciousness of the audience in Act III. Confronted with the fact that his peasant daughter, Luisa, has become involved with a noble in disguise whom she can never marry (shades of *Giselle!*—though this time by way of Schiller's *Kabale und Liebe*, which preceded the ballet by many years), Miller pleads with her not to commit suicide but to live, for his sake.

In a bill of particulars addressed to his librettist, Cammarano, when *Luisa Miller* was being planned, Verdi suggests: "Develop well the duet between the father and daughter, make a duet that will draw tears."[9] Cammarano did his work well, especially in pressing for attention on the word *"figlia!"* ("daughter!"). First, of course, it comes from Miller, in a desperate appeal to Luisa. Then—and this is the moment of real emotional climax—it comes from the mouth of Luisa herself as she says:

> "Ma sempre al padre accanto / la figlia sua starà"
> ("But always beside the father / will be his daughter").

And he exclaims, with passionate simultaneity (*as can only be done in music*)

> "Quel padre e quella figlia / Iddio benedirà, benedirà!"
> ("That father and that daughter / God will bless, will bless!").

It is elementary in any form of theater that to achieve an effect with an audience, the emotion must first be felt by the creator of it. Verdi's response to the heartrending "Figlia!" entrusted to Miller bears tears in the sound of it; by the time it has been repeated half a dozen times in the long scene, on the way to the climax quoted above, Verdi's directive to Cammarano has been fulfilled beyond resistance. It opened flood gates of emotion within Verdi that reached barrier-bursting levels in his next new project, *Rigoletto* (after he finished *Stiffelio*, which was already under way). And with *Rigoletto*, Verdi's name became for the first time (in 1851) of worldwide identity.

If filial relations led to eloquent results whenever touched upon by Verdi, key words were an even more immediately provocative incitement to musical ends. "Figlia!" ("Daughter!") was one, "Madre!" and "Padre!" ("Mother!" and "Father!") two others, and "Dio!" and "Gran' Dio!" ("God!" and "Great God!") still others. As for "Patria!" ("Country!"), it is, along with "Figlia" and "Padre" a three-word synopsis of *Aida*.

These were not merely common coin of the emotional realm which Verdi cashed for profitable audience response. They were keys to unlock his own emotional reserve, which flowed over with the drenching kind of Verdian melody almost as often as he called upon it. Each had a deeply personal part in his own life, of which "figlia" strikes me as the one which was closest to his heart.

After all, it was the death of two offspring in their infancy that left him childless in his mid-twenties, and the death of their mother not long after that left him wifeless. In a biographical sketch given years later (verbally) to his publisher, Giulio Riccordi, who subsequently circulated it in published form, Verdi recalled that the first child to die was Icilio, then Virginia, then his wife, Margherita—all "in a very little over two months."[10] Verdi misremembered not only the period during which the disaster occurred (two years rather than two months), but the sequence of deaths: Virginia's preceded Icilio's.

Art, of course, is built on what is remembered, rather than the facts of what actually happened and when. Out of the storehouse of the past as he recalled it, Verdi drew the ecstasy and the tears for a subject that is "closeness" personified: the father-daughter relationship of the court jester Rigoletto and his daughter Gilda. One of the most perennially popular and least destructible operas ever written—it can be played with an orchestra of two dozen and little better than student singers and still make an effect—it would astonish some of its greatest admirers to know that it was written with a doctrinaire purpose in mind.

Verdi's intentions came to light in a letter by the composer to the husband of the soprano who was to sing Gilda at the first performance in Rome in September, 1851, several months after the premiere in Venice. It was the fond husband's fond wish that Verdi write a new aria for his wife's personal purposes. The composer replied:

> If you were convinced my talent is so limited that I can do no better than I have done in *Rigoletto*, you would not have asked for an aria for this opera. Wretched talent! you may say. I agree; but there it is. If *Rigoletto* can stand on its feet as it is, a new number would be superfluous. And where is it to be placed? Verses and notes can be written, but they would make no effect without the right time and place. . . .

After some other observations on property and propriety, Verdi let the husband of soprano Teresa Borsi in on a secret:

> But to revert to our first question, let me add that my idea was that *Rigoletto* should be one long series of duets without airs and without finales, because that is how I felt it. If any one retorts: "But one might do this or that or the other" and so on, I reply: "That may all be very well, but I did not know how to make a better job of it."[11]

Thus, thanks to Mme Borsi's importunate husband, we have an insight into Verdi's creative concept of how *Rigoletto* should be constructed, and, inferentially, of how he responded to the practicalities of the theater when he concluded that things would not—or, perhaps, could not—work out that way. There were, of course, censor problems, and one scene, at least, had to be omitted. This took out what today might be called the "specific" connotation of the Duke (originally King) as a libertine, and may have impelled Verdi to give him two character arias instead. One is the jaunty "Questa o quella" in Act I; the other, the boastful "La donna è mobile" in the tavern scene. For the soprano, he wrote the delightful, delicate, and innocently different "Caro nome," which is, in effect, a part of the finale to Act I (as it stands in the score, the separation of the first scene from the second is—as in the case of *Il Barbiere*—arbitrary and unnecessary to all in the theater except the man who has the bar concession).

Otherwise, Verdi did adhere, in large part—from the second scene on—to his concept of one long series of duets. Out of thirteen vocal "numbers" in the score, five are formally described as "Duetto." The first scene, as it stands in the finished score, does not lend itself to such a purpose: it is a mélange of fun and laughter, into which a few serious incidents intrude. Rigoletto suggests to his employer, the Duke, that he add the Countess Ceprano to his conquests by throwing the Count in jail, and he mocks Monterone for protesting the Duke's seduction of his daughter. Each has its place in the drama to follow: the offended Ceprano vows to track down the girl Rigoletto is hiding in town and Monterone responds to the jester's derisive remarks delivered from the ducal throne with a malediction "for deriding the grief of a father," which terrorizes Rigoletto.

But the second scene of the act is, indeed, what Verdi intended it to be—a long series of duets. No. 1 is the encounter of Rigoletto, on his way to his daughter's home, with Sparafucile, the *bravo* who assures him he has a "spada" (sword) for hire, should he need one, and Rigoletto promises to keep him in mind; no. 2 is the emotional visit of Rigoletto with his daughter, whom he implores not to leave the house, for there are those who would do him damage, through her; no. 3 is the amorous outpouring of the Duke (another nobleman disguised as a commoner!) who has seen her in church and hopes to see her in less public surroundings. After their "Addios!" Gilda goes off to her bedroom musing on the "Caro nome" ("Dear name") of Gualtier Maldè that the Count has given himself to cover his identity, and the vengeful Ceprano leads the raiding party to kidnap Rigoletto's "mistress" (as they believe Gilda to be). It is as father, rather than lover, that Rigoletto returns to find the house empty and the fears that drew him back all too swiftly justified.

There is nothing but drama in the second act—the Duke expressing his dismay at Gilda's disappearance (he, too, had returned to the house and found her gone) via "Parmi veder" which is half declamation, half aria; the courtiers surprising him but telling him the "body" is his; Rigoletto responding to the taunts of the kidnapers that the girl they have seized is not his mistress but his daughter; and then the incandescent outburst of grief, remorse, and finally terrible rage. This is duet no. 4, in which Gilda, ravaged and ashamed, rushes from the Duke's bedroom to her father's arms, shares his grief, and pours out her remorse for having disobeyed his instructions, and then joins him in his trumpeting call for "Vendetta, tremenda vendetta" ("Revenge, terrible revenge"). Rigoletto is bent on the Duke's destruction; Gilda is imploring him to forgive the only man she has known and the one she still loves—a prime instance of Verdi's craft in combining two conflicting emotional statements in a single span of dramatic time.

Act III pursues its relentless course as Rigoletto brings Gilda to Sparafucile's tavern in an effort to persuade her that the Duke is unworthy of her love. According to Verdi's directions, which may or may not be literally carried out by today's designers, the tavern is visible through the ruins of a two-story house, with a wall dividing one part of the stage from the other. Thus the audience can see the action at the right and at the left, though the performers cannot. To the left of the audience, Rigoletto and Gilda discuss their problem; to the right, the Duke (dressed as a cavalry officer) bent on an assignation with Maddalena (Sparafucile's sister).

The famous sequence goes its ghoulish, Hugoish way (the story was adapted from his *Le Roi s'amuse*); Gilda hears enough of the Duke's easy, amorous discourse with Maddalena to persuade her that she has been wrong about him; Rigoletto instructs her to put on the man's clothing he has prepared for her and ride to Verona where he will meet her on the following day. In her absence, Rigoletto makes his deal with Sparafucile. Rather than going to Verona, Gilda returns to the tavern and overhears Sparafucile discussing his assignment to kill the Duke with Maddalena, who has taken a liking to him. The latter persuades Sparafucile to waylay a passerby and Gilda decides to sacrifice herself for the man unworthy of her love. Duet no. 5 is the final mournful episode in which Rigoletto discovers that his thirst for vengeance has brought tragedy to himself and death to "Mia figlia! . . . Dio! mia figlia!" ("My daughter! God! My daughter!"), while she summons dying breath to console him with visions of her mother whom she will soon join in heaven.

Five duets in a single opera, relatively few arias in an instantaneous success and a lasting favorite? This achievement must be rare among Italian operas to that time; it supports wholly Verdi's judgment that his way was indeed the right way to deal with this subject matter. But there are, in fact, seven rather than five duets in *Rigoletto*. Mention has been omitted of the famous episode in Act III when Gilda still has hopes that the Duke's love for her is sincere and, with Rigoletto at her side, overhears his conversation with Maddalena. This grouping adds, by any count, to four, and it comes to musical life when the Duke begins the renowned quartet with "Bella figlia dell'amore" ("Beautiful daughter of love"), addressed to Maddalena.

Technically, the episode qualifies as a quartet; but, having shown his skill at combining two different emotional expressions in one time span at the end of Act II, it is no problem for Verdi to utilize the text of Francesco Maria Piave to write what might be called a double duet. On one side of the stage, the Duke is spinning his seductive net around Maddalena, who is not disposed to be enmeshed merely in sweet talk; on the other side, Gilda is discovering unhappy proof of her mistaken faith in "Gualtier Maldè" as her father plots a course of revenge that will take in Sparafucile.

Whether as a quartet or a double duet, this great ensemble is the fulfillment of a scheme that only such a master of melodic invention as Verdi had become at thirty-eight could make wholly convincing. In his early days as a music critic, George Bernard Shaw derided the allegation that "the quartet in *Rigoletto,* with its four people expressing different emotions simultaneously was . . . an innovation of Verdi's. Such concerted pieces were *de rigueur* in Italian opera before he was born. The earliest example that holds the stage is the quartet in *Don Giovanni* 'Non ti fidar.' "[12] This is the moment in the first act in which Elvira has interrupted the Don's plans for the seduction of Zerlina, and taken her off stage, in custody; then Donna Anna and Ottavio appear, and when Elvira returns, he undertakes to persuade them that Elvira "è pazza; non badate" ("is crazy: don't believe her"). It is, indeed, just what Shaw says it is: "a concerted piece" with Donna Anna and Don Ottavio singing mostly in thirds, Elvira carrying her own line, and Don Giovanni performing his effort at persuasion, none too convincingly.

One cannot, of course, conceive of Mozart operas without their vocal ensembles: from the opening duet of Figaro and Susanna in *Le nozze* to the later "Crudel perche finora" for Susanna and the Count, or "La ci darem la mano" for Don Giovanni and Zerlina in *Don Giovanni,* to the intertwined voices of Fiordiligi and Dorabella in *Così fan tutte* (a miracle of euphony). But they are, for the most part, vocal chamber music, which makes for heavenly music rather more than for good theater. What they lack, in my view, is precisely what Verdi accomplishes so successfully: the use of intermingled voices to create a *dramatic effect.* In *Rigoletto,* the characters are physically separated, their widely differing emotions depicted in music reflective of each, yet part of a whole, formed into a quartet.

Victor Hugo, who somewhat resented the changes that had to be made in *Le Roi s'amuse* to make it acceptable as a subject (under censorship) for an Italian opera, eventually saw the result in Paris and acknowledged its superior qualities. He was particularly taken by the quartet, of which he said: "If I could only make four characters in my play speak at the same time, and have the audience grasp the words and sentiments, I would obtain the very same effect."[13]

Verdi could, and did, employ a similar scheme in a number of later scenes, including the brilliant one in *Falstaff* where he applies the deftest of touches to blend anger and *amour* within the same musical framework. At the climax of Act II, as the Wives of Windsor and their companions search the house of Alice Ford for the miscreant Falstaff, Fenton and Nanetta, off to one side and behind a screen, exchange loving lines and kisses. Anger boils in the orchestra, but youthful love rides the storm serenely.

Certainly the *Rigoletto* quartet provided the guide lines for Puccini's treatment of another final scene, in Act III of *La Bohème*. The participants are again four—Rodolfo, Mimi, Marcello, and Musetta. But it, too, is a double duet: Rodolfo consoles Mimi in her consumptive misery as Marcello and Musetta row over their congenital inability to get along on any permanent basis—all within the same time span and in the same musical container.

4

Why did Verdi, initially, and Wagner very soon afterward, veer more and more to duets, trios, and larger ensembles and depend less and less on arias? (Wagner had it both ways—first defending *Lohengrin* to Schumann as being like other operas, later contending that he had given up that sort of thing in the *Ring*, despite the inclusion in the *Ring* of a Forging Song in *Siegfried*, a Spring Song in *Die Walküre*, and Siegfried's narrative in *Götterdämmerung*.)

The trend is closely parallel to the trend in design generally, articulated most often by Frank Lloyd Wright and his great progenitor Louis Sullivan: Form follows function. As the function of the plot in opera veered more and more from the setting out, merely, of the formalities of old events (mythological and legendary) to depicting, in all their variety, the real problems of people in whom the audience could see themselves and their own problems, so composers sought out ways of dealing with their characters that tended more and more to actuality, less and less to artificiality.

In this regard Verdi is decidedly the predecessor of Wagner, in recognizing the duet as a highly productive means to a desirable end. The duets of *Tannhäuser* and *Lohengrin* tend to have the characters singing separately *at* each other, rather than *with* each other (such obvious exceptions as the Bridal Scene in *Lohengrin* aside). Certainly what Verdi accomplished in 1851 in *Rigoletto* was more advanced, musically and psychologically, than what Wagner was doing at the same time.

But when Wagner began to broaden the functions of the texts he wrote for his own use, and began to find, in the mythology on which the *Ring* was based, parallels for many of the things that were bothering him in his own life, the musical means he chose for arriving at his dramatic ends became decidedly more subtle and sophisticated. *Das Rheingold* is an allegory setting forth (as a good prologue should) the premises on which the *Ring* dramas are projected. But *Die Walküre* is full of elements that aroused Wagner to his greatest music: individual liberty, compassion as well as passion, responsibility as well as privilege, and loyalty to a father's directive as well as a need for his love. All these deep impulses flow through a sequence of duets as structurally pervasive and at much greater length than those in *Rigoletto*.

The whole first act of *Walküre* might be called a *duet à trois* prefaced by Siegmund's appearance in Hunding's hut, the richly promising (in the emotional sense) exchanges with Sieglinde when she enters, the variations in tone but not in procedure when Hunding arrives, followed by the brief solo interlude when Siegmund is left alone and falls to wondering what the next day will bring. And then, with the reappearance of Sieglinde, the gathering, glowing sense of love between them that erupts into one of Wagner's most expansive duets and is climaxed by the discovery not only of the sword that resolves the weaponless Siegmund's dilemma, but of the family tie that makes them brother and sister as well as lovers.

The second act is again almost exclusively another sequence of duets, interrupted by the appearance of new characters required to keep the story moving. First, there is the brief exchange between Wotan and Brünnhilde, in which father gives daughter her marching orders for the day; then the appearance of Fricka, furious at the unseemly conduct of Wotan's own offspring and shaming him into withdrawing his protection from Siegmund in his forthcoming duel with that good man Hunding; the reappearance of Brünnhilde and the agonizing episode in which Wotan tells her that even a god is responsible to a higher power (in this case, Fricka and her "honor"); the arrival of Siegmund and Sieglinde; and into the great confrontation in which Siegmund declines Brünnhilde's offer of an afterlife in Valhalla if Sieglinde cannot be with him, and Brünnhilde, moved by this assertion of love, decides to defy her father's instructions and thereby alters the shape of her own life.

The third act surpasses—unbelievably—the ensemble content of its predecessors. Not all the episodes are duets; there are mechanics to be manipulated and preliminary matter to be disposed of (including the

"Ride of the Valkyrie" to their rock, the arrival of Brünnhilde and the bewildered Sieglinde, and the great duet in which she informs the distraught victim of Hunding's wrath of her destiny to bear Siegmund's son, to be known as Siegfried). When all these happenings have been resolved, there ensues the greatest drama of all: a dissertation of differences between angry father and contrite daughter that runs for nearly three quarters of an hour of overpoweringly beautiful music. I have, with some purpose, characterized "Wotan's Farewell" as one of the "arias" written by Wagner against his own protestations of not indulging in such vanities. The composer could have responded, had he wished, that this was really one more duet, of a highly sophisticated sort, between Wotan and the recumbent daughter he had just put to sleep with a kiss.

Such a sequence of stupendous music flowing from one pair of performers to another, in endless variety and eloquence, could only be surpassed by a whole *work* in which the *same* performers claim the attention of an audience from start to finish. Musically and philosophically, Wagner came as close as he wished to in *Tristan und Isolde—* surely he could have carried through the sense of the story and sustained the attention of the audience by a musical dualogue for Tristan and Isolde *alone*, had this been for Wagner (in Verdi's phrase about *Rigoletto*) "the way I felt." Even so, Act I is, with minor interruptions, Isolde's act *against* Tristan (until her intention of sharing a death potion with him is contravened by Brangaene), as Act III is Tristan's act *without* her, and Act II is, of course, their act *together*, in unquestionably the longest, most affecting love duet ever conceived. It may be noted finally, that neither Isolde nor Tristan is ever really alone on stage—much of Act I is framed as a duet between Isolde and Brangaene (her companion) as Act III is framed as a duet between Tristan and Kurvenal (his companion).

The passing mention of the *Ring* as containing parallels to "many of the things" that were disturbing Wagner "in his own life" has a bearing, also, on his development of musical means "decidedly more subtle and sophisticated" to arrive at his "dramatic ends." It is widely known that *Tristan und Isolde* was written during a time in which he was sharing a closely guarded, secret relationship with the wife of his Zurich benefactor, Otto Wesendonck. It is much less well known that the attachment between Richard Wagner and Mathilde Wesendonck took hold—in some close, if not consummated form—when Wagner was writing the first act of *Die Walküre*, at least two years earlier.

There exists, to those who have seen the manuscript now in the

Bayreuth archives, no less than sixteen inscriptions, notations, and coded designations on the manuscript of the *Walküre* which bear this out. It is clear, as Newman has noted, that Wagner "constantly saw himself and her in his Siegmund and Sieglinde." The great English biographer of the composer cites half a dozen, among them the following:

> After Siegmund's cry to Sieglinde, "Die Sonne lacht mir nun neu" ("But sunlight laughs on me now") Wagner has written "I.l.d.gr." ("Ich liebe dich grenzenlos" "I love you infinitely"). At the point where Siegmund and Sieglinde "Look into each other's eyes with the utmost emotion" we find "L.d.m. M??" ("Liebst du mich, Mathilde?")[14]

If, as Newman proposed in his insidiously rational way, Wagner wrote *Tristan und Isolde* not because he was "in love" with Mathilde, but, rather, he was in love with Mathilde *because* he was writing *Tristan* and needed to live out the emotion by which he was motivated, the logic should prevail *vis-à-vis Die Walküre*. Without regard for this ingenious argument for cause and effect, one has to agree that the two greatest examples of the operatic duet bringing performers "closer together" were related in no minor way to people whose own lives had become totally, and rather desperately, interrelated.

VIII

"Heilige Braut"
(The Manners of the Love Duet)

1

The lore of operatic creators is, in the nature of things, better documented than the lore of operatic re-creators. The operas and their creators are eternal, the re-creators ephemeral. On the other hand, for every chucklesome anecdote of what Puccini said to Caruso after he first heard him, as an unknown tenor, audition "Che gelida manina" from *La Bohème* ("Who sent you? God?"), of what Mozart replied to the royal critic who said of *Le Nozze di Figaro* that he liked it but it had too many notes ("Not one too many, Majesty"), there are ten that recall what Caruso said to John McCormack when they met in the lobby of a Boston hotel and McCormack inquired, "How is the world's greatest tenor this morning?" and Caruso replied, "Since when have you become a baritone?" or how the late Richard Tucker, when asked much the same question by an admirer, responded, "It's a great responsibility." The written documentation is less, but the verbal file is greater because for every composer of durable operas there have been ten times as many outstanding performers.

It is also demonstrable fact that many of the best revelations of the performer, as personality, have to do with duets, or two people in a situation that brings them "closer together" than they are to any others on earth save husband, wife, sweetheart, or business manager. The chemical nature of the human being is such that any such great escalation of emotion as occurs in *Rigoletto, Aida, Die Walküre,* or *Manon Lescaut* over a three- or four-hour period will necessarily induce some sense of intimacy, whether the man and woman have, otherwise, one particle of affection, or even esteem, for the other. The highest praise one singer can pay to another is not to praise voice, musicianship, or artistry—these are all tools of the trade which some have in greater abundance, some in less. It is, rather, to say that he (or she) is a "good colleague."

This accolade (and the word may come out "KOL-league" when the speaker is American or English born or "kol-LEAGUE" from a European whose language contains exactly the same word) conveys that the person in question (when male) is considerate of his collaborators; does not eat garlic before a performance; can be depended upon to show a lady the courtesy of taking her bow before he takes his; is not inclined to hold a high tone longer than has been prearranged with the conductor; will sense whether his partner is in strong voice or not and, in consequence, will not bellow a top note when she is not up to doing the same; doesn't mess with phony *amour* in a clinch, but keeps strictly to the etiquette of not nuzzling a cheek but faking the smooch; doesn't ruffle a costume by excessive pressure in an embrace, or muss a hairdo with a careless gesture—in short, behaves as sensibly as an opera singer can, if he tries.

If the performer in question is female, many of the same general strictures prevail, *vis-à-vis* eating habits, breath, vocal etiquette, and so on. But there are certain specific ones that come into play when the circumstances arise in which *two* ladies share a duet (*Norma*) or when one of them is impersonating a male (as in Strauss's *Der Rosenkavalier* or Rossini's *The Siege of Corinth*). When the two ladies are, indeed, *ladies,* the more famous performer who is also a "good colleague" doesn't pre-empt the applause for herself, but shares it graciously (or as graciously as she can) with her fellow performers. When one of them is impersonating a male, such as Octavian in *Der Rosenkavalier* or Neocle in *The Siege of Corinth*, it is both good manners and good artistry for her to stay in the frame of the action, which is to say, to give the female character the deference that would be due her from a bona fide male performer in the same circumstance. Sometimes a *faux pas* can occur in reverse circumstances, such as the occasion when a "gala" performer of *Die Fledermaus* included a series of "guests" who entertained Prince Orlofsky's gathering—and, incidentally, the audience—in Act II. All went well until a celebrated basso entered to perform his solo, and with all the deference due the lady impersonating Orlofsky—but not the male part she was playing—kissed her hand. It took some time for order (especially on stage) to be restored.

In many instances, being a "good colleague" goes against the grain, because learning to be a good opera singer is so time-consuming it is all but impossible to learn very much else. This is not a humorous put-down, but an occupational condition that must be reckoned with in a profession populated by so many talented, insecure, ill-educated people. Even the latitude afforded the public at large of hearing as wide a span of operas as their curiosity warrants is not readily available to many singers. In a season when they are performing themselves, the day's routine and the evening's requirement for early retirement—to begin the next day properly refreshed—do not lend themselves to much attendance at works in which they are not performing. At other times, the probability is that the singer is either concertizing or engaged in learning new roles for his/her own repertory.

On the other hand, being a "good colleague"—for a male in the profession—derives from acquired knowledge and from learning, by experience, that in work done at such close quarters, a soprano or mezzo must learn not only how to protect her interests in a ladylike way, but all the nasty little tricks that go into giving back better than she receives. As an instance, when Mary Garden was being victimized by an egotistical Don José who insisted on kissing her passionately on the mouth during their embraces in *Carmen*, she growled, "Do that once again and I'll bite your tongue so hard you won't sing again for a month." Whether she would, in other circumstances, accept such compliments is not the point. On stage, the blatant kiss smeared her makeup, and Garden—like many other first-class performers—was fastidious about the way she looked in character.

Another singer of whom I have knowledge told me her indoctrination in one aspect of the operatic art came about the hard way. As a very young performer, unexperienced in the perils of the profession, she made an appearance in company with the great Giovanni Martinelli. Both flattered and awed by the veteran's concern for her well-being during an embrace, she discovered—to her maidenly surprise—that she was encountering a rigid male organ poking her in the groin. As she instinctively recoiled, he squeezed her hand in a gesture of reassurance and said, "Pardona, signorina. È'naturale!" Martinelli was, indeed, a prince of good colleagues. To see him, as Rodolfo in *La Bohème* in the 1920s and '30s, offer his arm to Mimi as they prepared to leave the stage at the end of Act I, was to recognize a poet who may never have made it to the Sorbonne, but had acquired, at some higher institute of human relations, all the arts and graces of pleasing a woman.

In the instance of stealing bows or making a splash with a long-held note at the end of a duet, a tenor or baritone may discover that woman's wiles are not restricted to unwanted *amour*. On the occasion of a celebrated *Lucia di Lammermoor* in Mexico City that caused a small *scandale* in the operatic world, Maria Callas found that the sharp-pointed heel of the costume shoe she was wearing made an excellent instrument of caution when placed "accidentally" on the toe of the non-colleague who was annoying her. She was also disposing all the weight of her "heavy" period at the time. Sharp fingernails may be fairly effective also.

The love duet at the end of Act I of Puccini's *Madama Butterfly* may, on occasion, arouse a strain of fond affection that impels a tenor to carry Cio-Cio-San over the threshold of their honeymoon house. It is, however, advisable that it not be a spur-of-the-moment improvisation, but an action that is rehearsed. One such impulsive action by the young tenor Daniele Barioni ran afoul when he put his arms in the classic positions, and then discovered that the soprano's well-muscled body was more than he could lift! Reminded of this mishap recently, the Cio-Cio-San (Dorothy Kirsten, who is an excellent golfer and keeps herself in shape with many hours on the links) said, "It was the most embarrassing moment of my career."

On the whole there are more "good colleagues" than the other kind. These, incidentally, are rarely described as "bad colleagues." The negative is usually conveyed by the use of such terminology as "cretin," "porco!" ("pig!"), or "What do you expect of a tenor?" The best of the good colleagues lend gloss to the stage and class to the occupation, and they are fondly remembered long after they have left the "profession" (as it is usually described by those no longer in it).

Among recent Wagnerian tenors, the late Wolfgang Windgassen got high marks from performers who worked with him, especially from Birgit Nilsson, with whom he sang innumerable *Tristan*s, *Götterdäm-merung*s, and *Tannhäuser*s. She particularly cherished a matinée *Tristan* in Vienna on an afternoon when a championship soccer game in which they were both interested (it was Germany vs. Sweden) was being broadcast. He rushed on stage at the appropriate moment for Tristan's entrance in Act II, crying, as the audience expected him to, "Geliebte! Geliebte!" Then, as he smothered Isolde-Nilsson in his arms, he said into her ear, "Germany is beating Sveden, 2–0."

2

Perhaps this suggests the cynicism of a cynical age, of singers spoiled by jet planes, hardened to their calling, and pampered into philistinism

1a. "Preparation"; 1b. "Immolation"; 1c. "Relaxation." Taken at the "Farewell to the Old Met" gala on April 16, 1966, these pictures of Birgit Nilsson are a study in perfect posture, bodily control and vocal discipline. The Nilsson position does not alter, whether preparing to sing, performing the demanding "Immolation" scene from Wagner's *Götterdämmerung*, or responding to the applause of the audience. (*photos by E. Fred Sher*)

2. Sarah Caldwell at an early stage of her career as a conductor-producer-impresaria of the Opera Company of Boston. (*photo courtesy Opera Company of Boston*)

3. Nicolai Gedda. "El Vino" (Nicolai Gedda in Bellini's *La Sonnambula*). (*photo by Louis Melançon courtesy Metropolitan Opera*)

4a, 4b. Maria Callas as Norma in her first American appearance on November 1, 1954, with Nicola Rossi-Lemeni as Oroveso. (*photos courtesy Chicago Lyric Opera*)

5. George London listens as Wieland Wagner (right) coaches him in the role of Vanderdecken in Wagner's *Der Fliegende Holländer* at the Bayreuth Festival of 1959. (*photo courtesy Bayreuth Festival*)

6. A memento of a Metropolitan Opera performance of Bizet's *Carmen* attended by Albert Einstein. From left to right: Giovanni Martinelli (Don José), General Manager Giulio Gatti-Casazza, Maria Jeritza (Carmen), and Einstein. (*photo by Carlo Edwards*)

7a, 7b. The noted German director Carl Ebert at work during a staging of Strauss's *Ariadne auf Naxos*, with Leonie Rysanek. (*photos by Eugene Cook*)

8. The Art of Stage Direction: Five decades of Mozart's *Le Nozze di Figaro* at the Metropolitan, as Cherubino sings *Voi che sapete* in Act II. 8a. In the production of 1916, Susanna (Frieda Hempel) is at the left, with the Countess (Margarete Matzenauer) in the middle, and Cherubino (Geraldine Farrar) at the right (*photo courtesy Metropolitan Opera Guild*); 8b. In the 1939 production, Susanna (Bidú Sayao) is in the middle, with Cherubino (Risë Stevens) at the left, and the Countess (Elisabeth Rethberg) at the right (*photo courtesy New York Times Studio*).

8c. In the production of 1959, Susanna (Elisabeth Soederstroem) is at the extreme right, with Cherubino (Mildred Miller) at the left, and the Countess (Lisa della Casa) in the middle (*photo courtesy Metropolitan Opera—Louis Melançon*); 8d. In the Metropolitan National Opera Company's production of 1965, Susanna (Mary Beth Peil) has completed the cycle and is once again at the left, with the Countess (Nancy Stokes) in the middle, and Cherubino (Dorothy Krebill) at the right (*photo courtesy Martha Swope*).

9. Opera-goers enjoying an interval in the gardens of the Glyndebourne Festival grounds in Sussex, England. (*photo courtesy British Travel and Holiday Association*)

by greater demand than there is supply. I have myself wondered whether such things were common in an older time. I wondered no longer after coming across an account by Ignatz Moscheles, the great pianist, less great composer, and good friend of Beethoven, Chopin, Mendelssohn, and others, of the first performance of Beethoven's *Fidelio* in London, on May 18, 1832. It was doubly distinguished by the début in England of Schröder-Devrient and by an audience so enthusiastic that the overture, canon quartet, Prisoners' Chorus, and finale were encored. Wrote Moscheles of the happening:

> The following comic episode will perhaps be new to some of our readers:—that deeply tragic scene where Madame Schröder-Devrient (Fidelio) has to give Haizinger (Florestan) a piece of bread which she has kept hidden for three days for him in the folds of her dress, he does not respond to the offer: she in rather strong language whispers to him, with a coarse epithet: "Why don't you take it? Do you want it buttered?"[1]

Schröder-Devrient has already been identified as an exemplary artist, a singer beloved of Schumann, Liszt, Grieg, Wagner, and Weber (not to mention Beethoven himself), and a paragon of her time. She was neither flippant nor irresponsible to her "art" in addressing a tart remark to the dilatory Florestan. Indeed, as Moscheles makes note, Schröder-Devrient's brusque reminder that some physical response was required from her fellow performer was, like Windgassen's remark to Nilsson, strictly between them: "All this time," he adds, "the audience, ignorant of the by-play, was intent solely on the pathetic situation."[2]

This, indeed, is the kind of operatic anecdote I value most: down to earth, full of *Gemütlichkeit*, essentially *copèrto di terra* ("earthy"), and above all in good humor. Such a swift interjection has the ring of authenticity, like the account of Mary Garden, slithering over to the cistern in Strauss's *Salome* and saying to the Jokanaan of the evening, the much-loved Marcel Journet, whom she had not seen previously that day, "Bon jour, Papa." This has its counterpart in a variety of forms, including the mute. One, involving the legendary tenor and formidable practical joker Leo Slezak, concerns another performance of *Salome* in which the Jokanaan was a bass-baritone celebrated to the Vienna opera personnel as a hypochondriac, one who often complained of ear pains and stuffed the aching area with cotton. When the severed head of the Baptist was delivered to the Salome of the evening, it was complete in every physiological detail—including, carefully placed there by Slezak's contrivance, a cotton plug in each ear.

This was, clearly, not the improvisation of a moment, but the outcome of careful, loving planning, in which there had to be complicity and consent by the prop man. And Slezak had to know his Salome well enough to be sure that the joke would not backfire—*à la* Barioni in *Madama Butterfly*—and leave her laughing, compulsively, unable to sing.

It was doubtless his conviction that, however unexpected, the reaction would be momentary and the performer's instinct to perform in any and all circumstances would take precedence over all else. Opera singers are so alert to the possibility of the unexpected being expectable that adrenalin is in strong supply and ever ready for emergencies. Such a readiness came to the rescue some years ago at a performance of *Die Walküre* at which I was present. All ears were alert and eyes concentrated on center stage for Frida Leider to begin her appeal to Wotan for fatherly consideration. After a momentary indecision, those closest to the situation detected that the initial "War es so schmählich?" ("Was it so shameful?") came, not from the center, but from the side, and so it continued for the next six or eight measures. Leider, it was later learned, suffered a momentary blockage of the throat and was unable to sing. The capable, thoroughly experienced Dorothée Manski (one of the evening's Walkürin, who should not even have been standing in the wings, because her evening's work was done) sensed immediately what had happened, and instinctively picked up the words Leider was unable to sing.

The most remarkable part of the episode is that Wagner has written these measures for the soprano to sing *a cappella*—which is to say, without accompaniment. Manski had to make her own entrance, unsupported by the orchestra, and sustain the all-important measures to an audience to whom nothing else was audible. Leider thus had a few moments in which to clear her throat, and begin to sing again—as I recall it—when the orchestra was once more playing, and could support her.

Stage mishaps are by no means infrequent in *Siegfried*, especially where the trip mechanism holding the anvil together until Siegfried delivers a shattering blow with the sword he has just "forged" fails to give away and the anvil remains in one piece. Some Siegfrieds I have seen strike it again, but a better solution was provided by one who gave it a contemptuous kick, causing it to fall apart. It was only recently, in a performance of *Die Walküre* in which Jon Vickers as Siegmund appeared for the first time with Birgit Nilsson as Sieglinde, that another sort of contretemps intruded into the stormy climax to

Act I, when the plastic handle of the sword Siegmund draws from the tree parted company with its blade. Under the whipping motion Vickers had imparted to his wrist, the blade shot through the air toward the footlights and skidded along the floor.

Disgust was clearly written on Vicker's features when he was left, not with Nothung to wave triumphantly in the air, but with nothing in his hand except a plastic fragment. Hardly an instant elapsed—a few measures of music, perhaps—until the triumph (minus prop) flared up in his voice on "Als Brautgabe bringt er dies Schwert" ("As bridal gift he brings this sword") as he prepared to dash off with Sieglinde.

As for Nilsson, how did she treat this intrusion into a duet whose climax had been built on the strength of some of the greatest singing it had had in years? My attention shifted to her the moment the blade took off from Vickers' hand, and the light glinted on its steel-tinted plastic surface. Would she kick it away? Pick it up and pretend it was part of the action? Fall to her knees and somehow cradle the object to her, in order to carry it off as the act ended?

She did none of the negative things, only the positive—by remaining exactly in the duet's ongoing mood, ever-rising emotional tide, and cresting musical wave. She had, it seemed, the iron will to respond with a quick, instinctive, reflex *inaction*, as appropriate to these circumstances as Manski's reflex *action* had been to hers. Nilsson's determination put in preeminent position the first law of survival in meeting a stage emergency: "Don't try to retrieve the irretrievable." If damage has been done, chances are that half the audience may have been looking elsewhere or at the conductor or at another character; that half of the half who saw what happened might have thought it was a "new" detail of staging and the rest would have been too sophisticated to care.

But bending down to pick up the pieces, or deviating in any way from her set posture, would only have alerted those who didn't know that something out of the ordinary had occurred. (In the aftermath of the occurrence, it developed that Nilsson's "iron will" took in more than control of a stage situation. She was acutely aware that if she hadn't moved, impulsively, *upstage* a moment before, she would have been directly in the path of the flying object, and it could have struck her body.)

Sometimes one kind of theatrical instinct can challenge another; then it is good to have a stagewise partner at hand to control major action at the risk of a minor inconvenience. I have in mind a performance of *Der Rosenkavalier* in whose closing moments of Act III, Risë Stevens (Octavian) and Hilde Gueden (Sophie) were about to leave the stage. The action calls for Sophie to drop her handkerchief to the floor, where it will be retrieved a few moments later by the Marschallin's servant. As they were singing their final phrases, Stevens noticed that Gueden was edging toward the place on the floor where the handkerchief lay—slightly away from the designated spot—to push it with her foot or perhaps even pick it up and drop it again.

Here was an instance in which the manners of the love duet called for an assertion of male prerogative. The two conflicting considerations were, on Gueden's side, a concern that the servant might not spot the handkerchief in the unexpected place, and the curtain action be spoiled, and on Stevens' side, a sharp awareness that the real need was to protect the immediate situation, and let the hypothetic problem-to-come resolve itself. She took masculine command by whispering *urgently* to Gueden, "Pick it up and I'll slap you." The duet ended happily, and, of course, so did the performance.

3

If there is an immoral to all these slips that pass in the night, it is this: to the performers, opera is far from the beglamoured, star-studded occupation it may appear to a member of the audience. It is work, hard and difficult work, with a lot of chancy possibilities that things may go wrong. Who remembers Lotte Lehmann's first Tosca at the Metropolitan? I remember it not because it was such a great performance of *Tosca*, but because, in the hurly-burly of Cavaradossi's efforts to evade Scarpia's henchmen, the wig of the tenor (Martinelli) was dislodged. Here were two people of world repute—Lehmann in a frenzy of concern for her lover, Martinelli in a desperate effort to protect his dignity as a performer—victimized by circumstances they had both been through a hundred times before.

The so-called glamour of the occupation was revealed to me for what it is on another *Rosenkavalier* occasion when Elisabeth Schwarzkopf performed her superb Marschallin in New York for the first time. The performance was embellished by the participation of Sandor Kónya, as the Italian tenor in Act I. He sang the aria "Di rigori armato" uncommonly well, and I noticed, when he walked to the Marschallin's dressing table—as the action requires—and bent to kiss her hand, Schwarzkopf said a few words to him.

As he had no further function in the opera, Kónya had shed his costume and donned his street clothes and was standing in the lobby of the old Met when the first act ended. The man with whom he was talking was a mutual acquaintance. I walked over, was introduced, and (knowing Kónya spoke fluent English) I asked—half-expecting to hear some dazzling compliment on his artistry in the Italian aria—"What did Schwarzkopf say to you when you walked over to her?" Kónya laughed and answered, "She said: 'My throat is dry.' "

These are among the humors and mysteries that make one side of the footlights off limits to the other—the inside aspect of the set of circumstances which may prompt a Tristan to hold an Isolde in his arms longer than is ordinarily observed, not because he is overcome with emotion, but because she has whispered, "My zip is undone," and he is fumbling with the back of her gown in order to correct the condition. Nor was it romantic ardor or insensate lust that drove Lawrence Tibbett to a particularly vigorous pursuit of Ljuba Welitch when he performed Scarpia to her Tosca. Mme Welitch (fondly known to her fans and colleagues as "the hellcat") was throwing chairs at his feet as they pursued their (unrehearsed) way through the action late in Act II, and Tibbett finally caught up with her to say, "Madam, I am not a stagehand!"

For that matter, it could have been the same lack of rehearsal which cost Fritz Reiner, a great perfectionist of the baton, a moment of indignation during a performance of *Die Meistersinger* in which Ferdinand Frantz, a Hans Sachs new to him, was about to sing the "Fliedermonolog." He gave him a broad warning of what was to impend, only to discover that the Sachs had picked that moment to bend over with his back to the audience, and the cue was aimed directly at the singer's ample rump.

I have termed this chapter "Heilige Braut" because the phrase pertains to one of the greatest moments in Wagner, in which the stricken Siegfried remembers his discovery of the sleeping Brünnhilde. It comes in Act III of *Götterdämmerung* after the hero has been stabbed in the back by Hagen, but summons superhuman strength to remember the events of his past that had been obscured by the forgetfulness potion he had drunk in the hall of the Gibichungs. It is perhaps the most beautiful, satisfactory, and well-mannered of duets, because Siegfried sings of his love for Brünnhilde, but not to her.

Beautiful, yes, but so atypical. Of all the stories of this high-flown, glamorous collaboration of two artists pouring out their love for each other, the one I cherish as most typical is also the briefest. It concerns the moment when the soprano went through all the intricacies of a Verdi duet, then turned to the tenor and nodded. Quoth she: "Okay, Baum. Now it's your turn."

IX

Finale Ultimo

1

Contemporary opera-goers are so accustomed to the idea of a finale being final that they may be surprised to discover that there is also such a thing as a Finale Ultimo. The existence of such a compositional structure may be confirmed by a glance at the table of contents of a work first performed in Paris as early in the nineteenth century as Rossini's *Le Siège de Corinthe* (October 9, 1826) or as late as Meyerbeer's *L'Africaine.* In the tradition of a time when a *grand opéra* was a five-act affair, it may be that composers ran out of patience with such terms as *finale primo, finale seccondo,* and so on. The term endures and may be found (perhaps by some editorial accident) in the scores of such great works of the American musical theater as Jerome Kern's *The Cat and the Fiddle* and *Roberta;* Richard Rodgers' *Carousel, South Pacific,* and *The King and I;* and Lerner and Loewe's *Paint Your Wagon.* All end with a segment designated finale ultimo.

Whether or not the words are present and visible, they may be discerned—were one a mind reader—graven in the consciousness of every true opera composer. The finale ultimo is not merely the finale of an act, which is to say, of a category; it is the categorical end to the thing as a whole. For such careful plotters and conscientious collaborators as da Ponte and Mozart, Boito and Verdi, Hofmannsthal and Strauss, Wagner the librettist and Wagner the composer, this last finale was the putting in place of a capstone to the whole carefully elaborated structure, the dotting of *i*'s and the crossing of *t*'s which brought, in their opinion, a suitable resolution to all that has preceded.

In this respect it could be described as a counterpart to the overture, which serves as an introduction to all that is to follow.

One historic confusion should be clarified at once. It is common belief that, with certain notable exceptions, all operas have unhappy endings. The natural consequence of such endings is operatic agony, in which mortally wounded tenors prop themselves up to an elbow to intone a lengthy farewell to the world, sopranos about to expire of strangulation or poisoning find the breath to sing a duet, and mezzos—the rare ones who have not been disposed of prior to an opera's last scene—still possess (in the manner of Azucena in *Il trovatore*) enough energy to declaim their triumph, even if it is, in Azucena's case: "Sei vendicata, o madre!" ("Thou art avenged, O mother!").

To be sure, a concentrated quantity of some of the most popular operas do have such unhappy endings. But, considering that opera will attain its four hundredth anniversary of Monteverdi's *Orfeo* in 2007, this gravitation to the tragic end could be described as relatively recent. For a good part of the nearly four hundred years in which it has existed, opera was afflicted with a contrary malaise known as the *lieto fine*.[1] This provides a remote but living link to the art form known today as the *opera sapone*, or "soap opera." Put into the vernacular, the *lieto fine* would be the "happy ending," for which there are such other contemporary equivalents as the "up-beat" ending, the ending "on a note of hope," or as Norman Corwin, the founding father of television aesthetics called it, "On a Note of Triumph."

Contrary to all reason, for example, Euridice did not expire, in the Calzabigi-Gluck treatment of 1762, when Orfeo violated his pledge not to look back at her until they were safely out of the underworld. The gods loved him for his love of her and arranged a second miracle. Despite all their difficulties in *The Magic Flute*, Pamina and Tamino are united at the end, as are the original partners in *Così fan tutte* (the males "forgive" the females for being human enough to succumb to the deception foisted upon them, thus carrying illogicality to divinely absurd heights).

Even da Ponte's *Don Giovanni* has a *lieto fine*, in the sense that the audience is quite content to have the Don dragged down to hell after three hours of indulging appetites for drinking, feasting, and roistering which they might envy but could not possibly emulate. Lest this implication be left unclarified, the opera is not yet at an end. The *lieto fine* comes in the *Scena ultima* (as it is described in the score) in which the six remaining characters gather before the curtain to remind the audience that "in this life scoundrels / Always receive their just deserts," and Mozart demonstrates that he retains enough creative energy, after all that has preceded, to write a dazzling (double) vocal fugue for Donna Anna and Don Ottavio, Donna Elvira, Leporello, Masetto and Zerlina.

The turn toward what is now considered by some to be the unvarying unhappy operatic ending came in the early decades of the nineteenth century. Along with the intrusion of *la pazzia*, they brought with them the blend of realism and fantasy called romanticism. This tying-together of realism and romanticism may seem to some more farfetched than most fantasies. But romanticism made much of the fragility of life, which can be terminated under the compulsion of a strong enough passion. Thus the two ideas are intimately interrelated.

To describe the nineteenth as the century which began with romanticism and ended with verismo is to identify it as the operatic century sans peer. Each of the categories deals, in its own way, moodily or violently, with the narrow line separating life from death. As all humans cherish life, the ones who give it up under the stress of a compelling impulse are making the greatest, most expensive decision of which man is capable.

History remembers Cleopatra better than her predecessors because she loved Antony more than life itself and invited an asp to provide the solace he no longer could. Many biblical heroes performed deeds of valor that gave them and theirs the rewards of a full, happy life. Few are more revered than the blinded Samson, led by a child, who found the strength to push apart the pillars in the temple of Dagon and to accept death as the cost of destroying the enemies of his people.

This is, perhaps, the epitome of the finale ultimo: an ending which is certainly not happy, but also not unhappy. It is a curious intermingling of the one and the other, a shimmering concatenation of a cymbal struck lightly in the midst of an arpeggio on the celesta, with a low tone in the double bass, pizzicato, as the final vibration.

We are, for the while, converted into something nobler than ourselves when we share the tragic grandeur of Brünnhilde's Immolation in Wagner's *Götterdämmerung* or the mad ecstasy of Elektra's finally fatal death or the response of Aeneas to the call of duty which takes him from Carthage to Italy in Berlioz' *Les Troyens*. Approximately seven decades separate Gluck's *Orfeo ed Euridice* from Bellini's *Norma*, but the ideological gulf could not be wider were the distance seventeen. Both the hero and the heroine—Orfeo and Norma—enter into a pledge

freely taken and with a sure understanding of the punishment that
awaits one who violates its terms. Each breaks the vow. The gods
forgive Orfeo for human error, but Norma faces her failure courage-
ously and pays for it with her life.

Der Rosenkavalier is, by its creators' designation, a *Komödie für
Musik*. If it were a comedy and nothing more, it would lack a half,
at least, of what makes the work endure. Had Hofmannsthal's text
identified the Marschallin's participation in the plot to expose the
lechery of Baron Ochs as a means of preserving Octavian for herself,
Der Rosenkavalier would be just another lively farce set to lively music.
It is Hofmannsthal's projection of the Marschallin as a woman who has
come to recognize that her young lover's life now belongs to a girl
of his own age (Sophie) that prompts Strauss to transcend the music
he had previously written in this score and draw the audience to a
pitch of total participation in the work's emotional climax. Together
the creators have made the Marschallin an object not only of love but
of admiration. She has demonstrated the ability to make the kind of
self-sacrifice any of us might be called upon to perform but would be
likely, for selfish reasons, to reject.

But, as with da Ponte and *Don Giovanni*, the play is not yet ended.
It is the grace of Hofmannsthal and Strauss to finalize the finale in a
way that makes it, however high-minded, congruent with all that has
preceded. The Marschallin has gone out to her carriage, the young
lovers have sung their endearing duet in clinging, Mozartean thirds and
sixths, and the stage is empty. Somehow, the curtain persists in not
coming down. It is trapped, immobilized, suspended, as though reluctant to end that magical moment.

Then the reason becomes apparent. Mohammet, the attentive Moor
who had interrupted the amorous communion of Octavian and the
Marschallin in Act I to deliver his mistress's morning pot of chocolate,
reappears, candle in hand. He dances about, clearly in search—of what?
It is Sophie's handkerchief, which had dropped from her hand during
her last embrace with Octavian. The servant finds the tiny object on
the floor, flourishes it aloft, and bears it off in triumph. Through all
this episode, Strauss, like a master draftsman expunging one image to
replace it with another, has light, deftly, restored the mood to gaiety
and sparkle by paralleling each movement of Mohammet with a pattern
of sound, a chatter of woodwinds, a dash of percussion and a sprinkle
of strings as swift as the *now*-falling curtain.

Such a concept of balance and contrast was so new to America when the work was first performed at the Metropolitan in 1913, that the closing conceit was judged to have "ended badly" what had not been welcome from the beginning. Even though Octavian was not allowed—for reasons of prudery—in that first performance and many that followed, to share the bed with the Marschallin as the curtain rose, the first words they exchanged were all too indicative of what had preceded. The involvement of the fat, vulgar Baron Ochs and the female-as-male masquerading as a male-as-female servant fed an irritation that was carried over, by some members of the press, to the very end of the work.

"A lamentable piece of bungling" one termed it; "after the story is completed they . . . maunder on nearly ten more minutes and finish with a ridiculous piece of pantomime, evidently, for the sake of doing something unexpected. . . ." For another New York critic, however, the third act included some of Strauss's "most successful passages," and he described the pantomime at the end as "a quaint touch." The passage of time and hundreds of performances have only enhanced the visual and audible resonances of this deft, delightful scene.

That it is Mohammet who retrieves the handkerchief tells us many things left unsaid: the Marschallin has made peace with herself, welcomed the young lovers to her carriage as guests, and, with the greatest civility, has dispatched her own servant to pick up the lost handkerchief and so to speed them all on their way back to Vienna—in a total of twenty-one measures! How much more can be said, without using a word, than is conveyed in this consummate example of the capstone securely in place, if rakishly tilted in a way becoming to the subject matter?

2

The moments of comparable perfection are hardly legion, but the contenders for excellence in the treatment of opera's second hardest problem (next to "How to Begin") are as various as they are numerous. Much depends, of course, on the composer's own temperament and taste. For some, the preferable scheme of design may be all structure and no capstone.

Outstanding among them, without question, is Giacomo Puccini, whose closing episodes are seldom more than the termination of what has preceded, rarely its culmination or summation. He is generally admired as "a man of the theater" (a vague term of praise that implies,

I suppose, that others are "men of the studio"). In Puccini's case, the description might relate to subject matter and how he came to choose it, rather than to what he did to make it something other than what it was when he found it.

In the case of *Madam Butterfly* it is well known that Puccini set his heart on making an opera from David Belasco's play after absorbing its content wholly by eye from a London production (1900) of which he understood scarcely a word. It is less well known that he had been led to *Tosca* in much the same way, by seeing Sardou's *La Tosca* performed in French by Sarah Bernhardt in Florence in 1895.[2]

In both instances (as with Belasco's *The Girl of the Golden West*, which he saw in New York in 1907 and made into *La Fanciulla del West*) Puccini was impressed with his ability to understand the story without knowing either English or French. Perhaps he reasoned that if the action was intelligible to him despite his language limitations, it would, if converted into an Italian opera with his kind of music, be no less intelligible to a non-Italian-speaking viewer-listener.

What resulted from Puccini's choice of subject matter by such trial and error was at least two of the most successful operas ever written (*La Bohème*, their equally successful predecessor, was derived from a novel by Henri Murger, which also had a history as a play). Both *Butterfly* and *Tosca* are, essentially, operas of situation rather than character. They lend themselves to the kind of incisive, lucid, and appealing music that is Puccini at his best, and they just as certainly narrowed his task to what involved the listener in the action of the drama rather than what motivated the characters to their course of action.

The curious contradiction is, that in addition to creating three of the most successful operas ever written, Puccini settled for seven (when *Manon Lescaut*, *La Fanciulla del West*, *La Rondine*, and *Turandot* are included) of the weakest, least subtle, most obvious dramatic endings ever espoused by a major opera composer. The fourth act of *Manon Lescaut* is, aside from the principal character's despairing "Sola, perduta, abbandonata," all but dispensable. It plays on what the text describes as "a vast plain on the borders of New Orleans," for reasons adequately described in Abbé Prévost's story, but not in the Praga-Oliva-Illica libretto. Was an amplification of content more than Puccini's impetuosity tempted him to reckon with at this point? Perhaps. Massenet's *Manon* has her dying on the road to Le Havre, thus eliminating the American episode altogether.

As a group, a substantial majority of Puccini's operas have what might be called a *mezzo-lieto fine*—a half-happy ending. In addition to *Manon,* the heroines of his Big Three (*Madama Butterfly, Tosca,* and *La Bohème*) all die in the end. The "half-happy ending" is descriptive of the circumstances that, in each case, it is predictable. Mimì expires of the tuberculosis with which she has been suffering from the first time we met her; Butterfly, by hara-kiri with a dagger that we have seen among her possessions in Act I; and Tosca, by a leap from the parapet of the Castel Sant' Angelo that is altogether in keeping with her theatrical nature.

The perceptive Mosco Carner (whose biography is by far the best work on Puccini and his creations) says of the last-mentioned finale: "Tosca's realization of her deception by Scarpia would, one imagines, have inspired Verdi to one of his greatest monologues—Puccini, regrettably, dispatches this scene with more 'situation' music and in a rather perfunctory manner, for that matter."[3] Clearly, for Puccini the matter that had fed his mind and nourished his appetite in *Tosca* had been consumed, digested, and absorbed as the climax approached. To say that he had lost interest in the subject would be incorrect. It was, simply, an expression of a trait in Puccini as a creator that endeared him to countless admirers. Sir Thomas Beecham found it summed up in an opinion he gathered in his wide travels. When he asked what it was about Puccini they liked, the answer—whether from cab drivers, hotel attendants, or head waiters—was: "He doesn't keep us waiting. He gets on with it."

The matter of structure and capstone has a curiously applicable part in the belated success of *Turandot.* Outside of Italy, this opera has only within the last decade and a half attained and retained the rate of repetition associated with the best of its predecessors. The reasons for its renewed popularity are double: the demonstration by Birgit Nilsson that Turandot's music held sumptuous appeal when performed by an instrument as splendid as hers (Maria Callas ventured it in the fifties and sang it all over Italy "hoping to God that I wouldn't wreck my voice . . . it's a rather nasty part, and it keeps on singing in a nervous way")[4] and the resolution of the third act's finale ultimo problem.

For years the terrors of the high range of the music by Puccini for the Princess Turandot put it in the category of inhumane and unattainable, save for such an exceptional soprano as Eva Turner, who made her fame with the role, beginning in 1929 or Maria Nemeth, who served the theaters of Central Europe well between 1926–1940. Thirty years later, Nilsson demonstrated that the part was neither inhuman nor unattainable for a singer who also performed the ordinary repertory (if in an extraordinary way). Now it is performed by singers who perform the ordinary repertory (in an ordinary way). In this way it has been brought within the perimeter of repertory works (even for a company on the scale of the New York City Opera) with a frequency of repetition to match.

The resolution of the finale ultimo problem in *Turandot* came about in quite a different way, because of circumstances different than those which prevailed in Puccini's other operas. Because Puccini succumbed, during an operation of throat cancer in 1924, before finishing the last scene, *Turandot* was presented at its premiere in La Scala on April 25, 1925, as an incomplete work. At a point after the death of Liù, conductor Arturo Toscanini lay down his baton, turned to the audience and said, "Here, at this point, Giacomo Puccini broke off his work."[5] On the next evening, the opera was performed in full, with an ending derived by Franco Alfano (1876–1954) from Puccini's sketches.

Following the first flurry of interest in America, *Turandot* had a double burden of disfavor to bear: it was, in part, unsingable, and it had been left "unfinished." Giulio Gatti-Casazza, under whose general managership of the Metropolitan *Turandot* was introduced to America in 1926, contributed his share to that burden when he wrote, after his retirement from the Metropolitan Opera in 1935: "*Turandot* was a brilliant success for two seasons: the public was particularly curious to see this work after Puccini's death. The performance and the mise-en-scène were very successful, but unfortunately, the opera was not finished—Puccini had not the time. He was a capable and self-critical man and would undoubtedly have smoothed out the rough spots in the opera, which cries out for a final revision. I find the first act not of great dramatic interest and the last act mediocre. But the second is effective."[6]

If these deficiencies were, indeed, present in the work when Puccini died, what has brought about their resolution? The usual frustrating, but readily available remedy: time. Measured against such predecessors as *La Bohème, Butterfly,* and *Tosca, Turandot* may lag here, sag there. But its aims are so much higher in dramatic concept, chorus, and orchestral writing, and Puccini achieved so substantial a quantity of them, that we now take the opera for what it is, and on the same basis as we cherish friends—not because they are perfect, but because we have learned to love them, and to live with their shortcomings.

Turandot is not quite the old Puccini, absorbed with situations and largely indifferent to character (even to the extent that one can pick up a radio broadcast of a Puccini recording and take a moment to decide: Is it *Bohème?* Is it *Butterfly?* or perhaps the later part of *Manon Lescaut?*) Here is the same man, striving to be a different, if not a new, Puccini, and to a large extent succeeding.

The lady who describes herself as "Gèlo che ti dà foco" ("the ice that gives you fire"), in the last of the three riddles the Unknown Prince Calaf is required to solve to win Turandot or lose his life, is certainly one of Puccini's most absorbing female characters. But it is Liù who is more completely realized. She begins, humbly, as the slave girl weeping for the Prince's decision to risk his life by challenging the riddles. She ends, nobly, with her life-sacrificing lesson to Turandot —to learn what love is, and to honor the pledge she made to marry the man who solved the riddles (as the Unknown Prince Calaf has). Puccini's capacity, in the last work of his life, to deal even-handedly with the unfathomable impulse of the one woman and the wholly human motivation of the other proclaims a man finding within himself depths he had never before reached.

As for the heights he might have scaled in the finale, the musical structure has been so soundly built, so surely supported by the hidden resource Puccini built into his best scores that, in the end, it can stand squarely in place without the finalizing touches he doubtless would have provided. Among those "hidden resources" was a poker player's skill in holding, in reserve, a melodic ace or an emotion-laden queen to put into play at an appropriate time late in the action.

Sometimes, as in *Manon Lescaut* and *Tosca*, the new element is an aria that provides the surge of life required to carry the action to the final curtain. Sometimes, more subtly, it is a new motive or emotional outcry which screws tighter the cap on the vessel containing the explosive dramatic charge. In *La Bohème* the carefully husbanded resource comes late in Act III (page 206 of the score) as Rodolfo describes to Marcello, in the most heartfelt strain of the whole opera and one which has not been heard before, Mimi's "uno terribile tosse" ("a devastating cough"). That Mimi overhears the conversation and realizes that her death sentence is being pronounced, only adds, of course, to the grip the music imposes on the situation. In *Butterfly*, the infusion of new musical life is held even longer in reserve—it comes on page 231 of a score which ends on page 266, when the long-absent Pinkerton returns to the house he has shared with Butterfly, against a new melodic strain almost accusatory in its poignance. The phrase is eventually sung by Sharpless (page 236) to the words "Io so che alle sue pene non ci sono conforti" ("I know that for such misfortune there is no consolation"). It thus becomes the tugging thread of emotion from which Puccini weaves the fine ensemble in which Sharpless is joined by Pinkerton and Butterfly's favorite companion, Suzuki.

In *Turandot*, Puccini secretes his trump-to-come in the orchestra at the end of Act II when Calaf makes his generous counter-offer to Turandot: since she has failed to accept him in marriage even though he has solved *her* riddles, he will offer one to her in exchange. Should she be able to answer correctly what his name is, he will release her from any obligation. The motive becomes a prime element in Calaf's stirring "Nessun dorma!" ("No one sleeps"), Puccini's last aria for tenor and one of his greatest, in Act III. In its rising sequences capped by the words "Tramontate, stelle! All'alba vincerò! Vincerò! Vincerò!" ("Set, you stars! At dawn I shall win! I shall win! I shall win!") lies the last resource guarded so carefully by the composer.

The vacillations of the Princess as the third act proceeds might have been resolved more adroitly, with a creator's second thought, than they were by Alfano, with an editor's first and final option. But when Turandot has finally responded to the Calaf's generous identification of *himself* by saying that her name for him is "Love," it is just in these sequences from "Nessun dorma!"—now sung to the words "O Sole! Vita! Eternità! Luce del mondo è amore! Ride e canta nel Sole / l'infinita nostra felicità! Gloria a te! Gloria a te! Gloria!" ("O sun! Life! Eternity! Light of this world and love! We rejoice and celebrate with song in the sunshine our great happiness! Glory to thee! Glory! Glory!")—that Puccini builds for Turandot's overjoyed subjects a triumphal hymn of rejoicing as the curtain falls. If this was, in every way, Puccini's Finale Ultimo, it was one whose capstone was almost dwarfed by the structure which supported it, but was nevertheless a part of it.

3

Such an outcome is, of course, much more surely arrived at if planned dramatically *and* musically from the outset, rather than being left to chance or happy accident ("inspiration"). Wagner personified the best of all possible procedures by—as noted—collaborating with himself in a total way. In writing his texts, he frequently jotted down musical ideas as they occurred to him, and left areas for sizable symphonic interludes (as in *Götterdämmerung* and *Parsifal*), thus weaving a cohesive texture throughout. Verdi followed exactly the opposite course for much of his career, taking subject matter that was offered to him. Gradually he asserted his own right of consent to the subject matter and close supervision of the textual content. Eventually, of course— though he was by then seventy—he found, in Boito, a dramatist who was almost as much an alter ego to Verdi as Wagner the litterateur was to Wagner the musician.

In Wagner the sense of climax was so well developed that there is scarcely a work of his maturity that one can leave before the end and not miss some of its finest music. Each of the *Ring* dramas is so plotted that the finale surpasses almost everything that has preceded: the "Entrance of the Gods into Valhalla" (in *Das Rheingold*); the end of *Walküre* to which reference has already been made; the duet of Brünnhilde and Siegfried at the climax of *Siegfried*, and the whole last *half act* of *Götterdämmerung* beginning with Siegfried's "Mime heiss ein mürrischer Zwerg" and going through to the "Funeral March"; the "Immolation Scene" and the final return of the Ring to the Rhine.

Verdi's sense of summarizing tension increased steadily as he took a larger hand in the selection of materials to work with, as may be read in the shaping of *Aida* to a superb summation in the Tomb Scene and the choice of *Otello* with its double tragedy at the end. Verdi also expressed an interest, after completing *Otello*, in Sardou's *La Tosca*, before the play became the property of Puccini. Two things deterred him. He considered himself "too old"—at eighty-one—to undertake a major new project, and he would require that Sardou allow him to change the last act. Carner relates that Gino Monaldi (author of a Puccini biography) discussed with Verdi his thoughts about the third of *Tosca* and characterized them as "most beautiful." "Unfortunately," writes Carner, "Monaldi . . . omitted to record them in his book."[7] The clear fact is, however, that what Puccini found satisfactory, Verdi did not.

There was, of course, an even later project that Verdi did attack eagerly, though by the time he began writing *Falstaff* he was approaching eighty. But the mood and the circumstances were different. Here, finally, was the *comédie humaine* for which he had been yearning all his life. He would amuse himself with it. If the results were to his satisfaction, fine. If not, he was under no obligation to anyone but himself. He could throw the manuscript into the fire and let it go at that.

From the start, the collaboration with Boito proceeded splendidly. As has been mentioned, Verdi found the sense of it all so irresistible that he dashed off a finale before all else. But his sharpening sense of climax found one phase of the libretto unsatisfactory, and described it so to his collaborator. The third act (in which Falstaff is lured into a forest by a new promise of an assignation and is subject to new indignities) Verdi complained, was "chilly."

Boito responded: "No doubt about it—the third act is rather chilly: a pity. Unfortunately that is the law of the comic theater: in tragedy it is the opposite that happens. Getting closer to the final catastrophe (either foreseen as in *Otello* or unforeseen as in *Hamlet*) the interest grows enormously as the end is terrible. Hence the final acts of tragedies are the most beautiful. In comedy all that happens is that the knot will be untied, and the interest wanes, as the end is happy." After instancing examples to this point in works of Shakespeare, Molière, and Beaumarchais, Boito adds: "In comedy a point is reached when the audience says: 'It is over': but on the stage all is not yet over."[8]

One of Italy's leading Wagnerites in his youth, Boito perhaps forgot—or did not consider it apposite to mention—one exception to his maxim "The knot is untied in comedy: it is broken or cut in tragedy." This is *Die Meistersinger*, a comedy so abundant in its content and fecund in its musical invention that it is not merely the longest of operatic comedies but one of the longest of all operas. Late in Act III when—in Boito's analogy—the knot is about to be untied, Wagner finds a way of giving the drama another twist and so sustaining interest for still another musically magical moment.

I have said that Wagner's sense of climax "developed" to the sharpness it attained in the *Ring* and in *Tristan und Isolde*. A specific example of that development may be cited in this third act of *Die Meistersinger*. Like a number of other projects, *Die Meistersinger* was sketched in his thirties, but not fulfilled by Wagner until he had passed fifty. In a book devoted exclusively to the conception, birth, and growth of *Die Meistersinger*'s content (*Wagner and Die Meistersinger*, Oxford University Press, 1940) Robert M. Rayner provides an insight into certain crucial differences between the early version and the one with which we are familiar.

The changes pertain in large part to the character of Hans Sachs, whom Wagner first sketched as a rather rough-mannered, ironic man, and later defined as a still somewhat gruff but far more mellow, and understanding, philosopher. Thus, in the moment of climax in the comedy when Walther has won his bride but angrily rejects the laurel wreath making him a fellow to the guildsmen who had turned him down for membership in Act I, the new Sachs does not rebuke him "half in earnest, half ironically" as Wagner had earlier written. Now the older man admonishes the younger one seriously but with warmth and compassion—"taking him strongly by the hand" reads Wagner's stage direction—"Verachtet mir die Meister nicht" ("Disparage not the masters to me"), reminding Walther that the masters have made music what it is and enabled him to win the prize (Eva Pogner) for which he had competed.

Thus in the midst of a scene of which Boito had said, as a rule, "the interest wanes as the end is happy," Wagner found a way to sustain that interest and to put all the content of the drama into a new perspective. This comes at the very end—the Scena Ultima of the Finale Ultimo of this truly *lieto fine*—as Eva takes the laurel wreath from Walther's head and, slipping stealthily behind him, puts it on Sachs', as the crowd raises its voices in praise of the true hero of the drama, their beloved shoemaker.

Does, then, a great final moment make a great opera greater? Not necessarily—but it can add a glow of artistic satisfaction if what has preceded has already earned our attention, appreciation, and admiration. The great climax of the steadily mounting tension of Berg's *Wozzeck* comes with the great orchestral unison on C after Wozzeck has plunged the knife into the throat of his faithless paramour, Marie. Berg could have made it his final curtain, but he has another kind of finale ultimo to communicate, when Wozzeck has returned in search of the knife he has thrown into the pond, wanders beyond his depth, and is drowned. The scene changes to the street where Marie has lived and where the child Wozzeck has fathered is playing with friends. A new arrival to the group whispers news of Marie's death, and one of them calls out, "Hey, your mother's dead." They rush off toward the pond, and the child, still riding his hobby horse, trots after them crying, "Hipp hopp, hipp hopp" as Berg's murmuring music reminds us who the real victim of the tragedy is.

Büchner's play (it was titled *Woyzeck* and never wholly completed) was written in 1837. The words set by Berg have so much flavor of the pre–World War I German literature that some degree of adaptation by the composer would strike one as having been inevitable. But the publication, in the Bantam Library of World Drama (entitled *Tragedy: Ten Major Plays from the Greeks to Modern Times*) containing Theodore Hoffmann's translations of the Büchner text, establishes that Berg's alterations of the original, if any, are minor. The play begins, as does the opera, with Wozzeck shaving the Captain and the officer cautioning him, in the familiar words "Langsam Wozzeck, Langsam" ("Easy Wozzeck, Easy"). And the drama proceeds twenty-five scenes later, to the street, the children playing, and the unfortunate son of Wozzeck's union with Marie on his hobby horse.

Berg might have missed the dramatic effect of his ending had he felt a slavish obligation to Büchner. But it was his decision to eliminate a further scene, in the original, showing a group of officials examining Marie's body and a policeman saying, "A real murder, a first-rate murder, as beautiful a little murder as you could ask for. It's a long time since we had one like this." This scene clearly belonged to the part of the play the dramatist didn't finish, rather than the play that Berg finished, enduringly, with his music.

On the other hand, as great a finish as Gustave Charpentier devised for his *Louise* did not assure lasting favor for all that preceded. Like some other composers of the immediate post-Wagnerian decades, Charpentier wrote his own text on a theme well known to him—the romance of a poet, Julien, and the seamstress, Louise, who could not marry at the turn of the century because her parents withheld the consent then required under French law. She agonizes with that decision for the first two acts, finally leaving to share Julien's quarters as she rejoices in her new happiness "Depuis le jour où je me suis donnée" ("Since the day I gave myself to you"). The idyll is interrupted when Louise's mother seeks her out to say that her father is dying, and that perhaps her return will restore his will to live. She returns, only to encounter all the old recriminations: the unworthy poet, the Bohemian life, and all it implies are not good enough for the child they reared; to which Louise asserts she is no longer a child, but a woman. In a fury the father orders her out, fully expecting she will stay. But as the moments pass and Louise does not return, the father shakes his fist at the scene below the window, denouncing the villain of the piece, in the outburst "O Paris!"

It is a great scene and has been embodied superbly by bassos from Charles Gilibert, who made his fame by performing the role of the bearded, pipe-smoking father, to Ezio Pinza (a particularly fine character study enhanced by his height as well as his voice). But Charpentier burdened his own work disastrously by specifying no less than forty separate, *named* characters for the scenes of Parisian life and festivity which come and go during the story. The high promise of such an eloquent episode as "Depuis le jour" is never quite fulfilled in the score's other major melodic content, and the workshop scene is tamer now than it was fifty years ago. But the end is an excellent example of a *mezzo-lieto fine*—happiness for Louise, tragedy for the father.

Perhaps the most debated and least understood conclusion to any regularly performed opera is the last scene of Moussorgsky's *Boris Godunov*. Surely, the average opera-goer will contend, the death of Boris is the end of the opera, and anything beyond it must be anticlimactic. There are always opera impresarios and conductors who will accept this "tradition" (the average performer of Boris requires little persuasion) and drop the final curtain on the crumpled figure of the once all-powerful Czar. It is dramatic, it is impressive, and it is finalizing for Boris.

But it is not finalizing for *Boris Godunov* as Moussorgsky conceived it. For him the artistic imperative was simple. Boris is not the history of the Russian people, he is merely an incident in that history. The true heroes of *Boris* are the Russian people who were—when Moussorgsky wrote the opera in the 1870s—centuries remote from the time of Boris's death (1605) and still miserable, still unhappy, as they are even now, another century later. All this is summarized in the final scene in the Kromy forest depicting the people rallying to form an army behind the false Dimitri for his march to Moscow and power, as the Simpleton—age-old symbol of the truth speaker, however else he may be mentally incompetent—wails:

> O soul, soul of poor Russia. Soon the foe will come
> and the darkness nears. Shadows hide the light, dark
> as darkest night. Sorrow, sorrow on earth: weep, weep,
> Russian folk, poor starving folk.

The composer's own views on the subject are contained in the memoirs of Vladimir Stasov, musician, author, and father of the expression "Moguchaya Kuchka"[9] (the "Mighty Handful" or "The Five," as Moussorgsky, Rimsky-Korsakov, Cesar Cui, Alexander Borodin, and the founding figure Mily Balakirev became known):

During the winter of 1870–71, Musorgsky made another decisive change in his opera. He decided not to end with the death of Boris, but with the scene of the rebellious people [at Kromy], the triumph of the Pretender and the cry of the Simpleton about poor Russia. How much the opera gained by this conclusion, in stunning and tragic force, and in menacing significance! This important change was suggested to the composer by his friend V. V. Kikolsky. Musorgsky was in raptures, and in a few days he reconstructed and fitted this final scene. I admit I felt despair and a profound feeling of envy that it was Nikolsky and not I who suggested such a splendid idea to Musorgsky. . . .[10]

It was Gustav Mahler who, in an everlasting operatic epigram, defined "tradition" as "the last sloppy performance." The Western "tradition" of performing Boris for Boris's sake rather than Moussorgsky's can be isolated not only as to time and place but as to the Russian impresario who imported the example from Russia, a Boris and a highly qualified dissenter. Writing in the Comoedia Illustré of which he became music critic in 1912, Maurice Ravel challenged the forthcoming presentation of a new Boris production under the supervision of Sergei Diaghilev in these words:

Mr. Dhiaghilev intends to produce for us the inn scene, never before shown in France. Why not have the courage to dare a little more? Why not restore the omitted passage in the fifth scene, where the parrot escapes and there is the vision of the tolling bells? Otherwise the musical commentary to this scene is unintelligible. Why has he deleted the short yet significant role of the Jesuit Rangoni? Why does he continue to destroy the dramatic sense of the work, the populace as principal actor, by inverting the sequence of the last two scenes?[11]

The production was made memorable for Paris by the Boris of Chaliapin, and internationally acclaimed as the beginning of the work's worldwide acceptance. The first American production was at the Metropolitan in 1913, as previously noted, in the sequence sanctified by Diaghilev-Chaliapin, and immutable for decades thereafter. A little counterattack was launched in the fifties, but the propaganda for a purer, less diluted Boris began to gather force on the Continent in the sixties and seventies. Munich saw a Boris in the proper sequence with Martti Talvela in 1972, and the same artist was the principal of productions in San Francisco (1973) and New York (1974) in which, finally, all the pieces were properly in place. Either, I think, would have delighted Ravel, even to the imposing presence of Talvela. Thus has "tradition" been repulsed; but it will take a while for those reared in it to find their way to a true appreciation of the meanings and the merits of what prompted "raptures" in Moussorgsky.

4

If the finale is the domain not of the singer but of the director, then the Finale Ultimo is the domain of neither, but wholly of the composer. It is his to scheme, to shape, to manipulate; to leave, in a shattering fortissimo or even more shattering pianissimo, the last, best vista of himself. To judge from the widespread practice composers have of inscribing the date on which they achieve the safe haven of that last double bar, finalizing the finale is an objective tantalizingly remote, long deferred, and ardently embraced.

But it is one not arrived at save by individual means and personal methods. Until Wagner developed the *Leitmotif* it was not considered good musical form for a composer of a serious work (*opéra-comique* was responsive to different rules) to repeat musical ideas more than infrequently. Inferentially, this restriction would apply also to the Finale Ultimo, demanding that the inventive process go on and on. This pattern could be described as the step-by-step, block-by-block method of rearing a structure, or, perhaps, as shaping a pyramid with the Finale Ultimo as its tip.

The Wagnerian innovation brought with it a new freedom of action as well as a new mode of procedure. The common idea (parodied by even so well-informed a composer-critic as Debussy) that the motive is automatically reprised each time the character appears (in the manner, wrote Debussy, of a "harmless lunatic who, on presenting his visiting card, would present his name in song")[12] differs sharply from Wagner's fully developed practice. Mr. Siegfried, for example, is not always identified by the same form of the notes that introduced us to him (even before he is born) when Brünnhilde, in Act III of *Die Walküre*, gives the famous word to Sieglinde that she bears within herself "the highest hero in the world."

The Siegfried theme is one thing in the hero's youth, when he is forging a sword, killing a dragon, and talking to birds. It becomes something quite different—stronger, longer, and more mature—when he has found a bride, been deceived, suffered a mortal wound. When his life is spent, and he is borne back to the Hall of the Gibichungs on his shield, the incredible burden is carried to the sound of funeral music

which seemed an absurd presumption for the German radio to broadcast in memory of a mere Adolf Hitler in 1945. The overpowering
climax is achieved through still another transformation of the theme
once heard (in *Siegfried*) as a carefree horn call and now the generative
force of an elegy such as few composers have ever equaled.

But this is barely the slow introduction to the symphonic structure
(with voice) that Wagner evolves in the Immolation Scene, the epic
ode that ends *Götterdämmerung*. Here is not merely a web, but a
tapestry of tone, a Gobelin of reminiscence woven from the innumerable musical motives of the *Ring*. It summarizes not only the four
hours of music which have preceded, but all four nights of the cycle.

It is, of course, not vital to an appreciation of the *Ring*'s majestic
climax to identify the musical mottos with specific names or events.
But it does add mightily to understanding, appreciation, and enjoyment
to relate a primary handful of them to a happening, a person, or an
idea. Such is the one welded into an overreaching arch at the very end
of *Götterdämmerung* when Wagner reaches back to the great phrase
on the words "O hehrestes Wunder" with which Sieglinde thanks
Brünnhilde (in Act III of *Die Walküre*) for telling her that she will
bear the fallen Siegmund's son. It is an arch that spans all of Siegmund's
life and the best of Brünnhilde's, summarized in a musical phrase that
epitomizes high promise and mortal heartbreak.

It is perhaps less necessary for us to know the source of the
scampering passage with which Strauss brings the swishing curtain
down on Act III of *Der Rosenkavalier* to appreciate the effect the
music has created. But knowing its source does, assuredly, add a
dimension to enjoyment and provide access to the full measure of
Strauss's wit: what is being implemented is a combination of the figure
with which Mahommet was introduced in Act I, with a transformation
of the very first notes that were heard when the opera began. I refer
to the rapturous eruption in the horns which, legend tells us (and if it
is not true, it ought to be), is Strauss's riotous evocation of what the
Marschallin and her young lover have been doing to while away the
night. If one can relate the first and the last, and realize that Strauss is
not only ending an opera brilliantly but closing a cycle of life, our
entry into his thought is so much the keener.

Mention has already been made of Verdi's heightening discrimination in endings and climaxes as he matured. The same applies to his
mastery of musical means. The step-by-step, bit-by-bit procedure was,
for some years, Verdi's *modus operandi*, with a new, late-blooming

strain serving the ritual of finalization. The most immediate example is in *Rigoletto*, in which the sound of the supposedly dead Duke's voice ripping off the buoyant reprise of "La Donna è mobile" sends a shock of fear through Rigoletto, and through us, the audience. The tune tells us, by immediate association, that something has gone wrong with the tidy plot for punishing the seducer, and that someone else's body must be crowded into the sack at his feet.

Verdi was undoubtedly the greatest learner in operatic history. By the time he had arrived at *Otello*, he was not content to resolve the double tragedy with an invention of the moment, however eloquent. He reaches, instead, for the music of the crowning moment of happiness that Otello and Desdemona had enjoyed together, the sensuous, soaring phrase that caps the love duet at the end of Act I. Contrast and commentary on the sad, unhappy, wholly unnecessary trend of events that had converted them from one into two could not be more perfectly conveyed.

When we have heard enough operas enough times and can separate those whose promise is fulfilled in the final, ultimate detail from those in which we have to settle for second, third, or tenth best, one thing becomes clear. It is not necessary for a composer to be a master of symphonic structure, as Wagner was, or a melodic genius with the inventive power of a Verdi, or even such a jolly good workman as Strauss, to command the flash of light that distinguishes a great Finale Ultimo from a commonplace one. He need merely have the good judgment and theatrical instinct of Bizet, who plays off the jubilant sounds from the bull ring against the agonizing outcries of the trapped Carmen screaming for her life to escape Don José's blade, while the orchestra nails all exits closed with the "Fate" motive.

This great final scene wears, as its coat of arms, a knife poised in midair with a bull rampant, and it has served innumerable Carmens and Don Josés well. The episode is also identified with one of the most memorably operatic of all operatic happenings. This occurred in a performance by the New York City Opera Company in the Chicago Civic Opera House on November 19, 1953. In a fit of temper at the competing conducting of Joseph Rosenstock, the Don José of the evening (the twenty-eight-year-old David Poleri) threw down his knife and marched offstage, bellowing at the conductor, "Finish it yourself." It was the only time in history that Carmen died of a heart attack.

Poleri picked for his departure the moment when Don José sings, desperately: "Mais ne me quitte pas, O ma Carmen" ("O Carmen, do not leave me now"). "Then," in the aftermath of the affair his partner, Gloria Lane, said, "he walked off, and I had to sing 'Laisse-moi' ('Let me go') but no one was holding me."

Even before Rosenstock had time to ponder Poleri's advice, the music swept on, and the end was at hand in the relentless "Fate" motive. Bizet had already "finished it himself" in music that tells us, even if the lights failed and the stage were pitch black, that Carmen had found the resolution promised to her in the Prelude. It is there, between the swank of the "Toreador" march and the bright bustle of the music heralding the opening scene of a square in Seville, that the "Fate" motive first made its dark presence known to Bizet. Or did it? Preludes, like overtures are, after all, traditionally written—after all.

EPILOGUE

X

A Perfect Season

1

For those whose interest in opera has been fostered by repertory companies, here and abroad, the average season is, more often than not, the "patchwork" to which reference has been made previously. What is offered can, of course, be supplemented by the samplings in depth offered by such specialized festivals as those of Bayreuth (Wagner), Munich (Strauss), Salzburg (Mozart, plus), and Glyndebourne (likewise). But festival-going is, for the average person, limited to occasional indulgences at lengthy intervals.

In the American cities where opera is regularly heard—San Francisco, Chicago, and New York (primarily); also Boston, Baltimore, Houston, Dallas, Santa Fe, Kansas City, Seattle, and so on—variety of fare is almost directly related to length of season. The number of works heard in San Francisco and Chicago in their twelve- or fourteen-week seasons is rarely more than ten or twelve. The statistics would suggest that the Metropolitan, which has averaged rather more than twice as many weeks in the last dozen years (plus a month's tour), should have a repertory nearly three times as large.

Such, however, is not statistically the case. The Metropolitan's repertory has steadily dwindled, over the decades, from a bulging forty-eight works in the pre-depression twenties to a paltry twenty-three or -four (depending upon fragmentations into double or triple bills). At the outset of the Rudolf Bing administration, the cutback was defended by the self-serving contention that less quantity would promote greater quality, that doing fewer works would "buy time" for upgrading the standard of all.

This argument could be described as a logical conclusion based on a false premise. The false premise is that more time for preparation would *guarantee* a higher quality of result. For a Fritz Reiner, a George Szell, a Dimitri Mitropoulos, a Georg Solti, or a Karl Böhm, unquestionably true. Conductors of this calibre hone and refine, shape and mold, polish and perfect. For a Bruno Amaducci, a Bohuslav Klobucar, a Gabor Ötvös, or Leif Segerstam (all unsuited to the repertory in which they have been heard during recent Metropolitan seasons), no quantity of rehearsal would have improved the results they were *qualified* to achieve. As much can be said for the larger number of singers whose limitations have been optimistically underrated or ignorantly misappraised.

It is in the nature of the operatic cosmos that the one indispensable component in its solar system is not a vocal star but a musical sun and moon—a competent conductor. He can do more to upgrade an indifferent ensemble than a great singer, and his absence can do more to bring down the quality standard than even an inept cast. Given such a permanent center of gravity, even a sinking ship may be kept on an even keel.

A classic illustration of this truism occurred on the occasion when Gustav Mahler came to Hamburg for the first time (in March, 1891) as a way point on the long artistic journey which would subsequently take him to Vienna and New York. Circumstances required that Mahler should begin his six years in Hamburg with performances of *Tannhäuser* and *Siegfried*, both without rehearsal. Present at the second was Hans von Bülow, who, in addition to being first conductor in Hamburg and thus Mahler's superior, was a celebrated pianist, disciple of Wagner, friend of Brahms, son-in-law of Liszt, and partisan of the young Richard Strauss. Some days later he wrote to his daughter Daniela: "Hamburg now has a new first-class opera conductor, Gustav Mahler (a serious, energetic Jew from Budapest), who, in my opinion, equals the greatest (Mottl, Richter, etc. . . . .). Recently I heard *Siegfried* conducted by him . . . and felt deep admiration for the way in which—without a single orchestral rehearsal!—he forced those rascals to dance to his tune."[1]

Conducting *Siegfried* without rehearsal is certainly not to be recommended to anyone, including Gustav Mahler. But Bülow's imagery of a conductor capable of forcing "those rascals [the orchestra] to dance to his tune" is a comforting one. It pictures a Mahler only thirty-one but already with eleven years of solid experience behind him, dominating a situation, however troubled, and holding the Wagnerian line firmly in his grasp.

For lack of rehearsal or other exigencies of the operatic involvement, there is no substitute for competence. One memory of the late Fritz Busch that stands out in a round of fine performances under his direction, here and abroad, of operas by Mozart, Strauss, Wagner, Verdi, Donizetti, and so on, occurred during a Metropolitan *Nozze di Figaro* in which Ezio Pinza was Figaro. Uncommonly—for though he never learned to read music, he was almost always letter-perfect in his performances—Pinza lost his place in a second-act ensemble. Instantly sensing the problem, Busch held up his left hand, palm facing the stage, in a message (directed toward Pinza) from the international sign language meaning "Stop!" as he continued to beat time with his right arm. Having extricated Pinza, at least, from causing further danger to those in the ensemble, Busch waited for a moment until Pinza-Figaro had a clear entrance. Then, confident that Pinza had been alerted to a word cue by the prompter, Busch aimed a finger at his Figaro, the sound came forth at the right moment, and the performance went briskly on.

No one learns such subtleties of procedure in a conservatory or by studying scores in a studio. Behind Busch at this moment of crisis in 1946 was nearly forty years of experience in the theater. All this armed him with the means to combat, not only the momentary confusion in *Le Nozze di Figaro*, but also the occurrence later in the season when Ramon Vinay, on the way to becoming an outstanding Otello, sang the role for the first time as an emergency replacement for Torsten Ralf. There was no time for an extended review of the music problem or even a run-through at the piano. Busch and Vinay met for twenty minutes before the curtain went up, consulted on tempi and dynamics at key spots, and went to work in an opera in which the principal tenor is rarely offstage from curtain rise to curtain fall. Doubtless Busch has made his share of mistakes during his long career, but he made them where brilliant talents are expected, even permitted, to make them—in the obscurity of Riga (where Busch began at the age of nineteen) or Gotha or Aachen, before he reached Stuttgart at the age of twenty-four on the way to Bayreuth at thirty-four.

This was a far cry from the circumstances in which Zubin Mehta, presuming to conduct *Carmen* from memory at the new Met (in 1968) forgot there was a repeat and second ending in the "Toreador Song." He began to signal the rallentando (ritarded pace) for the *next* episode, during which Mercedes, Escamillo, and Carmen exchange their gradually more intense toasts to "L'Amour." Fortunately, the orchestra and chorus ignored Mehta's signals and went about their business of the second stanza of the "Toreador Song," thus keeping *him* from losing their places.

Two ever-growing shortages—competent conductors and experienced singers—are among the reasons the repertory has contracted as the seasonal playing time has lengthened. Together they produce a formula whose inevitable outcome is dullness and depletion of interest. When Gatti-Casazza had forty-eight works available for a twenty-four-week season, he could present *each* weekly subscriber with a *different* opera over a two-year span. As for those who shared a subscription with a friend, they might not hear the same work in a four-year span. Admittedly, the presentability of these works varied greatly (some scenery was shabby, some casts were makeshift, others were under-rehearsed). But the breadth of Gatti's repertory permitted a place for Meyerbeer, for Weber, for Gluck, for Smetana, for Delibes, even for Pergolesi. In today's scheme of things, where a smaller repertory is manipulated across an even longer seasonal span, these niches are usurped (even at the State Theater, where the New York City Opera's enterprise in reviving works of Delius, Donizetti, Handel, Janáček, Monteverdi, and Korngold is a community blessing) by Puccini, Puccini, and more Puccini.

In the extended period in which the Metropolitan's playing time has lengthened and its repertory has contracted—the decades of the fifties and sixties—the prime works of Puccini have risen from a respectable, traditional third place behind Verdi and Wagner to an astonishing primacy over both. Ten works of Wagner had, during this period, a total of 387 performances, or nearly 150 *fewer* than the total of only *three* works of Puccini: *La Bohème, Madama Butterfly,* and *Tosca.* The same three works of Puccini led the top three Verdi operas (*Aida, La traviata,* and *Rigoletto*) 532 to 516. Adding the figures for *Manon Lescaut, La Fanciulla del West,* and *Turandot* to the Puccini column would increase his total for *six* works to an incredible 277 performances *more* than for Wagner's ten works, or nearly two thirds again as many (664 to 387).

Nor does there appear to be a contrary trend impending. For the first time in a decade, in the mid-seventies, a Metropolitan Opera has been reduced from more than thirty weeks to twenty-seven. But until the repertory is *expanded,* this decline is not likely to alter the general reality that the longer the season, the greater the probability, *not* of good performances, but of indifferent, lax, or poor ones. In this recent period, it is not the number of interesting, uncommon, or exceptional operas whose performance totals increase, but the most hackneyed, marginal, and threadbare.

This is polite language for *La Bohème, Tosca,* and *Madama Butterfly* as they have been seen and heard in this era of overproduction and undernourishment. Each has been performed twenty times (or slightly fewer) in a single season recently, not because these are the best productions the company has, or the works for which the best personnel is available, or even the ones in which there is the greatest public interest. They are merely the operas that represent the most inviting path for the impresario (whatever his name) in need of *quantity* of performances, the way traditionally and correctly known as the line of least resistance.

As a measure of comparison, 1974–75 was the Year of the *Tosca* at the Metropolitan, with a total of eighteen performances. In the period between 1923 and 1927, this quantity would have sufficed for nearly *four* seasons (for which the total was twenty-one). Perhaps, it might be suggested, the Metropolitan had no outstanding Tosca in those years? The question is irrelevant, really, for the Metropolitan had no outstanding Tosca among the half dozen who appeared in 1974–75. But the record shows that the Metropolitan's Tosca in the twenties was merely Maria Jeritza, the greatest popular favorite in the role New York has known, with Martinelli or Gigli for Cavaradossi, and Antonio Scotti the most eminent of Scarpias. But there was a different premise, another order of mentality at work, then than there is now.

2

The old attitude was based on the conviction, evolved over decades of international opera in New York (including lavish years of French operatic experience at Oscar Hammerstein's Manhattan Opera House, followed by lengthy visits of the equally French-oriented Chicago Opera Company), that an opera season in such a cosmopolitan as well as metropolitan center should adhere to a central plan. The repertory should contain, if not something for every taste, at least things with which a person of good taste should be acquainted.

Let us recognize that there no longer exists, as there did in the twenties, a post-Verdian wave of new Italian works, for which there was a degree of valid curiosity. Let it be granted that the economic situation of today is a world away from what it was then, and that a manageable repertory has to be, say, twenty-five works rather than nearly fifty. And there is ready agreement from me that the shallowness of the talent pool—both of experienced conductors and qualified singers—is very real, and not a managerial fiction.

Nevertheless, a wide latitude of choice exists among the old and the new, the established and the not yet tested, the fast favorites of yesterday and the tired war-horses of today whose prominence, or lack of it, could, in such a repertory, be productively inverted. Such a mixture would vary vastly the offerings of the American Big Three companies from what they have, in the aggregate, mounted in recent years. It would, in addition, broaden the operatic outlook of the average attendant. That, in turn, would make him/her receptive to still wider digression from the usual.

The following listing is primarily alphabetical, within the framework of an opening and closing opera. The name of each is followed by a capsule comment, and the reason for its inclusion. Note that there are, in every instance, plural justifications.

A PERFECT SEASON

COMPOSER	TITLE	LAN-GUAGE	COMMENT
1) Mozart	Die Entführung aus dem Serail	German	Gaiety and sublimity in the same package
2) Beethoven	Fidelio	German	Indispensable
3) Berg	Lulu	German	Inimitable
4) Berlioz	Benvenuto Cellini	French	Ignored
5) Bizet	Les Pêcheurs de Perles	French	Unknown
6) Britten	Turn of the Screw	English	Unique
7) Charpentier	Louise	French	Time for a revival
8) Debussy	Pelléas et Mélisande	French	Full of unrevealed values
9) Delibes	Lakmé	French	Gallic, delightful, neglected
10) Donizetti	La Fille du Régiment	French	Unregimented
11) Dvořák	Rusalka	English	Unjustly slighted
12) Granados	Goyescas	Spanish	Time for reconsideration
13) Handel	Giulio Cesare	Italian	Self-identifying
14) Humperdinck	Hänsel und Gretel	German	The ideal "first opera"

15) Massenet	*Manon*	French	The quintessence of *l'amour française*
16) Moussorgsky	*Boris Godunov*	English	One of a kind
17) Paisiello	*Il Barbiere di Siviglia*	Italian	Dawn of Beaumarchais
18) Puccini	*Manon Lescaut*	Italian	The most of the promise, with the least cost of the fulfillment
19) Rossini	*Le Comte Ory*	French	Genius with a difference
20) Smetana	*Prodaná Nevěsta (Bartered Bride)*	English	Diversion supreme
21) Strauss, J.	*Der Zigeunerbaron*	English	Rarely given its due
22) Strauss, R.	*Capriccio*	English	The summation of a great composer's experience
23) Verdi	*Don Carlos*	Italian	The opera *complete*, as rarely heard
24) Verdi	*Falstaff*	Italian	No season complete without it
25) Wagner	*Die Meistersinger*	German	The best of his best

LANGUAGE TOTALS

German (5) French (8) Italian (5) English(6) Spanish (1)

Predominance of French relates to recent neglect of this literature; quantity of English texts relates to my suggestion that such seldom-heard (in America) works as *Lulu, Der Zigeunerbaron, Capriccio, Rusalka,* be given in the vernacular. This leaves one (*Turn of the Screw*) composed for an English text and one (*Boris*) which suits it better than any language other than Russian, and suits the audience better than all other languages.

Die Entführung aus dem Serail (Mozart): Dawn of German operatic comedy (*Singspiel* department, meaning spoken recitative) and Mozart's first major operatic success. Admirers included such royalty as Joseph II and Christoph Willibald Gluck. One of the world's most abundant melodic bouquets, with a mighty aria for every performer (high soprano, florid soprano, lyric tenor, comic tenor, basso robusto— who also sings trills when he is in the mood). Effortless audible enjoyment, with inviting opportunities for exterior and interior decoration, harem-style. A treat to behold, and be exalted by. Nicest way I can think of to spend an operatic opening night.

Fidelio (Beethoven): A counterpart to the preceding in respect to German operatic evolution, though the point need not be labored to the extent of discouraging enjoyment. The Olympian Beethoven at his most humane, identifying himself with a jailer and a jailer's daughter, their emotional responses when confronted by crises of life and death, misplaced love and the agony of non-response to it. Broadly speaking, the opera with the greatest concentration of music per minute of elapsed time.

Lulu (Berg): The last unexplored frontier of conventional opera for many Americans, Berg's creation offers challenges of staging, decoration, and character creation which can engage any talents hardy enough to confront them. To speak of Berg's derivative from the *Earth Spirit* and *Pandora's Box* of Frank Wedekind in terms of "conventional opera" may suggest a purposeful pursuit of paradox, but it is defensible fact. Berg's objectives were basically the same as Wagner's, expressed in an extension of the *Tristan* vocabulary. If *Wozzeck* has now absorbed into most operatic repertories, it is a mere matter of time until *Lulu*—pitiless and pitiful, exotic and profound—joins it.

Benvenuto Cellini (Berlioz): Much less of a theatrical handful than *Les Troyens*, *Benvenuto Cellini* (in the sequence devised for his recording by Colin Davis, which by-passes some complications of Berlioz' libretto and effects better juncture of others) is a potent combination of history, histrionics, and high-spirited music. Everybody knows at least a part of it—the famous "Carnival Romain" ("Roman Carnival") overture, which was written as an interlude and escaped to the wider world of the concert hall. As the fame of the "Royal Hunt and Storm" music from *Les Troyens* came, finally, to be accepted as indicative of the quality of what surrounded it, rather than as an exception, so the "Roman Carnival" typifies what there is waiting to be heard and enjoyed in *Cellini*.

Les Pêcheurs de Perles (Bizet): Few composers have suffered so unjustly from the success of one atypical work as Georges Bizet. His absorption of the Spain he never visited, in *Carmen*, has blanketed consideration of several other stage works of which, by general agreement, the best is *The Pearl Fishers*. A product of Bizet's youth when he had barely finished his Prix de Rome years, it is a derivative of the current (1863) fascination with strange happenings in exotic lands. These pearl fishers flourish in Ceylon, where—local mores to the contrary—they become involved with a priestess (Leïla) who causes one of them to fall in love with her, and another to resent his rival's success. If, perhaps, the background is as nonrealistic as that of *La Fanciulla del West*, Bizet's talent—no less than Puccini's—immerses his story in a soaking solution of his own musical solvents which charms the ear. Nadir's "Je crois entendre encore" is, of course, one of the famous tenor arias in the French literature; Leïla's cavatina "Comme autrefois" is delicate and delightful; the whole is pleasant—and unfamiliar—diversion for anyone who can forget that it was written by the man who created the "Seguidilla," the "Air de fleur," and the other immortal matter of his well-imagined, never-never-land Seville (in Spain, *Carmen* is seldom performed).

The Turn of the Screw (Britten): One of the most successful of the prolific Britten's stage works, this treatment of Henry James invites attention for its quartet of singing roles (the Governess, for mezzo-soprano; the housekeeper, for soprano; Miss Jessel, a former governess, also soprano; and Quint, a former manservant, tenor) and of course, the children, Miles and Flora. Can such young voices be heard in a large theater? If carefully selected, yes—as demonstrated in such roles as the Shepherd in *Tosca* or the Tzarevitsch in *Boris*. Peerless for atmosphere and for musical interrelationship to an absorbing drama, *The Turn of the Screw* is a logical extension, in repertory usage, of the Britten conditioning now achieved for a miscellaneous audience by several revivals of *Peter Grimes*.

Louise (Charpentier): The previous deprecation of this work as a whole, in some prior productions, does not exclude the possibility that its individual merits might produce a different sum, in a new, more fluid form of presentation. This would include a liberal share of projections related to the art of the period (1890s) and the surroundings (Montmartre) in which Charpentier himself lived and worked. Indeed, the whole opera could be evoked as a reminiscence of the composer as a young man, seen through the eyes of the poet Julien, for whom Charpentier was his own prototype. If the vignettes of Parisian life (including the "Couronnement de la Muse"—"Coronation of the Muse of Montmartre") and the prelude to Act II ("Paris s'eveille"—"Paris awakens") could be presented as flashbacks or cinematic abstractions, the dramatic pace of the whole could be accelerated. In all, a scheme worth the effort, especially on behalf of a new generation of young sopranos who, given luck, might invoke the bygone spirit of a Grace Moore, a Ninon Vallin, or a Mary Garden.

Pelléas et Mélisande (Debussy): Polemics are unnecessary on behalf of this work's right to be included in a perfect season—the score has argued its own case in theaters large and small the world over (the best-sounding version I ever heard was in Glyndebourne, seating 799; the best-looking in the Lincoln Center Metropolitan, seating 3,880). But the work requires some exposure, still, for its special distinctions to be appreciated by that portion of the opera-going public which regards an evening without arias as an evening without opera.

Lakmé (Delibes): Those who assume that there is little to *Lakmé* beyond the florid "Bell Song" (and that is hardly worth the cost of a production) can scarcely have appraised the matter more than super-ficially. There is also the attractive role of Mallika (Lakmé's slave), who fortunately sings mezzo and thus can share the delightful bar-carolle "Dôme épais" with her mistress; a good male lead (Gérald, an English officer—tenor); a strong baritone part for his friend, Frédéric; and, of course, the basso Brahmin priest Nilakantha (Lakmé's father). As for ballet music, in its traditional French *opéra comique* place in Act II, who is better qualified to produce it than Delibes, the master craftsman of *Naila* (From *La Source*), *Coppélia,* and *Sylvia?* A sure winner—but please not Joan Sutherland . . . there *is* more to the role than the Bell Song.

La Fille du Régiment (Donizetti): Of Donizetti's *opéras bouffes,* this one is richest in invention and broadest in presentation, because it was, indeed, written to be performed in Paris, not converted from an original named *La Figlia del Reggimento.* When spared such farcical, antiquated addenda as a cutout horse with a spastic addiction to kick-ing, or a Sergeant Sulpice with an alcoholic's passion for tippling during business (duty) hours, the opera's vivacious *vivandière* (Marie, "daugh-ter" of the Twenty-first Regiment of Grenadiers) and droll Tonio (who aspires to becoming the Regiment's "son-in-law" by marrying Marie) have enough beautiful music to sing—alone and together—to satisfy any melomaniac's craving. Let's, by all means, again have Joan for this one.

Rusalka (Dvořák): Though it is considered fashionable to extol the Dvořák of the *New World* and G major symphonies as the composer of much beautiful chamber music "unjustly" neglected (which is unquestionably true), there are few voices to be heard on behalf of Dvořák as the composer of operas universally ignored outside his native country (which is manifestly unfair). A good point of beginning would be with the next to the last of them, created in 1900. A composite of the familiar Undine (Ondine) of folk tale, or Mélusine, or Andersen's Little Mermaid—which is to say, a water sprite who aspires to human form and entices a Prince to enable her to fulfill her longing—*Rusalka* is not well served in its opening pages, in which a group of watery witches commune in a language which suggests a cousinly relation to Wagner's Rhine Maidens. Too, the introductory remarks of her father, ruler of the moist underworld, characterizes him as a sub-surface Wotan. However, the appearance soon after of Rusalka's "O moon in the deep sky" sustains the attention until Dvořák sheds his subservience to the Wagnerian presence of the time and becomes his own, eloquent man. Acts II and III are full of the richest kind of Dvořák, and that, by definition, is music that no well-balanced opera repertory can do without.

Goyescas (Granados): Admittedly a problem child, *Goyescas* was the offspring of a World War I mating of Granados' famous piano pieces based on portraits of Goya and a dramatic scheme unequal to the needs of a story suitable to the music. Originally produced at the Metropolitan (because the Paris Opéra, to which it had been promised, was immobilized by war), the premiere was preceded by tales of frantic reorchestration, emendation, and alteration. Whatever Granados might have learned from the experience, and however he might have intended to rework *Goyescas*, the whole project became a casualty of war when the vessel (the *Sussex*) in which he was returning to Europe was torpedoed in the English Channel. Neither Granados nor his wife survived. What is urgently in order is a reworking of the whole subject. Some of the music is, in its present orchestral form, enormously attractive, and all of it (considering its sources in the piano literature) is remarkably singable. Someone with an instinct for the style should filter the clear essence of Granados from the muddy matter in which it is sometimes entrapped (the lame story line). Perhaps that someone could find a purpose in rebuilding dramatic interest around Goya and his famous lady friends. There is ample other music of Granados to make a full evening's work from a score first paired with *Pagliacci*.

Giulio Cesare (Handel): No contemporary opera repertory can now be considered complete without a work of the Baroque period. Of the many composers whose literature presents itself for consideration, Handel's is the worthiest as a point of beginning. Within that spacious realm, *Giulio Cesare* stands out for vitality of dramatic content and richness of musical fulfillment, not to mention proven theatrical worth. Now that it has been demonstrated (by Julius Rudel of the New York City Opera) that name singers of other standard operatic matter (Beverly Sills and Maureen Forrester, as the most prominent) can readily adapt themselves to Handel's requirements, there is no valid reason why others cannot conform. For optimum outcome, *Giulio Cesare* should be performed in the Italian text for which Handel wrote, with a proper scenic appreciation of the work's full title: *Giulio Cesare in Egitto*.

Hänsel und Gretel (Humperdinck): My characterization of *Hänsel und Gretel* as the "perfect first opera" pertains to its clear story, engaging action, picturesque atmosphere, and triumphant conclusion: a *lieto fine* prompted by a detonation (of the witch's oven and, of course, of the witch herself) hardly surpassed in the operatic canon. Its enduring place in the repertory and the reason why it can be seen and heard again and again (since it was first performed under the baton of the young Richard Strauss in 1893) rests on the superlative skill with which Humperdinck realized his purpose. This included a whole range of Wagnerian sophistications (the composer assisted, at the age of twenty-seven, in the preparation of *Parsifal* for publication) artfully applied to the orchestra, while restricting the vocal line to the artless simplicity appropriate to it.

Manon (Massenet): Once the composer with the largest quantity of different operas performed in America (circa 1910, the high noon of French repertory in New Orleans, New York, and Chicago, and the low ebb of Verdian proliferation), Massenet has been retrograded to one household favorite—but what a favorite! Included as the "perfidious darling" more to be loved than either pitied or censured, is

Manon, every soprano's dream of what her specialty should be; Des Grieux, the tenor hero who sings "Le Rêve" with the most honeyed sound he can command and then declaims "Ah! fuyez, douce image" ("Leave me now, Lovely dream") in the best manner of Jean de Reszke and Edmond Clément he can muster; and the Comte des Grieux, father to the Chevalier, a role for which no bass can be too stately. This is less a roster of roles than a gallery of portraits which, when perfectly matched, can provide an insight into the skills and aptitudes with which Massenet filled his operas with whole beings, ready to be animated by artists capable of bringing them to life. As they have dwindled, so has his place in the repertory—but never *Manon*'s.

Boris Godunov (Moussorgsky): Excluding Russian opera from a "perfect season" would be akin to banishing caviar from a gourmet repast—save that, at its best, Russian music is earthier, with a broader appeal to aural taste buds. In such a general category, the earthiest and broadest in appeal is unquestionably *Boris Godunov*. Now that its preferable musical form and order of scenic statement have been universally established, there are new values of pictorial interrelationship and tonal vocabulary (preferably Moussorgsky's own) to be appraised and absorbed. These provide not only a renewed incentive for audience attention, but a new urgency for character creation by its performers, whether the roles are small or large. Nevertheless, when the Bolshoi Opera made its historic first appearances in the United States in 1975, it performed its *Boris* in the now superseded edition of Rimsky-Korsakov. So much for nativity as a warrant for authenticity.

Il Barbiere di Siviglia (Paisiello): For the cost-conscious impresario, this score presents the possibility of a second dividend on the expensive production of Rossini's *Il Barbiere* that occupies space in every repertory opera company's scenic warehouse. As the time and place are also identical, Paisiello's work could be played in the same costumes, further minimizing the expense of installing a score of warmth, wit, and melodic freshness in a seasonal scheme. To be done properly, it should be directed by a French theater man well-versed in the practices of the 1775 Théâtre Française, where the Beaumarchais prototype was first produced. Certainly it should not be undertaken by an Italian director inclined to regard it as a "forerunner" of Rossini.[2]

Manon Lescaut (Puccini): Enough has already been said to require little more about this work and its special place in the lore of Puccini.

More to the point, "A Perfect Season" should include at least one opportunity for a soprano to match some historic feat of the past. This would be permitted by a week including the two *Manon*s, with but a single Manon.

Le Comte Ory (Rossini): As Massenet's time of favor in the repertory theaters of the world recedes into the past, Rossini's gives every indication of rising. A swing in taste? A response to a new wave of performing personnel? Either way, it hasn't yet made way for the last of Rossini's comedies (his only later opera was *Guillaume Tell*) and one of his best. *Le Comte Ory* is a wily rascal who has disguised himself as a hermit—holy man—to receive the confidences of medieval ladies (with, nevertheless, timeless needs) whose husbands have gone off to the Crusades. Needless to say, he is not reluctant to offer amorous consolation to the neediest. This is achieved, in part, by Ory and his cronies, when they disguise themselves as nuns and take up residence in the castle where the husbandless wives of the neighborhood have banded together to wait out the Crusades. What happens thereafter by way of resolution really does not matter—Rossini oils this elegantly farcical vehicle with some of his most unctuous music and speeds it on his way with arias and ensembles. *Le Comte Ory*'s crowning glory is the trio "A la faveur de cette nuit obscure" ("Favored by that dark night") which Rossini's biographer Francis Toye describes as "worthy of Mozart at his best."[3] If this may strike some as partisan praise, harken to the voice of Berlioz—whose poor opinion of Rossini and his use of the big bass drum is well known—who declared that *Le Comte Ory* had "enough stuff in it to make the fortunes of two or three ordinary operas."[4] If so, it should appeal to those American impresarios who have shown little awareness of its existence, even with a perfect Fernandel of a role in Comte Ory himself. Can one imagine Luciano Pavarotti as a hermit giving counsel to woebegone ladies? What is more, as a nun? I can; and can't—wait.

Prodaná Nevěsta (Smetana): Opera-going knows no greater pleasure— hence no greater deprivation when it is denied—than Smetana's *Prodaná Nevěsta*, *Verkaufte Braut*, or *Bartered Bride*, depending on which language and title is preferred. For me, the preferred tongue is German, perhaps because that is the way I learned it, especially in versions that included one of the great operatic impersonations of a lifetime, Michael

Bohnen as Kezal, the broker who barters the bride. Even without Bohnen (indeed *with* a Kezal who spoke Czech to Jenik [Hans], the hero who appears to be selling out his beloved), an English-language version in Boston a few years ago was totally charming, not only for the wise choice of Mary Costa to impersonate Marenka, but also for the inspired selection of Emmett Kelly as a non-singing, non-speaking adjunct of the circus whose presence winds in and out of the action. This was a spectacular—but hardly unique—instance of Boston *impresaria* Sarah Caldwell's genius for realizing an opera composer's intentions even though they are nowhere indicated in writing. From the first note of the overture, Miss Caldwell as conductor implemented every gesture, movement, and device that Miss Caldwell as director had called into being. Only she, perhaps, knew before the curtain went up how the two would go together—but once it did, everyone in the theater realized that she was inviolably, inevitably, incontrovertibly right. An extraordinarily gifted woman, she could doubtless conduct every work of this "perfect season" and do most of them better than anyone I can otherwise think of would do four or five. For all the fact that the performance took place in an antiquated movie house, with no stage to speak of, Miss Caldwell made us all feel we were in Prague, savoring the best of which the Czech National Theatre was capable.

Der Zigeunerbaron (Johann Strauss): As the country cousin to the citified pleasures of *Die Fledermaus*, Johann Strauss's other great stage score has had far less than its due on the English-speaking stage. I say "other great stage score" rather than "second-best" score because some of it (such as the great finale to Act I) rises to heights even *Fledermaus* does not attain. Anyone who has ever heard the late Richard Tauber sing "Als flotter Geist" or "Wer uns getraut?" with an appropriate female companion, or joined in the above-mentioned finale with such super-appropriate female companions as Lotte Lehmann and Karin Branzell, will not willingly settle for less. This may seem to rule out any ready reconsideration of its merit, but such resources exist and need only be marshaled. The singular circumstances—an unsuitable conductor, a wildly improbable Zsupan (Walter Slezak, whose speaking voice could hardly be heard beyond the first ten rows), the far too elegant Lisa della Casa as Saffi—which restricted the Rudolf Bing venture to a mere two performances (the all-time low for any production of his administration) should not be held against the mistreated masterpiece. Clearly *The Gypsy Baron* needs not only proper casting but a thorough textual revision of the libretto. But such insights have been profitably applied before to other book-weary projects (Offenbach's *La Périchole,* as an instance) and will be again.

Capriccio (Richard Strauss): The first time I heard Strauss's last (1942) composition for the musical stage was in postwar (1951) Vienna. No score was available, of course, nor a German text. I found it, aside from an occasional stretch of solidly Straussian music, and with even so great an artist as Paul Schoeffler in the key role of La Roche, an excruciating essay in ennui. Three exposures later (all in English, and with the appropriate study material—score, libretto, recording—all investigated and digested), *Capriccio* has become one of the most refined musical pleasures of which I know. First impressions, when unfavorable, can be overcome. The moral is that, in this ripe work built around the age-old question "Prima le Parole, dopo la musica" or "Prima la musica, dopo le Parole"? ("First the word, then the music," or "First the music, then the word"?), if the words cannot be understood, the issue cannot even be argued. In one of his verbal commentaries on the subject, Strauss admonished: "Considering the importance given to the spoken word in this particular work, it would not seem inopportune to suggest that, before study of the score begins, the producers should arrange a few thorough reading rehearsals (solely based on the text) with special emphasis on the clearest possible pronunciation of consonants: e.g. of the letters at the beginning and end of words—readings which should moreover be repeated without any music before the last stage rehearsals (from two to three days before the dress rehearsal)."[5] Trust Strauss, the conductor, to have the answers for the problems of Strauss the composer! A product of his seventy-seventh year, when he had lost interest in virtually all the common subjects for opera, *Capriccio* deals with the one subject that held interest for Strauss—opera itself, and the materials from which one could be created. When all the aspects of the subject have been argued (through an eighteenth-century composer and poet who are trying to persuade their Countess-patron that each is more important to the outcome of her commission than the other) the answer comes clear (if only by inference). Each with the aid of the other becomes something greater than he is alone; together they give birth—in a manner known to nature generally—to a thing which blends the best of both. When enriched by some of Strauss's ripest, raptest music, even two uninterrupted hours of leisurely, sophisticated *causerie* is not too much.

Don Carlos (Verdi): For many American opera-goers, Elisabetta in *Don Carlos* has been a late-blooming love, a romance entered into when the *inamorata* was well along in years, but still able to exercise a mature charm for those who had previously been attached to her older, but more vivacious, sisters (Violetta, Gilda, and so on). Now that they have grown to know her in all her vitality and variety, they have only one impediment to a wholly happy relationship: she insists on keeping a secret, from her American admirers especially, about some incidents of her life in France before she came to Spain as the wife of King Philip II, days when she was deeply in love with his son, Carlos, and he with her. There are references, in the version of the opera with which we are thoroughly familiar, to those days—they are talked about passionately, and it is clear that if she, for reasons of state, has put them behind her, Carlos, for reasons of another state—the state of love—hasn't. When the episode that depicts them prior to Elisabetta's marriage to Carlos is brought up, some Verdians familiar with it say, "Oh yes—the Fontainebleau scene—you don't want to know all about that, it's really not important." But all of this evasion suggests to me a conspiracy of silence designed to conceal something discreditable to Elisabetta and *Don Carlos* itself. If Verdi wrote the scene—and he assuredly did, for the original production in Paris—he subsequently decided when further changes were made for *Don Carlos*'s production in Italy, that, with the Fontainebleau scene, the opera had become too long. Today it is the privilege of the opera's now fast friends to decide for themselves whether Verdi's later view should be the final one. If, indeed, the complete version I propose were to be billed as "The Truth about Elisabetta," *Don Carlos* might have a new round of box office appeal.

Falstaff (Verdi): Lightning in a bottle, mercury dancing on the point of a needle, fireflies imprisoned in flight—these are some of the visual images that come to mind in reviewing the audible magic that makes me say of *Falstaff*: "No season complete without it." Here is a realm, not of gold (which Keats discerned "On first looking into Chapman's 'Homer' ") but of wit and tears, song and laughter, an old man looking back from the last artistic act of his long life-drama and regarding another old man's folly with an understanding but no less penetrating eye. The most singular fact about *Falstaff* is, of course, the speed at which the music moves. Padding was anathema to Verdi whenever, in earlier works, he could avoid it; but there are more than a few minutes of expansion and digression in almost all those prior to *Falstaff*. Everyone can make up his/her own list of candidates for exclusion (in a recent colloquium, Maria Callas allowed as how *La traviata* could be improved by the omission of the elder Germont's "Di Provenza il mar, il suol" ["The province of sea and sun"]—the one opportunity during the evening the baritone has to express himself in a solo). There is virtually nothing anyone would have excised from *Falstaff*, for two reasons: there are really no superfluous words in Boito's text, and there was even smaller time for note-spinning at Verdi's advanced age (seventy-seven when he began, eighty when he finished the score). In addition, *Falstaff* is more than brilliantly orchestrated—it is orchestrally *conceived* from first to last. Verdi's command of the orchestra is so great that he can set it to jingling when coins are mentioned or have it chatter mischievously when the wives are reading each other parts of Falstaff's letter. If *Hänsel und Gretel* is the ideal first opera, *Falstaff* is the reward waiting in the distance when the novice become enthusiast, then devotee, eventually connoisseur, attains the aural palette to appreciate it . . . a treat for the musical gourmet become epicure.

Die Meistersinger (Wagner): As *Die Entführung* strikes me as the prime embodiment of gaiety and sublimity with which to open a perfect season, so *Die Meistersinger* contains the summarizing qualities of humor and profundity with which to terminate it. The wise burghers of Munich, where *Die Meistersinger* had its first performance ever in 1868, honor their good fortune by initiating every year's musical promise with a mid–New Year's Day performance of *Die Meistersinger* in the Bavarian National Theater. The good fortune of the Bavarian burghers cannot be claimed by others elsewhere, but the good taste and judgment could be emulated. Song, of course, is the essence of opera, but in no other opera as centrally as it is in *Die Meistersinger*, of which song is both the subject and the object. No matter how often one has been exposed to this great and good work—and in these times, the opportunities are far fewer than they used to be—the opening of the huge warehouse of musical pleasures-to-come, with one of the greatest overtures ever written, cannot fail to galvanize attention and stimulate anticipation. If there is truth to the contention that Richard Wagner was the son of the Jewish actor Ludwig Geyer rather than of the non-Jewish minor public official Carl Friedrich Wagner, one is tempted to believe that it was the Jewish blood in Wagner that flowed into *Die Meistersinger* (hardly into *Parsifal!*). A central justification for this supposition might be found in the Talmudic figure of Hans Sachs, who is as good a shoemaker as he is a poet (Beckmesser not to the contrary); as good a friend to Veit Pogner (in preventing the elopement of his daughter, Eva) as to Walther von Stolzing (in stage-managing the events that enable him to win Eva according to the rules of the song contest); a man, withal, possessed of the humanity and the wisdom to include his apprentice, David, among those to whom his favor is dispensed. In several other salutations, individual aspects of *Die Meistersinger* have been extolled. This is the place in which to rejoice in it as a totality, to ponder the miracle that a mind capable of *Die Walküre* could also create *Parsifal*, and write both *Tristan* and *Die Meistersinger* within a ten-year span.

3

An average aroused opera-goer, perhaps even an unaverage, avid opera lover, might find the preceding discourse beguiling, amusing, even mouthwatering—and then pose the hard question: to what extent is such a perfect season related to pragmatic, rather than visionary, considerations? Can it be done short of combining the resources of Salzburg, Munich, La Scala, and Glyndebourne? (As only one Wagner score is included, Bayreuth's aid need hardly be invoked for *this* perfect season, although it might very well enter into another, or for someone else's list.)

The season could be done without the participation of any European resources, indeed hardly any other than those available on Manhattan Island or creatable within the span of the Metropolitan's operational planning. No less than eleven, or nearly half the total of works included, are within the Metropolitan's power to activate. Five more productions could be borrowed without going off the island or beyond Boston: *The Turn of the Screw, Giulio Cesare, Lulu, Bartered Bride,* and *Capriccio.* That leaves nine—*Die Entführung, Benvenuto Cellini, Les Pêcheurs de Perles, Louise, Lakmé, Rusalka, Goyescas, Le Comte Ory,* and *Der Zigeunerbaron*—to be built. As the average number of new productions built by the Metropolitan in recent years has been four or five, approximately half the missing total could be provided in what is described as "the span . . . of operational planning." Furthermore, to bring about an innovation of this magnitude, an effort could be made to raise the funds for *two* seasons' new productions to be implemented in a single calendar year.

Very well, says the moderately mollified reader, the production problem is not impossible; indeed, it could be comprehended within the formula of old, new, borrowed, made. So much for the physical adjuncts. How about the even more essential human resources, particularly the all-important "competent" conductors of which so much was made in part 1 of this chapter? Where does one find them, and how many would be required—particularly in the currently tight sellers' market—to assure a respectable level of leadership?

Whatever the number you may have in mind for proper attention to twenty-five works, the number I have in mind is smaller. This would bring into play at least two factors: the total number of works assumed by each individual conductor, and the extent to which they accord with his enthusiasms. Most conductors spending an important segment of time in a foreign capital would rather conduct three or four operas than one. This range of activity provides more earning power per time allocated and a higher level of artistic satisfaction by sustaining the effective level attained during rehearsal.

Given such a pooling of effort as I visualize, division of repertory should be not too much of a problem, especially if the group of collaborators were limited to no more than five. I am talking about *conductors*, not about coaches, repetiteurs, those "responsible for the musical preparation," and so on. Clearly all this would have to be planned four or five years ahead—but the public favor thus to be gained would be well worth the effort.

I am talking, even more specifically, about conductors with an identity, and a known disposition for key works. In their separate ways, each of the following five (plus) have abilities above the average, with known capacities *vis-à-vis* half the works assigned to them, and a sound reason for believing that the other half would be congenial.

CONDUCTORS			OPERAS		
BARENBOIM	*Fidelio*	*Rusalka*	*Hänsel und Gretel*		*Meister-singer*
BONYNGE	*Lakmé*	*Manon*	*Giulio Cesare*	*Fille du Regiment*	*Les Pêcheurs de Perles*
CALDWELL	*Goyescas*	*Louise*	*Bartered Bride*	*Lulu*	*Falstaff*
COLIN DAVIS	*Entführung*	*Pelléas*	*Le Comte Ory*	*Benvenuto Cellini*	*Turn of the Screw*
GIULINI	*Don Carlos*	*Boris*	*Manon Lescaut*	*Il Barbiere di Siviglia*	
ERNST MÄRZEN-DORFER	*Capriccio*		*Die Zigeunerbaron*		

Märzendorfer, of Vienna, was responsible for an excellent *Capriccio* by the New York City Opera the last time the opera was heard in New York (1969). Having the fewest number of works on the season's schedule in his care, he could also assume responsibility of one or more of Barenboim's, in an emergency. Similarly, where *quality* is a primary consideration, it is not unlikely that others committed to the plan would be willing to direct a colleague's production in an emergency. It has happened with Toscanini, Serafin, Leinsdorf, and others during their New York careers; why not with Giulini, Bonynge, Caldwell, Davis, and Barenboim in 1983?

The resolution of the leadership problem gives next highest priority to the question of performing personnel. Again, giving prominence to persons of ability in specific roles (for which they have a known or presumptive affinity) the roster of those desirable would be—in terms of the operas specified—something like this:

OPERA	PRINCIPAL SINGERS	CONDUCTOR
Entführung	Sills, Blegen, Schreier, Macurdy	Davis
Fidelio	Dernesch, Blegen, Vickers, Macurdy, Schreier	Barenboim
Lulu	Lear, J. Simon, Fischer-Dieskau	Caldwell
Benvenuto Cellini	Gedda, Bacquier, R. Soyer	Davis
Les Pêcheurs de Perles	Sills, Gedda, Bacquier, Macurdy	Bonynge
Turn of the Screw	Niska, Reynolds, Shirley-Quirk, S. Burrows	Davis
Louise	Caballé, Domingo, Macurdy	Caldwell
Lakmé	Blegen, Gedda, Macurdy, Gramm	Bonynge
Pelléas	Blegen, Gedda, Macurdy, McIntyre	Davis
Fille du Régiment	Sutherland, Pavarotti	Bonynge
Rusalka	Zylis-Gara, S. Burrows, McIntyre	Barenboim
Goyescas	Caballé, Carreras	Caldwell
Giulio Cesare	Sills, Verrett, Shirley-Quirk	Bonynge
Hänsel und Gretel	Blegen, Von Stade, Chookasian, Gramm	Barenboim
Manon	Kanawa, Domingo, Bacquier, Macurdy	Bonynge
Boris	Talvela, Burrows, Macurdy, Verrett, Nagy	Giulini

OPERA	PRINCIPAL SINGERS	CONDUCTOR
Il Barbiere di Siviglia	Milnes, Blegen, Carreras	Giulini
Manon Lescaut	Caballé, Domingo, Bacquier	Giulini
Le Comte Ory	Sills, Pavarotti, Shirley-Quirk	Davis
Bartered Bride	Costa, Burrows, Macurdy	Caldwell
Zigeuner- baron	Zylis-Gara, Gedda, D. Gramm	Märzendorfer
Capriccio	Zylis-Gara, Gedda, Fischer-Dieskau	Märzendorfer
Don Carlos	Kanawa, Verrett, Domingo, Macurdy, Talvela, Fischer-Dieskau	Giulini
Falstaff	Evans (Glossop?), Burrows, Milnes, Chookasian, Blegen	Caldwell
Meister- singer	Moser, Burrows, Gramm, Dunn, Macurdy, Schreier	Barenboim

The attentive eye of the well-informed opera-goer will isolate one detail without much prompting: virtually every singer on the list for principal roles is well known to American audiences. The sole innovation is the manner of their assignment and combination—all with conductors who have, with the exception of Barenboim and Giulini, also performed their specialties in this country.

The one conspicuous exception to such familiarity, among the vocalists, is, of course, Dietrich Fischer-Dieskau, familiar though he is as a master in the concert hall. Past efforts to bring him into the activities of the Metropolitan have been frustrated by his desire to make a New York operatic debut in an Italian opera, rather than, once again, as a German specialist. This could readily be accomplished by presenting him either in *Falstaff* or as Posa in *Don Carlos* leading thereafter to Oliver in *Capriccio* and Dr. Schön in *Lulu*, both roles in which he is an acknowledged specialist.

My cherished objective and crowning event of this Perfect Season was, for long, the even-longer fostered hope of Fischer-Dieskau as Hans Sachs in *Die Meistersinger*. For me, the possibility existed as long ago as 1951, when a Beecham-conducted *Meistersinger* at Covent Garden promised the unfamiliar "Dieskau" as one of its participants. Before rehearsals began in earnest, the then twenty-six-year-old singer decided the time was not yet right for him.

It was not until a full twenty-five years later, on March 12, 1976 that the long-awaited event came to fulfillment in the Deutsches Oper in Berlin. By a curious set of circumstances, I was among those who crowded the house for a long, memorable evening with Eugen Jochum as conductor. Though it was Fischer-Dieskau's first appearance anywhere as Hans Sachs, the characterization was impressively his own: wise, thoughtful, yet clearly animated by an emphasis on the self-denial embodied in Sachs' renunciation of Eva, but as clearly sung in a volume of voice more appropriate to Wolfram than to Wotan; which is to say, with a reserve of power suitable to Continental theaters of the Deutsches Oper size (capacity 1900) but not to the American variety, of which the Metropolitan (capacity 3880) is more than twice as large.

But it is the nature of the operatic involvement that the twilight of one bright, unmanageable prospect may become the dawn of another manageable one. What bass-baritone with a studious mind, a rich voice, a fine command of languages, and a great gift for characteriztion could become the *next* prime exponent of the poet cobbler? My nomination— and it will not come as a surprise to him, as it has been urged by others —is Donald Gramm. An American-born singer who made his debut at the New York City Center as long ago as the 1952–1953 season, Gramm has moved steadily, securely, from one career plateau to the next higher one. The mere improbability of his ascension to the highest level to which a bass-baritone can aspire is no more than a mystical, perhaps even mythical, barrier between the untried and the unimaginable. That, indeed, would make *his Meistersinger* a proper end to my "Perfect Season."

XI

A Portrait of a Paragon

1

The eye that detected Fischer-Dieskau's name in several points of preferment in the preceding cast page may also have noted the tenor whose name appears most frequently in the same sequence. Depending on the reader's degree of operatic indoctrination, such frequent mention could have been either surprising or expectable. Both possibilities exist for the man whose thoroughness, intelligence, and vocal artistry have made a name for him as Nicolai Gedda.

Would he have made the same name for himself as Nicolai Ustinov? Perhaps, but probably with a little more difficulty and a lot more confusion. At the time he emerged to world prominence in the later 1950s, one Ustinov was already at large and making a substantial name as the author, director, and principal performer of a play called *Romanoff and Juliet*. To add another Ustinov to the one already prominent in the performing world would have caused endless confusion to copy editors, proofreaders, and caption writers required to explain why Peter was singing opera or Nicolai was writing a play. The opera community can be grateful that the second Ustinov is, as Gedda, unique in name as well as in talent.

Contrary to some possible presumption, "Gedda" is not a manufactured name, an acronym, or even a contraction of something else. The surname derives from the tenor's mother's maiden name and identifies her as the Swedish part of his mixed parentage. A native of Sweden, where he began his public career, Gedda ascribes his choice of the name he bears (professionally and personally) to his desire to identify himself to the world as a Swedish artist.

If, as Wordsworth contended, the child is father of the man, the man who fathered this child was much responsible for the manner of man he became. You might have seen that father on the stage of the concert halls of Europe and America during the twenties, not in white tie and tails but in the white blouse, dark knickers, and black, high-heeled boots of the Don Cossack Choir. Mikhail Ustinov—like most other "white" Russians who made up the Original Don Cossacks—made his home far from Russia. His preference was, as noted, Stockholm, where Nicolai was born in 1925.

Because he had a young son to look after, Ustinov gave up his traveling career in the late twenties. Indeed, when his son was three, Ustinov accepted a position as the cantor of a Russian Orthodox Church in Leipzig. Being brought up in a bilingual home gave young Nicolai two languages to start with, Russian and Swedish. Being taken, by accident of parental occupation, to Germany as a child gave him a third (languages are, traditionally, most readily learned when young). This was a fair kind of conditioning for a tenor whose gift of tongues is one of his highest professional credentials.

The child began to sing almost as soon as he began to speak. When some routine tests—preliminary to inclusion in the choir of the church where his father was employed—revealed that the boy had absolute pitch as well as beautiful soprano sound, he was marked for serious musical training. As they had a beginning in the home, his studies included the balalaika as well as harmony and ear-training. Within a few years, the boy became a companion to his father in entertaining at parties, weddings, and similar social events.

What would have happened had the Ustinovs remained in Leipzig? A digression to the choir school of Bach's St. Thomaskirche perhaps, an eventual training as an expert in German *Lieder*? Fortunately for the world opera community, the option was never offered. The onset of the Hitler terrors in the early 1930s cost father Ustinov his job at the Russian Church in Leipzig. As Sweden was still home to his wife, the family returned to Stockholm in 1934, taking with them a nine-year-old fluent in German, with a knowledge of Russian liturgical music and an indoctrination in the *a capella* writing of Machaut, Dufay, Josquin des Prés, and other great polyphonists.

Latin and English came into his growing stock of languages at the

Soedra Latin School after his return to Stockholm. At sixteen, the expected change of sound occurred with an added detail: it not only changed—it disappeared entirely. The death of father Ustinov made it necessary for the son to find work to contribute to the family's support. He found a job in a bank, spent some time in army service, and became a tall, thin, six feet four. At eighteen, nature gave him back the voice she had temporarily suppressed, having converted the beautiful boy-soprano timbre into a promising adolescent tenor. As a young, tall tenor, Gedda dreamed of becoming a *Heldentenor*.

Nature, however, had other plans. The sound was good, but it failed to gain the body or power for a *Heldentenor*. By chance, Gedda's emerging interest in opera led him to records of Tito Schipa and Tito Gobbi. Together they provided a persuasive example that singing in the Italian manner was not a bad compromise. It was as a *lirico-spinto* (strong lyric) that Gedda was trained, and trained well, by Karl-Martin Oehmann. Also a product of the north country, Oehmann had progressed far enough in his own career to make a reputation in the German theaters of the post–World War I period, to be heard on records (excerpts from *Die Meistersinger*, among others), and to share the stage (as Laca Klemen) of the Metropolitan Opera House with Maria Jeritza when Leoš Janáček's *Jenufa* was introduced to America on December 6, 1924. Gedda's job in the bank continued, as a means of sustaining family support; vocal lessons were paid for by a patron who believed in him.

Between the ages of twenty-two and twenty-four, Gedda won several competitions, which contributed further to his confidence that an operatic career was not out of reach. In 1950, at the age of twenty-five, he was accepted for the opera school of the Stockholm Conservatory. His steady progress, his size, and the promise of his voice carried him to a debut at the Royal Opera at twenty-seven. His role was in an opera revived on behalf of young Gedda's high voice, and strong top: Chapelou in Adolphe Adam's *Le Postillon de Longjumeau*.

This was sufficient in itself to mark 1952 as the year of years for Gedda, but a hardly less memorable event occurred even before the debut. Walter Legge, who, as recording supervisor for English Columbia and products distributed on the Angel label, has unquestionably created more great operatic recordings than any other man, was furthering, in England, a project he had craved for years to accomplish: an all-Russian *Boris*, built around the great talents of Boris Christoff. On a recording, Christoff (who was Bulgarian-born and Slavic-trained)

could sing not only Boris, but Pimen and Varlaam. This left, nevertheless, a few other male roles to be accounted for.

For his conductor, Legge had selected Issay Dobrowen. To further
their plans and to accompany his wife, Elisabeth Schwarzkopf, on a
concert tour to Scandinavia, Legge went to Stockholm where Dobrowen was conducting. It was spring, 1952.

As Legge tells it: "My wife and I were met at the airport by
friends, and of course, press. The questions were of the usual kind,
including one about whether I would listen to Swedish singers. 'Of
course,' I replied . . . little knowing what that would mean. The
story was all over the press that day, and by morning I had a list of 80
singers who had called to have their names considered. I asked the
director [a fine bass-baritone of the 1930s and 1940s, Joel Berglund]
if I could have the use of the opera auditorium for the auditions. That
wasn't possible, but he did offer the use of a room in the opera house.

"Among the earliest applicants was a tall, thin young man. I asked
what he would like to sing, and he said 'Air de fleur, *Carmen*.' And
he sang it with astonishing beauty of sound, all except the last note—
which was too loud [it is a D flat, in a phrase that begins with a
pianissimo, proceeds to a swell and diminuendo on C, and ends quietly].
I explained what I wanted him to do, the swell and diminuendo, and
so on. Then I said, 'Do it again.' He sang it beautifully again, and did
the ending *exactly* as I had suggested.

"My next question was: 'Do you sing any Mozart?' He replied:
'Both arias of Don Ottavio in *Don Giovanni*.' 'Do them' I said. He
did both arias more beautifully than I had ever heard them, except
from Richard Tauber and on the John McCormack record. I asked
him to come back later in the day, as I wanted my wife to hear him.
She was equally bowled over.

"I sent two cables," continued Legge, "one to von Karajan, the
other to Ghiringhelli at La Scala. They read: 'Just heard the greatest
Mozart singer in my life. Name is Nicolai Gedda.' Of course I signed
him for Grigory [the young monk who emerges as the false Dimitri,
the pretender to the throne who succeeds Boris]."

It was many months before the *Boris* was completely cast, the company assembled in Paris, the recording made. Additional months passed
before it was edited, mastered, pressed, and publicly distributed, in
1953. Nevertheless, the sound that can be heard from Dimitri is the
sound of Gedda at virtually its purest—sweet yet incisive, fully formed
but floating on a stream of air that never seems to require replenish-

ment, and adroitly inflected to the Russian text which Gedda pronounces better, perhaps, than anyone else in the cast.

2

Needless to say, when Legge first auditioned Gedda in Stockholm, he had little knowledge of the singer's background, save that his father had been a member of the Don Cossack Choir and that the family was obviously—to judge from the six feet four Gedda's skin-and-bones appearance—in straits. But he could detect instantly, a prime product of his background—musicality, a quick intelligence, and the ability to comprehend an instruction and execute it instantly. All of these are attributes to endear a singer to the heart of a recording supervisor with Legge's stiff standards, as they would to a demanding conductor.

It is not difficult, in these days of a vast record market and a highly competitive quest for salable merchandise (to serve a world of record enthusiasts with products from such a central point of supply as London that flow westward to the Golden Gate and eastward to Japan) to find a sequence of disks that trace a career from the start to its ultimate resolution. You can, for example, do "The Rise and Fall of Giuseppe di Stefano" from the time he was recording with a dance band under the name of Nino Florio (he does a charming chorus on "Voglio Sognar") in the late forties, through the glowing debut-at-the-Met sound of "Ah non credevi tu" from Ambroise Thomas' *Mignon* and the memorable Callas recordings of the fifties, every step along the primrose path to the latest, if not the last, echo of a priceless endowment. And with patience, one can assemble from Swedish, English, and American sources every link in the long chain that leads from the late Jussi Bjoerling's youthful sound in "Love Me and the World Is Mine" (1931) to his last recorded opera (*Turandot*), issued in 1960. But there are few, besides Gedda, who have performed, before they were thirty, so revealing a role as Dimitri in a production of *Boris* that must be included in any list of the greatest opera recordings ever made.

On the basis of a discography that can be comprehended in half a dozen long playing records, Conchita Supervia is esteemed as one of the great mezzos of the century by people who were unborn at the time of her death (1936). As the rank of "greatest tenor in the world" passes from a Caruso to a Gigili to a Bjoerling, or from a di Stefano to a Pavarotti, or from a Tucker to a Domingo, it is altogether likely that Gedda will retain a rank all his own as a paragon of extraordinary and unusual artistry.

The reasons for this opinion are neither speculative nor obscure. They are inherent not merely in Gedda's vocal endowment or in his ability to compete in the lunge to the auditory solar plexus with which the great names above achieved their unquestioned triumphs. Gedda is not possessed of a sound with which he was born to conquer. He was, rather, born with a brain that enables him to shape the sound at his disposal into the words, the images, and the nuances of tone from which conquest can be commanded.

As Legge responded to his exceptional promise not only because he was a tall, thin Swede with an amazing range, but because he could also sing in authentic Russian, others elsewhere have found in his equipment no less perfect answers to a dilemma, no matter the language in which the word was pronounced. Soon after their meeting in Stockholm, Legge's cable to La Scala earned Gedda an audition before its director, Ghiringhelli, and his musical staff. The verdict, delivered by Ghiringhelli to Legge when they later met was, of course, favorable, with a codicil: "His was the most perfect Italian of any foreigner who auditioned at the Scala during my administration." Gedda's first great international fame came from his early (1954) association with the Paris Opéra, especially for his ability to challenge the frightfully high-lying role of Huon in Weber's *Oberon*. The three-year contract that resulted was not because he was simply a tall man with a fine presence and the ability to sing C sharps and Ds. He was valued in Paris for all these things and one thing more—he could qualify as the leading tenor of a theater that then transacted all its artistic business in French.

My small share in the saga of Gedda (whom I do not know and had not met when these words were written) came during the *Oberon*-Huon period in Paris. A mutual acquaintance of the musical profession mentioned that Erich Leinsdorf was recruiting talent for his first season as general director of the New York City Opera Company (to begin in fall, 1956) and with typical good judgment, had offered an engagement to Gedda. Question: Would it be a good move for him to accept, as a way of introducing himself to New York? My answer was an unequivocal "No!" Though I had not yet seen Gedda in a live performance, what I had heard of his recordings pointed clearly to an uncommon career in the making. A man of his ability would always be welcomed by New York's "second" company. It would be far more advantageous for him to await an expression of interest by the Metropolitan, which was certain to come—sooner or later.

That Gedda's Metropolitan opportunity came sooner rather than later was not because Rudolf Bing was specifically looking for a tenor to sing Faust in a new production during the opening week of the 1957 season. It was also because Gian Carlo Menotti had been scouting tenors to sing the leading male role of Anatol in the premiere, later that season, of Samuel Barber's *Vanessa* (for which he had written the text) and was impressed with what he had heard of Gedda in Paris. One could surmise from Gedda's bearing and buoyant personality that he could muster the charm to make plausible Anatole's easy conquest of Erika shortly after his arrival at the country house where she lived with the aging Vanessa; likewise, his shift of affections to Vanessa when it suited his purpose. But it remained for the dress rehearsal to show that he could sing the English text more understandably than any of the other principals—all of them Americans.

The records show that Gedda made his New York debut as Faust on November 1, 1957 (he had made his American debut in Pittsburgh the previous April as Faust in a production directed by Richard Karp which also included George London and Louis Quilicó, en route to San Francisco to sing in the Ninth Symphony of Beethoven). He also performed his excellent Don Ottavio in *Don Giovanni* on November 13, and nothing else until Anatol on January 15. (Nothing like solving three casting problems with one artist who excels in the styles and texts of operas in three different languages!) It would not be an exaggeration to say that, good as Gedda was in *Faust* and *Don Giovanni*, his special qualities as an artist were most engaged in *Vanessa*.

Just as Gedda solved Legge's *Boris* problem at least in part because of his Russian, was a blessing to La Scala because of his excellent Italian, and a rare acquisition for Paris because of his command of French, he was an unalloyed treasure to Bing, Barber, and Menotti because of his English. In a series of projects, in and out of the Metropolitan, that followed, Gedda became known as an artist whose command of English enunciation was not only superior to that of his American colleagues of the *Vanessa* cast (primarily Rosalind Elias, Eleanor Steber, and Giorgio Tozzi), but almost any others with whom he was associated.

This superiority became the central subject of an interview with Gedda a few years later (February 26, 1961) by John Briggs, a member of *The New York Times* music staff who had himself studied singing. The substance of Gedda's comment was that Americans tend to believe that "because one can speak English one can also sing it," which, in turn, results in the almost universal unintelligibility of opera-in-English when sung by native Americans. It is, of course, an unspoken reality that Americans speak a dozen different varieties of English—in support of Bernard Shaw's contention that "England and America are divided by a common language." They range from Down East (New England) to Deep South, New Yorkese as distinguished from Brooklynese, Middle West, Southwest, Northwest, and so on. On all of these is superimposed, for professional purposes, a kind of "singing teacher's English" which does indeed blot out regional differences, but also the distinctness of enunciation that makes for intelligibility. As a result of this defloration, or elimination of specific identity, individual inclinations among American singers are reduced to a kind of mass non-identity and almost total non-intelligibility, save for such an occasional exception as yesterday's George Meader or today's Donald Gramm.

To Gedda's mind, as revealed by Briggs, Italian is the "ideal vocal language," because it has many open vowel sounds and few consonants that end syllables. French comes close, despite the complication of the "nasalized letters." Like German and his own Swedish, English has more consonants than are comfortable for the palate. Add to difficulties of English those disagreeable diphthongs ("mixtures of two or more vowel sounds") and the consequence is a language "not very comfortable for singing." In the case of the bothersome *r* sound, the Gedda solution is pragmatic: trill the *r* "firmly and forcibly." If the result tends to be artificial, contends Gedda, so be it. The objective is to be clearly understood, not to produce a result comparable to conversational English. (John McCormack, with a slight flavor of Erin on his rolled *r*'s, was a model of intelligibility for any singer in English.) In other words, emphasize the five vowel formations "ah," "ee," "eh," "oh," and "oo" on which a vocal sound can be evolved, and other things will take their course—but don't forget final consonants.

The citations of these principles is not so much to endorse them as incorruptibly valid as to underline the extent to which Gedda has penetrated to the essence of a problem that cuts across all gradations of singing. Maria Callas never has sung in English on stage (she did, indeed, turn down Vanessa for that expressed reason) because, though born and partially educated in New York, she doesn't regard it as a singer's language. Though born in Australia and vocally matured in England, Joan Sutherland never has sung intelligible English because her vocal method (whether the language is Italian, French, *or* English) abhors the consonants that give almost every spoken word its formal demarcation from every other.

Here, in sum, is a measure of the degree to which Gedda's approach to the art of singing is *consciously* different from most others. His effort is directed toward the solution of problems; those of most others, to the evasion of them.

3

If this dissertation suggests a performer devoted, in the main, to some form of artistic ventriloquism in which the vocal instrument is programmed—one can hardly say computerized—to give a kind of Univac quack of recognizable syllabification, whatever the language and without regard for a musical essence, it is false, misleading, and totally erroneous. My point is, rather, that verbal clarity is among Gedda's *special* distinctions, over and above all the merits of a vocal discipline second to none during the span of his career and a range of artistic adaptability no tenor of living memory has commanded.

Merely to enumerate the roles Gedda has sung at the Metropolitan (*subsequent* to the first three, each in a different language) is to categorize him as unique. In sequence (and with a parenthetical I, E or F, for Italian, English, or French) they have been: Singer in *Der Rosenkavalier* (I), Hoffmann in *The Tales of Hoffmann* (F), Tamino in *The Magic Flute* (E), Lensky in *Eugene Onegin* (E), des Grieux in *Manon* (F), Barinkay in *Gypsy Baron* (E), Alfredo in *La traviata* (I), Admetus in *Alceste* (E), Dmitri in *Boris Godunov* (E), Pinkerton in *Madama Butterfly* (I), Nemorino in *L'Elisir d'Amore* (I), Pelléas in *Pelléas et Mélisande* (F), Kodanda in *The Last Savage* (E), the Duke in *Rigoletto* (I), Don José in *Carmen* (F), Roméo in *Roméo et Juliette* (F), Edgardo in *Lucia di Lammermoor* (I), Rodolfo in *La Bohème* (I), Arrigo in *I vespri siciliani* (I), and Riccardo in *Un ballo in maschera* (I).

It is because of Gedda's extraordinary ability to sing those things which most other tenors sing and a wide range of things that they prefer not to sing, that the grand total shows almost as many roles in English as in Italian (10 to 7) and only three fewer in French. One more role must be added (it has been set aside because of the special circumstances in which it was performed). When Joan Sutherland was to be produced for the New York public in her surpassingly fine portrayal of Amina in Bellini's *La Sonnambula*, casting of the male role opposite her found most tenors inclined to look the other way. The part

(Elvino) is not only full of fearfully high and exposed top notes, but lies in a tessitura (the *average* range of the voice writing) that suited very well the abilities of the great Rubini, for whom it was written, but not many contemporary tenors. Clearly, this was singing in a range that was not comfortable for Gedda, and the effort told in the white, rather colorless sound he produced. But he applied to the part all the professionalism at his disposal, and the result was dignified but not really distinguished—save for some beautifully shaped phrases which identified a singer with a true feeling for Bellini. It was not until I looked into Gedda's background for the purpose of this chapter that I discovered he had never sung a note of Bellini in public previously. It was, clearly, out of his long-spun phrases for Mozart, which excited Legge's attention, that his adaptability to the Bellini cantilena was formed. He was, incidentally, uniquely rewarded for his application to the needs of Elvino, whose tranquility is disturbed by Amina's sleep-walking. One paper's comment came out commending him for his work in the difficult role of El Vino. No tenor could find that designation less than beguiling.

What Gedda has done at the Metropolitan is not the whole story of what he has done in New York. That would include a concert version of Bellini's *I Puritani* in 1963, a version in similar style of Berlioz' *Benvenuto Cellini* in 1965, and programs of the Friends of French Opera which have included the fourth act of Meyerbeer's *Les Huguenots* and Massenet's *Werther*. For the San Francisco Opera, he was all but indispensable for the title role when a production of Auber's *Fra Diavolo* was in the planning for 1969. He has sung the version for a tenor Orphée which Gluck made for Paris in 1775, and he has been heard in *Tales of Hoffmann*, not only as Hoffmann, but in the role of Nicklausse, Hoffmann's faithful companion, according to a local tradition in Stockholm. Vienna heard him as Orfeo to Joan Sutherland's Euridice when the long-lost version of *Euridice* by Joseph Haydn was rediscovered and revived in 1967.

His repertory of rarely heard, seldom reperformed operas is second, perhaps, only to the long-lived Hugues Cuenod's list. In addition to the works of Adam, Weber, Auber, Barber, and Menotti previously mentioned, Gedda has been heard in a range from Lully's *Armide* (at Bordeaux in 1957) to Orff's *Trionfo di Aphodite* at La Scala and Rolf Lieberman's *School for Wives* at Salzburg, where he has, of course, also sung the great Mozart roles for tenor.

If there is a tenor who has sung more leading roles in more recorded operas than Gedda, it is not a name which comes readily to mind. Here he has performed widely not only down the broad highway of normal repertory (including Don José to the Carmens of both Victoria de los Angeles, under the baton of Beecham, and Maria Callas, with Georges Prêtre conducting) but in such byways as Glinka's *Life for a Czar*, Peter Cornelius's *The Barber of Bagdad*, Rameau's *Platée*, Bizet's *Les Pêcheurs de Perles*, Delibes' *Lakmé*, Berlioz' *Benvenuto Cellini*, Rossini's *Il Turco in Italia*, and Gounod's *Mireille*. As with Kurt Herbert Adler, for San Francisco's venture with *Fra Diavolo*, "getting Gedda" under contract may well precede all other considerations for fleshing out a difficult recording.

To this point, the recitation of Gedda's merits have been restricted to his career as an opera singer, and an exceptional one. There are at least two other Geddas, either of whom could have made an illustrious career without ever putting a foot on an opera stage. One is the Gedda who began childhood training in the choir school singing *a capella* Dufay, des Prés, and so on. He matured to become one of the world's leading participants in the concert hall literature of choral works by Bach (B minor Mass and *St. Matthew* Passion), Beethoven (*Missa Solemnis* and Ninth Symphony), Berlioz (*Damnation de Faust* and *Requiem*), Janáček (*Slavonic* Mass), Mendelssohn (*Elijah*), and Verdi (*Requiem*). He has not merely sung these once, twice, or occasionally—he has, indeed, recorded all of them with the greatest of his contemporary colleagues.

The other Gedda is more difficult to trace to a childhood conditioning. Had his father spent the years from 1928 to 1934 in Vienna rather than Leipzig, it would be simple. But it was not the case. It was the case, however, that, while growing up in Sweden and amassing tenors with whom he had a special affinity, he discovered not only the recorded literature of Schipa, but also that of Richard Tauber. To his own surprise, he had the opportunity to become everybody's favorite performer ("everybody" may not include a few tenors who are competitors) of the operetta literature more familiar at the Volksoper than at the Staatsoper on Vienna's Ring.

Some light on this side of Gedda was shed in another comment by Legge. It has long been a tradition for the European company that produces Electrola records to engage, promote, and hold exclusively to itself the best tenor it can command for the great operetta favorites of the Central European public. Early on, Electrola decided that Gedda was the man it wanted to carry on the Tauber–Wittrisch–Peter Anders

–Rudolf Schock tradition. "Within two years," recalled Legge, "Gedda had become a master of this literature." His new specialty included not only such marginal works as Flotow's *Martha*, Lortzing's *Zar und Zimmermann*, and the afore-mentioned *Barber of Bagdad*, but the whole canon of high-style operetta from Johann Strauss to Franz Lehár. Included, as a matter of course is *The Merry Widow*—which Gedda has sung in America only in concert—and the greatest of all musically (in my view), *Das Land des Lächelns* (*The Land of Smiles*). The version for Angel supervised by the much-mentioned Legge which brings together Schwarzkopf as Lisa and Gedda as Prince Sou-Chong is not only impeccably well sung, it is possessed of a patina, a luster, a mixture of charm and sparkle rarely encountered in any performance, least of all in the recording studio.

For those not acquainted with the work, the action plays first in Vienna and then in Peking. So adept is Lehár in this score (made famous by his greatest pair of interpreters, Richard Tauber and Vera Schwarz) in differentiating, musically, one locale from the other, and so responsive are all the performers to the direction of Otto Ackermann, that one is spiritually and mentally transported from the Danube to the Yellow Sea by sound alone.

I could not begin to speculate which Gedda is the one for whom I have the highest respect or the greatest admiration. The Gedda of *Lakmé*? The Gedda of Strauss's *Capriccio* (as Flamand)? The Gedda of *Orphée* or Mozart's *Entführung*? Certainly the Gedda who impersonates Prince Sou-Chong in *The Land of Smiles* is one to cherish when all the others have been appraised and evaluated.

But there are, even as I write this, other Geddas in process on recordings still to come, and in the opera house. He has lately performed for the first time in America the part of Riccardo in Verdi's *Un ballo in maschera*. This is, of course, an opera whose locale is Sweden, and whose leading tenor is a king who was assassinated during a masked ball in—a Swedish royal opera house. His recent activities will also lead to such typically diversified record releases as Adolar in Weber's *Euryanthe*, Gerontius in Sir Edward Elgar's mystical *The Dream of Gerontius* and a remake, after nearly twenty years, of Johann Strauss's *Wiener Blut*.

As this list of activities coincided with his fiftieth birthday, it seemed appropriate—after more than twenty years' acquaintance with the artist's work—to seek out the man and find out how much interaction there was between them, or, perhaps, how little. Either is a possibility, depending on native gifts, temperamental disposition and intellectual inclination. I have been acquainted with some artists so prosaic offstage that they might have been stockbrokers or pharmacists; others, who were so flamboyant that they could hardly have been anything else but operatically employed.

Gedda, it came to pass, belongs to neither one *genre* nor the other. Still as tall (six feet four) as he had been when Legge first encountered him, but properly fleshed out, he was, to the unknowing eye, certainly engaged in some artistic endeavor. The manner, the walk, the casual dress were all components of an individuality that spelled the theater, the *atelier*, the gallery. But when he opened his mouth in a greeting, the secret was out. An actor? Perhaps. But the quality was right there between the eyes, so to speak, a well-placed head tone of greeting in a properly tenorial registration.

Reference to his Riccardo at the Metropolitan prompted his observation that somehow, for all the fact that it was an intensely Italian opera, Verdi had penetrated an essence of Swedish character, at least in the part of Riccardo. "I feel very at home with him," he said. "All of what I have read of Gustav III is there, to be made of what one can." His reference brought my countering comment that, of all the Riccardos (as Gustav III is known in the Italian original, because of censorship strictures against possible offense to the Swedish court) I had heard, my favorite remained—Jussi Bjoerling.

Gedda's eyes lit up at the mention of Bjoerling. "Did you know him?" I inquired. "Oh yes," he replied. "There were some years after my debut before he died [in 1960]. Tragic that it should have been so early. He was singing better and better, and should still have had years in his career [Bjoerling was fifty-three when he died of a heart attack at his home on an island in the waters off Stockholm]. I didn't see him much in Sweden, but we often met in Europe or here. I am still very friendly with his family."

Were there other languages in his future? How about Spanish. "Yes," he answered. "I have been learning Spanish. Not to speak it. I am too lazy. I can get along in Spain with Italian, so I am not learning to speak it. But to sing, in recitals, in such works as Turina's *Poema en forma de canciones*." He had missed last year (1974–75) in New York, hadn't he? "Yes," he replied. "It was a year mostly in Europe. But whenever I come back, I am so much impressed by what the Met does with performances in the original languages, even *Boris* is Russian. You know, you don't find that anywhere else. And I must say they have one strength that is rarely encountered in other companies. I am speaking of the great quality of the coaching staff. Men like Jan Behr, Walter Taussig, formerly Ignaz Strasfogel, who is now in Strasbourg, also Martin Rich. They are of great value to younger artists, as well as to more experienced singers like myself. They have not only great knowledge, but a rich background with outstanding conductors of the past such as Bruno Walter, Mitropoulos, Fritz Reiner, and so on. This is a most uncommon thing to find in a theater today."

An even more uncommon thing to find in any theater, any time, is a singer of great accomplishments who also has the will power not to leave undone the one thing that would undo all that he has done. That is to forebear diluting, by acceptance of random roles and assignments of marginal suitability, the solid reputation for quality established in the ways herein described. Already there are signs of persuasion and pressure in Gedda's recent recorded output—roles as dissimilar as Almaviva in Rossini's *Il Barbiere* and Tybaldo in Bellini's *I Capuleti e I Montecchi*—which detract from, rather than enhance, his reputation.

When the question was broached, in a general way, to Gedda, about a timetable for retirement or an alteration of activity, he responded, "No timetable," apparently unruffled by the suggestion that such a thought might be impending. "I will sing as long as I can measure up to the standard I like to think I have. I hear my records constantly and I listen to myself quite critically. I would say that after a few more years I would not—in these times—consider it proper for me to appear as Des Grieux in *Manon* or Roméo at the age of fifty-five. Romantic roles? Fewer of them. Character parts? As long as practical. As for concerts and recitals, I will do those as long as I can."

Some with a keen ear for the semantics suitable to a paragon might wish that Gedda had said not "as long as I can" but "as long as I should." How can the difference be assessed? By the measure of such prior nonpareils as John Brownlee and Edward Johnson. The former, whose participation in the matchless Mozart recordings produced in Glyndebourne during the mid-thirties, and in more than five hundred performances with the Metropolitan between 1937 and 1957, qualifies him for rank as a baritone Gedda, walked out of the stage door, his reputation intact, into another world altogether (as president of the Manhattan School of Music). The latter, who married young and had a daughter who also married young, told her when she announced her matrimonial plans to him, "Fine. But don't make me a grandfather while I'm still singing Pelléas." He avoided that dire happening by also walking away from an ongoing career to quite another, which took him, sooner than he could have imagined, into the General Manager's office of the Metropolitan in 1935.

The decision is Gedda's to make: to be a paragon with a postscript, or a permanent member of a small club whose charter members, for our time, include Brownlee and Johnson.

XII

The Vocabulary of Ignorance

1

When the present coterie of newspaper critics in America gives way, eventually, to another, it will be recognized that, in a time when certain kinds of vocalism were being reborn on the world operatic stage, expressions of opinion in this country were more attuned to instrumental values than they were to vocal. This view does not imply that the quality of such vocalism was ignored or underrated; rather, that its characteristics were too often grossly misstated or inadequately interrelated.

I have in mind the specific instances of superiority represented, over a twenty-year period (1954–1974), by Maria Callas, Joan Sutherland, and Beverly Sills. To judge from the frequency with which these names have been grouped or referred to in a breath, it could be concluded that one was much the same order of singer as the other. To be sure, they are female sopranos who, inevitably, must have some roles in common and have been active concurrently.

But common courtesy demands the recognition that one of them was the leader, the other two the followers. When Callas made her momentous London debut in 1952—after half a dozen years of performing such an incredible range of roles as Isolde and the *Walküre* Brünnhilde (in Italian), Abigaille in *Nabucco*, Fiorilla in Rossini's *Il Turco in Italia*, and Elena in *I vespri siciliani*—Sutherland was a minor performer of small parts . . . specifically, the small part of Clotilde to Callas's first Norma on the Covent Garden stage (November 8, 1952).

At the time of Callas's notable debut in her native land (also as

Norma, in Chicago in the fall of 1954), Miss Sills was so far from prominence that she had not yet been accepted as a member of the New York City Opera Company (then with ten years still to go in its West Fifty-fifth Street home). When she was accepted, some months later, her abilities were so far from special that she made her debut, in the fall of 1955, as Rosalinda in an English-language version of Johann Strauss's *Die Fledermaus*. More years were to pass before Sutherland emerged from the status of an all-purpose soprano at Covent Garden (Helmwige in *Die Walküre* and Olympia in *Les Contes d'Hoffmann* at the extremes of assignment) to challenge a new career as a dramatic coloratura in *Lucia di Lammermoor* in 1959. Even more years elapsed before Sills was to reap the reward of arduous, painstaking work when she appeared in Schumann's *Scenes from Faust* with the Boston Symphony Orchestra under the direction of Erich Leinsdorf (March, 1966) on the way to her rendezvous several months later (September, 1966) with Handel's *Giulio Cesare* (and destiny) in the New York State Theater of Lincoln Center.

It is abundantly clear that Callas was singing her *soprano d'agilità* kind of Norma more than a decade before Sutherland, and the broadly structured kind of Lucia, for which Sills has become known, all of twenty years previously. She was performing both roles with a dramatic insight and a flair for verbal distinction hardly aimed at, thus scarcely achieved, by the others. Callas did not, in the shaping of her career, have what was readily accessible to both Sutherland and Sills: a prototype, a model, a living proof that what she aspired to accomplish was well within the reach of a woman armed to do battle. All three met, eventually, on the common ground of Lucia, of Norma, of Violetta; but, *together*, Sutherland and Sills do not command the breadth of repertory that made Callas unique in her active years—and perhaps, shortened her professional life span.

Hers was a repertory that need merely be recalled to be categorized as bold beyond the dictates of common sense, and ambitious to the point of recklessness: Isolde and Amina in *La Sonnambula;* the terror of Medea and the laughter of Rossini's *Il Turco in Italia;* womanly self-sacrifice (Elena in *I vespri siciliani*) and unbridled fury (Lady Macbeth); plus a command of recitative to match her passionate predilection for melodic flow.

Conceivably, a singer could possess all these attributes and still leave one looking the other way when she stepped on stage. But once Callas had put her physical house in order (by losing seventy-five of the

excessive pounds she was carrying when she auditioned, without outcome, for General Manager Edward Johnson of the Metropolitan
Opera in 1945), she begged no question, asked no quarter, craved no
indulgence for a sight unserved, an illusion faulted, a visual need left
unattended. Her Violetta was a credible courtesan, not because of a
fluttery fan and a giddy manner suitable to her calling, but because she
assimilated every hint and inflection—*"un fil di voce"* ("a thin voice")
is one—that Verdi poured into his characterization. Flattered as she was
by Alfredo's attentions, she was no less aware of the harm her attachment to him might cause the nameless daughter on whose behalf
Germont, senior, asked her to renounce his son. Pained as she was by
Alfredo's insulting return of the money she had spent on their life
together, she was still worldly enough to understand his act of temper,
and forgive him for it.

Perhaps it would be sufficient to say that if, for all their vocal
virtues, neither Sutherland's Norma nor Violetta are wholly persuasive,
it is because Callas has been there first with a thrust of intensity, a
sound of human credibility that no later singer has equaled. With Sills,
as Elvira in *I Puritani* or as Lucia, the depth of emotion may be in the
performer's heart, but it does not resound in a voice whose lower
range has been sacrificed for brilliance at the top.

In another time, and with another such colossus dominating the
world operatic stage, it would all be in the verbal record, available for
the guidance and instruction of those too young to have experienced
the phenomenon that was, successively, Maria Kalogeropoulos, Maria
Callas, Maria Meneghini Callas, and just plain Callas. All too much of
her productive public life was spent (between fourteen and twenty-
four) in wartime Greece or waging the struggle for survival and recognition in Italy. Now, on the other side of an ill-advised, failure-
doomed concert tour, she is, at little more than fifty—an age at which
many great sopranos are just about to draw a career's second breath—an
all-but-extinct volcano. Her literary likenesses thus far, save for an
excellent but early biography by George Jellinek, exist primarily in
effusive outpourings of the fan coterie, a kind of writing which cap-
tures the shadow of Callas but not the substance.

Thus one must speculate, independent of any useful printed literature, on the flaw (geologically speaking) that gave rise first to problems, then to difficulty, and finally to an inability to perform. Was it
in her vocal endowment? In the method with which it was used? Or
in herself? Those who deplore the lack of *authoritative* evaluation in

English (a single, searching article by Teodoro Celli published in *Saturday Review*, January 31, 1959, is about the sum of it) can still go to the sources and find out for themselves.

I refer not to the commercial recordings—which can be edited, amended, and reorganized to produce a result that never really existed —but to another branch of electronics that might be termed the New Realism. There is, in being, for those with the means and the interest to investigate it, a total of more than 80,000 "live" events (spanning the period from the early 1930s, when radio came in, through the sixties and seventies when portable tape recorders began to yield credible results) that have been brought to book. Opera performances are in the largest supply, but the quantity of concert music is also considerable.

The Callas file takes in the Verdi *Vespri* directed by Kleiber at the Maggio Musicale Fiorentino of 1951 that ignited the flame of her Italian fame; the Mexico City *Lucia* of June 10, 1952; the *Traviata* with di Stefano as it sounded in La Scala on May 28, 1955; and the Dallas *Medea* of November 8, 1958 (among, of course, others).

Such documentations can be bought, owned, studied, evaluated. They are all what Callas herself calls "trapeze" parts, a telling term that is singularly suitable not only for the picture of danger it paints, but of the result that awaits failure—a fall from grace, with no net below.

Putting all the evidentiary matter together—beginning with the "live" Norma in Chicago in 1954, many others elsewhere thereafter, and the products of the New Realism—my answer to the self-posed question would be: the flaw in Callas was, primarily, in the individual herself; secondly, in the way the voice was used; least of all, in the voice itself. She was, to run the sequence in the opposite order, blessed with responsive cords (the ability to sing Santuzza in *Cavalleria Rus-ticana* in Greece at the age of fifteen proves that) which had been more than adequately trained for the exceptional uses to which they would be put. But her own fierce desire to excel, the pressure she put on her throat to make it yield every ounce of drama for which she strove, and the inability to coast, to finesse, to meet challenges other than head on, undercut the resource without which Callas was no longer Callas. When the all-important vocal exclamation point with which she drove home her vocal oratory was no longer a triumph but a trial—when, in other words, her searing, soaring top voice seared but did not soar—her vocal statements were truncated, incomplete, devoid of the burning touch of human emotion that made them unique.

It is in the nature of a re-creative urge that burns fiercely to be self-consuming. The artist whose effort is classically poised, delicately balanced, and always under tight restraint will, almost invariably, outlast the one whose impulse is stronger than the will to hold it in check. The truism was expressed poetically in what might be called Edna St. Vincent Millay's Law: "My candle burns at both ends, It will not last the night . . ." but while it does, "it gives a lovely light."[1] The Callas equivalent was expressed in her own way in 1972, when she was working hard to make a return to vocal performance a reasonable reality. A friend suggested it be done by easy stages, with a trial performance in some out-of-the-way place. "No," she said, in a manner that brooked no contradiction, "I want to look the lion in the eye. I will go to London."

In the recollection of his twenty-two years as general manager of the Metropolitan Opera, Rudolf Bing bracketed Callas with Herbert von Karajan as "the complete artists of my time," adding, "I can criticize myself most effectively by complaining how few performances we had from either—from Callas, only twenty-one altogether."[2]

2

Bing's assumption of blame is hardly grounds for a general amnesty from shame, considering that it was his impulsive act in "firing" Callas in November, 1958, that deprived New York audiences of a season in which she would have added more than half again to that total of twenty-one performances. Again, had he lauded her as the "complete artist" he now acknowledges her to be—rather than including her among the "outstanding artists the Met always presents" and pouring fuel on the fire by adding that "Mme. Callas' artistic qualifications are a matter of violent controversy between her friends and foes"—the controversy might have been resolved long before the end of the six Callas-less seasons that ensued.

But it is a matter of record that the response of the New York press to this "complete artist" encouraged, rather than opposed, the rash act of the headstrong administrator. To be sure, Paul Hume declared in the *Washington Post* that it was Bing who should be fired, not Callas. But his was not a voice the Metropolitan's directors were called upon to heed. From the time of her New York debut as Norma on October 29, 1956, there was little effort to separate the artist from the vocalist, or both from an outspoken personality whose loose tongue was her worst enemy. Those baffled by the conflict between the irascible person and the sovereign artist found it easy to rest their case on citations from the vocabulary of ignorance to which vocal appraisal was increasingly dependent in this time.

To the commentator of one important paper who had, apparently, not before encountered a dramatic *soprano d'agilità* (that is to say, a vocalist who combined a sound of dramatic power with the flexibility for ornaments, embellishments, runs, staccati, and a florid, flaring top) it was a "puzzling voice." Another thought the voice had "many limitations." He praised the "nicely rolled coloraturas" (a grammatical mismatch, as *coloratura* is an Italian, not an English term) in "Casta diva" but decided they were "at times punctuated by high notes that were not well placed."

In a summarizing statement, the person who had pronounced it a "puzzling voice" concluded: "In the Casta Diva and the third act scene with the children when she did not force, her voice had delicacy and point."[3] This recourse to the one term regularly invoked when all others are insufficiently vague to cover a critical quibble is the vocabulary of ignorance at its zenith.

To judge from the episodes selected by the writer, my conclusion would be that he is equating the use of color for dramatic purposes with the sinful inclination to "force" the voice. I understand "to force" (a terminology I shun) to mean "to apply excessive muscular power to achieve a bigger sound than is available through normal means of production." The equivalent would be a pianist's application of muscular strength on the keys to achieve a sound not available to him by normal, well-regulated weight and pressure. In either case, the outcome is a strangulated, nonvibrant output which relates more to *noise* than it does to *tone*.

To fine-point the objection, the writer should be prepared to state not only *where* the singer was inclined to "force," but how. Was there excessive use of the neck muscles? Was there strain in the lips? Was the tongue pushed down? Was the palate pulled high? It is common knowledge that there are three elements to singing: the *activator* (or lungs which provide air), the *vibrator* (or "cords," where a sound is generated), and a *resonator* (mouth, pharynx, nasopharynx and nasal cavities), which forms a trumpet-like thrust to project a sound to the listener. Ideally, the tone should be the product of an unconstricted *vibrator*, heard from a *resonator* functioning without tension, with a steady stream of air from the *activator*, which is supported from the diaphragm, pushed upwards by the abdominal muscles.

Reading the objection to Callas stated by the writer who described her voice as "puzzling," I would conclude he is describing a small-voiced singer striving for the power to make herself heard in large surroundings and thus driven to "force." Callas could hardly be accused of inaudibility in any auditorium in which she commonly performed (the Chicago Civic Opera House, the old Met, Carnegie Hall, or Covent Garden).

Was it possible that these and other reviewers who complained of harshness in her tone or coarseness in her recitatives were simply averse to vocal color, dramatic accent, a constant striving for verbal emphasis, and a total devotion to emotional intensity?

Even were such the case—and it would be a merciless condemnation of any press corps to allege such indifference to the one singer among hundreds whom the author of *5,000 Nights at the Opera* singled out as "the complete artist"—twenty-one performances spread over a dozen years should have produced something more memorable than can be found in print. During those years (1954–1965) there were still eight New York newspapers regularly reporting on the musical scene. It was not until after the old Met had passed from the scene, when three papers that had combined in a last struggle for survival collapsed together and two others also failed, that the total fell to an insupportably meager three (1967). Nevertheless, one can find little to be described as sharp journalistic observation, even less, distinguished criticism in their columns.

Did she sing flat? Did she sing sharp? An answer to such curiosity might, on occasion, be found—but not necessarily the correct one. A distinguished musicologist who was required to grapple with this problem offered his judgment: "There is a byproduct of her vocal enunciation, a sort of resonance, that often veils the clear soprano timbre and even threatens true pitch. As a matter of fact, Miss Callas' sense of pitch is not always secure. She is not exactly flat or sharp, but neither is she always on the dot."[4] This, I submit, is a prime instance of a man striving uncomfortably to describe something he has not clearly perceived. The "sort of resonance" to which he refers is doubtless descriptive of the covered method of production Callas—and others—use to darken the sound and invoke an ominous quality for which "a clear soprano timbre" would be wholly inappropriate.

On another occasion, when it was Verdi's *La traviata* to which Callas addressed herself, the same commentator wrote: "There was a moment during the first act duet when the pitch was dropping so alarmingly that I expected soprano and tenor to end up in the lap of Fausto Cleva, the conductor. . . ." The presumption would be, from the order of mention—"soprano and tenor"—that it was Callas who was weighting the scales so heavily from her higher register that the tenor was being pushed down and down, despite all effort to the contrary.

A dozen lines further down in the comment, however, we are informed, as something of an afterthought: "Mr. Barioni [the previously-mentioned young Italian christened Daniele, who enjoyed a transistory fame in the mid-fifties] has a fine voice which he pushes mercilessly. It sounds agreeable, even impressive when used within its natural boundaries, but becomes pinched and flat when it is forced [?]. *The near-disaster mentioned above was largely his responsibility, for he pulled Miss Callas with him.*" (Ital added)

I cast a glow of the spotlight on these words not because what happened in a performance nearly twenty years ago (1958) has any lingering significance, but because the statement defies logic. If the man was "pushing mercilessly"—and also, for this day's usage, "forcing"—the usual consequence would be to *raise* the pitch, *not* lower it, as it indeed did. Barioni was singing off pitch, and Callas' firm adherence to the proper intonation did, indeed, cause a dissonance—but it was because he was singing *sharp,* not flat.

To answer all arguments, quash all countercontentions, the account of the Callas Violetta is summed up in the statement "She was in turns appealing and ardent and her stage presence is electrifying, but her voice is just not a beautiful organ. . . ."[5]

This is, of course, the unvocal approach to singing, at its most instrumental. If Emerson endorsed the plurality of human comeliness by asserting, for all time, "Beauty is in the eye of the beholder," so there can realistically be the premise that "Beauty is in the ear of the auditor." We can readily agree that one set of sounds can be described in different acoustical terms than another, especially when they are machine-tuned—as in the piano, organ, or harp—or responsive to keys, valves, or screws—as are the stringed instruments, woodwinds, brass, and timpani.

But if the pipes are not those of Pan, but of the muscle and blood that form windpipes, and the bellows are human tissue, not wood and leather which pump air into a harmonium, and the diaphragm is not a synthetic stretched skin-thin but the "muscular and tendinous partition separating thorax from abdomen in mammals" (Oxford Concise Dictionary), then every combination of these entities within the human body must necessarily be different from every other combination of them. Which combination of which (when used together with all the accessories) comprises "a beautiful organ" is subject to an infinite variety of shadings that can only be wholly defined by someone who has made a close, intensive study of the subject and the vocabulary appropriate to its characterization.

I do not include myself in that category, and recognize that my own qualifications could be rated inadequate. I can, I am sure, claim greater credibility for my description of the late David Oistrakh's Carnegie Hall debut (at about the same time in the 1950s) than I could for Callas's at the Metropolitan: I have studied the violin and know what goes into its manipulation. In addition, everything about the result could be visually observed as well as audibly heard. That is only the beginning of the ways in which the tangible, visible violin, piano, or cello differs from the invisible, intangible, impalpable vocal organ.

3

If there exists, today, a whole generation of critics who write about such nineteenth-century singers as Giulia Grisi and Giuditta Pasta as though they were, indeed, present when they performed at the Italian Opera in London, it is wholly because there was one who was present and whose words have outlived him by a century. That is the same Henry Fothergill Chorley to whose words I have made reference several times before. The temptation to do so, in the present context, is made irresistible by such specimens of Chorley's *vocalizing* a singer's performance as the following:

"Never has so beautiful a woman as Madame Grisi been so little coquettish on the stage," records Chorley about the year 1835, from the vantage point of 1861. "I remember no solitary instance of smile or sign which could betray to the closest observer that she was attempting any of those artifices which are so unpleasing to all who love art and who do not regard the theatre as a slave-market. . . . And what a soprano voice was hers! rich, sweet, equal throughout its compass of two octaves (from C to C) without a break, or a note which had to be managed. . . ."[6]

In his choice of the last dozen or so words—"without a break, or a note which had to be managed"—Chorley is clearly of the opinion that he is writing for a reader as keenly conscious of voice and vocal values as he is himself. "Without a break" goes to the point, of course, that the professional singing voice is *evolved* over two or more registers, that the passage from one register—low, middle, high—to the other has to be equalized (smoothed over, joined, blended) to avoid ugly discrepancies in timbre and weight, which is to say (to resume the quoting of Chorley) that they may have "a note which has to be managed."

"When the passion of the actress was roused—as in *La Gazza*, during the scenes with her deserter father, with the villainous magistrate, or in the prison with her lover, or on her trial, before sentence was passed —her glorious notes, produced without difficulty or stint, rang through the house like a clarion, and were truer in their vehemence to the emotion of the scene than were those wonderfully subdued sounds in the penetrating tenuity of which there might be more or less artifice."

So much for praise of the palpable. Chorley was no less eloquent in his characterization of an impalpable which might lastingly have denied all praise to a singer less resolute than Pasta: "The ninety-nine requisites of a singer (according to the well-known Italian adage) had been denied to her. Her voice was originally limited, husky and weak, without charm, without flexibility, a mediocre mezzo-soprano. Though her countenance *spoke,* the features were cast in that coarse mould which is common in Italy. Her arms were fine, but her figure was short and clumsy. She walked heavily, almost unequally. . . .

"It has been said that Giuditta Pasta was more than overlooked— openly flouted—in this very Opera House of ours, in the year 1817, and by a wardrobe woman. . . . At all events, whether roused by it or not, she subjected herself to a course of severe and incessant vocal study, to subdue and to utilize her voice. To equalize it was impossible. There was a portion of the scale which differed from the rest in quality and remained to the last "under a veil" to use the Italian term. There were notes always more or less out of tune, especially at the commencement of her performances. Out of these uncouth materials she had to compose her instrument, and then to give it flexibility. Her studies to acquire execution must have been tremendous: but the volubility and brilliancy, when acquired, gained a character of their own from the resisting peculiarities of the organ. There was a breadth, an expressiveness in her roulades, an evenness and solidity in her shake, which imparted to every passage a significance totally beyond the reach of lighter and more spontaneous singers."[7]

By application not only of the admirable vocabulary at his command, but also of his sharply defined mental image of each singer, Chorley can almost auralize, for us, two performers long dead and of whom not even so much as a whisper remains: Grisi, whose voice "without a break, or a note which had to be managed" is the image of the ideal instrument; Pasta, denied "the ninety-nine requisites of a singer," the archetype of the performer who makes her way despite, rather than because of, the gifts with which she was endowed.

We have, of course, known both types in recent times, but they could hardly be more lastingly categorized than Chorley did, decades ago. We who reach for such analogies as a trumpet for the voice of Flagstad or a clarinet for the even-fingered scale of Sutherland, from dusky *chalumeau* in the rich lower ranges to reedy fullness in alt. (which means not some derivative of *alto,* as might be supposed, but *altissimo,* or G above "high" C), can only envy the skill with which Chorley could instrument *his* allusions. Thus, in searching for a detail with which to support his contention that Mme Löwe "was the best Donna Elvira in *Don Giovanni* that I have ever seen" because the "*harpsichord* quality of her voice told well, rather than ill, for the opera— the *quill*-tone in it (musicians will understand my word) giving a sort of fantastic excuse for the Don's vicious vagaries in favour of something sweeter."[8] My own preferment, from among all the Donna Elviras I have heard, for Elisabeth Schwarzkopf, did not go at all, I must say, to the plectral.

There are, as I have noted, some English disciples of Chorley who are quite persuaded, from study of his words, that they have themselves heard Grisi or Pasta and will argue the merits of a contemporary singer on such terms. Nor is it a paradox to praise his invocation of an instrumental analogy for a singing effect, and denounce others for *evaluating* singers instrumentally. In Chorley's case, the reference is overt, as an extension of vocal terminology; in the other cases, the procedure is, not merely covert, but the *only one* at the writers' command.

This is all too unfortunate, for a skilled exposition of a singer's long suit as well as his/her shortcomings, can make for spirited reading when administered with the finesse of W. J. Henderson's evaluation of

Luisa Tetrazzini's Violetta in *La traviata* at the Manhattan Opera House on January 15, 1908. After several introductory paragraphs, Henderson declared:

> Mme. Tetrazzini has a fresh, clear voice of pure soprano quality and of sufficient range, though other rôles must perhaps disclose its furthest flights above the staff. The perfectly unworn condition and youthful timbre of this voice are its largest charms, and to these must be added a splendid richness in the upper range. Indeed, the best part of the voice as heard last evening was from the G above the staff to the high C. The B flat in "Sempre libera" was a tone of which any singer might have been proud. The high D in the same number was by no means so good, and the high E flat which the singer took in ending the scene was a head tone of thin quality and refused to stay on the pitch.
>
> In colorature Mme. Tetrazzini quite justified much that had been written about her. She sang staccato with consummate ease, though not with the approved method of breathing. Her method is merely to check the flow between tones instead of lightly attacking each note separately. But the effect which she produces, that of detached notes rather than of strict staccato, is charming. Of her shake less can be said in praise. It was neither clear in emission nor steady, and the interval was surely at least open to question.
>
> Descending scales she sang beautifully, with perfect smoothness and clean articulation. Her transformation of the plain scale in the opening cadenza of "Sempre libera" into a chromatic scale, though a departure from the letter of the score, was not at all out of taste, and its execution fully sustained its right to existence.
>
> The ascending scales in the same number were sung in a manner which would not be tolerated by any reputable teacher in a pupil of a year's standing. They began with a throaty *voce bianca* and ended in a sweep into a full medium, with the chest resonance carried up to a preposterous height.
>
> The most notable shortcoming of Mme. Tetrazzini's singing as revealed last night was her extraordinary emission of her lower medium notes. These were all sung with a pinched glottis and with a color so pallid and a tremolo so pronounced that they were often not a bad imitation of the wailing of a cross infant. This style of tone production she carried into most of her recitative, till she seemed to be inclined to think that Violetta ought to show that fondness for "baby talk" which is sometimes accepted as a charm among her kind.[9]

In what might be called, were it printed in *The Congressional Record* "an extension of remarks," Henderson went on to characterize Tetrazzini's command of cantilena "furthest below the demands of supreme vocal art," her use of "cold color" (a "pitiless description of her infantile delivery of 'Dite alla giovine' would read like cruelty"), and her "tricks of phrasing in short and spasmodic groups." Certainly it is clear that this lucid, balanced, discriminating evaluation of a memorable event was written by a man who knew singing well enough to discuss, in detail, the art of Lilli Lehmann, Jean de Reszke, and Marcella Sembrich—with the singers themselves. As with Chorley, Henderson was of the opinion that he wrote for people who knew the voice and its values.

Voce bianca? Emission? Glottis? Staccati? Chest resonance? These all have readily intelligible meanings in lay language—but to whom? And in what percentage are they readers of a contemporary newspaper? As there were far more newspapers in New York in 1908 than there are decades later, the presumption would have to be that there are also far fewer readers today who are versed in such terminology. Has so much changed about musical education over those years, or are there fewer people interested in singing and singers now? Yes and no—but not evasively. On the primary level, I would have to believe that musical education is far less demanding and far less productive now than it was in the 1920s, but the interest in singing and singers is as great as, or even greater than, it was those fifty years ago.

The curious paradox—and it is a baffling one—is, simply: in the present era, when almost any subtlety of vocal execution can—by electronic means—be auditioned and evaluated in the home, the discriminating discussion of its fine points has all but vanished from the general press of this country.

Does this mean that the public is content merely to enjoy, via records and radio, what it likes and cares little about informed discussion of it? Or is it possible that the response—intelligent, informed, discriminating—to the abundance of aural experience now so readily available will make itself apparent in the next generation of critics?

3

In the meantime, it would contribute mightily to the enlightenment of the non-Italian audience were its access to opera to be made as close, genuine, and direct as it is in the country where the art was born. An all but hopeless presumption? Not really. If the Japanese can learn to comprehend baseball and perform it with great skill, why should not a similar indoctrination produce, among Americans, an equal understanding of opera?

Whether the town is Naples or Perugia, Milan or Parma, Italians begin to know their opera almost as early in life as Americans begin to throw a baseball. Indoctrination in these communal pleasures all stem from the same, parental source. Is it the answer, then, to perform all opera in English? No. The answer is to bridge the gap between the experience and those to whom it is alien by making the American listener as keenly conscious of the lore, the traditions, and the criteria of operatic performance as he is of the sport he has grown up with since childhood.

It is widely agreed that baseball has vastly expanded its audience among women since the radio, through such a persuasive, well-spoken intermediary as "Red" Barber, brought the lore, the traditions, and above all, the criteria of the game into the home. Many of them have become so expert in their appreciation of the game's fine points that, with the advent of the televised picture in the home, they can turn down the huckster's voice on the sound track and derive enjoyment from the picture alone. I agree that it is, on the whole, desirable to restrict comment on an opera broadcast to the time when the curtain is down, or the action suspended. But, in special circumstances and with proper forewarning, it would be useful to have a person with the proper qualifications to have the option, during an opera of the length of *Don Giovanni*, say, to commune with the audience (via a *separate* channel and in a golf-championship whisper) now and then:

> And now, ladies and gentlemen of the radio audience, a brief bit of background to the aria we are about to hear. . . . Wesley Parks, our Don Ottavio, is approaching stage center. It is the middle of Act II, and Parks has had an erratic, not to say, trying day. . . . In "Dalla sua pace" he went at the vocal line in good style, but tailed off in a couple of passages where shortness of breath let him down—he should do more leg and lung work to build up that very necessary element in singing Mozart. . . . Moreover, the aria comes on andantino sostenuto, and slow stuff tends to bother him. . . . He did have a better grip of that prominent phrase "Grazie di tanto onore" ("Many many thanks for the honor") just before the Mask Trio, but the two ladies, Anna and Elvira, were there to pick him up if he should falter. . . .
>
> OK—while I was filling you in on Parks earlier at bats, we've heard him do the first phrases of "Il mio tesoro"—good control, nice level delivery—that's where his strength is, in the middle register—now—he had a good run at "Cercato" first in the direct attack and then into Mozart's really deceptive, curling figuration—upp!! he couldn't resist the temptation to overpower it, and, of course, it

threw him as he pushed the phrase out of line. . . . Too bad these young singers don't learn from the example of "Raef" Schipa, who was known as Tito but was born Raffaele, or Jack McCormack, how to work around the tight spots—what a pair! Neither had what you could call a powerhouse punch, but when it came to making it in the clutch, they had the diaphragm to do the work for them—it was like having an extra man in the lineup—right there in the gut, the real extra bit of support to get that breath column in where it would do the most good and knock the line for six—pardon me for the cricket allusion, I mean six measures. . . .

Now, then—if the young man were to ask my advice, as an experienced singer, I would suggest to Parks that he forget those fans up in the top gallery, and stop laying into every note as if he wouldn't be heard. . . . He'd find that not only did his delivery carry farther if he didn't squeeze on every note, but he'd attract more attention if he made the listener come to *him* more, rather than going to the listener with every phrase. . . . Those are the things about singing that make it sport for the pros, and an ordeal for the would-be pros. . . . Now this is your good, old friend Jan Peerce, saying *addio* and *arriverderci*, until next time. . . .

Farfetched though it may appear, there is more affinity between effort and result in these two unrelated forms of endeavor than would seem possible. Preparation, coordination, command of the technical means to execute a basic physical discipline, a sensible understanding of personal strengths and weaknesses, a candid insight into one's limitations—all of these are as vital to success in one line of work as in another. But what about the personal input, the factors of character and imagination that differentiate one performer's "Il mio tesoro" from another's? This personal dimension can be likened to the same human impulse that produces a great competitor in one athlete and a routine response to challenge in another.

The lore of both endeavors is replete with brilliant prospects, fast starters, persons of wonderful endowments destined for memorable careers—all forgotten after five years of day-to-day, intensive pressure. Curiously enough, durability in both opera and baseball may be measured in similar time spans—five years or less for the morning glories; ten years or so for the good, sound professionals; fifteen years, at least, to qualify as a star; twenty years for consideration as an all-time great. More years than that are proof that an individual has a combination of identity, consistency, *and* durability which must be measured in fractions of a century rather than merely in decades, as for example Peerce, whose Metropolitan career embraced the years from 1941 to 1965.

Is it possible for a well-qualified observer, coming upon a performer not yet identified as an established star, to form a reliable, perceptive evaluation that surpasses, for acuity and perception, the generality of opinions being circulated at the time? Reviewing the early years of the Callas career vs. the Vocabulary of Ignorance, I have come upon one such candidate for consideration.

The words that follow were written for *Opera News*, the inter-member organ of the Metropolitan Opera Guild, for an issue dated October 27, 1952. The writer is Robert Lawrence, whose qualifications for pursuing a career either as a critic or a conductor have many documentations. How he came to be present in Mexico City I do not know. What he wrote, speaks for itself:

> Not in a long time has any one singer stirred so much controversy as Miss Callas. One faction—the management of the *Opera Nacional* and a generous segment of the Mexico City musical press—hails her as a kind of deity. "La Callas" wrote one newspaper this summer, "is the diva of the century. She is a phenomenon to be compared with the *aurora borealis*." Another group, whose opinions are more prevalent in the lobby of the *Bellas Artes* than in the press, finds the lady over-rated. There seems to be no middle ground.
>
> To pin-point the reason for this controversy, it should be explained that Miss Callas has the billing of *"prima donna assoluta."* There is no phase of the soprano repertory, be it dramatic, lyric or coloratura, which she is not prepared to explore. A hundred and fifty years ago, this was common practice in the lyric theater. Today, in an era of specialization, our sopranos confine themselves to a limited gamut, singing either high and fast or the reverse. Not, however, the intrepid Miss Callas, who tried Gilda one week and Tosca the next.
>
> Miss Callas has much of the vocal technique necessary for such diversity. Her legato is expertly controlled, her agility (especially in semi-tone scales) quite dazzling, when coupled with the sonorities of a big, full-bodied voice; and her musicianship is formidable. Few other singers are so accurate in every mechanical aspect of their roles. Her vocal resources are not, however, unlimited in their adaptation to every part. Miss Callas is fundamentally a *lirico spinto*. Hers is the type of voice for *Aida*, *Trovatore*, and *Tosca*. In the higher and more active altitudes of both *Rigoletto* and *Lucia*, the coloratura arias were taken at somewhat less than their usual speed so that all the notes could apparently fit into the design. . . . Both these roles she is said to have learned in a week. Up to a high C, Miss Callas' top tones are impressive; beyond that, they tend to become shrill.
>
> There seems to be no general admiration, even among the

strongest Callas fans, for the basic timbre of the voice. It is her method, her virtuosity that command the plaudits; and the current debate centers about the extent of this virtuosity. As to communicative power, her interpretations are intelligently planned, sincerely carried out, but—perhaps—lacking in spontaneity. Great emotional summits, such as the "Amami, Alfredo!" of *Traviata*, miss the expressive impact. Miss Callas is at her best in archaic pieces like *Puritani*, which demand her marvelously equalized scales and superb control of the legato line. She is less successful in standard repertory.[10]

This strikes me as very rightfully the tone, the attitude, the point of departure to be taken *vis-à-vis* a performer not yet thirty, clearly possessed of extraordinary objectives, and still burdened by the weight that made her ungainly, impeded rather than assisted by her physical presence (the diet did not occur until the following year). No idolatry, even less any hostility: it is a portrait of a performer drawn in swift, accurate strokes, to which some power of divination had to be applied. Above all, no recourse to the Vocabulary of Ignorance . . . not even a single "forced."

Lawrence's comment proves that it is reasonably possible to do, assuming that the writer is musically educated, attuned to the values that pertain to singing, and disposed to report his impressions as he receives them. In May of 1961, Callas responded to an invitation to appear before the Court of St. James by performing a short, but exacting, sequence of arias. The command performance was in St. James's Palace, with Sir Malcolm Sargent (with whom she had appeared on British television during the previous October) as her accompanist.

The following report appeared in *The Sunday Times* of London on June 4, 1961. In the part that related to Callas, it read:

There could hardly be a greater contrast than the four tremendous operatic arias which Maria Callas then sang, accompanied by Sir Malcolm Sargent. It was a brave action for Madame Callas to undertake to sing these testing works in so intimate a setting. Not unnaturally she sang the first aria "Casta diva, che inargenti" from Bellini's *Norma*, with some reserve, emphasized by the slight cold from which she was suffering.

But then, as the next three arias followed each other, we heard the ringing power of Madame Callas' voice developing and felt the dramatic force of her personality. The characteristic quality of her lower register emphasized the grief-stricken character of the words "Pleurez mes yeux, tombez triste rosée" in that aria from Massenet's *Le Cid*. It was the last two arias "Tu che le vanità" from Verdi's

Don Carlos and "L'altra notte" from Boito's *Mefistofele* which
demonstrated the range of her voice, the clear low notes, the soft
high singing and the perfectly controlled intervals. Every performance was stamped with the high intelligence which governs all
Madame Callas' singing. It was a remarkable experience to be able
to see and hear this in such intimacy.[11]

Discriminating, discerning, well worthy of *The Sunday Times*,
whose principal music critics have, from 1920 to 1975, been only Ernest
Newman and Desmond Shawe-Taylor. The writer was neither of
them. Newman, of course, died in 1959, and his successor, Shawe-
Taylor, was, I presume, not on the guest list. But the Rt. Hon. Edward
Heath (M. P. from Bexley, Lord Privy Seal, not yet Prime Minister)
was, and favored all Britain with a demonstration of the musical literacy
with which his constituency had long been familiar.

XIII

The Sight for the Sound

1

In whatever guise, from whatever source, opera appeals to its audience today on two levels: sight and sound. Why the specification of "to-day?" What is there about the contemporary audience that is different from its predecessors? The answer is not a complicated one. Traditionally, opera has been primarily an aural experience, intensified by the recorded reproduction of excerpts which have, in recent times, been extended to complete works. Today's audience, however, is the most eye-minded in history, if still somewhat laggard by comparison with the super-sophisticated ear.

Film provided the first adjunct for the eye comparable to sound reproduction for the ear. But it was not until the development, first of black and white, then of color television, that the eye began to have a home source of information and education worthy of a sound system capable of reproducing records and tapes. Should the video disc and video cassette fulfill their potential to enable the user to choose his own programs to view whenever and as often as he can play a record, the eye will achieve parity with the ear. Already, however, its standards and criteria have been transformed.

In its early (nonmusical) aspects, opera catered to the audience through a trinity of collaborators: an architect who designed a theater, an artist who decorated its stage (frequently the same person), and an engineer who devised the mechanical means to bring the stage alive. Broadly speaking, the same separation of function prevails today (with a subdivision of "designer" into scenery and the lighting of it), just as there are still orchestral players, solo singers, and chorus, with a conductor to give unity and purpose to their combined efforts.

Indeed, given Divine Intervention, a composer such as Rossini, Donizetti, or Bellini could walk into theater where *La Gazza Ladra* or *Lucrezia Borgia* or *Norma* was being performed and take charge of the overture with little problem of musical adjustment. But when the curtain rose, he might react to what he saw with shock, surprise, rage—or delight. I have stated the chances of a pleasurable reaction as one in four because it would be sheer luck if it occurred.

There was no such question of "luck" with the *mise en scène* when the works mentioned above were first performed. In all three instances, the original scenery was the work of a man who had actually, physically, collaborated with the composer. It is no accident, either, that the man was the same on each occasion. He was Alessandro Sanquirico, a painter who had digressed to scenic design, with special influence on the works that were produced at La Scala between 1817 and 1832.

On the other hand, had Mozart, by similar Divine Intervention, been allowed to participate, posthumously in a famous (1815) performance of *Die Zauberflöte* in Berlin, what he saw would doubtless have pleased him enormously. After a suitably serious and finely phrased playing of the overture under the composer's direction, the curtain would rise on the first of a series of highly original but intensely appropriate stage pictures. Outstanding among them was the vaulted, starry night sky, spread out like a blue and white blanket over the Queen of the Night. The scenic concept has frequently been reproduced as a model of imaginative design, so often, indeed, that one might suppose it originated at the work's premiere.

A reasonable guess, but inaccurate. The artist, Karl Friedrich Schinkel (born in Neuruppin, near Berlin in 1781) and best known as an architect, did collaborate with Mozart, but in a way different from Sanquirico with Rossini, Donizetti, and Bellini. Schinkel's collaboration was of the other, one-out-of-four variety, that could be described as psychic, or spiritual. It was the compelling effect of Mozart's *work* that aroused Schinkel to a veritable visual counterpart. The interaction might be likened to the kind of spiritual, psychic collaboration that enables one conductor (of insight, and some divination) to look at a page of black and white markings and re-create the audible counterpart of what lies buried in them. To another, of less insight and no divination, the marks remain simply symbols of note values. The difference, in our time, is that most conductors are bound, by training and disposition, to strive for the authentic equivalent of the printed page, but most designers of today incline, by training and disposition, to use the stage to serve their own purposes rather than the composer's.

Such being the case, it might be asked, why could not a great production of the past be more often reproduced as a satisfactory solution to a constantly recurring problem? This would first: be an evasion of a recurrent responsibility; second: substitute slavish imitation for creativity in an area where change is not only possible but welcome; and third: require the strength of character possessed by Richard Strauss when, as head of the Vienna Opera in 1919 with a new production of *Die Zauberflöte* pending, he said (in effect), "Let's do Schinkel again." It is a rarity when so satisfactory a solution to the scenic problem as Alfred Roller's original settings for *Der Rosenkavalier* remain a model for most later ones.

In a larger sense, however, the reasons for change go beyond the merely egotistical or self-centered. By a curious division of functional response, the ear is constant in its demands, capable of extending its resources to accommodate change, but holding fast to basic centers of pitch, color, dynamics; the eye is a radical, adjusting its criteria to what it sees about it, rejecting today something that pleased it two or three decades ago, or, in the main, what pleased its predecessors of a century ago. Sometimes a massive change in visual perception comes as a result of developments that alter life itself. Nothing so drastically altered nineteenth century scenic design as the advent of electricity.

The new, unprecedented source of energy provided, immediately, a more stable source of illumination than gas ever did. It provided, thereafter, power for moving, lifting, and hauling that revolutionized stage machinery. It made possible the introduction of the stage turntable (pioneered in Japan) to revise and refine swift scenic changes; it brought in the improved cyclorama, that huge semicylindrical expanse of canvas at stage rear which is rarely identified but is indispensable for the illusion of a deep, infinite sky or a horizon far in the distance. Above all, the swift availability of abundant light, or *the absence of it*, made possible the *suggestion* of a locale as an alternative to the realistic representation of it. This vastly reduced the importance of the scene painter, who had the world of the stage in his hand during the nineteenth century.

As the twentieth century progressed, electricity became basic to a whole series of innovations and elaborations previously mentioned. Each new resource made a contribution to revising the perceptions of the ever-sensitive eye; together, they created new criteria for the acceptance or rejection of realism. Film was a first beneficiary, when electricity brought the input of power to make a truly "moving picture" possible. It is a mere statement of priorities that "light" precedes all else in the famous trinity of "Light! Camera! Action!" Eventually, after silent film and film with sound, film with sound *and* color brought the images of far-off places to millions who had never been fifty miles from home. When jet travel brought millions of previous non-travelers to those far-off places, criteria of what was a believable likeness became much more acute.

Unquestionably, a titanic source of energy, both mechanical and aesthetic, had been released. As with all such sources of raw power, from gunpowder to nuclear fission, electricity could be utilized for good or for bad. It gave to the producers of opera, as the twentieth century progressed, a resource such as they had never before possessed. The challenge to them is the one already stated: Would they use such resources to collaborate with the composer toward wholly valid objectives or would they turn them inward, toward ends primarily self-centered?

2

Nature, which abhors a vacuum, sensed one when the architect was separated from his dual function of builder-designer in the early nineteenth century. The bigger the theater, the more specialized the knowledge required to satisfy high standards for public safety, fire control, ventilation, sanitation. It was no longer a work for one man and a handful of associates, such as those who designed some of the greatest examples of Italian Baroque theater building in the eighteenth century. It became concerted labor on a large scale, in every detail from digging a foundation to the secure surfacing of a roof. Add, as time progressed, a sprinkler system; air conditioning that should be silent as well as effective (when I first visited the new Vienna State Opera House on a June evening in the fifties and found it as warm inside as it was outside, I asked an attendant whether it wasn't, in fact, air-conditioned. He replied, "Yes, but we cannot use it during the performance because it creates too much noise"); two side stages to make possible a swift movement of scenery from act to act; escalators, elevators, projection rooms, and electrical control panels; and the building of a contemporary opera house has almost more to do with engineering than with aesthetics.

Into the void vacated by the architect-designer stepped the scene designer, who collaborated with the composer, as Sanquirico did with Rossini, Donizetti, and Bellini. When the composer was no longer present to act on his own behalf, his function fell to his musical surrogate (Toscanini in Milan, Mahler in Vienna, Beecham in London). But as the line of connection to the musical source frayed and broke, into the new void has come the large, presumptive person of the "producer." He has become to the opera scene of the twentieth century what the castrati were to the seventeenth and eighteenth and the virtuoso conductor surrogates were to the late nineteenth and early twentieth centuries—the acclaimed prima donna who, at the end of a premiere, drains applause from those who have sung, played, conducted, or danced. He has made a career of being an indispensable non-performer, all-knowing, all-powerful. We have all heard of the "Felsenstein productions" in East Berlin. Does he design the scenery and the costumes, too? If not, who does? The talented, short-lived Rudolf Heinrich was one of his best scenic collaborators; but his name was little-known to opera-goers elsewhere until he began to work outside of East Berlin.

In its inception, like many things, the role of producer arose in response to a need. The man who assumed it possessed a capacity denied to others, the ability to convert a miscellany of collaborators into a disciplined company of co-workers—in other words, he was a "producer" (one who was productive). When, however, his role is self-assigned on the basis of some other specialty, danger impends. When it occurs to such a conductor as Herbert von Karajan to combine, as producer, the supervision of the stage and its lighting (as he did in a production of *Tristan und Isolde* I saw in Vienna in 1959) and it further occurs to him to make the conductor the most visible participant in a scheme that ranged, on stage, from dark to darker (with an occasional spotlight to pierce the gloom), danger no longer impends. It has been wholly, disastrously realized.

If others were at a loss for words to describe the results, Birgit Nilsson, the largely invisible Isolde, was not. During a lull in a recording of *Turandot* in Rome a few weeks later, I asked what her impressions of the Karajan *Tristan* were. She confined herself to the musical aspects of the production to say, "It was like a wax rose. Beautiful, but without perfume."

Richard Wagner was, to some extent, the prototype of the producer (on the grandest possible scale, since he was also the poet-composer of the works he staged). He recognized the new importance of spectacle in opera, from his days in Paris. When his works began to be performed in places where he could not be present, he wrote and published long dissertations "To the scene painter" and "the Machinist." The one entitled "On the performance of *Tannhäuser*" takes up forty printed pages in the third volume of his *Prose Works.*[1] Verdi entered actively into the selection of the principal performers for the premieres of his later operas. He also conceived the idea for the double stage used in the concluding scene of *Aida*.

This was as practical a contribution to the resources of stage craft as Wagner's creation of the previously mentioned split, or "Bayreuth," curtain. What Wagner saw as primarily applicable to his own works has become, in a number of theaters elsewhere, the preferable form of fore-hanging for the operas generally. Its principal advantage is that the *rate* of rise or fall can be controlled to suit the dramatic situation at the beginning and end of a scene or act. The roller curtain does not provide such flexibility.

The growing complexity of operatic compositions opened the way for producers in the wake of Richard Wagner, not only in Western Europe, but in Russia, where Serge Diaghilev elevated the function to embrace ballet as well as opera. Among the first non-composers, non-musicians to fulfill the role of producer on an important musical occasion was Max Reinhardt, born at Baden (the one near Vienna) in 1873. He began an acting career in a small company (the Stadt Theater, Salzburg) at twenty, playing—according to immemorial custom—character parts, old men, and so forth. He soon progressed to the theater world of Berlin, where he found an outlet for his unrouted spirit in the "Überbrettl" (Cabaret) movement (which also provided an outlet for such other unrouted spirits as Arnold Schönberg and, at a later date, Kurt Weill). By 1901, still less than thirty, Reinhardt had a theater of his own. Not only was he producing works of August Strindberg and Frank Wedekind, but also Oscar Wilde's revolutionary *Salomé*, which set Richard Strauss on the way to writing his operatic treatment. Reinhardt's succeeding production of *Elektra* not only gave Strauss a successor to *Salome*, but brought him together with Hugo von Hofmannsthal, the most important happening of his life as a composer for the stage.[2]

It is thus hardly surprising that Reinhardt came to be so highly valued as a collaborator in an operatic project that one of its principal creators threatened to withdraw if he were not included. The circumstances arose in the aftermath of the triumphal introduction of *Der Rosenkavalier* in 1911. Fearful that the aristocratic action of this *Komödie für Musik* might suffer in the hands of a less imaginative director, Strauss and Hofmannsthal induced Reinhardt to supervise the premiere. The work has become famous in the action Reinhardt devised (though the program at the first performance bore the name, as director, of Dresden's resident producer, Georg Toller, whom Reinhardt had superseded).[3]

To reward Reinhardt for his nameless participation in the birth of *Der Rosenkavalier* (well known though it was in the theater and opera world of the time), Strauss and Hofmannsthal chose, for their next collaboration, a work singularly suited to Reinhardt's talents as a dramatic craftsman. The work was even conceived in Hofmannsthal's mind (if not in Strauss's) as a production for Reinhardt's Deutsches Theater in Berlin. This was, of course, *Ariadne auf Naxos,* with its complicated combination of a play with incidental music (Molière's *Le Bourgeois gentilhomme*) followed by a musical *tour de force:* the *simultaneous* performance of a serious treatment of the mythological subject of Ariadne, Bacchus, and the island of Naxos, with a commedia dell'arte.

Wrote Hofmannsthal to Strauss in December of 1911: "The subtly conceived exiguity of this play, these two groups acting beside each other in the narrowest space, this most careful calculation of each gesture, each step, the whole like a concert and at the same time like a ballet—it will be lost, meaningless, a tattered rag in incompetent hands; only in Reinhardt's, yours and mine, can it grow into a singing flower, the incarnation of dance."

Strauss's opinion of Reinhardt ("a real artist and not a theatrical manager") was hardly less than Hofmannsthal's. But his principal concern was with the *musical* problem; he feared that the Deutsches Theater lacked the physical space to accommodate his orchestra. "Surely," he wrote in response to Hofmannsthal, "it is not my fault that the theatre in the Schumannstrasse isn't an opera house."

Within a month, Strauss had produced what turned out to be the eventual solution. *Ariadne* would have its premiere, not in Berlin, which he ruled out, or in Dresden, where a suitably small theater was not available, but in Stuttgart, "provided they agree to the cast chosen by yourself, Reinhardt and me," he wrote to Hofmannsthal in January, 1912. . . . "The only thing now is that Reinhardt's got to come in with us, that Hempel and Destinn [Strauss's choices for the roles of Zerbinetta and Ariadne] must accept, if necessary I'll conduct myself— and then it could be launched with two model performances about the middle of October. After that we can have Dresden—the big opera house; Munich—the Residenztheater; Berlin—the Schauspielhaus—anything you like. The piece will have been staged twice in an exemplary production and that's the main thing."

Hofmannsthal had some pangs of dismay at the prospect of a premiere in Stuttgart—"that most God-forsaken spot on earth" he wrote to Strauss—with "ninety nine per cent" of those in the theater, seating eight hundred, sure to be "critics, envious colleagues, professionals: for the real public there will be literally no seats." When the work was produced on October 25, 1912, with Strauss conducting, the program bore the words: Responsible for the Production, Max Reinhardt. The whole history was crowned by a note written by Strauss to Hofmannsthal (in response to the latter's suggestion) reading: "I have inscribed the following dedication to Reinhardt in the full score: *Max Reinhardt in deep respect and gratitude* followed by both our names: mine first, in accordance with your wish, though I should have liked it better if the poet's name had stood first."[4] And so it reads today.

3

This documentation of a working partnership that included three rather than two equally important participants gives a vivid insight into the complexity of a creative project on the highest level. First was Hofmannsthal, determined that the dramatic content in *Le Bourgeois gentilhomme* and the combined *Ariadne*-commedia dell'arte not be debased; then Strauss, taking the position that, as a matter of course, the score should have a model *musical* presentation before being turned loose into the mainstream of opera; finally Reinhardt standing by patiently, surrendering the privilege of playing host in his own theater, accepting a relocation to Dresden, and going along, loyally, with the eventual solution in Stuttgart. All had their points of view and each had to accept some readjustment with the others' in order to share a collaboration in which the honorary rank of "first among equals" belonged, not to librettist, composer, or producer, but to the work itself.

Here was an instance of a collaboration that was both physical and psychic in which, regrettably, Reinhardt's part frequently fails to be credited, as it should, in today's revivals. Part of this neglect may be charged against the concept itself. The notion of presenting a spoken play as a prologue to a highly complicated opera performance proved to be beyond the performing capacity of non-German theaters (which, traditionally, house dramatic companies as well as opera ensembles) except under exceptional circumstances. Strauss and Hofmannsthal returned to the workbench, detached the play from the opera, evolved a sung and spoken prologue to the combination of commedia dell'arte and mythological lyric drama, and sent *Ariadne auf Naxos* on the way (in 1916) in which it is known, and loved, today.

The many able persons in the German opera world of Reinhardt's time included such producers as Wilhelm von Wymetal (at the Vienna Opera from 1908 to 1922, and later at the Metropolitan), Lothar Wallerstein (Vienna from 1926 to 1937, and thereafter—sometimes unhappily—also at the Metropolitan), and Otto Erhardt (1920–1927 at Stuttgart, Dresden 1927–1932, later with the New York City Opera). But the one who worked most closely in the spirit of a "third" to librettist and composer was Carl Ebert.

The nature of his participation on one specific occasion has already been described. It is instructive to note, in Spike Hughes' history of the famous Glyndebourne Festival, these words: "Not long after he accepted Christie's offer [to become music director of a new festival] [Fritz] Busch was conducting in Vienna and happened to tell Max Reinhardt about the Glyndebourne project. Reinhardt, who had always wanted to collaborate with Busch in a Mozart production, offered his services. . . . When the question of money came to be considered seriously, however, Reinhardt's enthusiasm for producing Mozart in England weakened considerably." Continues Hughes: "Instead of Reinhardt, Busch recruited a Reinhardt disciple . . . Carl Ebert."[5]

Thus was transferred to English soil, and to even more promising conditions than had prevailed when they last worked together in Germany, a community of spirit and a meeting of minds that made Glyndebourne one of the prime sources, in this century, of opera at its best rather than opera at its most familiar. The collaboration of Busch and Ebert began at the 1932 Salzburg Festival when, having been invited to conduct *Die Entführung aus dem Serail*, Busch agreed—Hofmannsthal-like—only if Ebert would join him as producer of Mozart's *Singspiel*. Their next venture together was a production of *Un ballo in maschera* (in Berlin, fall, 1932) which contributed much to the ongoing Verdi revival in Germany. Two years later, after their first season together in Glyndebourne, they were joined by a former assistant to Ebert in Berlin, who had been trying to relocate in the business side of Vienna's musical life, Rudolf Bing.

Together, Busch and Ebert typified the best form of psychic collaboration. They had little choice. Between 1932 and 1964 Glyndebourne provided the possibility of physical collaboration with a composer on only four occasions: Britten's *The Rape of Lucretia* (1946), Stravinsky's *The Rake's Progress* (1953), Poulenc's *La Voix Humaine* (1960), and Hans Werner Henze's *Elegy for Young Lovers* (1961). With Busch as the best kind of nonvirtuoso conductor-surrogate for the composer and Ebert as a highly qualified, quality-conscious counterpart on the stage, they made a glorious name for Glyndebourne. As a worldwide symbol of excellence, it commanded a devoted public which waited impatiently for it to be salvaged after the bleak days of the war and re-created in the fifties. From 1936 Busch and Ebert shared official responsibility for artistic direction (with Bing designated general manager).

Design was a coordinate part of their common purpose, with the name of Hamish Wilson most frequently credited with the "scenery." In 1948, the name of Rolf Gérard appeared for the first time as the designer of a new production of Mozart's *Così fan tutte*, followed in 1950 by *Die Entführung aus dem Serail* and *Le Nozze di Figaro*. Doubtless there were disagreements, perhaps even arguments about their choice of one "third party" rather than another, but contention was neither audible nor visible when the curtain went up.

In its American conversion, the Glyndebourne-Metropolitan pattern preserved Bing, now a most general manager, and some of those with whom he had been associated as co-workers: Gérard as the designer of a *Don Carlos* made memorable by the conducting of Fritz Stiedry and the stage direction of Margaret Webster of a cast that included Jussi Bjoerling, Robert Merrill, Cesare Siepi, and Fedora Barbieri as nearly ideal embodiments of their parts, and Delia Rigal as a decidedly non-ideal one of hers (Elisabetta).

In its adaptation to American soil, "producer" became a coordinate word for general manager, as it has been in Germany, on occasions, for intendant (and stage manager). Productions were planned several years ahead, more often for a singing cast than for a conductor. Some results were extraordinarily good, but the average was hardly fifty-fifty. The discovery that a good designer of interiors (such as Gérard's for Johann Strauss's *Die Fledermaus*) was not necessarily a good designer of exteriors (Gérard's for *Faust*) was painfully learned in the wrong place—when a set was hung on stage, rather than displayed as a *bozzetto* (sketch or model).

The truism that a *bozzetto* is only a gleam in the eye of the designer, not a promise of how the baby will look when it is born, must be uppermost in the mind of any producer charged with evaluating the possible success of a production. Picture books of opera are abundant with handsome renderings of productions of the nineteenth century in the sketch stage. Scepticism, even some doubt as to their final quality, begins to intrude when equally striking sketches of indifferent productions one has seen on the stage are added to the total. The beautiful baby imagined by the mother has become a small horror, disfigured by all the shortcomings—naturally—of the father.

In the final phases of his tenure, the Bing productions too often suffered from a form of gigantism, in which size was equated with effect, and too many lines of connection were loosely drawn. For each fine *Frau ohne Schatten*, *Pelléas*, or *Tristan und Isolde* there were two overstated, excessively ornate versions of *Lucia di Lammermoor*, *Luisa Miller*, *Il trovatore*, or *La traviata*. The inclination to equate *Il trovatore* or *Luisa Miller* with *Don Carlos* or *Aida*, in spaciousness and number of supers, because all are by Verdi, overlooked the root fact that *Don Carlos* was written for Paris and *Aida* was created for an ambitious new theater in Cairo.

More recently, however, the accelerated growth of latitude for the producer has gone forward in a manner a man with Bing's background in the continental world of opera could hardly have tolerated. The arc of flight, on many sides and in many places, is flat out, not merely jet-propelled but rocket-powered into visual outer space. In other words, any restraining payload pertaining to the producer's psychic collaboration with the composer can be jettisoned at will.

4

"Sicily is steps" firmly insisted a well-known producer to me not long ago when the treatment of familiar operas with that background was under discussion. The dogma can be accepted without argument, for the steep, spiky conformations of the rocky island are unmistakable. The question, however, is: "Whose steps?" Are they the broad flight of stony steps topped by the towering village church suggestively utilized by Franco Zeffirelli for productions of Mascagni's *Cavalleria Rusticana* here and abroad? Or are they the bleak, blank, black ladder-like abstractions Josef Svoboda has provided for more than one production of Verdi's *I vespri siciliani*?

One might argue the issue in terms of content. *Cavalleria Rusticana* is as close to basic *verismo* as one can get—the word, indeed, came into musical usage to describe the realism (*verista*) utilized by Mascagni and by Leoncavallo in *I Pagliacci*—whereas *Vespri* is something else again. This is an argument postulated on a non sequitur. *Vespri* may be "something else again" to someone with only a superficial knowledge of the subject matter. But to Verdi who labored long and hard to make its content worthy of the Paris stage on which it was performed, it was as close to realism as he could achieve.

Were Verdi to join Mozart, Rossini, Donizetti, or Bellini among the immortals granted leave for a day to view a production of one of his works a century after it was composed, we trust it would not be Svoboda's *I vespri siciliani*. If it were, the composer might wonder whether he had been privileged or sentenced to make the acquaintance of something in which music that was obviously his own was being combined with action in a surrounding totally indescribable . . . certainly unascribable to the action planned by Eugène Scribe.

One might say that Sicily isn't what it was when the famous uprising at the vesper hour occurred in 1282. But it really hasn't changed to the extent suggested by Svoboda. Palermo is still in the same place it was when Verdi wrote the eloquent aria in which Procida affirms his rare relief in being able once more to touch the soil of the land from which he had long been absent. But, to Svoboda, all "Tu Palermo" means is blank, bare, black steps. As for the later moment in which the hated French occupying troops (and some renegade Sicilians) sail by to taunt the oppressed natives on shore, all the audience is offered, visually, is the same, unchanging, ladderlike staircase. This could be described as making a charade of a simple, properly pictorial, dramatic incident. The Svoboda settings certainly don't assist Verdi to make his point to an audience unversed in the opera or the language in which it is being performed. Such a production is less a collaboration, psychic or otherwise, with the composer than a love affair with an abstraction of the designer's own devising.

If such mischief were limited to one city or one stage in one city, it could be considered a local curse by which the local inhabitants were being punished for any of a dozen good reasons. But producers are a clannish lot, worldwide, and what one does in defiance of reason and logic is not a cause for caution in others. Rather, each such misbegotten "innovation" is an incitement to another exaggeration in expressing an abstraction of an opera's central theme ("Sicily is steps") and to eliminate any petty relationship to the specific content over which such a composer as Verdi labored.

The European side of the cheapened coin was surveyed in the June 29, 1975, issue of *The Sunday Times* of London by Desmond Shawe-Taylor, its respected music critic. He noted, as a contemporary form of "cultural schizophrenia" that, even as an excessive effort is being applied on the musical side to restore, as nearly as possible, the manner of performance appropriate to an opera at the time it was written (embellishments, interpolated cadenzas, and so on), "the producer—in the past a sound craftsman generally known as the stage manager—now arrogates to himself, and his accomplice the designer, powers that grow steadily more arbitrary and extreme."

Continues Shawe-Taylor: "We are always being asked to applaud the fact that such-and-such a producer has brought to his task an entirely new and revolutionary conception of the work being entrusted to him; it is regarded as a point in his favor that he should just have encountered the work for the first time, and as a still greater advantage if he can claim never to have produced an opera before; if he has never so much as *seen* an opera, that is game, set and match."

As to the presumption that aberrations and absurdities are the penalty for living in one place rather than another, Shawe-Taylor asserts: "While we English opera-goers may feel that we have suffered our fair share of pointless eccentricities, a dozen pages of reports from abroad [in *Opera* magazine, for June, 1975] amply supported by hair raising photographs, suggest that we are in luck's way."

Among them Shawe-Taylor cites a production of *Das Rheingold* in Marseilles "in the style of a Victorian melodrama" designed by Jean-Pierre Ponnelle beside which the "cat-infested *Don Pasquale* that he designed for Covent Garden is moderation itself." Ponnelle's Wotan wears striped trousers and spats, and Fricka a black crinoline. The reader is invited to imagine what the rest of the *Ring* is likely to be, to look at. Ponnelle is quoted as saying he "doesn't know yet." Adds Shawe-Taylor, "Perhaps he hasn't yet had time to acquaint himself with Wagner's own continuation of the story."[6]

Also noted are a *Pelléas* in Cologne, in which a Mélisande of con-

ventional size is surrounded by a Geneviève, Arkel, and Doctor standing in stilts—the better to tower over you, emotionally, little girl. This
bit of Freudian suggestion fortunately did not occur to Maeterlinck in
time to incorporate it into his play, but what a producer wills, a
producer can do. If there was any psychic collaboration with Debussy
in this inspiration, it must have been carried on at a very long distance.

For those who would wish a word of warning against unsuspected,
unexpected invasions of their credibility by a producer more interested
in producing headlines in a newspaper than in serving the composer,
the following catechism may serve a useful purpose:

Has the century of the action been altered to permit "a more
interesting background" for the designer and costumer? Beware:
it is likely to produce some contradictions between the action
and the background. Even places like Verona and Mantua may
change—ever so slightly—from one century to another.

Has some scene been changed from an interior to an exterior
or vice versa for reasons either stated or unstated? Look out for
oddly inappropriate statements by one character to another, re-
ferring to *il giardino* when no garden is visible or to *Mondschein*
when the designer neglected to provide a moon.

Does the producer claim the basis of the production's "style"
to be found in "relevance" to some contemporary condition?
The primary relevance in Gluck's *Orfeo*, is to an almost in-
humanly high standard in the performance of Gluck's score.

Are the costumes *and* scenery by the same man? Don't expect
equal felicity in both. To excel in one craft is a sufficient burden
for one man to bear.

Finally, if the total production is the work of brothers, or
brother and sister, or man and wife—don't go. Family relations
have no place in the serious business of providing a suitable sight
for the rarefied sound.

XIV

The Unwritten Repertory

1

Had Jules Massenet acted on an impulse by which he was possessed at one point in his life, there would have been three, not two, operas based on Henri Murger's *Scènes de la Vie de Bohême*, thus depriving Ruggiero Leoncavallo of the distinction of having written the "other" *Bohème*. Had Georges Bizet possessed the courage and the confidence in his mid-twenties to go ahead with his idea of treating E. T. A. Hoffmann's *Le Tonnelier de Nuremberg*, there might have been an authentically French *Les Maîtres Chanteurs* rather than the one performed in France as a translation of Wagner's *Die Meistersinger*. As to how Claude Debussy's collaboration with Edgar Allan Poe (through Baudelaire as translator) in a double bill of *Le Diable dans le Beffroi* and *La Chute de la Maison Usher* might have turned out, one can only speculate.

These are some of the entries in the ghostly ranks of the Unwritten Repertory which obsess the mind and challenge the curiosity. The reference is not merely to projects that were started and abandoned by talented song composers or symphonic composers convinced that they had gotten hold of a "great subject for an opera." The reference is, rather, to subjects to which serious thought was given by composers who had passed the qualifying test for writing an opera—writing an opera. They represent something more of a tangible deprivation to posterity than the kind of unwritten repertory that includes the name of Johannes Brahms. Asked on one occasion why he had never written an opera, Brahms replied, "Beside Wagner it is impossible," a statement of basic truth which he may have reconsidered later in life when, in response to the same question, he answered, "Because I never found a proper subject."[1]

The Unwritten Repertory that tantalizes me is the one that exists, to a greater or lesser degree, in the plans of such men as Massenet, Bizet, and Debussy, whose capacity to write not merely a performable opera but a masterpiece is demonstrated fact. Unlike Wagner, who nurtured his scheme for an opera based on the song contest in Nuremberg from 1845, when he was thirty-two, until he plunged into it in 1862, when he was verging on fifty, Bizet never reverted to Hoffmann's tale. We have thus been deprived of such counterparts to Wagner as Maître Martin (Pogner) and "sa fille unique," Mademoiselle Rosa (Eva).

Debussy was Wagner-tenacious in his devotion to a project related to Poe, whose works exercised a powerful fascination for him almost from youth. In 1889, when he was twenty-seven, Debussy's attachment to Poe prompted him to plan a "symphony on psychologically developed themes based on the *House of Usher*." This, of course, simply identified Debussy with many other French artists of his generation. It is hardly an exaggeration to say that it was the French who discovered Poe for America as more than a writer of horror tales and chilling mysteries.[2]

The symphony or symphonic poem never came to fulfillment, but the fascination of *La Chute de la Maison Usher* remained with Debussy as long as he lived. In the early years of the twentieth century it became known that Debussy was at work on a stage version of *Le Diable dans le Beffroi*. The idea of joining it to *La Chute de la Maison Usher* surfaces not only in the Debussy literature but in the *Memoirs* of Giulio Gatti-Casazza, general manager of the Metropolitan Opera from 1908 to 1935.

Prior to assuming his duties, Gatti came to the United States (in late spring, 1908) to familiarize himself with the building and its operation. On his return to Europe, Gatti made a tour of the principal scenes of operatic activity on the Continent, including Paris. "I paid a visit to Debussy to pay my respects to him and to find out whether he had anything ready or in his mind [*Pelléas et Mélisande* had, only a few months before, provided the rival Manhattan Opera House with a great *succès d'estime* at its first American performance on February 20, 1908]. The composer received me in a very friendly manner and told me that he was really considering three compositions: 'The Legend of Tristan,' 'The Devil in the Belfry,' and 'The Fall of the House of Usher,' the last based on the story by Edgar Allan Poe. But it was impossible to say when any one of these works would be ready to be presented in the theatre. Although this news was not encouraging, I did not fail to request from him priority for the production of these works at the Metropolitan. In return for these rights Debussy did not make any impossible demands. We agreed on a very small advance."[3] (*La Légende de Tristan* was to be a collaboration with Gabriel Mourey derived from Joseph Bédier's version of the chronicle of the Middle Ages.)

In response, perhaps, to the interest of Gatti and the prospect of a production in New York, Debussy did considerable work on his commitment in the next year or two. His absorption with the Usher family is reflected in several letters to Durand, his publisher, including one in which he expands on some of his musical ideas. Dated June 26, 1909, it reads: "These last days I have been working on *La Chute de la Maison Usher* and have almost finished a long monologue for poor Roderick. It is sad enough to make the stones weep and as it happens there is a question of the influence of stones on the state of mind of neurasthenics. The music has an attractive mustiness obtained by mixing the low notes of the oboe with harmonics of the violin. Don't speak of this to anyone for I am rather proud of it."[4]

All the evidence points to the conclusion that, in this period of his life, Debussy was literally living the life of the Ushers, as he more than once remarked to correspondents. Conflicting obligations were set aside or delayed as he would forget "the normal rules of courtesy and close myself up like a brute beast in the house of Usher unless I am keeping company with the devil in the belfry."[5] The recipient of this confidence was André Caplet, a conductor to whom he owed an overdue composition.

The treatment of *Le Diable dans le Beffroi* (a work of Poe so little known that it is not included in the 666-page *Portable Poe* published by the Viking Press, but it is to be found in the 1,026-page *The Complete Tales and Poems of Edgar Allan Poe* in the Vintage Books series published by Random House) concerns a Devil who takes over the belfry in a small Dutch village appropriately dubbed Vondervotteimittiss. One single action distracts the villagers from everything else and spreads consternation—the Devil causes the village clock to mark the hour of noon by chiming thirteen times. As late as 1911, the two projects were much in Debussy's mind. In a letter to a close friend, Robert

Godet, he confided (February 6, 1911): "The two tales of Poe have thus had to be postponed until I don't know when. Writing to you I will admit that I am not very sorry since there are many points of expression (*accents*) with which I am not yet satisfied . . . notably in regard to *Le Diable dans le Beffroi* where I would like to achieve an extremely supple and at the same time an extremely fluid manner of choral writing."[6]

To Debussy, the Devil was not "the spirit of evil. He is rather the spirit of contradiction." This is a fitting epitaph for a project of which Old Nick was a part. Despite the length of time in which Debussy was engaged on the two works (the libretto for *Usher* was finally completed in 1916), there was, at his death in 1918, a residue of only twenty-one pages of score—much of it illegible. Obviously the bulk of material that had accumulated since 1889 had been destroyed by Debussy, out of disaffection, or, more likely, the fear that it would be performed as an incomplete torso, or even worse, in company with something else—a possibility expressly forbidden in his contract with Gatti.

2

From a layman's point of view, the saddest lack in the French Unwritten Repertory is not a *Meistersinger* by Bizet or a double bill of *Le Diable* and *La Chute* by Debussy. It is the treatment of Murger's *Scènes de la Vie de Bohême* that Jules Massenet did not write. My endorsement of this view may strike some as decidedly plebeian, others as undecidedly controversial. I, too, share the general esteem for Bizet and Debussy. I would say, merely, that the quantity of pleasure in the world never equaling the demand for it, one more great opera by Massenet, equal in quality to *Manon*, would shed a quantity of vocal sunshine for which all of us—or nearly all of us—yearn.

The reasons for presuming to mention it longingly are contained in Massenet's own recollection of the circumstances which frustrated this wholly happy possibility. They concern the composer and his publisher, George Hartmann. In the manner of the Ricordis, Hartmann was something more than a tradesman who awaited the product of a writer and merely processed it into print. He was constantly in search of a new project with which, almost before Massenet had drawn the last double bar on a work in hand, he could entice him anew.

It was while he was engaged on *Werther* (in 1885) that the idea for a Massenet *Bohème* arose. The composer has written: "In order to encite me to work more ardently [on *Werther*] (as if I had need of it) my publisher . . . engaged for me at the Reservoirs at Versailles, a vast ground floor apartment on the level of the gardens of our great Le Nôtre. The table at which I wrote was the purest Louis XV. Hartmann had chosen everything at the most famous antiquarians. Hartmann had a special aptitude for doing his share of the work. He spoke German very well; he understood Goethe; he loved the German mind; he stuck to it that I should undertake the work."

Massenet continues:

So, when one day it was suggested that I write an opera on Murger's *La Vie de Bohême*, he took it on himself to refuse the work without consulting me in any way. I would have been greatly tempted to do the thing. I would have been pleased to follow Henry Murger in his life and work. He was an artist in his way. Théophile Gautier justly called him a poet, although he excelled as a writer of prose. I feel that I could have followed him through that peculiar world he created and which he has made it possible for us to cross in a thousand ways in the train of the most amusing originals we had ever seen. And such gaiety, such tears, such outbursts of frantic laughter, and such courageous poverty, as Jules Janin said, would, I think, have captivated me. Like Alfred de Musset—one of his masters—he had grace and style, ineffable tenderness, gladsome smiles, the cry of the heart, emotion. He sang songs dear to the hearts of lovers and they charm us all. His fiddle was not a Stradivarius, they said, but he had a soul like Hoffmann's, and he knew how to play so as to bring tears.

I knew Murger personally, in fact so well that I even saw him the night of his death. I was present at a most affecting interview while I was there, but even that did not lack a comic note. It could not have been otherwise with Murger. I was at his bedside when they brought in M. Schanne (the Schaunard of *La Vie de Bohême*). Murger was eating magnificent grapes he had bought with his last louis and Schanne said laughing, "How silly of you to drink your wine in pills."[7]

Murger, born in 1822 (in Paris, of course) died in 1861. Though steadily employed as secretary to Count Alexis Tolstoy (a writer and relative of Leo), Murger craved the independence of the free-lance life. This brought him directly into contact with the Left Bank and its inhabitants, about whom he began to write in 1845, for a publication called *Corsaire*. He was paid fifteen francs an installment and sold the collection of articles in 1848 for 500 francs (much less than as many dollars). The publisher reaped the profits from an immediate sale of

70,000 copies. However, Murger was not wholly impoverished by this lack of business judgment. He collaborated on a play derived from *La Vie de Bohême,* which entertained Parisians from 1849 on and made Murger a success.

In my opinion, had Hartmann kept his distance and not spoken his mind before Massenet had the opportunity to exercise his own judgment, the principal female part—and a great one—in his treatment of *Vie de Bohême* would *not* have been the flower girl Mademoiselle Mimi (as she is called in Murger) but the artist's model, Musette. In the first place, the pathetic, dependent female with whom Puccini fell in love (as he did with Madama Butterfly) hardly strikes me as a character to whom Massenet would have responded. In addition to the "courageous poverty" Massenet praised in the characters immortalized by Murger, he speaks fondly of "such gaiety, such tears, such outbursts of frantic laughter" as being among the qualities that endeared them to him. The latter, certainly, are much more characteristic of Musette than of Mimi. He also—at another point in his *Recollections*—makes pointed reference to his particular reason for being drawn to *La Vie:* "As I knew not only Murger but also Schaunard and Musette, it seemed to me that there was no one better qualified than I to be the musician of *La Vie de Bohême.*"[8]

Such being the case, it is altogether possible that in his opera entitled *Musette* (to go along with *Manon, Thaïs, Esclarmonde, Cendrillon, La Navarraise, Thérèse, Sapho,* and *Cléopâtre,* in his personal gallery of female portraits) there would have been a cross-fertilization of Murger's Musette by Massenet's knowledge of her prototype.

In the words of the unidentified writer of an introduction to an English edition of Murger: "Mariette, for such was was Musette's name, was remarkably well made, and was a model highly esteemed by both painters and sculptors. Her features were not so regular, and her face acquired a mocking aspect from the fact that when she smiled, the left side of her mouth was drawn up, while the right retained its normal position, a fact that led her friends to remark that she 'squinted with her lips.' She was fully conscious of her plastic value and was ready at the slightest provocation to reveal it."[9]

Massenet's reference to Schanne dovetails with his reference to knowing Murger and being acquainted with many of those on whom he had built his characters. Murger had, for purposes of fiction, christened him Schannard. The identity by which he is universally famous arose by a typographical error, the printer substituting "u" for the first "n," thus making it Schaunard. Schanne was a direct contemporary of Massenet's and wrote his own account of that interior circle. It was published in 1887, shortly before the author's death. Schanne, who was both a painter and a musician, recalled the real Mariette-Musette, in one provocative encounter:

> One evening at Lazare's [also a painter] a dozen of us were met, among whom was the austere Jean Journet, who had constituted himself in the name of the "phalanstere," the lay apostle of virtue. The idea struck our host to offer us the spectacle of the Temptation of St. Anthony, for to suggest it to him, he had on his mantel shelf among other trifles a herd of six little pigs in gingerbread. After he whispered to Mariette (Musette) she suddenly threw everything that covered her to the ground, and went and sat down on Jean Journet's knees. . . . The apostle remained for a moment confused and undecided. But he suddenly rose, which caused the temptress to slip to the floor. Then he rushed out like a mad man and the staircase echoed with his maledictions. . . .[10]

Of the later Mariette-Musette, the editor of the English *Bohemians of the Latin Quarter* writes: "Mariette ended by leaving the Latin Quarter for the Rue Breda, where she lived an irregular life in more regular fashion, and pursued the career she had chosen in the world more seriously. . . . She was careful without being miserly, and amassed a large sum. . . ."[11] According to this source material, Mariette died shortly after Murger himself, in approximately 1863. There would thus have been no obstacle to combining the facts of her own life with those embroidered around it by Murger.

Had Massenet been permitted to develop the line of his special interest in *La Vie de Bohème*, he and a chosen literary companion might have developed a basic script-structure from the following sequence of scenes:

ACT I

[From Murger's *Mademoiselle Musette*]: Musette, out of funds and behind in her rent, has been dispossessed from her flat. All her furniture has been stacked in the courtyard (an enclosed space). All this, with a party pending that night! Call it off? Not Musette. When the first male guests arrive, she instructs them gaily and with no air of concern, to lay the carpet, spread the furniture about—they'll have the party *al fresco*. Says Murger: "She had the courtyard arranged as a drawing room . . . prepared everything as usual, dressed to receive company, and in-

vited all the tenants to her little entertainment, toward which
Heaven contributed its illumination." She also sings (country
songs, her specialty, from the province of her birth) to entertain
her guests. . . . Among them is a poet Rodolfo (Murger himself) who had brought along a friend Marcel (modeled on two
painters, Lazare-Tabor). . . . He clearly is smitten and Mariette is not unresponsive. . . . As the party wears on, the guests
begin to drift away. . . . Rodolfo and Marcel linger, poised on
Mariette-Musette's dilemma. What to do? She cannot sleep in the
courtyard. . . . Rodolfo, who has his own dilemma with Mimi,
disappears. . . . Marcel offers hospitality. Musette, possessed of
a frankness paralleled in few operatic roles, gives him the answer
in Murger's words: "I do not beat about the bush to say what
my thoughts are. You like me and I like you. It is not love, but
perhaps its seed. . . ." An ending duet for Musette-Marcel, as
they stroll out of the courtyard, and morning begins to dawn.[12]

ACT II, SCENE I

[More from Murger]: A scene of loving content in Marcel's flat-
studio, several days later. Marcel has brought Musette a batch of
fresh flowers as a love token. She sings to him (in a scene not
unlike the Manon–Des Grieux duet at the beginning of Act II of
Manon, a form of dialogue at which Massenet was very good) of
her present mood: "I am going to stop here, and I shall stay here
as long as the flowers you have just given me remain unfaded."
"Ah," laments Marcel, "they will fade in a couple of days. If I
had known, I would have brought *immortelles* [evergreens]."
In a later scene we see that they have kept fresh, fragrant and
unfaded much beyond their normal life expectancy. Reason:
Musette rises early, tends them lovingly—perhaps even replenishes
them with others she brings in(?). Scene ends when she neglects
to tend them, and as the flowers fade, leaves a note telling Marcel
she must go. . . . A tender song, reciting her need to be on her
way, on her own. With words from Murger, ending: "My life
is like a song. Each of my loves is a verse, but Marcel is the
refrain" (implying that they will be together again—and providing a motif that will recur musically, as the opera progresses). . . .[13]

ACT II, SCENE II

[From Schanne, *L'Histoire de Mariette*]: Musette is established in
her own flat, her "irregular life now being on a more regular ba-

sis." But she has not forgotten her old friends. They are present at a party. Included are Jean Journet, the chemist of Carcassonnes, and, eventually, Marcel. He clearly hasn't lost his feeling for Musette. He offers her a large sum of money derived from selling his best painting, *The Passage of the Red Sea*. She thanks him, but declines the money. Schaunard premieres his new composition *Symphony on the Influence of Blue in Art* (there was such a composition by Schanne, in *three* flats, of which he said to a potential patron, "How many avaricious composers would you meet in life who would put in one, or two at most?"). The incident of the Temptation of St. Anthony. Murger's words: "The poem of her youth and beauty had never before been seen in a more seductive binding."[14] Marcel's outrage as he departs, Musette's amused defiance.

ACT III, SCENE I

[Murger: *Musette's fancies*]: Some time later. Musette at home, in the company of her kind. No longer the old friends. A coterie of rich guests, mostly male, of several ages—middle-aged verging on elderly, plain middle-aged and a scattering of young, mostly well-attired. She sings again, and wanders into one of her country songs. This attracts the attention of one of the *not* well-attired youngish, if not youthful, males. He is in the retinue of "her" Vicomte. They have a strain of sympathy, for he is a riding master from her part of France. The scene develops on two levels: the interest of the younger man in Musette, her waning interest in the Vicomte. Eventually she returns to the strain heard at the end of Act II, Scene I, now expanded to include Murger's words: "I need to breathe the air of that life from time to time," in yearning for the life she left behind. Then into "My life is like a song, each of my lovers is a verse, but Marcel is the refrain. . . ."[15]

ACT III, SCENE II

[More Murger]: Back to Marcel's studio. He is older, has painted well, and if not noticeably prosperous, is also well above the poverty level. A knock. Musette at the door. Mingled emotions. Can the old flame be rekindled? Musette thinks so, confident that it is in her power to do anything required to make a man respond. But Marcel is not so malleable. It is he who broaches the question of their future, if there is to be one, and Musette who, with her usual frankness, says her future is elsewhere, no longer with his paints and palettes, but with another kind of life, in another kind of place, the country from whence she came to Paris, with a person of the kind with whom she grew up—the riding master (groom) and his plans for a business of their own. Then it is Marcel's turn to tell her, in Murger's own words (of which Alexander Dumas *fils* said that he would willingly have given all his novels to write):

VERSE 6

Musette, when richer friends grew strange,
Bethought of him who loved her best
And returned a while for change,
The stray bird to the ancient nest
Alas! with e'en the greeting kiss
Our fond love vanished in a sigh
Each felt that something was amiss,
You were not you, and I not I.

VERSE 7

Farewell for aye! My lost, my dear
For you are dead and dead your lover,
And both our youths lie buried here
In this old almanack's torn cover.
'Tis only when we stir the dust
Of some dear day that in it lies,
That memory gives us back in trust
The keys of our lost paradise.[16]

End, as Musette leaves, and Marcel studies a canvas that he takes from his hidden stock: an unimaginably beautiful portrait of Musette in the prime of their lives together.

This brief scenario may strike some as incomplete for lacking reference to Mimi. Massenet was notably selective in rarely combining *two* women as competitors for attention. It may, for others, lack a touch of harshness required to make it "contemporary." But contemporary with who, and what? Let us remember it is such a script as might have appealed to Massenet in 1885, pre-Puccini, pre-Leoncavallo. For me, it lacks only one thing: a score whose rhythm, life, color, and melody would have made Massenet and Musette synonymous.

3

That Massenet, Debussy, and Bizet were all French composers is no more than a coincidence. The Unwritten Repertory is no less abundant in works we would cherish but have been denied by Italian and German composers. As an instance, Giacomo Puccini was even more prolific in subjects with which he had a brief flirtation than he was in those he espoused in artistic marriage. The reason for this was less a matter of whimsy or inability to make up his mind than compulsion. He, too, was constitutionally addicted to being constantly "with opera." Like Massenet, as soon as one was finished, or well on the way to being finished, he was restless until he was engaged—in more than the occupational sense—to another. There was thus a constant stream of possibilities under consideration. As his standards for acceptability were very high, the first flush of enthusiasm often turned, when really close study was applied, to disenchantment.

One project that we have been denied—if that is the proper term—was a *Pelléas et Mélisande* by Puccini. Incongruous as it may seem, Puccini not only sounded out Maeterlinck on the possibility of a collaboration, but actually paid him a visit. He was disappointed to learn that the rights had been granted to Debussy, who had been present at a single, private performance of the play in Paris in 1893 (Whistler and Mallarmé were also in the small audience) and had begun to write music for it almost immediately. It is a mark of Puccini's generosity as a man that, on an occasion in 1903 when he heard *Pelléas* at a performance at which Debussy was present, he sought out the composer and told him he was "greatly moved."[17] He also told the conductor, André Messager, that he was "surprised at the complete absence of pieces of vocal effect."[18]

Among the other subjects to which Puccini's attention turned from time to time, a special curiosity attaches to Ferenc Molnar's *Liliom*. Like *Madama Butterfly*, *Tosca*, and *La Fanciulla del West* (to a lesser extent, *Turandot* and *La Bohème*), *Liliom* satisfied one of Puccini's basic criteria: it had been, since its first production in 1910, a successful play in the contemporary theater. His interest was made known to Molnar, whose response was a paraphrase of the one which Bernard Shaw gave when he was asked to grant musical rights to *Arms and the Man*: "I want *Liliom* to be remembered as a play by Molnar, not as an opera by Puccini."[19] Molnar's attitude was quite different in 1944 when an intermediary suggested it as a subject for Richard Rodgers and Oscar Hammerstein II. He gave the response that made possible *Liliom*'s glowing rebirth as *Carousel*, a musical with a background in New England, while remaining a play by Molnar about a barker at an amusement park in Budaspest.

Had Puccini succeeded in writing operas around a tenth of the subjects that came to his mind, were suggested by others, or were thrust upon him in the form of complete scenarios or librettos, he would have doubled the number of those indispensable to the repertory, an inadequate six. In the index of Mosco Carner's invaluable biography, Puccini's unwritten list extends (alphabetically) from *Aphrodite* (Pierre Louÿs) to *Trilby* (Gerald du Maurier). It includes, among *fifty-six* others, such "additional" Puccini heroines as Anna Karenina, Daphnis, Marie Antoinette, Parisina, and La Rosa di Cipro (the last two from the hand of Gabriele d'Annunzio).[20] If one considers, among alternates, *his* choice of Madama Butterfly, Tosca, Minnie in *La Fanciulla,* and Turandot, one has to conclude that his power of self-diagnosis was uncommonly keen.

Would a *Faust* or a *Macbeth* by Beethoven have been a great masterpiece—or even, let us say, a greater *opera* than *Fidelio?* Beethoven did, indeed, consider such subjects seriously: *Faust,* in 1808 and again when he had his famous meeting with Goethe in Teplitz and very likely discussed a plan for an adaptation of the poem with its author. Memoranda exist of music for *Macbeth* which he sketched between 1808 and 1809, when Heinrich von Collin (for whose play on Coriolanus Beethoven had written one of his greatest concert overtures) was writing a German adaptation of Shakespeare. One can see, in either subject, opportunities that would have stimulated Beethoven to noble utterances, affecting encounters, heart-wringing climaxes, but, as inevitably, posed requirements for contrast and variety that might have taxed him even more than that "crown of thorns" (as he referred to *Fidelio*). Let us be grateful that he did not sacrifice other, more manageable projects on the altar of "another opera." A powerful but incomplete *Faust* by Beethoven might have deterred Berlioz, Schumann, Gounod, Boito or Busoni from what they did with the subject, as a gigantically fragmented *Macbeth* by Beethoven might have discouraged Verdi from challenging the same material.[21]

As for Mozart, the list of his contributions to the written, rather than the unwritten, repertory would very likely have been twice as long and as lovable as *Don Giovanni, Le Nozze di Figaro, Così, Die Zauberflöte,* and *Die Entführung,* had he been granted only one thing— another ten years of life. He was such a prodigious worker, with so long a list of "specialties" and so many demands on his waking hours that he had, to my knowledge, no subject unset, no commissions unfulfilled (save, perhaps, *Zaïde* or the unfinished *Requiem*) when he lived his last hours in the magic atmosphere of *Die Zauberflöte.*

Richard Strauss, who was quite willing to accept the view of his collaborator, Hugo von Hofmannsthal, that their new project (*Die Frau ohne Schatten*) "stands in the same relation to *Die Zauberflöte* as *Rosenkavalier* does to *Figaro*" had—so far as I can discover—no unfulfilled objectives for a different reason.[22] He had both the means and the longevity to weigh, carefully and at leisure, all the suggestions that were made to him. If neither the mood nor the suggestion was in tune or the wind and the weather not to his liking, he had the option of going off on another conducting tour, or performing profitably in recital with a favored singer. Indeed, Strauss knew himself and his interests so well that, when he was asked to consider operatic subject matter after *Capriccio,* which he completed in 1941 at the age of seventy-seven, he would reply, "I can only make one testament."

Unquestionably the most curious operatic project, written or unwritten, of which I have knowledge brings together Robert Schumann —and, if the subject is not too incongruous—*Tristan und Isolde.* Schumann was something more than a composer of great songs (and of unique instrumental music in all its forms) who had an incorrigible urge to write a good opera. He did actually pass the first test by completing *Genoveva* (after Tieck and F. Hebbel); he thought seriously of writing another, on Byron's *Corsair;* he responded to the same poet's *Manfred* with a great overture and much incidental music for a spoken performance of the drama; and he challenged Goethe in a series of *Scenes from Faust.* In totality, however, these works on dramatic subjects do not bear the conviction or sense of fitness he achieved in his best songs or instrumental works.

The long-buried plan for *Tristan* was brought to light and thoroughly documented by Friedrich Schnapp more than fifty years ago in an article for *The Musical Quarterly* (October, 1924). The date (spring, 1846) is consistent with Schumann's absorption, during this decade, with songs and several of the dramatic schemes previously mentioned. For those with an instant curiosity, this was nearly ten years before a treatment of the same subject began to ferment in Wagner's mind. It is improbable that Schumann's interest in Tristan was ever known to Wagner, any more than Wagner's familiarity with the guilds was known to Bizet (in the 1850s). Each subject was a part of the cultural stock of the time, whether at the great length of Karl Leberecht Immermann's epic *Tristan und Isolde* (published in 1840) or in the brief form of E. T. A. Hoffmann's *Le Tonnelier de Nuremberg.*[23]

Subjects treated by Moore, Byron, and Shakespeare (*The Tempest*) were other possibilities that were reviewed by Schumann and his collaborator Robert Reinick, before *Tristan und Isolde*. Once recalled, it took precedence over all other subjects. Reinick preceded with a sketch of subject matter which was among the documents discovered by Schnapp in the collection of Schumanniana in Zwickau, the city of the composer's birth. It is instructive to compare the unfamiliar scheme, for Schumann's purposes, with the classically familiar one made by Wagner from substantially the same material. We find, in Reinick, almost all the characters now so well known to us: Mark, Tristan (described as his "nephew"), Isolde, Morolt, even Brangaene. There is much mention of magic, of potions with extraordinary powers, of Isolde's interest in Tristan (though he had slain her uncle, Morolt), of her resistance to marrying the aging Mark, of a plan by Tristan for Isolde to escape with him. Eventually, it is Isolde who dies first and Tristan who "sinks down on her corpse with the cry 'Isolde' " (in the words of Reinick's text).

The details *are* all there—but not in the order or with the economy of Wagner's conversion of a historical legend of the fifteenth century into a celebration of love for both sexes and all the ages. Reinick required five acts (including one in Ireland) for what Wagner did in three. Once organized and on its way, Wagner's mind—and Schopenhauer's philosophy—began to weave garlands of embellishments about the legend that made the result, literally, as different from Schumann's as night (of which much is made in *Tristan und Isolde*) is from day.

One curious corollary remains. Years later, Clara Schumann—who kept a diary much of her mature life—attended a performance in Munich (after Robert's death) of *Tristan* by Wagner (for whom she had an abiding antipathy). Her comment reads: "It is the most repulsive thing I ever saw or heard in my life. To have to sit through a whole evening watching and listening to such love-lunacy till every feeling of decency was outraged, and to see not only the audience but the musicians delighted with it was—I may well say—the saddest experience of my whole artistic career. I held out till the end, as I wished to have heard it all. . . . The subject seems to me so wretched: a love madness brought about by a potion. . . ."[24]

What would Clara have said had her beloved Robert gone ahead with his plans for a *Tristan* opera, love potion and all, thirty years before, rather than putting it aside for a "later time" which had not arrived when he died in July, 1856?

4

That question is a minor, rhetorical one beside the profoundest of all the mysteries that surround the Unwritten Repertory. For those versed in the life and career of Giuseppe Verdi, the categorization in such exclusive terms can refer to only one unanswered question: "Whatever happened to Verdi's *Il Re Lear (King Lear)*?

To put it thus bluntly is to imply that there was indeed a Verdi's *King Lear*. No remaining musical evidence exists to prove there ever *was* such a work, but so much explicit, direct, and indirect evidence of Verdi's absorption with the subject over years exists and can be cited that the reality of such an opera is hard to disbelieve.

Certainly, it is tantalizing to imagine, in addition to Verdi's deep feeling for *padre, figlia,* and *patria* in other works, the musical expression he would have given to them in a drama on the epic scale of *Lear.* This great monarch had not one daughter, such as Rigoletto's Gilda or Simon Boccanegra's Maria (Amelia), Father Miller's Luisa, Amonasro's Aida or the Marchese di Calatrava's Leonora (in *La forza del destino*), nor two, such as Nabucco's Fenena and Abigaille, to motivate a filial firestorm, but the famous trio of Goneril, Regan, and Cordelia. From the first scene between the aging king and his daughters, in which Il Re Lear is prepared to share his kingdom in proportion to their love for him, Shakespeare sets forth their responses in words that sing, and cry out to be sung. As Bernard Shaw said of a much later work by Verdi: "Instead of *Otello* being an Italian opera written in the style of Shakespear, *Othello* is a play written by Shakespear in the style of Italian opera."[25]

Shaw was, of course, speaking as broadly and paradoxically as only Shaw could. He was aware that the readers of the *Anglo-Saxon Review* (in which these words were originally published in March, 1901) knew that Verdi did not set *Othello* as originally written, and that the text that inflamed him was perhaps the greatest literary achievement of that matchless poet-composer, Arrigo Boito. Unfortunately for all, Boito was born on February 24, 1842, and was thus only a year old when Verdi first began to fret, mentally, about an opera on a Shakespearean subject and nominated *King Lear* as his choice.

Verdi was then the composer of four operas, of which only *Nabucco* and *I Lombardi* have any identity today, and he was twenty-nine and possessed of indomitable resolution (for a composer who had not yet mastered the problem of *Ernani*). The Shakespearean aspiration had to be set aside because the commission of 1843 from the Teatro La Fenice, which he had thought to fulfill with *Il Re Lear*, didn't offer a low male voice to serve for the title role. That voice almost presented itself when a commission from London in 1846 included the great basso Luigi Lablache among its inducements. This time Verdi fell ill, and the commission was carried over to 1847. Lablache was still available, but so was Jenny Lind. The outcome was *I masnadieri*, with a star part for the soprano and a smaller one for the basso.

By 1850 Verdi has progressed sufficiently in his profession to originate projects of his own rather than to await the convenience (and the constriction) of a commission. He engaged Salvatore Cammarano, whose prior libretti included *Luisa Miller* as well as *Lucia di Lammermoor* (for Donizetti) to work, at his leisure, on an adaptation of *Lear*. Lest there be any misunderstanding of what he expected from Cammarano, Verdi provided him with a prose digest of the play. In an accompanying letter he stated: "You realize that there is no need to make *King Lear* into the usual kind of drama we have had up until now: rather, we must treat it in a completely new manner, on a large scale, and without regard for mere convenience. I believe the rôles could be reduced to five principal ones: Lear, Cordelia, the Fool, Edmund, Edgar [the contending natural and legitimate sons of the Earl of Gloster]. Two secondary female rôles: Regan and Goneril (though perhaps the latter would have to be made a second leading lady). . . ."[26]

In his scenario, Verdi compressed Shakespeare's five acts into four, and the much larger number of scenes in the original to eleven. The guide to Cammarano is studded with suggestions for musical episodes: Act I, Scene III: "The Fool with his bizarre songs mocks Lear for having trusted his daughters." Act II, Scene I: "Lear exclaims: 'What, have his daughters brought him to this pass? Couldst thou save nothing? Didst thou give them all?' (magnificent quartet)." And so on, through "Huge Chorus (in various verse metres)," "Very sweet sounds of music are heard behind the scenes," "magnificent duet," to "Ensemble in which Lear must have a leading part. End." Cammarano's work ended when he died in 1852. A year later, having been sounded out by another poet-playwright, Antonio Somma, on the possibility of a collaboration, Verdi directed his attention to *Lear* and added some further observations on the problems the play presented.

When Somma began to write his "treatment," Verdi commented:

"The opera is turning out to be too long, especially in the first two acts. . . . Do your best to be as brief as possible in the lesser scenes. . . . There are too many changes of scene. . . . The one thing that has always prevented us from writing more Shakespeare operas has been precisely this necessity to change the scene all the time. . . . The French have the right idea. . . . They plan their action with only one scene for each Act, and so the action flows freely without hindrance and with nothing to distract the public's attention."[27] At a later point, Verdi reminds Somma: "In the theater, lengthy is synonymous with boring: and, of all styles, that of boredom is the worst."[28]

The correspondence, in all its critical detail, is a seminar on the art of constructing a libretto. By March, 1855, Verdi is congratulating Somma with the words: "Now that you have finished 'Lear' could you find another subject which you would do for me at your leisure?"[29] But, more than a year later (April, 1856) Verdi is again dissatisfied: "I am not so sure that the fourth act of 'King Lear' is good in the form in which you have sent it to me, but I do know that you can't impose so many recitatives one after another, on the audience, especially in a fourth act."[30]

The nearest thing to a firm commitment to compose *Lear* came later in 1856 when Verdi was negotiating a commission for the Teatro San Carlo in Naples. He was looking ahead more than a year to October 15, 1857, and to March 15, 1858, and specified that his preferred Cordelia, Maria Piccolomini, should be put under contract for the total time period required for rehearsals and performances. He thought of Lear as a "big baritone" (another Rigoletto or Di Luna), "a soprano prima donna, not necessarily with a big voice, but with deep feeling, for Cordelia," a "very good contralto"[31] (for the Fool, which he thought of as a woman's role, no doubt—similar to the use of the Page, Oscar, in *Un ballo in maschera*—for contrast among the males with whom she would sing), and so on. But Piccolomini could not be promised by Naples, and Verdi angrily turned down the singer who was proposed in her place. The Somma libretto went into Verdi's portfolio, to be looked at from time to time, no doubt, and thought of as a possibility. In 1879 Giuseppina, his redoubtable wife, wrote to a friend who had inquired about the rumor that Boito's text for *Otello* had been completed: "Verdi must have liked it, for after reading it, he bought it, but . . . he put it beside Somma's *Re Lear*, which has slept profoundly and without disturbance for thirty years in its portfolio. What will become of this *Otello*? No one knows. I would like Verdi to be able to let it sleep like *Re Lear* for another thirty years and then find sufficient strength and courage to set it to music, to his own glory and the glory of art."[32]

The community of impulse represented in this portfolio must have crossed Verdi's mind when, finally, the musical content for *Otello* began to germinate in his mind and come to a full fruition five years later. Shakespeare and Verdi. Shakespeare, Verdi, and *Otello*. Why not Shakespeare, Verdi, and *Re Lear*? To a degree, I would say, for precisely the reason that was mentioned when Shaw pronounced his genealogy for *Otello*. The missing ingredient in the Somma text was the imaginative input and the verbal imagery Boito contributed to make *Otello* precisely what Verdi wanted in *Lear*—what is not lengthy, not boring (not only in *Otello* but in *Falstaff*).

Unbelievably, the desired outcome almost came about. "After the first performance of *Falstaff* in Rome," writes Walker, "Boito suggested *Antony and Cleopatra*, which he had translated for Eleonora Duse, as the subject for a new opera. There were persistent rumours, too, about *King Lear* and he certainly did some work on this subject. Nardi found the plan of a libretto in three acts [not lengthy, not boring!] and a fragment of the opening scene: there are annotations, too, in Boito's hand in his copy of the play, like those in his copies of *Othello* and the various sources of *Falstaff*. But nothing came of all this, after Giuseppina gave the anxious warning: 'Verdi is too old, too tired.' "[33]

The year was 1893, Verdi was eighty. Three years later the epilogue to the unwritten *Lear* was enacted when Mascagni, the newly crowned Heir Apparent as the composer of *Cavalleria Rusticana*, paid him a visit. As a tribute of regard for the new "rising man," Verdi offered him the synopsis he had written for Cammarano, also Somma's libretto. Mascagni had the presence of mind—so he said—to ask Verdi why, after all the years of cherishing the subject, he had never seen it through. The reply, as reported by Mascagni, was: "The scene in which King Lear finds himself on the heath terrified me."[34]

Those students of Verdi who cannot imagine him specifying specific details of musical treatment to his collaborators without having such matter at hand have a supporter in Charles Osborne. He cites specific passages in *Simon Boccanegra* and *La forza del destino* which suggest to him—a close scholar of Verdi's practices—adaptations, even paraphrases of material originally intended for *Lear*.

Another devotee who shared this opinion, on a more extensive scale, was the late Carolina Perera, a patron of chamber music in New York and a longtime friend of Arturo Toscanini, who, at his suggestion, turned her mind and financial resources to a study of Verdiana. Though it was officially declared that all of Verdi's unfinished works had, like Debussy's, been destroyed after his death, she was convinced that a manuscript of *Il Re Lear* did exist, and had been spared. For Carolina Perera, the mystery was still unresolved when she died in the sixties.

INTERMEZZO

Maria Callas had a secret—which, by now may be a non-secret in a paperback—about her practice in choosing roles. When a new opera was pressed upon her or when she was asked to consider an old opera unfamiliar to her, she had her own, private rule of procedure. That was to look first at the end of the work, to see how it all came out. This included not only the role she was being urged to perform, but the opera as a whole. If the end sustained interest, the beginning was worth considering. If it was not, why bother?

Callas's practice might imply, to some, a dismally self-centered approach to an undertaking that would involve a good many people other than herself. But her procedure went, rather, to a much more central fact of theatrical life: the simple proposition that anything—play, opera, musical—that begins well but ends poorly cannot be retrieved. But an opera with a weak or indifferent or *comme si comme ça* beginning can be salvaged, redeemed, or even made triumphant by a strong finish.

The principle applies also to a book. I wouldn't presume to judge whether the opening of this one was weak, indifferent, or *comme si comme ça*, but I will presume to take responsibility for the shape, the character, the impact of its ending. Much as Verdi restricted "La donna è mobile" from circulation prior to the premiere of *Rigoletto* in Venice in 1851, I wouldn't dream of permitting this statement to be circularized or otherwise reproduced prior to its publication in this specific place. What follows is, in effect, a Callas finale, an invitation to scrutiny *prior* to the reader's commitment to read any prior part of the book.

It is, in effect, a whale of a tail attached to a zebra that cannot change its stripes.

XV

The Operatic Bargain

1

The first chapter of Jean Jacques Rousseau's *The Social Contract* begins, if I am not in error: "Man was born free, and he is everywhere in chains."[1] The first law of "The Operatic Bargain" is—and I am sure it is not in error, for I have just written it—"Opera was born in riches, and it is everywhere (with the possible exception of the Soviet Union) impoverished." Long celebrated as second only to horse racing as the sport of kings, queens, princes, czars, and now commissars, every opera performance is of such complexity that it has a hundred and one reasons to fail, and only one to succeed—if everybody fulfills his or her function perfectly. If it is pointed out, painstakingly, that the arithmetic of this statement is illogical, that it would still leave a hundred reasons for a performance *not* to succeed, that proves nothing—except that opera is, inherently and by its nature, illogical.

Of the innumerable opera composers who ever dreamed of the ideal surroundings in which to have their works performed, only one in the nineteenth and one in the twentieth century saw the dream become a reality. Most others than Richard Wagner and Benjamin Britten took, for the most part, what circumstances provided. Certain of the elite attained the eminence to select the place for a premiere and to participate in its planning. As an instance Richard Strauss's *Ariadne auf Naxos*, for all the celebrity of Strauss, Hofmannsthal, and Reinhardt, ended up far from where its creators had first schemed to present it. One (the composer) urged that the little theater in the capital of Württemberg was, from his point of view, "another Bayreuth"; an-

299

other (the librettist) was heartily sick of the whole idea of Stuttgart for a premiere; the third (the producer) stood by dutifully to do his work wherever necessary. The outcome might be described as the Operatic Bargain in all its original sinfulness.

For all his satisfaction with Stuttgart for a premiere, Strauss did not escape the penalty for having written what eventually became a successful opera. Like all others who have achieved this supreme aesthetic accomplishment, he paid a price: the greater the success of what he had written, the more varied and even incongruous the surroundings in which it would subsequently be performed. Even Wagner, for all his foresight in shaping *Parsifal* to its predestined surroundings in Bayreuth, endowed what he called his *Bühnenweihfestspiel* ("A Stage-Consecrating Festival-Play") with qualities of popular appeal that defeated his intention of having it performed there and only there. Nor has Britten been an exception to the general rule. Hardly had the run of *Death in Venice* been completed in his own theater in Aldeburgh than it was off for performances in Edinburgh, Covent Garden, and the Metropolitan. Here it might, some season, find itself in a sequence after *Parsifal*, which had, in turn, been preceded by *Ariadne auf Naxos*. This would make a triple triumph for inappropriateness— three works for which the Metropolitan is either far too large (*Ariadne* and *Death in Venice*) or with a stage not large enough (for *Parsifal* as Wagner conceived it).

To a degree, opera differs little from the greatest chamber music (rarely performed in a "chamber") or orchestral music before Berlioz. The cross that concert music has to bear is, primarily, a problem of volume and balance. Orchestrally, volume and balance are the province of what Beecham has described as "an efficient conductor." Even a string quartet can achieve a livable compromise with non-chamber surroundings by enlarging its style of performance, provided it is content to play for an audience of hundreds rather than thousands. But no matter how well an "efficient conductor" does his work in the pit of an opera house, he cannot bring the scene closer to the eyes of those thirty rows away on the orchestra level or in the front row of the top gallery. These worthy people are participants in the Operatic Bargain at nothing like bargain prices.

Throughout the many decades and changing phases of its history, in only one period has opera enjoyed a harmony of means within a unity of space. Such conditions prevailed at the dawn of operatic time, as the art form native to Florence and popularized in Venice spread through Europe. The Italians not only chose the subjects, wrote the words, composed, played, and sang the music, but built the theaters in which opera was performed and designed the scenery to decorate them. It might be said that opera then enjoyed "gallery status"—it was hung and lit, as great paintings are, in a space suitable to the best enjoyment. In its prime form, Italian opera enjoyed an artistic hegemony which soon overran natural barriers and political borders.

The demand from those who had the means, the time, and the taste to make a personal pastime of Baroque opera kept whole families of Italian craftsmen busy and prosperous in the courts and palaces of Europe for decades. The great names among these artisans included Giovanni Burnacini, a pioneer architect-designer in the theaters of Venice in the early seventeenth century who became a favorite in Vienna and, when he died, was succeeded by his son Ludovico; Giacomo Torelli, an early co-worker of Burnacini in Venice who attained his greatest celebrity in Paris as the literal *deus ex machina* of the elaborate spectacles which became so characteristic a part of French opera; and the Quaglios. The last-named were Italians who also migrated north, to settle in Germany and flourish as scenic artists in Munich and elsewhere, century after century. An early Quaglio (Giovanni Maria) collaborated with Gluck on the Vienna *Orfeo;* a later one worked with Wagner in Munich. Eugen Quaglio died in Berlin in 1942.[2]

Probably the highest level of artistry was attained by the clan Galli-Bibiena, whose prominence spanned a dozen decades from 1650 to 1770. Fathers, sons, brothers, uncles, nephews, and grandchildren built and decorated the stages of theaters from Saxony to Spain. Their fame was crowned by the exquisite jewel of a theater that made Bayreuth a magnet for connoisseurs more than a century (1747) before Wagner decided on a nearby hilltop as the site of his Festspielhaus. Bayreuth's Italian baroque theater was created by Guiseppe and Carlo Galli-Bibiena for the Margravine Wilhelmine (a sister of Frederick the Great, with no less impeccable musical credentials).

The fame of the Bibiena masterpiece spread so rapidly that only three years later (1750), Elector Max Joseph III of neighboring Bavaria ordered an equivalent theater, in a more "contemporary" Rococo manner, to be built into his vast palace in Munich. It was designed by the Flemish-French François de Cuvilliés. The scene, in 1781, of the premiere of *Idomeneo* by Mozart (who makes no mention, in the letters to his father describing the preparation of the work, of the superbly decorated theater), Cuvilliés' creation was long known as the Residenztheater because it was part of the Elector's "residence." Since the restoration following World War II (during which the interior was dismantled and the irreplaceable carvings and paneling buried in a deep subsurface vault), it has been renamed in honor of its designer Cuvilliés, and is now used primarily for spoken drama.

For those who qualified for participation, either as composers or designers or performers, this was the high road in all the annals of journeys to an operatic Samarkand. The route was one on which all the expenses of the journey were prepaid, the cost of moving the cargo or equipage required royally disregarded. The low road, of course, was occupied by those restricted to building economically and for everlarger audiences, in order to produce opera in a way that would pay for itself, with little or no public or private underwriting. On the great, wide middle road moved the vast midstream of operatic traffic, for which there could be considerable or some or an unreliably large amount of assistance, but in which opera was nevertheless required to bear a fair (some would say unfair) share of its subsistence.

When opera came to America in the early eighteenth century, it was immediately on the low road. It has since attained the middle road, but it has only sporadically, fitfully, almost by accident—when the economic climate has been especially favorable—verged on the high road. New York had such a visitation, between 1910 and 1914; Chicago was blessed by the packing and manufacturing money to make it possible in the 1920s; San Francisco, perhaps in the thirties, when talent and money were in favorable conjunction.

At the present time, the middle road has become ever more crowded, for a simple if paradoxical reason. As changing economic and social conditions have caused more and more royal and lay sponsors to abandon the high road, where opera flourished in unashamed grandeur, so the same conditions have caused the low road to become barren and deserted because of opera's inability to be wholly self-supporting even in unashamed shabbiness.

For years and years there was, for those who lived in places as widely separated as Bridgeport, Connecticut; Canton, Ohio; or Milwaukee, Wisconsin—not to mention Boston, New York, or Cincinnati—a comfortably compatible operatic alternative to radio or records called the San Carlo Opera Company. It was a prime example of the low road at its highest flight, unsubsidized but hardly unsupported. The company had friends (in cities of suitable size) who impatiently awaited "their" week once a year. The orchestra was minimal, the chorus hardly larger, the scenery that served for *Rigoletto* one night likely to turn up (in part) for *Trovatore* the next. Its supernumeraries could have been brothers to the ones who walked around and around the stage in the performance of *Carmen* I saw as a teen-ager in Newark.

The San Carlo Opera, whose general director was the late Fortune Gallo, gave employment to well-known, aging singers and little-known maturing ones (the last of this description later to achieve star status was Dorothy Kirsten). The common fare was the bread-and-butter repertory (*Rigoletto, Cavalleria Rusticana,* and *Pagliacci*), extended from time to time by the meat and potatoes of *La Bohème, Madama Butterfly,* or *Aida.* The San Carlo had, in Coë Glade, a slender, dark-haired mezzo, a resident Carmen who sang the part perhaps more often than any American of her time, with an occasion Dalila to sharpen her wiles as temptress.

Now and then Gallo would add steak to his table. During a period when *Otello* was not in the Metropolitan repertory (which could have been anytime between 1913 and 1937, but was, actually, in the 1920s), I first heard Verdi's greatest tragedy as part of a New York "season" of the San Carlo company. The Otello (probably in the well-known, "aging" category) was Manuel Salazar. He was an able exponent of his demanding role. I remember still my first hearing of the fervent finishing prhase: "Un bacio . . . un bacio ancora . . . Ah! un altro bacio" ("A kiss . . . a kiss again . . . ah! another kiss . . .") from the expiring Otello to the expired Desdemona. It is my recollection that I paid less than a dollar to stand in the bygone Century Theater. This was the Operatic Bargain at its most equitable.

2

To speak of opera as peculiar, delightful, maddening, and irresistible is to reduce to four key words the many that have interceded since a taste for opera was described as "an aberration, a delusion, a deception, a delight, and a despair." Where else could one follow tracks that would lead to a live character saying to a desperately ailing one: "How silly of you to drink your wine in pills." Obviously, Alexander Schanne was born to become an operatic character, and so it turned out.

But is every Schaunard a Schanne? More particularly, how many performers of Schaunard know that there *was* a Schanne, and that there, but for the grace of God and a typographical error, goes a Schannard?

Perhaps it is a form of wishful thinking to suppose that every performer of a part that had a living prototype should know who the original was. I would settle for the awareness that the role *had* a living prototype. Such knowledge might lead the performer to an acquaintance with the literary work on which the opera was based and, perhaps, a little deeper knowledge of motivation, animation, and provocation than can be derived from the lines he/she delivers, or that are addressed to the character by others in the opera.

I backed away, somewhat, from hope of even this kind of awareness when, in the course of an informal discussion with a well-known soprano who had recently been performing Tatyana in Tchaikovsky's *Eugene Onegin*, I said, "You have, of course, read the story in which she is a character." "No," she responded, "I didn't know there was a story." I sent her, soon afterward, a copy of the paperback Pushkin, and promptly received an appreciative note. Unfortunately, the well-known singer didn't really like the role of Tatyana and hasn't sung it again since. Operatic Bargain Unconsummated.

I would insist, however, that just as life itself is founded on air, water, and a slender source of nourishment, and has given rise to astronauts, Channel swimmers, and gourmets, a small input of idealism in opera might grow to unexpected dimensions. The kind of idealism I dream of could swell and expand to provide a buffer against the impact of the Operatic Bargain in all its vexing give and take. It is too often forgotten that opera is—as well as being an entertainment, a diversion, a way of life—an art form. It is an art form which has served many great musical minds better than any other, but it depends, for its realization, on constantly fallible human faculties. That is the Operatic Bargain at its quintessential—the perpetual need to give something in order to get something. The idealism to which I refer would act as a layer of psychic immunization to withstand the anguishing shock that may arise from the inaudible absence of a right note in a key phrase or the audible presence of the wrong one. Then it is time for one to shudder and remember, "This is not Verdi's Violetta; this is Mme Bologna's Violetta"—and hope for better luck in her next solo.

An operatic cast that is well known for competence in all its parts is some warrant of security for a feeling that, for this night, the audience may be spared the Operatic Bargain in its quintessential form. But it is, ever and always, the lovable, irritating nature of opera to confound the expectable when least expected; security and insecurity are altogether relative terms. The instance of the disruptive non-climax to the first act of the first Vickers (Siegmund)–Nilsson (Sieglinde) *Walküre* previously described might have been contrived by an operatic Méphistophélès tired of taking the short end of his own Operatic Bargains.

There is the corollary happening, on a rare occasion, in which the affirmative rather than the negative unexpected may be encountered. Such was the performance that brought to an end the part of the Metropolitan's tour to Japan in 1975 in which Joan Sutherland was involved. The city was Osaka, the work was Verdi's *La traviata*, and the cast also included John Alexander (Alfredo) and Cornell MacNeil (Germont). All sound singers, in whose competence one could repose every trust, and from whom one could expect the same secure, evenly matched, nonvolatile effort heard earlier in the week.

There was much to commend in Richard Bonynge's direction of the Prelude and its playing by the Metropolitan orchestra, as there had been previously. With the rise of the curtain and Miss Sutherland's singing of "Flora, amici," the air seemed a little more charged, the atmosphere slightly more electric than it had been in the several preceding *Traviatas*, the soprano's sound distinguished not only by its customary poise, ease, and security, but by a timbre a trace more febrile than its norm. On the scale of body temperature it might be likened to 98.9° rather than 98.6°. Would it go as high as 99° or verge on an authentic if only mildly feverish 100°? Only the ebb and flow of the evening's performance could determine, even as the graph of Violetta's ailment might or might not build to an intolerable inner crisis. At its end, this performance of Violetta had become, without question, the most exciting, charged, even supercharged I had heard from Miss Sutherland over a dozen years' experience with her and it.

How to explain? There is no real explanation known to me. It was Miss Sutherland's and Bonynge's last performance of the tour. They were to be off the following day for England, by way of Tokyo and Anchorage, Alaska. The performance concluded a sequence of six given over a two-week period. But it would be pure speculation to associate any of these factual details with the artistic total. Perhaps the soprano was feeling above par, physically as well as musically, or, perhaps, even below par physically, but *above* par musically.

The latter circumstance is by no means impossible—but not to be counted on. Singers have been known to ask for the indulgence of an audience (in the formal manner of a printed slip reading: "Despite being indisposed, Mme Bella Nota has consented to perform in order not to inconvenience the management or disappoint the public") and then deliver the performance of their lives. Some tenors have reported that they never sing so well as when they have a slight head cold (the slightly congested passages give a sense of resonance and response they do not have when perfectly normal).

The word of critical importance here, of course, is "slight." How heavy a cold is a slight cold and how slight a cold is a heavy cold? The answer would, of course, vary from performer to performer. In some, the presence of a hazard—real or fancied—brings on a degree of caution not normally present.

If a singer is partial to stress and strain as a means to a vocal end, the procedure known as "singing over a cold"—which is to say, *avoiding* stress and strain, employing finesse rather than force to achieve the objective—can be a healthy antidote to an otherwise bad habit. Much that affects a career may hang on a singer's reaction to the circumstances of a single performance. Birgit Nilsson has said that learning how to get around a difficult physical condition in order to appear in a performance of the Verdi Requiem was a turning point in her career. She had a cold, but no substitute was available. "I was scared," she has said. "The whole day I kept thinking: I must discover a way to sing with a cold without hurting the voice. It came to me eventually that I should try putting up the voice into the head [a singer's terminology for what is called 'head resonance'].''[3] The plan worked in 1954, which is why she is still singing, healthily, twenty years later.

Those not versed in the psychology of singers may pardon a comment on a matter of phraseology in Nilsson's statement. Note that she says "*the* voice," not "my voice." This use of an impersonal, rather than a personal, construction is intensely typical of the singer's attitude toward the small, vibratory mass on which a career is dependent. The vocal cords are, certainly, *within* them, but hardly *of* them—something they have never seen, except in a mirror or on an X-ray plate. Also, there appears to be a superstitious avoidance of personalizing it as "*my* voice." The tendency is, rather, to treat it very respectfully, even circumspectly, in a manner to propitiate whatever dark spirits govern such matters, and not to take too much for granted.

That is eminently understandable in circumstances where even the steeliest vocal sound may, if misused, turn out to be just tissue and blood. Indeed, the *cordes vocales*, so called, is not really a cord at all. It has been defined to me by Dr. Leo Reckford, associate professor at the New York University School of Education who specializes in the diagnosis and therapy of voice disorders, as the mucular cushions or lips covered by fibrous tissue and mucuous membranes that protrude from the side walls of the voice box (larynx). They swing up and down like the vibrations of the lips of a trumpet player, responding to the air flow and their own muscular elasticity.

Ljuba Welitch, a great Salome, a strong performer of such roles as Aida, Tosca, Amelia in *Un ballo in maschera,* and an exuberantly vital Rosalinda in Strauss's *Die Fledermaus,* is said to owe the onset of her vocal difficulties and eventual decline to singing a searing Donna Anna in Mozart's *Don Giovanni* when she shouldn't have sung anything. It may have been specifically a matter of timing. Singers of experience can risk an apparently detrimental combination of roles if the sequence is comfortable and compatible with vocal realities (which vary from artist to artist). In Welitch's case, it might have worked better if the Donna Anna were before the Salome, rather than after. Needless to say, since the outcome of her venture was costly and eventually disastrous, she is—unlike Nilsson, who triumphed over her difficulty—not disposed to talk about how it happened. The two instances, together (with success in one case, failure in another), are examples—of which there could be many more—of the Operatic Bargain, for better or worse.

Perhaps the most used, least understood word in the operatic lexicon is "indisposed." My own acquaintance with it goes back to the twenties. Doubtless I first encountered it in the all-too-usual manner: an expensive ticket for a long-awaited opportunity to hear a favorite performer in a famous role, and the discovery, on arriving at the theater, that he/she is "indisposed," for which calamity there is, of course, not even so much as a refund on the ticket price. The term doubtless has a history stretching back into operatic antiquity.

I was long of the opinion that it must—because of its vaguely non-communicative, faintly euphemistic ambiguity—be of English origin. My belief in this was strengthened by a very recent discovery, in John Livingston Lowes' remarkable inquiry into the workings of the mind of Samuel Taylor Coleridge entitled *The Road to Xanadu,* an anecdote bearing on a happening in 1811. In a letter describing a social evening to which he had been invited, only to discover that he had to "wait dinner for an hour and twenty minutes," Coleridge notes: "After coffee, I was going" when "a Mrs. Jerningham sat down at the piano. . . . I could not, in civility, not sit down to listen . . . she continued playing a long hour. It was now eleven o'clock. As soon as I got out of the house, I felt myself indisposed, etc. . . ."[4] It might even be a terminology invented by a Briton—which is to say (according to the very British *Concise Oxford Dictionary*), a person belonging to "one of the race found by Romans in S. England." The lovely indefinition of "indisposed" is borne out by a definition in the same source reading: "indisposition n. Ill health, ailment (esp. of passing kind); disinclination (*to* thing, *to* do); aversion (*to, towards*)."

These words take in a range of possibilities almost precisely, specifically, and purposefully operatic. In the first place comes the very general matter of "ill health," a condition that requires a period of convalescence or removal to another climate than the damp and chill that may pervade New York, Chicago, London, or Paris during the winter season. Such a complaint invades the *total* body rather than the more special, localized areas that serve the singer. It is, in short, ill health to the personal as well as the professional debility of the performer.

Indisposition in its common form of an ailment "of a passing kind" is high on the list of those things periodically encountered in the Operatic Bargain that make the profession a drag, a bore, a mess (each often preceded by an adjective derived from a more vivid four-letter word). Some young performers are so constantly concerned about the state of "the cords" that they carry on (by use of mirrors, hand-held and otherwise) a constant, covert inspection of the throat area. They may, if not psychologically reeducated, worry themselves out of the ability to perform at all.

A dry throat on rising in the morning, a tickle that promises to become a cough, a nasal drip that threatens to seep into the throat—these are all signs of what, to you or to me, might evolve into an inconvenience. For the singer, any or all might be warnings of something more serious. Whether or not the worst comes to pass varies not only from individual to individual, but from type to type. It was long a tenet of vocal mythology that the shorter the cord (though it may only be a matter of fractions of a centimeter), the higher the voice range. Dr. Reckford observes that it is more the amount of the vibrating mass of the vocal cords (and not of their actual lengths), which is to say lengths and thickness: that sopranos and mezzos vary little in *length* of cords, rather more in the mass with which they have to work. High baritones and tenors are, again, quite similar in cushioning on the vocal muscle, but the mass may be dissimilar. Basses, of course, have the largest mass of all, and, from their often gigantic sizes—Hotter, Hines, Talvela, Siepi, Hans Sotin, to mention a few of recent identity—profit by the longest windpipes, largest larynges and biggest resonance chambers.

Nevertheless, it is true that tenors are the most indispositional of all male singers. Some tenors count a month without an indisposition something to sing about. How much of this is mental, how much medical? The candid answer would have to be: If a particular tenor thinks he is not well enough to sing, it doesn't matter whether the reason is medical *or* mental—he isn't going to sing. The next step beyond the questionable indisposition is the mental *disinclination* to do something, which can escalate into an *aversion* to doing anything. There comes a moment in such a progression when management takes recourse to the classic cure-all for a fancied complaint—a threat to replace the recalcitrant one with his most hated rival. If this has no effect, he has become the particular tenor least likely to perform.

Why the stress on tenors? Aren't other singers as "particular" as some tenors? The answer is: Perhaps they would like to be, but few can afford the same latitude of choice. There are rarely, if ever, enough good tenors to fill world demand. When Mary Garden became impresaria of the Chicago Opera Company in 1920, she brought together nearly a dozen of the best tenors that money (Harold McCormick's) could buy. The late Edward Johnson, the Metropolitan's general manager between Gatti-Casazza and Bing, had a particularly fond recollection of that year (being one of the dozen). "I was paid more for not singing than for singing," he once recalled. Did she need them all? Not really. She just liked having them available.

A company that has, at this time in the 1970s, a Corelli, a Domingo, a McCracken, a Pavarotti, and a Vickers (note that the sequence is alphabetical) simultaneously available has close to half the world's supply of desirable tenors in its custody. Eliminate two of these names, and the other three can all but write their own ticket for management indulgence, solicitude, and coddling.

Not all of the breed require such treatment, several are as dependable as the sturdiest bass. The late Richard Tucker rarely "canceled" (the professional term for asking out). But for a tenor who is both great and worrisome, the season may be one round of fretting, unhappiness, and complaint, even when he is on stage, six feet tall and apparently up to any physical feat in the world—but singing. It must be recognized that they do have a mental terror—mostly self-induced— called the High Note. There are few tenor roles without at least one, and for the tenor who rates success in terms of the response *his* High

Note generates vis-à-vis that of his rival, lack of confidence in the ability to produce it may give him a very negative attitude about the whole evening's work.

In prudent self-interest, those who have chosen the worst of all involvements with the Operatic Bargain—a job in, or close to, the seat of power where decisions are made—have evolved procedures to determine all questions relating to indisposition and its variants. In any large city where opera is regularly performed there are specialists in nose and throat complaints who have become even more specialized in looking after those whose livelihood depends on whether the "cords" look nicely clear, pink, and unclouded, or rough, red, and possibly infected, swollen, or congested.

One such doctor in whom management has confidence is usually asked to render a judgment when there is reason to doubt—from casual observation or sound—what the singer's condition is. To be sure, he cannot "make" a singer who thinks he or she is not up to performing, perform. But if the expert is well known for professional probity—which is to say, for having the welfare of the singer as much at heart as he has the interest of the employer—a yes from him which remains a no from the performer is likely to be noted and remembered when time for renewing contracts arrives.

Often enough a vocal malaise may be some other form of "indisposition" masquerading as the real thing. A random memory of instances in which a premiere was disrupted by the "indisposition" of a principal performer has, now and then, been certified later as really the singer's lack of disposition to do that particular role in the excitement and strain of a premiere—he/she simply didn't know it well enough. On the other hand, a famous instance of the opposite involved one of the great singers of this era who bore the burden of singing Aida in a new production though, it was confided to the press, she had spent a sleepless night with a bad tooth. Actually, it was later learned, her anguish was caused by a gall bladder attack, which was considered too indelicate an ailment for a vocal superstar. The gall bladder (perhaps also the "tooth") came out during the next off-season, certainly to the singer's relief and the benefit of her admirers.

Hardest to deal with when all else is under control is the psychic indisposition. It may afflict a performer well liked but high-strung, with whom everything has to be in order—with boyfriend, husband, or lover—or she cannot go on, for fear of not doing her best. Where the husband is also the teacher, only an extraordinary compatibility—

plus a perfect technique—can avert disaster. Marcella Sembrich, one of the great singers of florid roles in the last "Golden Age" (the 1890s and soon after), later a celebrated recitalist, was married to Guillaume Stengel, who had been her teacher . . . of piano. That worked well. One contemporary soprano of note sang under a strain for years because every performance was in the presence and under the scrutiny of her husband–vocal teacher. She began to relax more and sing better when she acquired not only a new teacher, but a different husband.

In some circumstances the condition may require the insight and counseling, not of a specially qualified M.D., but of an experienced, resourceful G.M. (general manager) who may even be required to resolve a problem bringing together a well-liked performer and an ex-husband. Both partners to the marriage, which had passed the unwinding point, were well-known performers. Difficult as the situation was on the personal level, it was even more of a dilemma artistically. Together they had commitments made years in advance to appear in roles they had made a specialty of singing together—Ochs–Octavian in *Der Rosenkavalier*, Telramund–Ortrud in *Lohengrin*, Fricka–Wotan in *Die Walküre*, and the Dyer and the Dyer's Wife (Farber and Färberin) in Strauss's *Die Frau ohne Schatten*.

The lady implored her general manager to release her from a longstanding obligation to play the part when her former husband appeared as the Dyer. He, too, hated the idea but felt he *had* to do it, professionally. It was a recitation of domestic difficulty too much like their own personal life for make-believe. In one important respect, life even transcended fiction. How could she answer, when the Dyer chided her for denying him the children he craved, a man whose children she had, indeed, brought into the world?

Pondering the schedule of performances for the time period in question, the general manager perceived a solution: a shift of roles, in which the world-acclaimed performer of the Färberin would sing Leonore in *Fidelio* instead of an equally acclaimed performer of Leonore, and the Leonore would replace her as the Dyer's Wife in *Frau ohne Schatten*. I saw both performances with the improvised arrangement. Neither was as good as it would have been had the original casting remained unchanged, but it was impossible to argue the necessity or the wisdom of doing what had been done.

This was the Operatic Bargain as a Kindness to All Concerned Save the Audience.

P.S. Both singers have since remarried, *not* to other singers. They now even appear in their specialties together. Question: Who do the children applaud—Momma or Papa?

3

Charles Frohman, a great figure in the theatrical world of both America and England until he was drowned in the sinking of the *Lusitania* in 1915, is on record as saying, "If you can find an actor that looks a part, be thankful; if you can find an actor that acts a part, be thankful; but if you can find an actor that looks and acts a part, get down on your knees and thank God."[5] Frohman was, of course, speaking of actors for New York's Broadway or London's West End theaters. What would he have said had he been challenged to produce a performer who not only looks and acts a part, but can *sing* the music as well?

He doubtless could have responded with a shake of the head and a fervent "God be with you." To produce such a prodigy requires not merely perseverance, perception, and patience, but a quantity of luck that is not so much doled out as dispensed in a fine mist that can be accommodated on the point of a needle. In terms of the Frohman sequence, opera singers who look a part are on a par, in scarcity, with those who can act a part. Periodically, a picture magazine or a supplement to a Sunday newspaper produces a layout captioned: "The New Opera Soprano: a study in contrasts." Here we have half a dozen comely young contemporaries, juxtaposed by half a dozen beefy favorites of Father's or Grandfather's day. The implication is that no audience of today would tolerate the oversized specimens of yesterday.

I use the word "periodically" because you can find a similar layout in a similar section when the late Lily Pons was in vogue in the thirties, or when Patrice Munsel first appeared in the forties, or when Roberta Peters had her success in the fifties, or the "new" Maria Callas and a slimmer, trimmer Renata Tebaldi gave style to their roles later in the same decade, or Anna Moffo made her debut in the sixties. All these have been, are, and always will be a deviation from, not the norm. Otherwise, how is it that we have *Götterdämmerung* with Rita Hunter (200 pounds, plus) as Brünnhilde, or Verdi's *La traviata* with Montserrat Caballé, of Tetrazzini's conformations, as Violetta, or Luciano Pavarotti, all 300 pounds of him, as the impoverished poet Rodolfo in *La Bohème*? For substantially the same reason that Father and Grandfather accepted an oversized Helen Traubel in the same role of Brünnhilde in *Götterdammerung*, or a robust Rosa Ponselle as the tubercular Violetta (one of the last roles in her abbreviated career), or a Leo Slezak as a comfortably corpulent Manrico.

The simple, basic fact of the Operatic Bargain, where bodily structure is concerned, is perennial and unchanging: Voice is no respector of person. The gift falls, almost like the gentle rain from heaven, on fat and lean alike, on the tall, the short, the ugly, *and* the fair of face. The chest for the sound and the legs for the sight are only by accident to be found in the same person. To demand otherwise is to ignore the late George Jean Nathan's memorable analogy of expecting a strawberry to smell like a rose. No matter how much he might like to, no impresario can put on a stage, to perform Marguerite in *Faust,* a ravishing young blond beauty who is mute. If he cannot find a young Farrar or Rethberg, a new Mary Garden or de los Angeles or a reincarnation of Hilde Gueden, he will settle for someone who can hold her own with the music and leave the rest to the indulgence of the audience. It is part of an implied compact with the ticket buyer that if he will put aside his notion of "the New Operatic Soprano" derived from magazines and picture supplements, management will gratify his ear by presenting him with a "Golden Age" voice, or as near as can be found in a Jet Age body.

This is not merely no Operatic Bargain, it is close to an aesthetic swindle. The last Golden Age, operatically, on which there is broader agreement than between an advertising copywriter and his client was the 1890–1905 era dominated by such male singers as the brothers de Reszke, Pol Plançon, Victor Maurel, Antonio Scotti, Jean Lassalle, and Francesco Tamagno, and such female counterparts as Lilli Lehmann, Lillian Nordica, Emma Eames, Emma Calvé, Ernestine Schumann-Heink, Marcella Sembrich, and Nellie Melba. These artists shared the capacities that mark the "Golden Age" performer at any time—they were singers who could act and actors who could sing. They would have welcomed Michael Bohnen and Lucrezia Bori of the twenties, Ezio Pinza and Kirsten Flagstad of the thirties, Lotte Lehmann and Jarmila Novotna of the forties—the pairings are random and by no means comprehensive—to their midst, likewise such more recent performers as Hans Hotter, Birgit Nilsson, George London, Maria Callas, Renata Scotto, Mirella Freni, Shirley Verrett, Christa Ludwig, Sherrill Milnes, and Jon Vickers.

The difference in "Ages" (Golden vs. Plastic) is less a matter of ability than of quantity. There is no lack of excellent voices in this decade or its predecessor or *its* predecessor. Too few of them, however, have been carefully, comprehensively conditioned to maximum productivity by people who also care enough to look their parts or to learn how to act them. There are few—as previously noted—who would qualify for the highest distinction in any time. This is simply to say that such distinction is not impossible, it is just too much trouble for the average performer interested in immediate results. Even a woman with so beautiful a voice as Caballé's, who was told, when she sought out Callas for assistance in learning Norma, "First lose thirty pounds," replied, "But I only want to sing a few years more."

A start toward the improvement of operatic artistry could be made on a collective, rather than an individual, basis, were the principal opera theaters of the world to make an agreement *not* to sign any new performers of leading roles for a five-year period. They would make do with the basses, baritones, and tenors, the sopranos and mezzo sopranos now in the world talent pool. If they found a person of un-common endowment, they would put him/her under option for a debut in three years, but only in subordinate parts, while learning the major repertory for his/her voice category (what the Germans call the *Fach*, a term derived from a word meaning "branch" or "profes-sional category").

The existence, in the German operatic world, of such systematized study of the basic roles required of a soprano or mezzo, tenor, baritone, or bass, is one reason why most performers reared in it are more proficient in their duties than those developed, in a more random way, elsewhere. As a recent example, Christa Ludwig, from her first per-formances on the world stage, was a more finished performer of Octavian in *Der Rosenkavalier* or Ortrud in *Lohengrin* or Brangaene in *Tristan und Isolde* than most other mezzos of similar age. So, too, is a current product of the same background, Brigitte Fassbaender. By contrast, Mignon Dunn, of American birth and City Opera and Metro-politan conditioning, did not begin to acquire total command of her essentially fine vocal material, or authority in the major roles for it, until she broke off the inadequate, improvised "career" she was pur-suing and spent the years in Germany required to master her *Fach*.

Conversely, I would stress the decline, in quantity and quality, of the French contribution to the world operatic scene (since the end of World War II) as the single greatest impoverishment it has suffered in the last thirty years. Attention has already been directed to its cost in a treasure of inimitable music. But it has also denied us the kind of intellectual and aesthetic stimulation that made the French-trained singers of the late nineteenth and early twentieth centuries qualitatively different from all others.

It is worthy of a reminder that, among the singers of the nineties extolled as representative of the "Golden Age," no fewer than half were French-trained—the two de Reszkes, Plançon, Lassalle, and Maurel among the men; Calvé, Eames, and Melba among the women. With the exception of Melba, whose distinction was more vocal than dramatic, they were all people who knew how to stand as well as to move; to declaim words as well as to sing notes; to wear a manner as well as a costume. In their wake, such an intelligent (if vocally limited) artist as the late John Brownlee derived much of the finesse that distinguished his singing of Mozart from the years (1927–1936) he spent at the Paris Opéra, as his countrywoman Marjorie Lawrence did for such a role as Rachel in *La Juive*. The last link to the light *leggiero* singing practiced in Paris years ago may be found in Beverly Sills, whose teacher, Estelle Liebling, studied with Mathilde Marchesi, who also taught Melba, Eames, and Calvé.

A whole vocabulary of vocal terminology—from *voix claire* to *voix sombre, coup de glotte, dans la masque, point d'appui*—has dropped out of currency for the primary reason that there is a pitifully small number of singers to whom the words could be applied. The first offenders are the French themselves. They appear to have forgotten how to train singers who could exemplify what these words mean. As for *physique du rôle*—which means "the body for the part"—the whole range of performance of French opera has been so degraded that the subtleties, preferences or priorities represented in such a concept are all but nonexistent.

How these values functioned or what they meant to the creators and re-creators of French opera in the nineteenth century may be derived from Massenet's description of how *Thaïs* came into being. He writes: "Louis Gallet [his collaborator] and Heugel [his publisher] proposed to me a work on Anatole France's admirable romance *Thaïs*. I was immediately carried away by the idea. I could see Sanderson [Sybil Sanderson, born in Sacramento, California, in 1865, Paris-trained —also by Marchesi—and a celebrated Manon, who unfortunately died at thirty-eight] in the role of Thaïs. She belonged to the Opéra-Comique so I would do the work for that house."[6] For Massenet to say "I could *see* Sanderson in the role" means that she had the *physique du rôle* he cherished. For him to mention that she "belonged" to the Opéra-Comique gives a clue to the kind of vocal writing (suitable to a smallish theater on the Rue Favart in which spoken recitative prevailed) he would stress. The French themselves finally put an end to such conscientious creativity by eliminating Opéra comique from its traditional home in 1972.

Operatic Bargains of the Massenet kind were not compacts to offset weaknesses (prizing voice above appearance or ability to act). They were artistic sales made to strengths, in a matching of matter to manner in a congruent collaboration with appearance, aptitude, and temperament. So little sense of this remains that operas with parts written for so specific a performer as Sanderson are "revived" for anyone—*lirico spinto*, dramatic soprano, *leggiero*—with the box office appeal to justify the "risk," and little sense of physical or emotional identity with the principal role. Indeed, the ability to *play* such a part as Tosca—which began, after all, in a play made famous by Sarah Bernhardt—is such a rarity at present on the major opera stages of the world, that Magda Olivero, now in her sixties and with scarcely an octave and a half of viable voice, can enthrall an audience simply by her ability to make Tosca dramatically credible.

4

Here, then, in *Thaïs* is an instance of the Operatic Bargain at Its Most Perfect: a work on a congenial subject by a master of his craft, written for a performer wholly qualified to satisfy its musical and dramatic requirements, for performance in a theater to which all were harmoniously attuned. But what a rarity among the list of Operatic Bargains that have been enumerated! The ones sequentially identified have included:

1) The Operatic Bargain in Its Original Sinfulness (the convenience of Strauss, the inconvenience of Hofmannsthal)
2) The Operatic Bargain at Nothing Like Bargain Prices (the oversized theater)
3) The Operatic Bargain at Its Most Equitable (an experience worth the price)
4) The Operatic Bargain Unconsummated (A Pushkin *Onegin* too late to help a Tatiana)
5) The Operatic Bargain at Its Quintessential (the need to give something in order to get something)

6) The Operatic Bargain at Its Most Mephistophélian (the prop that fails at a climax)

7) The Operatic Bargain for Better or Worse (the performance that may make or break a career)

8) The Operatic Bargain as a Periodic Drag, a Mess, a Bore (indisposition)

9) The Operatic Bargain at Its Worst Involvement (a job in, or close to, the seat of power where decisions are made)

10) The Operatic Bargain as a Kindness to All Concerned (save the audience)

11) The Operatic Bargain as an Aesthetic Swindle (the Golden Age vs. the Plastic)

12) The Operatic Bargain at Its Most Perfect (Massenet, *Thaïs*, and Sanderson)

Topping all of these in its demeaning effect on a historic art form—and properly bearing the malign, ill-favored number 13—is what I would call the Operatic Bargain as Indignity. My most vivid recollection of a first visit to the historic, beautiful Teatro La Fenice in Venice (in the thirties) is not of what was performed or who sang in it, but the delay in its starting time from the advertised 9 P.M.—at which hour the audience was assembled and waiting for the performance to begin—until 11 P.M. when Prince Umberto, then heir apparent to Il Re Emmanuel III as Mussolini's deputy, arrived. The audience that arose in ceremonious greeting to the miscreant didn't deserve more, but the opera did. I am quite sure that President Gerald R. Ford was on time for his ceremonial appearance at the Wolf Trap Theater (in Virginia, near Washington) for the opening of a recent outdoor opera season there. I wish, however, he would give something more substantial than lip service to the benefit of opera—such as administrative and financial support—in exchange for the publicity he received, nationwide, as a politician who was also a man of cultivated taste. Otherwise, the Operatic Bargain as Political Ploy is the greatest indignity of all.

Such being the disappointing tabulation of positives (2) and negatives (11) in the dismal dozen plus of Operatic Bargains, the reader may pointedly ask: Why devote so much space and invest so much time in detailing the condition of an art form so clearly unworthy of either? I could answer such a frank question with a frank quotation (from, of course, an opera). In paraphrasing Shakespeare for purposes of Verdi, Boito has Desdemona saying to Otello in Act I: "I have loved you for your misfortunes." These shortcomings and inadequacies that total to bad Operatic Bargains are less related to the immortals who created the works we love than to the mortals who do or do not re-create them, but desecrate them.

Opera breeds a kind of love which, if sometimes unrequited, is always capable of re-arousing an emotion that might have been temporarily frustrated. The peculiar fascination of opera was well summarized in a statement by the late Fritz Reiner, one of the truly complete conductors of his time (with a career span from Budapest in 1913, when he conducted the first performance in Hungary of *Parsifal*, to 1963, when he retired as conductor of the great Chicago Symphony Orchestra he had rebuilt during the preceding decade). Having given up his work at the Metropolitan to return in 1952 to his favorite pastime of orchestra building, Reiner was asked, "Which do you prefer, symphonic conducting or opera?" His answer was typically frank and revealing: "When I am doing opera, I always long for the symphony orchestra, but when I am doing symphony, I always miss opera."

This was not expressive of ambivalence or irresolution. Reiner's response went, rather, to the nature of the two art forms. As an opera conductor, Reiner had standards that he could—on the middle road to which he was confined during much of his American career—only infrequently achieve to his own satisfaction. A *Rosenkavalier* with Lotte Lehmann, Elisabeth Schumann, Emanuel List, and the Philadelphia Orchestra in the Academy of Music in 1934 (very, very high middle road!); a *Tristan* in San Francisco with Flagstad and Melchior; the *Salome* with Welitch; an *Elektra* with Astrid Varnay, whom he greatly respected; a *Falstaff* with Leonard Warren; a thoroughly rehearsed, carefully crafted production of *Carmen* with Risë Stevens at the Metropolitan; these were achievements that answered the needs in his heart. But always, then, came the letdown of repetitions, of revivals that did not revive (in line with the words of Erich Leinsdorf that "pot roast [i.e., *Tannhäuser*] can be reheated, but a *soufflé* [i.e., *Falstaff*] can never rise twice") or promising new productions that foundered on the rocks of inadequate personnel.

With the symphony orchestra, however, every program is freshly prepared, with a suitable amount of rehearsal time and no greater number of repetitions than can be accommodated with sustained interest by orchestra and conductor. A symphony orchestra is shared only with conductors who are selected by the music director, or invited with his consent: the orchestra remains the property of one man, the music director, for the duration of his tenure, and the personnel is responsive to his satisfaction—a very satisfying situation indeed. But where are the glow of the footlights against the curtain, the charm of the unknown as it begins to rise, the whole sense of theater by which the stage and its action are permeated?

They can be found, of course, only in the opera house. Opera has been described as a hybrid—king or queen—which brings to bear something about parentage and propagation. Is it then a mulish being which, I have read credited to "Author unidentified," "has neither pride of ancestry nor hope of posterity?"[7] No. It differs from other hybrids in being secure in its heritage but uncertain of its future. It is an art form whose perfect fulfillment is achieved only rarely, and with extreme difficulty. The essential bargain with which it is confronted is the need for its propagators to have as much conviction in its future as its progenitors. In short, what is accepted in the concert hall as a matter of course, is, in the opera house, the determining course of the matter.

In my own case, having never been required to make a decision between opera *or* symphony, symphony *or* opera, I have been free to flit from flower to flower, to gather nectar wherever it is to be found. To opera I owe not only an identity and a vocation, but an endless round of memorable experiences (to balance out the other kind), here and abroad. From a point of beginning on Manhattan Island, only blocks from where I was born, I have gone by car and train, boat and plane, to hear opera almost everywhere that it is performed.

I went to Salzburg and Munich to hear opera before I went to Boston, but I have since visited all three repeatedly. I have heard opera in Vancouver B.C., in Seattle, Washington; San Francisco and Los Angeles, California; Santa Fe, New Mexico; Chicago, Illinois; St. Paul, Minnesota; Cincinnati, Ohio, and Detroit, Michigan; Pittsburgh and Philadelphia, Pennsylvania; even in Newark, New Jersey. Adding Washington, D.C.; Wolf Trap, Virginia; and Caramoor, in Westchester County, New York, doesn't exhaust a list that also includes Hartford, Connecticut; Tanglewood, Massachusetts (the first American performance of Britten's *Peter Grimes* in 1945), and many, many visits to the Academy of Music in Brooklyn, U.S.A.

Random cataloging can be a bore, but cataloging with a purpose can be illuminating. An interest in opera has taken me to Mexico City and to Buenos Aires. One of the most picturesque operas in the world (Old or New), the Colon in Buenos Aires has a history in which I was reasonably well versed and which whetted my appetite for a view of its rose and cream interior. But I didn't realize, until I had been privileged to learn some local ways, that a surprisingly large number of the Colon's performances are broadcast, through a municipal station. Such consideration for those who have the interest but not the money to attend opera is worthy of imitation by every city, worldwide.

As a result of this interest (which I would hesitate to characterize as either a habit or an obsession, because even an alcoholic does not like to confess his addiction), I have active memory of opera not only in such likely places as London, Paris, Bayreuth, Milan, Florence, Rome, and Vienna, but in such less likely places as Edinburgh, The Hague, Amsterdam, Stockholm, and Copenhagen. I once heard four productions of Verdi's *Falstaff* in a single year, an opportunity, I fear, that will not come again in my lifetime. I have heard Mozart's *Così fan tutte* in Le Petit Trianon in Versailles (capacity 300) beside which the Redoutensalle in Vienna (seating 500), where the opera is given every year during the June Festival, is almost too large; the Glyndebourne Festival (where *Così* is a house specialty) stretches audibility for its 799 attendants; and the Metropolitan's 3,800 listeners require an output of sound twelve times greater than that which sufficed in the little auditorium—truly an *audi* torium—created for Marie Antoinette.

Curiosity about the Operatic Bargain in its more exotic forms has drawn me from the likely to the less likely to the least likely surroundings—Sydney and Tokyo. Like similar excursions elsewhere, the primary commitment to a musical objective has not ruled out attention along the way to Honolulu, the Fiji Islands, and Tasmania in one direction, Kyoto and Hong Kong in the other. Having heard opera performed in Japan in theaters seating 3,000 enthusiasts, I should not be surprised if the next great Salome or Elsa came from Tokyo or Osaka. I was surprised, however, to discover (in 1973) that a recital (with orchestra) by the great Birgit Nilsson did not sell out in Perth, Australia. I was reassured, however, when the manager who booked her said, "She's too new. If I could get Schwarzkopf back here, I could sell out even if she came in a wheel chair."

Beyond the geographic and the ethnic, what I have learned from opera touches on filial devotion (*Aida*), connubial loyalty (*Fidelio*), ingenuity in the face of difficulties (*Il Barbiere di Siviglia*), and obligation to an oath freely taken (Norma). Love, as a matter of course, could be assimilated in a range of shadings from total (*Tristan und Isolde*) to partial (*Madama Butterfly*) to fragmented (*La Gioconda*). I have never suffered the agony of having a daughter violated—I never had a daughter—but I have shared the experience because of *Rigoletto*.

There is hardly an act of humankind which does not have an operatic equivalent. From Marguerite's destruction of her child to the deaths of too many in more ways than are mentionable, it is all there: childhood (*Hänsel und Gretel*), adolescence (Gounod's *Roméo et Juliette*), discovery and disillusion (Wagner's *Lohengrin*), infatuation and greed (*Manon*), an insensate passion for personal liberty (Carmen). Anyone who can sit through an evening's examination of the poisonous jealousy that destroyed Otello, without misgivings about his own temperamental shortcomings, doesn't deserve a loyal wife.

We are, operatically, all fathers or sons, wives, mothers, and daughters, part of an ever-evolving, ever-revolving cycle of biological and chronological happenings, time eternal, world without end.

Considering the pleasure that can be provided by those who honor opera rather than the pain that can be caused by those who merely use or abuse it, the prognosis for opera's survival is, on the whole, good. While there is life in the works there can be hope for a brighter fulfillment of it. That is not too bad a bargain, operatic or otherwise.

Notes

I. OVERTURE

1. Eric Blom, ed., *Grove's Dictionary of Music and Musicians*, fifth ed. (London: Macmillan & Co.; New York: St. Martin's Press, 1954), vol. 6, p. 469.
2. Richard Wagner, *My Life* (New York: Tudor Publishing Co., 1936), p. 817.
3. *Ibid.*, p. 408.
4. Richard Strauss, *Recollections and Reflections*, ed. Willy Schuh, trans. L. J. Lawrence (London: Boosey & Hawkes, 1953), p. 150.
5. Frank Walker, *The Man Verdi* (New York: Alfred A. Knopf, 1962), pp. 497–498.
6. John Warrack, *Carl Maria von Weber* (New York: Macmillan Co., 1968), p. 288.
7. Prodaná Nevešta, *Bedřich Smetana*, intro. by František Bartoš (Prague: Artia, 1953), p. XXVII.

II. RECITATIVO

1. Lawrence Gilman, in *New York Herald Tribune* (November 30, 1929), vol. LXXXIX, p. 15.
2. Pitts Sanborn, in *New York Telegram* (November 30, 1929), vol. 62, p. 16.
3. Robert Magidoff, *Ezio Pinza* (New York: Rinehart & Co., 1958), p. 140.
4. W. J. Henderson, in *The New York Sun* (November 22, 1930), vol. XCVIII, p. 9.
5. Francis Toye, *Rossini: A Study in Tragi-Comedy* (New York: Alfred A. Knopf, 1934), p. 173.
6. Henderson, *op. cit.*, p. 9.
7. J. M. Barrie, *The Complete Plays of J. M. Barrie* (New York: Charles Scribner's Sons, 1928), p. 326.
8. Hermann Devries, Ronald L. Davis, in *Opera in Chicago* (New York: Appleton-Century, 1966), p. 150.
9. Charles Osborne, *The Complete Operas of Verdi* (New York: Alfred A. Knopf, 1969), p. 314.
10. *Ibid.*, p. 322.
11. *Ibid.*, p. 353.
12. Walker, *op. cit.*, p. 211.

13. Dyneley Hussey, *Verdi* (New York: Pellegrini and Cudahy, 1949), p. 176.

14. Wagner, *op. cit.*, p. 745.

15. Richard Wagner, *Tristan and Isolde*, trans. Stewart Robb (New York: E. P. Dutton & Co., Inc., 1965), p. 67.

16. Ernest Newman, *Wagner as Man and Artist* (New York: Alfred A. Knopf, 1924), p. 297.

17. Edvard Grieg, "Robert Schumann," *Century Magazine* (January, 1894), vol. 47, no. 3, p. 440.

18. *Ibid.*, p. 440.

19. Wagner, *My Life,* p. 44.

20. Robert Schumann, *On Music and Musicians* (New York: Pantheon, 1946), p. 156.

21. Martin Cooper, "The Songs," *Schumann Symposium,* Gerald Abraham, ed. (New York: Oxford University Press, 1952), p. 108.

22. Eric Blom, ed., *Grove's Dictionary of Music and Musicians,* fifth ed., vol. 7, p. 533.

23. Sir Thomas Beecham, *La Bohème* (brochure) (New York: Radio Corporation of America, 1956), p. 1.

24. Mosco Carner, *Puccini* (New York: Alfred A. Knopf, 1959), p. 63.

25. *Ibid.*, pp. 28-29.

26. Beecham, *op. cit.*, p. 2.

27. Jules Massenet, *My Recollections* (Boston: Small, Maynard & Co., 1919), p. 138.

28. *Ibid.*, p. 141.

III. ARIA, DA CAPO AND OTHERWISE

1. John Evelyn, F.R.S., *Diary and Correspondence of John Evelyn. F.R.S.,* ed. from the original Mss. at Wotton by William Bray, F.A.S. (London: George Bell and Sons, 1902), p. 211.

2. Henry Pleasants, *The Great Singers* (New York: Simon and Schuster, 1966), pp. 54-55.

3. Newman Flower, *George Frideric Handel: His Personality and His Times* (Boston and New York: Houghton Mifflin Company, 1923), p. 145.

4. Herbert Weinstock, *Handel* (New York: Alfred A. Knopf, 1946), p. 268.

5. *Ibid.*, p. 320.

6. Ernest Newman, *Gluck and the Opera* (London: Victor Gollancz, Ltd., 1967), pp. 191-192.

7. Emily Anderson, *The Letters of Mozart and His Family* (London: Macmillan & Co., 1938), vol. 3, pp. 1212-1213.

8. Eric Blom, ed., *Grove's Dictionary of Music and Musicians,* fifth ed., vol. 2, p. 2.

9. L. J. de Bekker, *Stokes' Encyclopedia of Music and Musicians* (Edinburgh: W. & R. Chambers, Ltd., 1911), p. 93.

10. Henry F. Chorley, *Thirty Years' Musical Recollections,* intro. by Ernest Newman (New York: Alfred A. Knopf, 1926), p. 22.

11. *Ibid.*, p. XVII.

12. Percy A. Scholes, *The Oxford Companion to Music,* ninth ed. (London: Oxford University Press, 1955), p. 142.

13. Hussey, *op. cit*, pp. 177-178.

14. Donald Jay Grout, *A Short History of Opera* (New York: Columbia University Press, 1947), p. 379.

15. Wagner, *My Life*, p. 394.
16. Walker, *op. cit.*, p. 264.

IV. SCENA

1. Schumann, *op. cit.*, p. 251.
2. Grout, *op. cit.*, p. 301.
3. Warrack, *op. cit.*, p. 103.
4. Wagner, *My Life*, p. 213.
5. Warrack, *op. cit.*, p. 195.
6. Wagner, *My Life*, p. 378.
7. Hussey, *op. cit.*, p. 166.
8. Rosa Newmarch, *The Russian Opera* (London: Herbert Jenkins), p. 44.
9. *Ibid.*, p. 86.
10. M. Montague-Nathan, *Glinka* (New York: Duffield and Company, 1917), p. 31.
11. Newmarch, *op. cit.*, p. 96.
12. Montague-Nathan, *op. cit.*, p. 64.
13. Alexander Pushkin, *The Poems, Prose and Plays of Alexander Pushkin*, ed. Avrahm Yarmolinsky, "Eugene Onegin," trans. Babette Deutsche (New York: The Modern Library, 1936), p. 174.
14. *Ibid.*, p. 171.
15. Newmarch, *op. cit.*, p. 389.

V. FINALE, FINALETTO

1. Jean Jacques Rousseau, *The Confessions* (Baltimore: Penguin Books, 1963), p. 357.
2. Lorenza da Ponte, *Memoirs of Lorenza da Ponte*, trans. Elisabeth Abbott (New York: Dover Publications, 1967), p. 151.
3. *Ibid.*, p. 133.

ENTR'ACTE

1. Irving Kolodin, ed., *The Composer as Listener* (New York: Horizon Press, 1958), p. 288.
2. W. J. Henderson, *op. cit.*, March 8, 1926, vol. XCIII, p. 30.
3. Kolodin, *op. cit.*, p. 289.
4. Herbert Graf, *Opera and Its Future in America* (New York: W. W. Norton & Co., Inc., 1941), p. 199.
5. Adolphe Appia, *Music and the Art of the Theatre* (Coral Gables, Florida: University of Miami Press, 1962), p. 1.
6. Geoffrey Skelton, *Wagner at Bayreuth* (New York: George Braziller, 1965), pp. 130–131.
7. *Ibid.*, p. 154.
8. Appia, *op. cit.*, p. 23.

VI. MAD SCENE

1. Herbert Weinstock, *Donizetti* (New York: Pantheon Books, 1963), p. 112, n. 113.

2. Alfred Loewenberg, *Annals of Opera 1597–1940* (Cambridge, England: W. Heffer & Sons, 1943), p. 346.

3. Chorley, *op. cit.*, pp. 106–107.

4. *Ibid.*, p. 212.

5. Cyril W. Beaumont, *Complete Book of Ballets* (New York: G. P. Putnam's Sons, 1938), p. 137.

6. H. L. Mencken, ed., *A New Dictionary of Quotations* (New York: Alfred A. Knopf, 1942), p. 732.

7. Michel Foucault, *Madness and Civilization: A History of Insanity in the Age of Reason* (New York: Random House, Vintage Books, 1973), p. 3.

8. *Ibid.*, p. 5.

9. *Encyclopedia Britannica,* fourteenth ed. (London: The Encyclopedia Britannica Co., 1939), vol. 3, p. 301.

10. Loewenberg, *op. cit.*, p. 12.

11. William Ashbrook, *Donizetti* (London: Cassell & Company, 1965), p. 23.

12. Herbert Weinstock, *Vincenzo Bellini: His Life and His Operas* (New York: Alfred A. Knopf, 1971), pp. 20–21.

13. *Ibid.*, p. 413.

14. W. J. Henderson, *op. cit.*, November 24, 1904, vol. LXXII, p. 7.

15. W. J. Henderson, *op. cit.*, February 23, 1926, vol. XCIII, p. 33.

16. Chorley, *op. cit.*, p. 198.

17. Hussey, *op. cit.*, pp. 54–55.

18. Wagner, *My Life*, p. 29.

19. *Ibid.*, p. 90.

20. Edward Albee, *Who's Afraid of Virginia Woolf?* (New York: Atheneum, 1962), p. 185.

21. *Ibid.*, p. 227.

VII. DUET

1. Toye, *op. cit.*, pp. 16–18.

2. A. W. Thayer, *Beethoven,* ed. Elliot Forbes (Princeton: Princeton University Press, 1967), p. 804.

3. Ernest Newman, *The Life of Richard Wagner* (New York: Alfred A. Knopf, 1941), vol. 3, pp. 12–13.

4. Edmond Michotte, *Richard Wagner's Visit to Rossini,* trans. Herbert Weinstock (Chicago: University of Chicago Press, 1968), pp. 44–48, 52.

5. Toye, *op. cit.*, p. 44.

6. *Ibid.*, p. 44.

7. *Ibid.*, p. 44.

8. Grout, *op. cit.*, p. 341.

9. Giuseppe Verdi, *Letters of Giuseppe Verdi,* ed. and trans. Charles Osborne (New York: Holt, Rinehart and Winston, 1972), p. 65.

10. Hussey, *op. cit.*, pp. 13–14.

11. *Ibid.*, p. 71.

12. Corno di Bassetto (later known as Bernard Shaw), *London Music in 1888–89* (London: Constable and Company, 1937), p. 393.

13. Franco Abbiatti, *Giuseppe Verdi* (Milano: Ricordi, 1959), vol. 2, p. 11. Also in *Letters of Giuseppe Verdi,* p. 230.

14. Newman, *The Life of Richard Wagner* (1939), vol. 2, p. 526.

VIII. "HEILIGE BRAUT"

1. Ignatz Moscheles, *Recent Music and Musicians: As Described in the Diaries and Correspondence of Ignatz Moscheles,* ed. by his wife (New York: Henry Holt and Co., 1875), p. 179.
2. *Ibid.,* p. 179.

IX. FINALE ULTIMO

1. Patrick J. Smith, *The Tenth Muse* (New York: Alfred A. Knopf, 1970), p. 196.
2. Carner, *op. cit.,* pp. 87, 120, 151.
3. *Ibid.,* p. 359.
4. Henry Wisneski, *Callas: The Art Behind the Legend* (Garden City, N.Y.: Doubleday and Co., 1975), p. 32.
5. Carner, *op. cit.,* p. 225.
6. Giulio Gatti-Casazza, *Memories of the Opera* (New York: Charles Scribner's Sons, 1941), pp. 276–277.
7. Carner, *op. cit.,* p. 98.
8. Abbiatti, *op. cit.,* vol. 4, pp. 384–385.
9. Eric Blom, ed., *Grove's Dictionary of Music and Musicians,* fifth edition, vol. 3, p. 149.
10. Modeste Petrovich Musorgsky, *The Musorgsky Reader: A Life of Modeste Petrovich Musorgsky,* ed. and trans. Jay Leyda and Sergei Bertensson (New York: W. W. Norton and Co., 1947), p. 155.
11. H. H. Stuckenschmidt, *Maurice Ravel* (Philadelphia: Chilton Book Co., 1969), p. 134.
12. Edward Lockspeiser, *Debussy,* Master Musicians Series (London: Dent, Ltd., 1951), p. 241.

X. A PERFECT SEASON

1. Henry-Louis de la Grange, *Mahler* (Garden City, N.Y.: Doubleday and Co., 1973), vol. 1, p. 232.
2. Cynthia Fox, *The Real Figaro* (New York: Coward-McCann, 1962), p. 84.
3. Toye, *op. cit.,* p. 135.
4. *Ibid.,* p. 136.
5. Strauss, *op. cit.,* pp. 106–107.

XII. THE VOCABULARY OF IGNORANCE

1. Edna St. Vincent Millay, "Figs from Thistles," from *Collected Poems,* ed. Norma Millay (New York: Harper & Row, 1956), p. 127.
2. Sir Rudolf Bing, *5,000 Nights at the Opera* (Garden City, N.Y. Doubleday and Co., 1972), pp. 246–247.
3. *The New York Times* (October 30, 1956), vol. CVI, p. 43.
4. *The New York Herald Tribune* (October 30, 1956), vol. CXVI, p. 20.
5. *Ibid.*
6. Chorley, *op. cit.,* pp. 76–77.
7. *Ibid.,* pp. 76–77, 87–88.
8. *Ibid.,* p. 132.

328 NOTES

9. W. J. Henderson, *The Art of Singing* (New York: The Dial Press, 1939), pp. 236–238.

10. Robert Lawrence, *Opera News* (New York: Metropolitan Opera Guild, October 27, 1952), pp. 5–6.

11. Edward Heath, in *The Sunday Times* (London: June 4, 1961).

XIII. THE SIGHT FOR THE SOUND

1. Richard Wagner, *Richard Wagner's Prose Works* (London: Routledge and Kegan Paul, 1894), pp. 167–200.

2. Huntly Carter, *The Theatre of Max Reinhardt* (New York: Benjamin Blom, 1914), pp. 42–45.

3. William Mann, *Richard Strauss, A Critical Study of the Operas* (New York: Oxford University Press, 1966), p. 102.

4. Richard Strauss and Hugo von Hofmannsthal, *A Working Friendship: The Correspondence Between Richard Strauss and Hugo von Hofmannsthal* (New York: Random House, 1961), pp. 109–111, 116, 131.

5. Spike Hughes, *Glyndebourne: A History of the Festival Opera* (London: Methuen, 1965), p. 43.

6. Desmond Shawe-Taylor, in *The Sunday Times* (June 29, 1975).

XIV. THE UNWRITTEN REPERTORY

1. Florence May, *Life of Johannes Brahms* (London: Reeves, 1905), vol. 2, p. 519.

2. Edward Lockspeiser, *Debussy: His Life and Mind* (New York: Macmillan, 1965), vol. 1, pp. 61, 139.

3. Giulio Gatti-Casazza, *op. cit.*, p. 157.

4. Lockspeiser, *op. cit.*, vol. 2, 142–143.

5. *Ibid.*, vol. 2, pp. 144–146.

6. *Ibid.*, p. 150.

7. Massenet, *op. cit.*, pp. 164–165.

8. *Ibid.*, p. 166.

9. Henri Murger, *The Bohemians of the Latin Quarter* (London: Vizetelly & Co., 1888), p. XIV.

10. *Ibid.*, p. XIV.

11. Henri Murger, *The Bohemians of the Latin Quarter*, trans. Henry Curwen (New York: Brentano's, 1901).

12. Murger, Vizetelly ed., *op. cit.*, pp. 73–76.

13. *Ibid.*, p. 255.

14. *Ibid.*, p. 241.

15. *Ibid.*, p. 255.

16. Murger, Brentano ed., *op. cit.*

17. Lockspeiser, *op. cit.*, vol. 1, p. 190.

18. *Ibid.*, vol. 2, p. 269.

19. David Ewen, *Richard Rodgers* (New York: Henry Holt Co., 1957), p. 235.

20. Carner, *op. cit.*, p. 497.

21. Thayer-Forbes, *Beethoven* (Princeton: Princeton University Press), pp. 602, 985, 441, 474.

22. Strauss and Von Hofmannsthal, *op. cit.*, p. 76.

23. Friedrich Schnapp, *Musical Quarterly* (New York: G. Schirmer & Co., October, 1924), pp. 485–486.

24. Clara Schumann, *Clara Schumann: An Artist's Life*, ed. Berthold Litzmann, trans. Grace E. Hadow (Leipzig: Breitkopf & Hartel, 1913), vol. 2, p. 312.
25. Corno di Bassetto, *op. cit.*, p. 394. Originally appeared in *The Anglo-Saxon Review*, March, 1901.
26. Verdi, *Letters of Giuseppe Verdi, op. cit.*, pp. 70–72.
27. Osborne, *The Complete Operas of Verdi, op. cit.*, pp. 79–80.
28. Verdi, *Verdi: The Man in His Letters*, ed. and sel. by Franz Werfel and Paul Stefan, trans. Edward Downes (New York: L. B. Fischer, 1942), pp. 185, 189, 190.
29. *Ibid.*, p. 189.
30. *Ibid.*, p. 190.
31. *Ibid.*, p. 202.
32. Walker, *op. cit.*, p. 476.
33. *Ibid.*, p. 502.
34. Osborne, *The Complete Operas of Verdi, op. cit.*, p. 81.

XV. THE OPERATIC BARGAIN

1. Jean Jacques Rousseau, *The Social Contract*, trans. Maurice Cranston (Baltimore: Penguin Books, 1968), p. 49.
2. Donald Oenslager, *Stage Design: A Studio Book* (New York: Viking, 1975), pp. 43, 50, 58, 92.
3. Irving Kolodin, in *Saturday Review* (February 22, 1966).
4. John Livingston Lowes, *The Road to Xanadu* (Cambridge, Mass.: Houghton Mifflin Co., 1927), p. 572.
5. Carter, *op. cit.*, p. 60.
6. Massenet, *op. cit.*, p. 189.
7. *A New Dictionary of Quotations*, sel. and ed. H. L. Mencken (New York: Alfred A. Knopf, 1942), p. 821.

Index

Prodána Nevěsta, see Bartered Bride, The
Prophète, Le, 85
Puccini, Giacomo, 12, 41–47, 189–90, 192–94, 287
  and Wagner's influence, 44
  his finales, 191–92
  See also La Bohème; Madama Butterfly; Il Trittico; Tosca; Turandot; Le Villi
Purcell, Henry, 138–39
Pushkin, Alexander, 93–94, 96–97, 150

Quaglio Family, The, 301

Rake's Progress, The, 69, 153
Rameau, Jean Philippe, 79
Ravel, Maurice, 200
Rayner, Robert M., 196
Recitativo secco, 20–21
Recitativo stromentato, 20–21, 32
Reckford, Dr. Leo, 307–08
Redoutensaal, 320
Reiner, Fritz, 318
Reinhardt, Max, 268–71
Residenztheater, 302
Rettenoper, 80
Ricordi, Giulio, 42
Rigoletto, 12, 28, 166–70, 203
Rheingold, Das, 8
Rienzi, 38–39
Rimsky-Korsakov, Nikolai, 94, 219
Ring des Nibelungen, 8–9, 202
Robert le Diable, 85
Roller, Alfred, 121, 265
Romani, Felice, 141
Roméo et Juliette, 44
Rosenkavalier, Der, 188–89, 202, 269
Rossini, Gioacchino, 7, 11, 23–27 52, 65, 147, 159–63
  and Beethoven, 160–61
  and Duets, 163
  and Wagner, 161–62
  See also Aureliano in Palmira; Barber of Seville, The; Comte Ory, Le; Cenerentola, La; Elisabetta, regina d'Inghilterra; Guillaume Tell; L'Italiana in Algeri
Rousseau, Jean-Jacques, 100
Rubini, Giambattista, 62–63
Rusalka, 217
Russian opera, 92–97
  influence of, 97
Russlan and Ludmilla, 94
Rysanek, Leonie, 40, 83

Sabina, Karel, 15
Salazar, Manuel, 303

Salome, 10, 153, 268
Salzburg Festival, 21, 82–83, 271
Sammartini, Giovanni Battista, 54
San Carlo Opera Company, 302–03
Sanborn, Pitts, 19
Sanderson, Sybil, 315–16
Sanquirico, Alessandro, 264
Sayão, Bidú, 46
Scala, La, 11–12, 192
Scarlatti, Alessandro, 52
Schiller, Friedrich, 87–88
Schinkel, Karl Friedrich, 264–65
Schipa, Tito, 144–45
Schoeffler, Paul, 90
Schönberg, Arnold, 268
Schröder-Devrient, Wilhelmine, 38–39, 179
Schumann, Clara, 290
Schumann, Robert, 37–38, 289
  and Gounod, 44
  and Wagner, 37, 78
Schumann-Heink, Ernestine, xiii
Schwarz, Vera, 241
Schwarzkopf, Elisabeth, 22, 182–83, 241
Scribe, Eugène, 274
Sembrich, Marcella, 6, 144, 311
Serafin, Tullio, 63
Serse, 52, 74
Serva padrona, La, 51, 99, 157–58
Shaw, George Bernard, 170, 291
Shawe-Taylor, Desmond, 262, 275
Siegfried, 8
Siepi, Cesare, 90
Sills, Beverly, 46, 64–65, 145, 246, 315
Simionato, Giulietta, 58
Simon Boccanegra, 12
Singspiel, 22, 24
Slezak, Leo, 179
Smetana, Bedřich, 15
Solera, Temistocle, 27
Somma, Antonio, 292
Sonnambula, La, 61
Staatsoper, *see* Vienna State Opera
Stage directors, 111–12
Stasov, Vladimir, 199–200
Steber, Eleanor, 46
Stevens, Risë, 58, 182
Stratas, Teresa, 40–41
Strauss, Johann, 16
Strauss, Richard, 10, 82, 153, 188, 268–70, 289
  See also Ariadne auf Naxos; Capriccio; Rosenkavalier, Der; Salome
Stravinsky, Igor, 94
Strepponi, Giuseppina, 31
Supervia, Conchita, 234